Evangelicals
and Empire

EVANGELICALS
and EMPIRE

Christian Alternatives *to the* Political Status Quo

EDITED BY

Bruce Ellis Benson *and* Peter Goodwin Heltzel

BrazosPress

a division of Baker Publishing Group
Grand Rapids, Michigan

© 2008 by Bruce Ellis Benson and Peter Goodwin Heltzel

Published by Brazos Press
a division of Baker Publishing Group
P.O. Box 6287, Grand Rapids, MI 49516-6287
www.brazospress.com

Printed in the United States of America

Library of Congress Cataloging-in-Publication Data
Evangelicals and empire : Christian alternatives to the political status quo / edited by Bruce Ellis Benson and Peter Goodwin Heltzel.
        p.   cm.
    Includes bibliographical references and index.
    ISBN 978-1- 58743-235-4 (pbk.)
        1. Evangelicalism—United States. 2. Christianity and politics—United States. 3. Christianity and international affairs. 4. United States—Foreign relations. 5. Imperialism. 6. Negri, Antonio, 1933- I. Benson, Bruce Ellis, 1960- II. Heltzer, Peter Goodwin, 1970- III. Title.
BR1642.U5E897 2008
261.70973—dc22   2008030574

Contents

5

Section III: Future

Foreword

NICHOLAS WOLTERSTORFF

Until recently, only those who wished to criticize America's role in the world described it as an empire. Those who applauded the U.S. role invariably resisted the charge. We Americans achieved our independence by breaking free from the grip of the British empire. We know first hand what's bad about empires. We will not be guilty of creating our own.

Times have changed. The neoconservatives who provided the ideology for the foreign policy of the administration of President George W. Bush, and thereby for much of its domestic policy as well, concede that America is an empire and boldly declare that that's a good thing. It would be even more of a good thing if we stopped telling ourselves that we are not an empire, acknowledged that we are, and unapologetically got on with the business of empire.

Most if not all previous empires were bad. Their goal was to subject other peoples to the control of the imperial center. The American empire is different, say the neoconservatives. Americans are good people; they have no interest in subjecting other people to their control. The goal of the American empire is to spread freedom around the world. Everybody wants to be free, politically and economically; God made human beings with the desire to be free. Tyrants and central planners inhibit this desire. Unfortunately, hortatory talks do not unseat tyrants and central planners; only the barrel of a gun works. So as the only superpower, America must use its military force to remove tyrants and central planners, hold at bay the terrorists who do not like freedom, and forestall the emergence of any power that might seriously contest this role of America in the world. Some say God has assigned America this role; others apparently think that morality requires it, given the historical emergence of this unique blend of supreme power and unparalleled goodness in America.

Hardt and Negri, in their two well-known books, *Empire* and *Multitude*, argue that political empires, such as America presently is and such as the neoconservatives want it to be, are becoming things of the past. What is now emerging is a global capitalist economy that eludes the attempts of states to control it, including the attempts of the United States. The United States may or may not be able to control Iraq; we don't yet know how the story ends. It certainly cannot control the dynamics of the global capitalist economy. When Hardt and Negri speak of "empire," it is the imperial reach and control of the global capitalist economy that they have in mind.

Unlike the neoconservatives, Hardt and Negri think that all empires, whether this emerging economic empire or the prior political empires, are bad. When they say what's bad about empire, however, one notices a curious convergence between the anthropology and morality they assume and that of the neoconservatives. What's bad about empire, whatever its form, is that it constitutes *domination*. Always in empire there is somebody or something telling people how to think and what to do, somebody or something exercising authority over people. What we need is a "liberatory politics" that will bring about a social order free from all such "transcendence." This is what human beings want, this is their desire, to be free from being told how to think and what to do. Thus it is that authority is inherently domination. One of the main innovations in the thought of Hardt and Negri is their claim that as electronic means of communication become more and more prominent in the global economy, it becomes just as impossible for business figures to control the lives of people as for political figures to control their lives. The dynamics of the new empire will lead to its destruction. Freedom and equality are at hand.

Hardt and Negri say next to nothing about the role of religion in the emergence of the new empire and in its projected demise. Obviously freedom as they understand it is incompatible with any acknowledgment of God as having authority over us. But evidently either they assume the truth of the secularization thesis, that under conditions of modernization religion will disappear, or they assume the truth of the epiphenomen thesis, that religion can be explained but cannot itself explain.

Evangelicals and Empire significantly advances the discussion by considering the role of evangelicals in empire, not only American evangelicals but evangelicals generally, and their role both in the American empire and in the newly emerging economic empire. That latter role proves both important and contradictory. On the one hand, evangelicalism, at least in its nondenominational forms, is almost a paradigmatic example of the sort of liberation that Hardt and Negri anticipate. When the evangelical who feels no denominational loyalty finds that his present church is trying to exert an "authority" over him that he doesn't like, he simply leaves and shops around for one in which what he is told to think and do meshes with what he was already thinking and doing. On the other hand, the great bulk of American evangelicals appear both to support the current American empire and to participate without qualms in the emerging global capitalist empire.

This support and this participation are strange. The Lord whom the evangelical professes to serve did not say, according to the scriptures that the evangelical holds as authoritative, that he came to bring freedom. He said he was anointed to inaugurate God's realm of justice. The person who has absorbed the scriptural understanding of what it is to be human, and the scriptural understanding of who Jesus was, will say both to the neoconservatives and to Hardt and Negri that liberation cannot be the fundamental social good. Justice within shalom is that. For liberty in the absence of justice is liberty for the lions and the eagles of the world. And as long as this world endures, there will be lions and eagles. Changing political and economic arrangements will not change that fact about human beings.

Ever since Hegel, domination and liberation have been the fundamental categories of social analysis and critique. An authentically evangelical voice in the discussion will question this and propose instead that justice and injustice be the fundamental categories. The fundamental social ill is not that people are not at liberty to do as they see fit; the fundamental ill is that we wrong each other.

Confronted with the present American empire, the person with an authentically evangelical sensibility will not be indifferent to the neoconservative preoccupation, whether it frees some people to hold elections. That will not be her fundamental consideration, however. Her fundamental consideration will be whether it serves to advance justice or whether instead it wreaks injustice. And when she hears American empire defended by appeals to the goodness of the American people, she will have ringing in her ears St. Paul's critique of all such naive claims to human goodness. Likewise, when confronted with the empire of a global capitalist economy, the person with an authentically evangelical sensibility will not be indifferent to whether such an economy promotes overall economic growth. But that will not be her fundamental consideration. Her fundamental consideration will be whether it operates in such a way as to advance justice. Does it lift up the downtrodden? Does it diminish poverty?

These are some of the matters discussed in the pages that follow. Peter Goodwin Heltzel and Bruce Ellis Benson deserve warm thanks for coordinating this engagement of evangelicalism with the empires under which we live.

Introduction

BRUCE ELLIS BENSON AND PETER GOODWIN HELTZEL

Both evangelicals and empire pervade the air and images in America today. Not very long ago, evangelicals were on the fringe of American society and largely overlooked. But for the past few years, it seems as if they've taken center stage. As evangelical President George W. Bush has led the nation as president, evangelical megachurch minister Rick Warren with rock star Bono are leading a new movement of evangelicals who are committed to embodying peace and justice in the world. Since the born-again Southern Baptist Jimmy Carter became president in 1976, evangelicals have risen to power with the rise of American empire. Given that coordinated rise, it is time to interrogate the deep connection between the two.

"Empire" has become an increasingly important metaphor for analyzing not just American political power but also global economic power. In terms of the United States, its political strength and economic vitality have granted it the status of the one remaining superpower nation-state. Yet ever since the end of the cold war, the United States has been trying to discern its role in the world. So far, it has wielded its power widely and acted primarily as "policeman of the world." As things stand, it would seem that the United States is at the height of its power. There is currently no nation that can challenge it militarily or economically. In its role of policing the world, the United States is currently engaged in "a war on terrorism" on three fronts: Afganistan, Iraq, and home. Although technically the United States is involved in these wars with "allies," the reality is that it went to war in flagrant disregard of the advice of some of its closest allies and friends. Moreover, it has acted—and continues to act—in ways that signal that it is "above the law," in terms of both international law

11

and international treaties (some of which it has refused to sign and others of which it has signed but then refused to honor).

In their books *Empire* and *Multitude*,[1] Michael Hardt and Antonio Negri challenge this conception of political empire, arguing that "empire" is much more complicated. On the one hand, they acknowledge that the United States does have this status as the remaining superpower. On the other hand, they question its power as a nation-state, given the emerging power of the global economy. With the ever-strengthening power of free-market capitalism, they argue that the power of the United States will inevitably fade. The result is that power will no longer be localized or even manageable, since the global economic empire belongs to everyone and no one.

This shift makes possible what Hardt and Negri call "multitude," a "set of *singularities*" that "remain multiple" yet is "not fragmented, anarchical, or incoherent."[2] Just exactly what that might look like is one of the questions this volume addresses.

As a result of the transformation of sovereignty in global actors, smaller networks of power—whether religious organizations or terrorist cells—are suddenly empowered. The world stood by as this was demonstrated on September 11, 2001, when a set of Al Quaeda terrorist cells organized an attack on symbols of U.S. military and economic power—the Pentagon in Washington, DC, and the World Trade Towers in New York City. While 9/11 vividly demonstrated the new and very public visibility of religion, it is only one specific instance of the ways in which religion has returned to the political scene. In this respect, it is not insignificant that sociologist Peter Berger has recently renounced his secularization thesis and admitted that religion is on the rise.

Today it is increasingly difficult to think of religion as something that is merely part of the "private sphere." Religious debates that used to take place within a particular religious community or organization are now becoming matters of public concern. One need only think of the considerable attention the media gave to the Episcopal Church of the United States of America's decision in 2003 to ordain a practicing gay bishop and bless same-sex unions. Similarly, questions regarding the role of Islamic leaders in public life are increasingly matters of public debate.

The rise of global Islam is an important expression of religion's new public visibility. Yet it also illustrates the deep-seated differences that one finds *within* Islam. Just as there is not one single expression of Christianity, so there is not just one expression of Islam. As in Christianity, one finds within Islam voices that call for a theocratic state, seeking to bring the public sphere under the

---

1. Michael Hardt and Antonio Negri, *Empire* (Cambridge, MA: Harvard University Press, 2000), and *Multitude: War and Democracy in the Age of Empire* (New York: Penguin, 2004).
2. *Multitude*, 99.

rule of religion. Yet this is merely one expression of Islam, and there are many Muslims who are deeply at odds with such a vision.

As global Christianity continues its meteoric rise in the Southern Hemisphere, it also presents us with competing visions of religion and public life. Scholars such as Dale T. Irving, Philip Jenkins, and Lamin Sanneh have argued that Christianity is experiencing exponential numeric growth in the Southern Hemisphere. We have seen this in the rise of global Pentecostalism in Africa, Asia, and Latin America. In Latin America, where there has been a strong tradition of liberation theology, many theologians have been challenging Christians in the United States to confront the downside of the neoliberal structure of the U.S. economy, as well as economic policy in the region. Confronting the negative consequences of economic globalization driven by U.S.-based multinational corporations has also been a primary concern of the global ecumenical councils, including the Lutheran World Federation, the World Alliance of Reformed Churches, and the World Council of Churches.

It has been difficult for many Anglo American evangelicals to confront these economic and political problems. For quite some time, Anglo American evangelicals have seen themselves as the keepers of Christian orthodoxy and have even viewed Christianity itself as a "Western religion." Yet the power of Anglo American evangelicals is quickly waning. Within the worldwide Anglican Communion, for example, African bishops have stepped in to correct what they see as heterodoxy in the Episcopal Church of the United States, and the power of non-Western Anglican bodies will only increase in the coming decades. We are likewise seeing the signs of global evangelicals beginning to critique and correct Anglo American evangelicals in various ways. For example, Justo González in his work *Mañana* argues that many American evangelicals are often unfaithful to the gospel by not living it out in every dimension of their life, including the economic and political.[3] This is merely the beginning of such critiques.

In our time, American political empire and evangelicals have increasingly come to be one and the same. Since the 1970s, we have seen the emergence of a strong conservative Christianity often refered to as the "Religious Right." While the term *Religious Right* is amorphous and difficult to define, there is no question that many evangelicals are part of this group. Even though the power of the Religious Right is on the wane, evangelicals are exerting their power in other ways. Evangelicals have learned what it is like to have political power, and they will hardly simply let go of that power. The only question is *who* and *what* evangelicals will support. True, the old guard of evangelicalism is losing its power, but there are many younger evangelicals ready to step

---

3. Justo L. González, *Mañana: Christian Theology from a Hispanic Perspective* (Nashville: Abingdon, 1990).

up and stake their claim for a much more progressive form of evangelicalism, one that is politically active and oriented toward social justice.

Inasmuch as some evangelicals work together with movements in the Religious Right that are perpetuating the dark side of empire—including U.S. practices of war and torture, neoliberal economic policy, and unilateral, isolationist foreign policy—they continue to participate in empire. Far too many evangelicals participate in empire without understanding the consequences of their behavior and the complexities of empire. Other evangelicals are quite conscious of these problems and intentionally seek to build empire, by supporting both the United States as a superpower and the economic and political practices that undergird it. Regardless of particular evangelicals' intentions, inasmuch as they participate in empire building that has negative impacts on the poor in this country and the poor throughout the world, the blood remains on their hands. At the beginning of the twenty-first century, American evangelicals and empire are deeply implicated together.

Yet what is an "evangelical"? As the plethora of literature on the topic demonstrates, not only is there no easy way to answer this question but even the term *evangelical* is increasingly used to describe various sorts of groups throughout the world. A traditional way of defining evangelicalism is that offered by David Bebbington and Mark Noll. Citing Bebbington, Noll writes that evangelicals are characterized by four factors: (1) a conversion to Jesus Christ, (2) holding the Bible as the ultimate authority, (3) an activism that takes the form of spreading the gospel and, to a lesser degree, social reform, and (4) an emphasis on the cross—Jesus's death and resurrection.[4] One might take issue with the very title of the chapter from which this definition is cited: is evangelicalism *really* the future of Protestantism? While the mainline denominations are hardly in the running for that title, Pentecostalism certainly is. Indeed, Noll goes on to speak about Pentecostalism at some length in his chapter. So are Pentecostals a subgroup of evangelicalism—or their own distinct movement? Such is a question that many of the chapters in this book address.

However, this question is indicative of a much broader question. As Noll notes, "Evangelicalism has always been *diverse, flexible, adaptable*, and *multiform*."[5] But, if such is the case, then how clearly can we define "evangelicalism"? As is evident from the chapter by Donald W. Dayton and Christian T. Collins Winn, there are alternative accounts of the genealogy of evangelicalism. However, many other chapters in this book also problematize the notion of "evangelicalism" in one way or another. Moreover, they put into question the relation between evangelicalism and what is currently called the "Religious Right." How much are evangelicals a part of that movement

---

4. Mark A. Noll, "The Future of Protestantism: Evangelicalism," in *The Blackwell Companion to Protestantism*, ed. Alister E. McGrath and Darren C. Marks (Oxford: Blackwell, 2004), 422.

5. Ibid., 424.

(if *movement* is even the right term)? The authors of these chapters—some themselves evangelical, some decidedly not evangelical—come to markedly differing conclusions. As editors, we see this as a strength of this text, not a weakness. For our goal is to create as open a space as possible to allow differing perspectives on evangelicalism and its relationship to empire to emerge, precisely because we think these differing perspectives reflect the complex and—at times—even contradictory or incoherent nature of evangelicalism. If there is any one message that this collection of essays conveys, it is that evangelicalism—or at least the millions of people throughout the world who self-identify as "evangelicals"—is not unified or cannot be described with easy generalizations. Perhaps there once was a time when such generalizations made sense, but that time is clearly over. Our volume challenges other volumes that attempt to depict evangelicals in broad strokes or, worse yet, simply characterize them as the "Religious Right."

This collection of essays examines the relevance of empire theory for politically and religiously interpreting both American and global evangelicalism. On the one hand, we seek to understand and analyze American evangelicalism's "Constantinianism" (i.e., the ways in which evangelicalism has both itself functioned as an empire and also aided the U.S. government in establishing and maintaining its empire status). On the other hand, we wish to consider what resources evangelism offers to counter or "subvert" imperialistic ways of thinking and acting. While some of these possibilities for subverting American and global empire lie within the United States itself, many chapters of this volume examine other manifestations of evangelicalism and Pentecostalism internationally that challenge empires of both types.

The volume is divided into three sections. Section 1, titled "Present," provides theoretical accounts of evangelical empire in conversation with Hardt and Negri. Section 2, "Past," presents historical perspectives on the evangelical empire in light of empire theory. Section 3, "Future," considers the relevance of this paradigm for the future of Christianity.

Opening section 1, Jim Wallis notes that the use of the word *empire* in relation to American power in the world was once controversial, often restricted to left-wing critiques of U.S. hegemony. But now, on op-ed pages and in the nation's political discourse, the concepts of empire, and even the phrase "Pax Americana," are increasingly wielded in unapologetic ways. To this aggressive extension of American power in the world President George W. Bush has added God, suggesting that the success of American military and foreign policy are connected to a religiously inspired "mission" and even that his presidency has been a divine appointment for a time such as this. As with the early church, our response is the ancient confession "Jesus is Lord." The contemporary evangelical church is called to live the truth that empires do not last and that the Word of God will ultimately trump the Pax Americana as it did the Pax Romana.

Helene Slessarev-Jamir and Bruce Ellis Benson argue that evangelicalism is "contested." Starting with an analysis of Wheaton College, they point out the differing visions—past and present—for what the term *evangelicalism* means. As Hardt and Negri point out, the "challenge of democracy" is acknowledging both commonality and difference. Such is also the challenge of evangelicalism. But Slessarev-Jamir and Benson argue that this "contestation" is neither simply negative nor positive: it turns out to be both. For the shifting definition of "evangelicalism" both allows for more diverse groups to take on that label and results in significant disagreements among those groups as to who truly stand as the rightful heirs of evangelicalism.

Gail Hamner's chapter investigates the biopolitical potential of U.S. evangelical Christians primarily through Hardt and Negri's claims about the "singularity" of multitude. She situates the challenge of *Empire* and *Multitude* to evangelicals between three critiques: the incompatibility of Christianity and democracy, the political undesirability of all forms of transcendence, and the impossibility of unified identity. The political strength of Christianity will come, she argues, through the display of its weakness.

Lester Edwin J. Ruiz and Charles W. Amjad-Ali's chapter explores several critical aspects of U.S. empire, in particular, the history of its sociopolitical and economic power and the kind of knowledge that this power has generated. They argue that U.S. theology has evolved in the context of U.S. imperialism and in the process has provided, and continues to provide, the fundamental moral underpinnings for this empire while justifying its contemporary manifestations. This theology is most fully expressed in the various strands of contemporary U.S. evangelical theology, which paradoxically is both a rebellion against Enlightenment epistemology and one of its most significant offspring.

In their chapter, Jennifer Butler and Glenn Zuber examine Hardt and Negri's definitions of multitude and empire in light of conservative white evangelical participation in United Nations activism and global NGO organizing. They argue that while often portrayed monolithically, white evangelical activism is quite diverse, making any hard-and-fast categorizations suspect. Nor can one predict whether this group will on balance provide greater support for empire or multitude. They contrast the work of humanitarian-focused and family-focused white evangelical NGOs to demonstrate the complexity of defining *multitude*.

James K. A. Smith considers the role and rubric of "freedom" in connection with empire—in relation to both free markets and militaristic foreign policy undertaken in the name of freedom. His argument cuts two ways: on the one hand, he argues that evangelicals, who find their legacy in Augustine, Calvin, and Jonathan Edwards, should be more cautious about the nonteleological notion of freedom that nourishes empire. On the other hand, he argues that

Hardt and Negri's account of the multitude's resistance to empire is insufficient precisely because they only radicalize the negative freedom of empire. What is needed to resist empire, he argues, are not just Augustinian tropes but a full-blooded Augustinian *ecclesiology*.

In his chapter "Liberality vs. Liberalism," John Milbank proceeds to think anew about liberalism and democracy in light of what he calls "the failure of secular ideologies." In this essay, Milbank contends that the liberalism so highly exalted by these ideologies must be challenged by a truer liberality. From the outset, this challenge must involve a rethinking of the *polis* and society in terms of an economy of exchange between persons, as opposed to the predominant theory of contractual relationships. Such a rethinking of the nature of society will, for Milbank, inevitably no longer result in a state oriented toward securing the private goods of private individuals but rather point toward a common and shared good. Finally, Milbank suggests that the modern state must move away from a political philosophy of pure democracy in which the majority of opinions will rule the day toward a "fusion of democratic dispersal with monarchic liberality and objectivity," where a "common good and absolute transcendent truth" guide the state and provide a liberality of the society at large against the tyranny of democracy.

Opening section 2, Patrick Provost-Smith argues that thinking historically about the relationship between evangelicalism and empire requires revisions in the way that we think of the legacy of evangelicalism and the writing of history. The objective of this essay is therefore not to "define" evangelicalism but to explore it genealogically. Provost-Smith argues that the Christian "evangelium" has long been articulated as in conflict with the forms of "imperium" that emerged from Roman civil theology in late antiquity and that were problematized anew in Catholic thought prior to the Reformation. In particular, it is argued that exploring the conflict from the point of view of the colonial experience, specifically through the lens of the Spanish empire in the Americas, provides new ways of thinking about the contemporary relationship of evangelicals and imperial ideologies.

Sébastien Fath's chapter compares and confronts the secular postmillennial worldviews of the neocons—and of most of George W. Bush's administration—with the evangelical premillennial emphasis. Through this particular lens, Hardt and Negri's notion of empire is translated in very different ways. On the one hand, U.S. empire appears to be defined as a coming paradise. On the other hand, the evangelical view of a coming empire seems mainly shaped by a very different ideological frame. Relying on a premillennial interpretation of the words attributed to Jesus Christ ("My kingdom is not of this world"), many evangelicals hold a far more pessimistic view of the political, economic, and cultural future of the global world. In that sense, Fath asks whether evangelical discourse could work as an anti-imperialist force.

In Kurt Anders Richardson's chapter, the political implications of key passages of the New Testament are reappropriated through practices of interpretation that can be called "evangelical biblicism." The early American theological and political theorist Roger Williams continues to provide an important resource for thinking about the politics of this nation. In contemporary evangelicalism, the relation between pneumatology (the doctrine of the Holy Spirit) and anthropology (the doctrine of humanity) can provide guidance for political orientation in the American empire where Hardt and Negri struggle to advance a constructive program.

Juan F. Martínez argues that Latinos have an ambivalent place in the United States, both because many became Americans due to U.S. imperial expansion and because their migratory patterns are directly linked to U.S. interventionism. Latinos became Protestants when U.S. missionaries sought to evangelize and Americanize them. Latino Protestants then developed an *evangélico* identity nurtured with immigrants from Latin America. This identity is difficult to maintain because of the links between U.S. evangelicalism and assimilation. *Evangélicos* have a limited space in U.S. evangelicalism, because if they assimilate they no longer have a clear *evangélico* identity, and if they don't they are not easily accepted by U.S. evangelicals. It is yet to be seen whether these stepchildren of empire will be part of Hardt and Negri's multitude that brings change to U.S. evangelicalism.

Eleanor Moody-Shepherd and Peter Goodwin Heltzel's chapter builds on Hardt and Negri's analysis of new social movements as constitutive to the emerging multitude but find their race theory problematic. They explore the relationship between Anglo American evangelicals, African American Protestants, and the economics and racism of empire, focusing on two contemporary social movements that have their roots in the Civil Rights movement of the 1960s: Jesse Louis Jackson Sr. and the Rainbow/PUSH Coalition and Jim Wallis and Sojourners/Call to Renewal. They argue that it is vital for evangelicals to embrace the struggle for racial and economic justice as an expression of the church's social witness and ministry of reconciliation. Christian social movements like the Rainbow/PUSH coalition and Sojourners/Call to Renewal provide a new trajectory where Anglo American evangelicals and African American Protestants can work together with Native Americans, Asians, and Hispanic/Latinos/Latinas for racial and economic justice for all.

Elaine Padilla and Dale T. Irvin explore a perspective on empire that comes from an indigenous grassroots Pentecostal community in Central America. In general, Pentecostalism has demonstrated that it can plant its roots both quickly and deeply in local indigenous cultures. In many places, it has freed Pentecostal believers from the sense of burden of western Christendom's colonial missionary heritage. A number of recent observers have noted the manner in which some sectors of the Pentecostal movement in Latin America today are collaborating in the construction of the new corporate or neo-liberal state that is emerging on the continent. Indigenous ways of negotiation present a more complex perspective on the relationship to both state and society that is critical to understanding further Pentecostalism and empire.

In a conversation format, Donald W. Dayton and Christian Collins Winn engage the question of evangelicals and empire by problematizing the dominant historical, theological, and ethical understanding of "evangelicalism." They question the validity and usefulness of the term as it is currently understood in popular and scholarly circles. In contradistinction to the synonyms *orthodox* and *conservative*, they raise the question of whether *pietism* and *revivalism* ought to be put forward. The latter make more sense historically and theologically for analyzing "evangelical" history and also problematizes and transcends categories like "orthodox" and "conservative" by pointing to a counterhistory of progressive radicalism, social action, and in some cases religious socialism, which would make a more robust contribution to an "evangelical" resistance to "empire."

Opening section 3, in his essay "Empire and Transcendence," Mark Lewis Taylor examines Hardt and Negri's notion of transcendence within the context of present struggle amid U.S. imperial powers. By reflecting on Ernesto Laclau's critique of *Empire,* Taylor challenges Hardt and Negri's claim that the emancipatory multitude rests on a thoroughgoing "refusal of transcendence." Instead of a comprehensive refusal, Taylor argues for a "transcendence of emancipatory politics," which can be distinguished from other modes of transcendence that often have supported, and still support, imperial enterprises. In fact, Taylor proceeds to identify several key points in the proposals of *Empire* and *Multitude* at which a transcendence of emancipatory politics seems much in evidence. The result is not just a critical view of Hardt and Negri (nor a rendering of them as closeted transcendentalists) but, more important, a critical challenge to U.S. theologians and ethicists today, urging that they break with modes of transcendence that reinforce imperial ideologies and practices and inviting them to reflect on the vital dimensions of transcendence present in the emancipatory politics of *Empire* and *Multitude.*

Corey D. B. Walker's engagement with evangelicals and empire offers a prolegomenon to a more robust project of developing a constructive theological proposal to challenge the foundations and norms of contemporary theoretical discourse. Developing the concepts of the ethics of opacity and theological thinking, Walker's argument investigates the broader phenomenon of the (re)emergence of the question of theology that has been firmly placed on the agenda for a variety of theoretical projects that seek to develop some form of alternative and/or radical political thought and praxis. Thinking with, against, and beyond Hardt and Negri as well as evangelicals, he presents a critical theoretical project that links ethics and epistemology in articulating an intricate critique of the geopolitics of theological knowledge that seeks to counter the "econo-epistemic" violence that is empire at the beginning of a new century.

In their chapter, Samuel Zalanga and Amos Yong interrogate the ideas of Hardt and Negri with regard to the possibility of Christianity in the United States and sub-Saharan Africa serving as a catalyst for social liberation. They argue that Hardt and Negri are right to assert that the human struggle for emancipation from the pervasive and hegemonic dominance of global market fundamentalism is one of the most serious challenges of our time. The authors maintain, however, that the struggle for social liberation is not just for the wider society alone: even the church of Christ needs to be liberated from being co-opted by this new religion of the market, a co-optation that is already under way in some respects. They maintain that it is an integral and prophetic role of the church to serve as a voice for the socially oppressed and marginalized. Failure to do this means, directly or indirectly, that the church is conspiring in legitimizing the global institutions and processes of market fundamentalism, which oppress many people in the world today. To explore the ramifications of Hardt and Negri's neglect of faith, Zalanga and Yong consider the increasingly influential role of Pentecostal Christianity in the global south. Beginning with some key themes from Hardt and Negri, they turn to a brief examination of the public role of Christianity in American society and the practice of Pentecostalism in sub-Saharan Africa, especially as it has been influenced by American Christianity. They conclude by suggesting how Christianity can and should subvert any "empire" project that constitutes idolatry from a biblical perspective.

After briefly setting out the rival accounts of the secular proposed by Milbank and Hardt/Negri, Michael Horton develops a covenantal account of the "two kingdoms" doctrine with its distinct appeal to natural equity. He suggests that by rehabilitating the secular as a site of legitimate concern distinct from the ultimate claims of the City of God, a theology of the secular can emerge that surrenders neither to secularism nor to "ecclesial communitarianism."

Mabiala Kenzo and John Franke claim that the thoroughly contextual nature of theology, while often acknowledged, has yet to take hold in the discipline as it is generally practiced in North American evangelical Protestantism. This situation is due in large part to two factors: (1) the enduring propensity of many evangelical thinkers to embrace the characteristics of modernity and (2) tendencies of modernity in the task of theological formulation, particularly those of foundationalism, and the tendency among the same evangelical thinkers to consistently overlook the fact that they belong to a dominant culture, which affects their theology and its reception in non-Western contexts. In response to this situation, Kenzo and Franke suggest a postfoundational and postcolonial model for the theological task. Such a model takes seriously the contextual nature of all human knowledge and the ecumenical vocation of the practice of theology. While remaining faithful to core Christian commitments, it draws on the insights of postmodern and postcolonial theories from the perspective of evangelical and ecumenical orthodoxy.

In his chapter, Paul Lim examines the tenability of Hardt and Negri's central thesis in *Empire*: the erasure of transcendence and the plausibility of constructing a biopower of "being against" utilizing immanence alone. He then proceeds to question the currently popular amalgamation of evangelicalism *and* Constantinianism, and demonstrates that the terms *evangelicals* and *evangelicalism* are in need of a more nuanced broadening of their semantic range to reflect the hemispheric shift within global Christianity. Finally, he offers a constructive forecast for the future in the philosophical and existential movement of "overcoming our xenophobia" toward *philoxenia*, the love of strangers that is embedded in the center of the Christian traditions.

In their chapter, Mario Costa, Catherine Keller, and Anna Mercedes examine the biblical basis and theological promise of love as a progressive political force, a mobilizing energy strong enough to persist in resisting the death drives of empire. Returning to the original notion of *evangelical* as "gospel based," able to constitute "good news" for those who desire freedom, justice, and healing, they take their cue from the Great Commandment to love both God and the neighbor. They argue for a hermeneutic of Christian love that exceeds the sentimental and finds its expression as an elemental force in the face of enmity. To that end, they deconstruct the traditional opposition between agape and eros, suggesting instead that only in its multidimensionality can love fulfill its potential as a theo-politics that is (in truth) evangelical.

To this multitude of voices are added some closing words by Michael Hardt and Antonio Negri. They observe that the interaction between the authors of this volume and themselves (neither evangelical nor Christian) is complex and cannot be described in terms of simple agreement or disagreement. For instance, they agree with those essays that argue that evangelicals both have resisted empire in various forms and have the power to do so in the future. Yet they take issues with various authors who argue that Hardt and Negri have no place in their theory for transcendence, arguing that they are willing to allow limited forms of transcendence.

The resulting volume well exemplifies the various ways in which evangelicalism can be interpreted and described—the diversity that *is* evangelicalism—and the multitude of ways in which evangelicalism supports and subverts empire. As editors our hope is hardly that this would be the last word on either evangelicals or empire. Instead, we hope to have opened a space for multiple conversations that are long overdue.

PRESENT

1

Dangerous Religion

George W. Bush's Theology of Empire

JIM WALLIS

Religion is the most dangerous energy source known to humankind. The moment a person (or government or religion or organization) is convinced that God is either ordering or sanctioning a cause or project, anything goes. The history, worldwide, of religion-fueled hate, killing, and oppression is staggering.

> Eugene Peterson (from the introduction to the book
> of Amos in the Bible paraphrase *The Message*)

"The military victory in Iraq seems to have confirmed a new world order," Joseph Nye, dean of Harvard's Kennedy School of Government, wrote recently in the *Washington Post*. "Not since Rome has one nation loomed so large above the others. Indeed, the word 'empire' has come out of the closet."[1]

The use of the word *empire* in relation to American power in the world was once controversial, often restricted to left-wing critiques of U.S. hegemony.

1. This essay was previously published by Jim Wallis as "Dangerous Religion," *Sojourners Magazine* 32, no. 5 (September–October 2003): 20–26.

But now, on op-ed pages and in the nation's political discourse, the concepts of empire, and even the phrase "Pax Americana," are increasingly referred to in unapologetic ways.

William Kristol, editor of the influential *Weekly Standard*, admits the aspiration to empire: "If people want to say we're an imperial power, fine." Kristol is chair of the Project for the New American Century, a group of conservative political figures that began in 1997 to chart a much more aggressive American foreign policy (see Project for a New American Empire).[2] The project's papers lay out the vision of an "American peace" based on "unquestioned US military pre-eminence." These imperial visionaries write, "America's grand strategy should aim to preserve and extend this advantageous position as far into the future as possible." It is imperative, in their view, for the United States to "accept responsibility for America's unique role in preserving and extending an international order friendly to our security, our prosperity, and our principles." That, indeed, is empire.

There is nothing secret about all this; on the contrary, the views and plans of these powerful men have been quite open. These are far right American political leaders and commentators who ascended to governing power and, after the trauma of September 11, 2001, have been emboldened to carry out their agenda.

In the run-up to the war with Iraq, Kristol told me that Europe was now unfit to lead because it was "corrupted by secularism," as was the developing world, which was "corrupted by poverty." Only the United States could provide the "moral framework" to govern a new world order, according to Kristol, who recently and candidly wrote, "Well, what is wrong with dominance, in the service of sound principles and high ideals?" Whose ideals? The American right wing's definition of "American ideals," presumably.

Bush Adds God

To this aggressive extension of American power in the world, President George W. Bush adds God—and that changes the picture dramatically. It's one thing for a nation to assert its raw dominance in the world; it's quite another to suggest, as this president does, that the success of American military and foreign policy is connected to a religiously inspired "mission" and even that his presidency may be a divine appointment for a time such as this.

Many of the president's critics make the mistake of charging that his faith is insincere at best, a hypocrisy at worst, and mostly a political cover for his right-wing agenda. I don't doubt that George W. Bush's faith is sincere and

2. See http://www.sojo.net/index.cfm?action=magazine.article&issue=soj0309&article=030911.

deeply held. The real question is the content and meaning of that faith and how it affects his administration's domestic and foreign policies.

Bush reports a life-changing conversion around the age of forty from being a nominal Christian to a born-again believer—a personal transformation that ended his drinking problems, solidified his family life, and gave him a sense of direction. He changed his denominational affiliation from his parents' Episcopal faith to his wife's Methodism. Bush's personal faith helped prompt his interest in promoting "compassionate conservatism" and the faith-based initiative as part of his new administration.

The real theological question about George W. Bush was whether he would make a pilgrimage from being essentially a self-help Methodist to being a social reform Methodist. God had changed his life in real ways, but would his faith deepen to embrace the social activism of John Wesley, the founder of Methodism, who said poverty was a matter not only of personal choices but also of social oppression and injustice? Would Bush's God of the twelve-step program also become the God who requires social justice and challenges the status quo of the wealthy and powerful, the God of whom the biblical prophets speak?

Then came September 11, 2001. Bush's compassionate conservatism and faith-based initiative rapidly gave way to his newfound vocation as the commander-in-chief of the "war against terrorism." Close friends say that after 9/11 Bush found "his mission in life." The self-help Methodist slowly became a messianic Calvinist promoting America's mission to "rid the world of evil." The Bush theology was undergoing a critical transformation.

In an October 2000 presidential debate, candidate Bush warned against an overactive American foreign policy and the negative reception it would receive around the world. Bush called for restraint. "If we are an arrogant nation, they will resent us," he said. "If we're a humble nation, but strong, they'll welcome us."

The president has come a long way since then. His administration has launched a new doctrine of preemptive war, has fought two wars (in Afghanistan and Iraq), and now issues regular demands and threats against other potential enemies. After 9/11, nations around the world responded to America's pain—even the French newspaper *Le Monde* carried the headline "We are all Americans now." But the preemptive and—most critically—*unilateral* foreign policy America now pursues has squandered much of that international support.

The Bush policy has become one of potentially endless wars abroad and a domestic agenda that mostly consists of tax cuts, primarily for the rich. "Bush promised us a foreign policy of humility and a domestic policy of compassion," Joe Klein wrote in *Time* magazine. "He has given us a foreign policy of arrogance and a domestic policy that is cynical, myopic, and cruel."[3] What happened?

A Mission and an Appointment

Former Bush speechwriter David Frum says of the president, "War had made him . . . a crusader after all."[4] At the outset of the war in Iraq, Bush entreated, "God bless our troops." In his State of the Union speech, he vowed that America would lead the war against terrorism "because this call of history has come to the right country." Bush's autobiography is titled *A Charge to Keep*, which is a quote from his favorite hymn.

In Frum's book *The Right Man*, he recounts a conversation between the president and his top speechwriter, Mike Gerson, a graduate of evangelical Wheaton College. After Bush's speech to Congress following the 9/11 attacks, Gerson called up his boss and said, "Mr. President, when I saw you on television, I thought—God wanted you there." According to Frum, the president replied, "He wants us all here, Gerson."[5]

Bush has made numerous references to his belief that he could not be president if he did not believe in a "divine plan that supersedes all human plans." As he gained political power, Bush has increasingly seen his presidency as part of that divine plan. Richard Land, of the Southern Baptist Convention, recalls hearing Bush say, "I believe God wants me to be president." After 9/11, Michael Duffy wrote in *Time* magazine, the president spoke of "being chosen by the grace of God to lead at that moment."[6]

Every Christian hopes to find a vocation and calling that is faithful to Christ. But a president who believes that his nation is fulfilling a God-given righteous mission and that he serves with a divine appointment can become quite theologically unsettling. Theologian Martin Marty voices the concern of many when he says, "The problem isn't with Bush's sincerity, but with his evident conviction that he's doing God's will."[7] As *Christianity Today* put it, "Some worry that Bush is confusing genuine faith with national ideology." The president's faith, wrote Klein, "does not give him pause or force him to reflect. It is a source of comfort and strength but not of wisdom."[8]

The Bush theology needs to be examined on biblical grounds. Is it really Christian or merely American? Does it take a global view of God's world or just assert American nationalism in the latest update of "manifest destiny"?

3. Joe Klein, "Blessed Are the Poor—They Don't Get Tax Cuts," *Time*, June 2, 2003, 25.
4. David Frum, *The Right Man* (New York: Random House, 2003).
5. Ibid., 148.
6. Michael Duffy, "The President Marching Alone," *Time*, September 9, 2002, 42.
7. Martin Marty, "The Sin of Pride," *Newsweek*, March 10, 2003, 32
8. Joe Klein, "The Blinding Glare of His Certainty," *Time*, February 24, 2003, 19.

How does the rest of the world—and, more important, the rest of the church worldwide—view America's imperial ambitions?

Getting the Words Wrong

President Bush uses religious language more than any president in U.S. history, and some of his key speechwriters come right out of the evangelical community. Sometimes he draws on biblical language, other times old gospel hymns that have deep resonance among the faithful in his own electoral base. The problem is that the quotes from the Bible and hymnals are too often either taken out of context or, worse yet, employed in ways quite different from their original meaning. For example, in the 2003 State of the Union, the president evoked an easily recognized and quite famous line from an old gospel hymn. Speaking of America's deepest problems, Bush said, "The need is great. Yet there's power, wonder-working power, in the goodness and idealism and faith of the American people." But that's not what the song is about. The hymn says there is "power, power, wonder-working power *in the blood of the Lamb*" (emphasis added). The hymn is about the power of Christ in salvation, not the power of "the American people," or any people, or any country. Bush's citation was a complete misuse.

On the first anniversary of the 2001 terrorist attacks, President Bush said at Ellis Island, "This ideal of America is the hope of all mankind. . . . That hope still lights our way. And the light shines in the darkness. And the darkness has not overcome it." Those last two sentences are straight out of John's Gospel. But in the Gospel the light shining in the darkness is the Word of God, and the light is the light of Christ. It's not about America and its values. Even Bush's favorite hymn, "A Charge to Keep," speaks of that charge as "a God to glorify"—not to "do everything we can to protect the American homeland," as Bush has named our charge to keep.

Bush seems to make this mistake over and over again—confusing nation, church, and God. The resulting theology is more American civil religion than Christian faith.

The Problem of Evil

Since 9/11, President Bush has turned the White House "bully pulpit" into a pulpit indeed, replete with "calls" and "missions" and "charges to keep" regarding America's role in the world. George Bush is convinced that we are engaged in a moral battle between good and evil and that those who are not with us are on the wrong side in that divine confrontation.

But who is "we," and does no evil reside with "us"? The problem of evil is a classic one in Christian theology. Anyone who cannot see the real face of evil in the terrorist attacks of September 11, 2001 is suffering from a bad case of postmodern relativism. To fail to speak of evil in the world today is to engage in bad theology. But to speak of "they" being evil and "we" being good, to say that evil is all out there and that in the warfare between good and evil others are either with us or against us—that is also bad theology. Unfortunately, it has become the Bush theology.

After the 9/11 attacks, the White House carefully scripted the religious service in which the president declared war on terrorism from the pulpit of the National Cathedral. The president declared to the nation, "Our responsibility to history is already clear: to answer these attacks and rid the world of evil." With most every member of the cabinet and the Congress present, along with the nation's religious leaders, it became a televised national liturgy affirming the divine character of the nation's new war against terrorism, ending triumphantly with the "Battle Hymn of the Republic." War against evil would confer moral legitimacy on the nation's foreign policy and even on a contested presidency.

What is most missing in the Bush theology is acknowledgment of the truth of this passage from the Gospel of Matthew: "Why do you see the speck in your neighbor's eye, but do not notice the log in your own eye? Or how can you say to your neighbor, 'Let me take the speck out of your eye,' while the log is in your eye? You hypocrite, first take the log out of your own eye, and then you will see clearly to take the speck out of your neighbor's eye" (7:3–5). A simplistic "we are right and they are wrong" theology rules out self-reflection and correction. It also covers over the crimes America has committed, which lead to widespread global resentment against us.

Theologian Reinhold Niebuhr made the point that every nation, political system, and politician falls short of God's justice, because we are all sinners. He specifically argued that even Adolf Hitler—to whom Saddam Hussein was often compared by Bush—did not embody absolute evil any more than the Allies represented absolute good. Niebuhr's sense of ambiguity and irony in history does not preclude action but counsels the recognition of limitations and prescribes both humility and self-reflection.

And what of Bush's tendency to go it alone, even against the expressed will of much of the world? A foreign government leader said to me at the beginning of the Iraq war, "The world is waiting to see if America will listen to the rest of us, or if we will all just have to listen to America." American unilateralism is not just bad political policy; it is bad theology as well. C. S. Lewis wrote that he supported democracy not because people are good but rather because they often are not. Democracy provides a system of checks and balances against any human beings' getting too much power. If that is true of nations, it must also be true of international relations. The vital questions of diplomacy, intervention, war, and peace are, in this theological view, best left to the collective judgment of many nations, not just one—especially not the richest and most powerful one.

In Christian theology, it is not nations that rid the world of evil—they are too often caught up in complicated webs of political power, economic interests, cultural clashes, and nationalist dreams. The confrontation with evil is a role reserved for God, and for the people of God when they faithfully exercise moral conscience. But God has not given the responsibility for overcoming evil to a nation-state, much less to a superpower with enormous wealth and particular national interests. To confuse the role of God with that of the American nation, as George Bush seems to do, is a serious theological error that some might say borders on idolatry or blasphemy.

It's easy to demonize the enemy and claim that we are on the side of God and good. But repentance is better. As the *Christian Science Monitor* put it, paraphrasing Alexander Solzhenitzyn. "The gospel, some evangelicals are quick to point out, teaches that the line separating good and evil runs not between nations, but inside every human heart."[9]

A Better Way

The much-touted Religious Right is now a declining political factor in American life. *The New York Times'* Bill Keller observed, "Bombastic evangelical power brokers like Jerry Falwell and Pat Robertson have aged into irrelevance, and now exist mainly as ludicrous foils."[10] The real theological problem in America today is no longer the Religious Right but the nationalist religion of the Bush administration—one that confuses the identity of the nation with the church, and God's purposes with the mission of American empire.

America's foreign policy is more than preemptive, it is theologically presumptuous; not only unilateral but dangerously messianic; not just arrogant but bordering on the idolatrous and blasphemous. George Bush's personal faith has prompted a profound self-confidence in his "mission" to fight the "axis of evil," his "call" to be commander-in-chief in the war against terrorism, and his definition of America's "responsibility" to "defend the . . . hopes of all mankind." This is a dangerous mix of bad foreign policy and bad theology.

But the answer to bad theology is not secularism; it is, rather, good theology. It is not always wrong to invoke the name of God and the claims of religion in the public life of a nation, as some secularists say. Where would we be without the prophetic moral leadership of Martin Luther King Jr., Desmond Tutu, and Oscar Romero?

In our own American history, religion has been lifted up for public life in two very different ways. One invokes the name of God and faith in order to hold us accountable to *God's intentions*—to call us to justice, compassion,

9. Jane Lampman, "New Scrutiny of Role of Religion in Bush's Politics," *Christian Science Monitor*, March 17, 2003.

10. Bill Keller, "God and George W. Bush," *The New York Times*, May 17, 2003.

humility, repentance, and reconciliation. Abraham Lincoln, Thomas Jefferson, and Martin Luther King Jr. perhaps best exemplify that way. Lincoln regularly used the language of scripture, but in a way that called both sides in the Civil War to contrition and repentance. Jefferson said famously, "I tremble for my country when I reflect that God is just."

The other way invokes God's blessing on *our activities*, agendas, and purposes. Many presidents and political leaders have used the language of religion like this, and George W. Bush fell prey to that same temptation.

Christians should always live uneasily with empire, which constantly threatens to become idolatrous and substitute secular purposes for God's. As we reflect on our response to the American empire and what it stands for, a reflection on the early church and empire is instructive.

The book of Revelation, while written in apocalyptic language and imagery, is seen by most biblical expositors as a commentary on the Roman Empire, its domination of the world, and its persecution of the church. In Revelation 13, a "beast" and its power are described. Eugene Peterson's *The Message* puts it in vivid language: "The whole earth was agog, gaping at the Beast. They worshiped the Dragon who gave the Beast authority, and they worshiped the Beast, exclaiming: 'There's never been anything like the Beast! . . . No one would dare to go to war with the Beast!' . . . It held absolute sway over all tribes and peoples, tongues, and races" (Rev. 13:3–4, 7b). But the vision of John of Patmos also foresaw the defeat of the Beast. In Revelation 19, a white horse, with a rider whose "name is called The Word of God" and "King of kings and Lord of lords," captures the beast and its false prophet.

As with the early church, our response to an empire holding "absolute sway," against which "no one would dare to go to war," is the ancient confession "Jesus is Lord." And to live in the promise that empires do not last, that the Word of God will ultimately survive the Pax Americana as it did the Pax Romana.

In the meantime, American Christians will have to make some difficult choices. Will we stand in solidarity with the worldwide church, the international body of Christ—or with our own American government? It's not a surprise to note that the global church does not generally support the foreign policy goals of the Bush administration—whether in Iraq, in the Middle East, or in the wider "war on terrorism." Only inside some of our U.S. churches does one find religious voices consonant with the visions of American empire.

Once there was Rome; now there is a new Rome. Once there were barbarians; now there are many barbarians who are the Saddams of this world. And once there were the Christians who were loyal not to Rome but to the kingdom of God. To whom will the Christians be loyal today?

2

The Contested Church

Multiple Others of Evangelical Multitude

HELENE SLESSAREV-JAMIR AND BRUCE ELLIS BENSON

The multitude is composed of a set of *singularities*—and by singularity we mean a social subject whose difference cannot be reduced to sameness, a difference that remains different. . . . The multitude, however, although it remains multiple, is not fragmented, anarchical, or incoherent.[1]

Michael Hardt and Antonio Negri are well aware of the complexities of their notion of "multitude," including "differences" within multitude. But they still see the multitude as constituted "not on identity or unity . . . but what it has in common." As they point out, the challenge of recognizing both commonality and difference is the very "challenge of democracy" itself.[2] Yet the question is whether the evangelical multitude is not just multiple but also (*pace* Hardt and Negri) truly "fragmented" and perhaps even somewhat "incoherent"— *despite* holding things in common.

---

1. Michael Hardt and Antonio Negri, *Multitude: War and Democracy in the Age of Empire* (New York: Penguin, 2004), 99.
2. Ibid., 100.

Here we want to argue that evangelicals—both in the United States and across the world—are truly fragmented into numerous groups. Moreover, many of these groups (not the least of which are upper-middle-class Caucasian, "Constantinian" evangelicals) want to define evangelicalism in their respective ways. The result is a "contested" church. The logic of this "contestation," though, is neither simply positive nor negative; rather it is both. On the one hand, the competing varieties of evangelicalism—and even that very state of contestation—have often served to strengthen rather than weaken evangelicalism as a whole. For they have allowed the development of a multitude of evangelicalisms. On the other hand, because of the possibility of construing the gospel in a way that largely focuses on personal salvation (and thus focuses on personal responsibility often to the exclusion of social responsibility), a crucial component—the social dimension of the gospel—has been largely ignored. This has been particularly true of the dominant American[3] version of evangelicalism that, for the most part, lacks a concern for justice and does little to promote peace or the welfare of the least of society. Yet this contestation (and thus incoherence) within the structure of evangelicalism demonstrates that it is an example of Hardt and Negri's multitude, which may hold *some* things in common but definitely not others. Further, it is precisely due to the logic of contestation that the chance for transforming American evangelicalism is a real rather than merely utopian hope.

The Fragmented Church

As a starting point for describing this "contested church," it is worth noting that we both teach[4] at what could arguably be described as the flagship educational institution of American evangelicalism. As a community, Wheaton College in its present form is overwhelmingly dominated by "Constantinian" voices. On the one hand, it quite self-consciously trains students to become part of American empire. It is no accident that both George W. Bush's former chief speechwriter Michael Gerson, and the former speaker of the House of Representatives, Dennis Hastert, are Wheaton graduates. On the other hand, our students generally come from families that have bought in heavily to the global economic empire, and most are quite comfortable with that relationship. To a large extent, they and their families are the beneficiaries of America's global reach, which they often believe their personal virtues have entitled them to enjoy. If it can be said that American evangelicalism takes itself to be

---

3. Given the common usage of *America* and *American* to denote the United States of America, we will mostly follow that usage here. However, we find these terms misleading and hegemonic, all the more so because their use is only infrequently noted and questioned.

4. At the time this chapter was written.

paradigmatic not merely for evangelicalism in general but also for the (true) church itself, then it is not too much of a stretch to say that Wheaton College takes itself (again, arguably, and with some qualifications) as paradigmatic for the church. While no one at Wheaton would probably own up to as bald an assertion as that, we think it is safe to say that such thinking is prevalent at Wheaton.

But immediately we realize just how problematic such thinking is. It is not just that many other groups within evangelicalism are vying for the opportunity to style their particular brand of evangelicalism as paradigmatic (to which we turn in the next section); it is that Wheaton itself is fragmented. Even at Wheaton, there are pockets of resistance to both American and global empire among faculty and students. Indeed, the past several years have witnessed a marked increase in student and faculty activism on issues of peace, global AIDS, and hunger. These differences are certainly not outside the range of what we have in common. No doubt Wheaton faculty and students agree on the basic tenets of orthodoxy—and, in the case of faculty, subscribe to a rigorous doctrinal statement. While that document states that part of the believer's task is to be "actively seeking the good of everyone, especially the poor and needy,"[5] there is significant disagreement at Wheaton concerning just how central that call is to our community as a whole. Is it merely one small part of how Christians should act in the world? Or is it, instead, at the very heart of the gospel itself?

As an institution, Wheaton once was prophetic in terms of social justice. We think it is safe to say that our first president, Jonathan Blanchard, would have seen acting out such social justice as absolutely central to living out the gospel.[6] Yet that is exactly not where Wheaton stands today. Those prior commitments have been largely replaced with a triumphalism that regards America as the nation blessed by God, the New Jerusalem, the upholder of good and freedom in the world. On the whole (and we certainly admit that there would be notable exceptions to this generalization), Wheaton students are more or less comfortable with American empire in its guise as "the city on a hill," or "manifest destiny," or the "the good superpower." They are also comfortable with the "Pax Americana" that, as Hardt and Negri realize, is simply a continual state of war. Yet for our students these notions are filled with idealism—and many come from families and home congregations where such ideas are deeply ingrained. Still, there are those of us at Wheaton who wish that it would once again turn in a more prophetic direction and recover that prophetic role. We worry—along with Lamin Sanneh—that "the cultural captivity of Christianity in the West

5. *Wheaton College Catalogue 2007–2008*, 4.

6. Wheaton's first president, Jonathan Blanchard, was a radical social reformer, particularly in regard to slavery.

is nearly complete, and with the religion tamed, it is open season on the West's Christian heritage."[7] However, we are heartened by the pockets of resistance to empire that we find within evangelicalism—and certainly within the wider church.

Here we have merely one instance of fragmentation, but it turns out to be exemplary of the larger global evangelical community. Even the term *evangelical* is open to significant dispute.[8] It is precisely because the church is so contested that Wheaton College cannot realistically take itself to be paradigmatic of evangelicalism. Evangelicalism—and the body of Christ more generally—has a certain degree of hybridity or alterity within itself. That hybridity and alterity are *central* to the very notion of the church. For although Paul notes that in the church "there is no longer Jew or Greek, there is no longer slave or free, there is no longer male and female" (Gal. 3:28), Paul also speaks of the various members of the body that have different gifts and different roles (Rom. 12 and 1 Cor. 12). While we do not mean to suggest that some believers should naturally gravitate toward American and global empire (to quote Paul: "may it never be!"), we do want to point out that the church neither is now nor ever has been simply unified. Or, to put it differently, when George W. Bush had the temerity to say "You are either for us or against us," that was simply a false dilemma, not just politically but also religiously.[9] We may be either for or against Christ and the good news, but the forms that takes may vary considerably.

From its very beginning, the *ekklesia* has been a site of contestation. Admittedly, Acts 2 gives us a picture of a group committed to radical social justice: "All who believed were together and had all things in common; they would sell their possessions and goods and distribute the proceeds to all, as any had need" (Acts 2:44–45). Yet Paul's stern words to the Corinthians demonstrate that not all the early Christians were so united and so concerned for those with lesser means. In Corinth, the sacrament that was supposed to draw the body together—the Eucharist—was being unequally divided.[10] That Paul had to write to correct this problem shows just how out of hand it had gotten. Moreover, Paul makes it clear that the Corinthians' lack of concern for justice (shown in this and many other respects) was profoundly at odds with the gospel.

7. Lamin Sanneh, "The Defender of Good News: Questioning Lamin Sanneh," interview, *Christianity Today,* October 2003, 112.

8. It is indicative of where evangelicalism currently stands that Wheaton's current president—in a recent address to the faculty—wondered aloud whether the term *evangelical* meant anything definite enough for it to be a useful way of describing the college.

9. Posted by CNN on November 6, 2001, at 10:13 p.m. EST (0313 GMT). See http://archives.cnn.com/2001/US/11/06/gen.attack.on.terror.

10. Paul writes: "So then, my brothers and sisters, when you come together to eat [the Eucharist], wait for one another" (1 Cor. 11:33). Evidently some believers were coming early and finishing off the meal, leaving little or nothing for those who came later.

The Terrain of Resistance

Hardt and Negri believe that the very global interconnectedness created by the collaborative, iterative production of knowledge that constitutes empire in the postmodern age creates the possibilities of new forms of resistance. Furthermore, "the creation of the multitude, its innovation in networks, and its decision-making ability in common makes democracy possible for the first time today."[11] In effect, they are arguing that the multitude's creation of democratic practice and voice is a source of life in an age of empire that is now characterized by the constant threat of war and the suspension of democracy.

The multiplicity of evangelism allows it to simultaneously serve as the bulwark of empire as well as the moral foundation of resistance to empire. In *The Next Christendom*, Philip Jenkins describes the rapid spread of Christianity throughout Latin America, Africa, and Asia.[12] He argues that much of it is truly orthodox Christianity yet at the same time indigenous to its local non-Western context. A significant portion of the growth is taking place outside the boundaries of the religious institutions established by the former Western colonialists. In fact, some local church leaders openly reject any teaching from the West, because they fear it contains the seeds of its own destruction. Church leaders from the global South are beginning to speak on behalf of peace and justice for their people in ways that will challenge the hegemony of Western Constantinianism. The recent successes in the campaign for debt relief are at least in part the result of growing global collaboration and exchanges between Christian and secular advocates in the United States, United Kingdom, and those Two-Thirds World countries burdened by debt.[13] Giving voice to Africa's poor, Archbishop Njongonkulu Ndungane of South Africa noted: "Our objective is a clean slate—a total cancellation of odious and unpayable debts owed by African countries."[14]

Looking closer to home, we see signs of resistance to the Constantinian marriage of religion to the politics of empire among people who live on the margins of American society. Rather than embracing the dominant evangelical image of America as "the city on the hill," the African American faith tradition

11. *Multitude*, 340.

12. Philip Jenkins, *The Next Christendom: The Coming of Global Christianity* (New York: Oxford University Press, 2002).

13. In mid-June 2005 the finance ministers of rich country governments represented in the Group of Eight (G8) announced a deal on 100 percent debt cancellation of International Monetary Fund (IMF), World Bank, and African Development Fund debt for some impoverished nations. The limited debt relief provided since 2000 has doubled poverty alleviation expenditures in the countries that received it. Savings from debt relief have more than doubled school enrollment in Uganda, provided three extra years of school for Honduran children, and provided resources to fight HIV/AIDS in Mali, Mozambique, Senegal, and Cameroon.

14. From a sermon titled "I Hunger No More: An Interfaith Convocation," given at the Washington Cathedral (June 6, 2005).

has long seen America as "Egypt," the land of slavery. Though not necessarily consciously anti-imperial, the majority of African American Christians remain people of the Old Testament for whom the oft-repeated stories of Moses, the exodus, Nehemiah, Isaiah, and the other prophets keep a "prophetic imagination" alive. To quote Walter Brueggemann, the black church's prophetic tradition is a "means of evoking the cries that expect answers, learning to address them where they will be taken seriously, and ceasing to look to the numbed and dull empire that never intended to answer in the first place."[15] Similar resistance exists among America's most marginalized immigrants, many of whom carried their faith traditions with them on their arduous journey across a border into territories that the United States seized from Mexico in the 1848 Treaty of Guadalupe-Hidalgo. Theirs is a form of Roman Catholicism shaped by centuries of interaction with indigenous cultures and influenced by strains of liberation theology that emanated from resistance to the old order in Latin America. Situated in large urban immigrant communities in the United States, this reading of the gospel message as God's preferential option for the poor empowers various forms of localized resistance to the domination of empire. This resistance has been manifested in the new wave of union organizing among low-paid service and factory workers, many of whom are immigrants. Indeed, Hardt and Negri applaud the Justice for Janitors campaign as "one of the most successful and creative union organizing efforts in the United States."[16] Yet they appear unaware of the centrality of faith-based support for these organizing campaigns occurring among the United States' most vulnerable workers. It is fair to say that there are relatively few major unionizing drives occurring among low-wage workers in the United States in which faith-based support is not present to some extent. Lacking the strength to win bargaining rights for very vulnerable workers, local unions rely on collaboration with the broader constituencies reached by faith communities. Furthermore, contrary to the traditional Marxist notions of "religion as the opiate of the people," many immigrant workers are also active members of local parishes from which they draw considerable sustenance during their sojourn in a strange land. For immigrant faith communities, the command to love one's neighbor takes the tangible form of marching on picket lines in front of hotels, grocers, and restaurants that deny bargaining rights (basic democracy in the workplace) to their workers. Many priests serving Hispanic immigrant parishes, while native-born Americans, spent years working in the barrios of Latin America as missionary-priests before being called back to the United States.

In the months leading up to the U.S. invasion of Iraq, people in cities around the globe staged demonstrations against the threat of preemptive war. Here again Christian voices were prominently in evidence, as there is a long tradition

15. Walter Brueggemann, *The Prophetic Imagination* (Minneapolis: Fortress, 2001), 13.
16. *Multitude*, 214.

of Christian activism on behalf of peace. According to Jim Wallis in *God's Politics*, "In a demonstration of unity never seen before, virtually every world church body in the United States and the world that spoke out on the prospect of war with Iraq (with the notable exception of the American Southern Baptists) concluded this war was not a 'just war.'"[17] One of the statements issued by church leaders in the United States and United Kingdom called for the disarming of Iraq without war. These efforts at peaceful conflict resolution have drawn inspiration from the South African Anglican Church's leadership in bringing a peaceful end to apartheid, as well as the central role of churches that served as "free spaces" in the nonviolent downfall of the regime in the former German Democratic Republic. Again we see how, given the global nature of Christianity, the church is an embodiment of both singularity and multiplicity, giving it the potential to serve as a vehicle in creating the power of the multitude.

Pockets of Resistance within Evangelicalism

We noted that even at Wheaton there are pockets of resistance. Yet one need only consider the myriad activities of resistance within the evangelical tradition itself. Wallis and *Sojourners* are one of the best examples at present. It wasn't that long ago that Wallis and *Sojourners* were relatively marginal in the evangelical world. But with their campaign proclaiming that "God Is Not a Republican or a Democrat" followed by the tremendous response to *God's Politics* (it remained on the *New York Times* best seller list for sixteen weeks), many more evangelicals began to take Wallis and *Sojourners* seriously. The appearance of *The Great Awakening* has only further demonstrated Wallis's reach into the heart of evangelicalism. Wallis has begun to talk of the presence of a *kairos* moment in which religious leaders from across the globe and across the theological spectrum in the United States are coming together with a unified moral voice calling on the wealthy nations to initiate concrete steps to end world hunger in the next decade. In an e-mail sent out to supporters of *Sojourners*, Wallis reflected on a meeting of American religious leaders with Prime Minister Tony Blair several weeks prior to the G8 summit held in July 2005.

> We spoke of how for the first time the world has the knowledge, information, technology, and resources to substantially end extreme poverty as we know it, but that what is still lacking is the moral and political will to do so. And we agreed that to generate such moral will is part of the job of the religious community. . . . Despite our many deep and sometimes painful divisions, the

17. Jim Wallis, *God's Politics: Why the Right Gets It Wrong and the Left Doesn't Get It* (San Francisco: HarperOne, 2005), 113.

growing crisis of the world's most vulnerable people is serving to bring many of us together.[18]

More widely, there are many congregations and faith-based community and labor organizations that are subverting empire (of both kinds) by pushing for peace, life, and love. Although many of these groups can be found in the United States, they are even more plentiful abroad. Of course, these groups are often not well known. They have not (yet) learned how to gain the media attention afforded the American Religious Right, whose leaders have become so skillful in making themselves seem like the sole owners of the Christian tradition. Further, one of the difficulties in our era is that terms like *conservative* and *liberal* are less and less helpful in defining where people really stand. It is "conservative" to be "pro-life" but "liberal" to be against capital punishment. Yet such leaders as Cardinal Joseph Bernardin have been able to articulate a "seamless" position that affirms life from beginning to end. Many evangelicals want to emulate that position, but they are only beginning to find their voice.

According to Hardt and Negri, our current global state is one of war. One might say this is true of the contested church—not war in a strong sense but certainly in a weak sense. The various factions of the church are constantly working to make their vision of Christianity hegemonic. Writing in the *New York Times*, John Danforth, former Republican senator from Missouri and an Episcopal priest, laments: "In recent years conservative Christians have presented themselves as representing the only authentic Christian perspective on politics."[19] One can see this in the divide between the older mainline denominations and the newer "nondenominational" denominations, as well as within denominations as liberals and conservatives exchange heated condemnations of each other. But for the sake of Christ's church, it seems appropriate to push beyond dichotomies of liberal-conservative, Republican-Democrat, and us-them.

Such a push is beginning to be felt even in the centers of evangelicalism itself. Of course, the evangelical house divided has—paradoxically enough—been both a source of strength for evangelicalism and a serious weakness. Although David Brooks is actually talking about *political* conservatives when he writes the following, we think it applies to evangelicals as well: "Conservatives have not triumphed because they have built a disciplined and efficient message machine. Conservatives have thrived because they are split into feuding factions that squabble incessantly. As these factions have multiplied, more people have come to call themselves conservatives because they've found one faction to agree with."[20] So a strength of evangelicalism—and we would say

18. Jim Wallis, "A Kairos Moment on Poverty," SojoMail, June 9, 2005.

19. John C. Danforth, "Onward, Moderate Christian Soldiers," *New York Times*, June 17, 2005.

20. David Brooks, "A House Divided, and Strong," *New York Times*, April 5, 2005.

this is true in both the United States and elsewhere—is that there are so many varieties and that it is capable of adapting to fit the needs of local contexts. Hardt and Negri's description of multitude as "legion" can be aptly applied to evangelicalism.[21] Moreover, their characterization of multitude as "always and necessarily an open, plural composition" seems to rightly describe the body of Christ.[22]

Yet this situation of "feuding fractions that squabble incessantly" has also seriously compromised evangelicalism. While debate and "squabbling" is healthy and absolutely essential to a living, growing tradition, the possibility of being able to define evangelicalism by selectively accepting only those biblical injunctions that suit our purposes has resulted in an American evangelicalism in which the second greatest commandment ("love your neighbor as yourself") is not taken nearly seriously enough, and "neighbor" is all too often defined in the most conveniently narrow way possible. It has often resulted in churches that include only people "just like us." Michael Crosby, who has written on the spirituality of the beatitudes, puts it as follows: "Despite the hard data showing the present form of globalization to be unjust, such people end up with ears to hear and eyes to see, but keep from acting on this information and accepting its consequences, because their 'heart has grown dull' (Matt. 13:15)."[23] Even those evangelicals who do not officially subscribe to the "health and wealth" gospel often do so implicitly, for it is the logic behind their faith. All too frequently, American evangelicals believe that they are blessed by God because of their individual (and corporate, meaning national) virtue.

Rather than standing as critics of the modern consumer-driven culture that undergirds the American economy, many Christians embrace it. Consequently, they look down on the poor, since, to quote William Stringfellow, "where money is an idol, to be poor is a sin."[24] Jesus's words of rebuke to his disciples in Mark 14:7, "You will always have the poor with you," is oddly used by some Christians to justify doing nothing, even though it seems clear that Jesus envisioned his disciples to always be among the poor. To dismiss concern for the poor at a time when the gap between the wealthy and the poor is growing across the globe is not just a result of the personalizing of sin and redemption. It is also the triumphalism of empire. The structural causes of poverty tend not to be acknowledged in the United States, because to do so would undermine the triumphal notion of America as a nation anointed by God.

---

21. *Multitude*, 140.
22. Ibid., 190.
23. Michael Crosby, *Spirituality of the Beatitudes: Matthew's Vision for the Church in an Unjust Society* (Maryknoll, NY: Orbis, 2005), 32.
24. William Stringfellow, *A Keeper of the Word: Selected Writings of William Stringfellow*, ed. Bill Wylie-Kellermann (Grand Rapids: Eerdmans, 1994), 245.

Having said all that, if Brooks is right that "this feuding has meant that the meaning of conservatism is always shifting,"[25] then perhaps we are in the midst of a shift in which American Constantinianism may be overthrown— or at least seriously questioned—as new voices come to the foreground. So far, Constantinianism has won the day; but its days may well be numbered. As Danforth calls for in his editorial, "It is important for those of us who are sometimes called moderates to make the case that we too, have strongly held Christian convictions, that we speak from the depths of our convictions, and that our approach to politics is at least as faithful as that of those who are more conservative."

Furthermore, if Hardt and Negri are right that "immigrants invest the entire society with their subversive desires," then the immigrants (many of whom are fleeing the devestations wrought by NAFTA) coming into the United States may prove to be the salvation of evangelicalism in a new form.[26] Hardt and Negri envision a multitude as "legion," comprising "innumerable elements that remain different, one from the other, and yet communicate, collaborate, and act in common." They go on to say: "Now that really is demonic!"[27] Yet under the guidance of the Holy Spirit, such collaboration might instead be a new Pentecost in which a holy host of new prophetic voices—speaking in hundreds of tongues—would emerge.

Given the pattern of church growth across the world, such a Pentecost actually seems almost inevitable. No doubt just as the Jewish religious leaders must have been greatly alarmed by the outbreak of the multiplicity of tongues described in Acts 2, so American evangelical leaders will likely become alarmed by this newly emerging Pentecost. And yet as sons and daughters prophesy and young and old have visions and dreams, the church will have to take serious account of these prophesies and dreams. The result will be a contested church, not just in the sense that different groups will be presenting different versions of what true righteousness is but also in the sense that the very notion of the church—at least as defined by the West—will be contested. Out of this contestation will grow new visions for how Christians need to act in the world in order to be true to the gospel and to Jesus Christ. The West desperately needs to hear that message, however unwelcome it may be.

25. Brooks, "House Divided."
26. *Multitude*, 134.
27. Ibid., 140.

3

Acting in Common

How the Flesh of Multitude
Can Become Incarnate Words against Empire

M. GAIL HAMNER

This essay delineates the challenge posed by the work of Hardt and Negri to contemporary U.S. Christian evangelicals. Assuming that evangelicals *can* offer biopolitical resistance against the biopower of empire, I contend that it will entail embracing a desire for democracy that should be recognized as contradictory to many practices currently associated with evangelical Christianity. Every Christian lives as both believer and citizen, and these religious and social roles crucially shape political action and social vision. I will argue that the habits and pragmatic affiliations associated with being evangelical and being American are contradictory to one another, a fact that raises the question of how Hardt and Negri's critique of transcendence can align with an evangelical social project that prioritizes the sovereignty of God.

Let me begin with three preliminary explanations.

First, the specific practical challenges presented by *Empire* and *Multitude* require theoretical clarification. Hardt and Negri derive their concept of 'biopolitical potential' from Michel Foucault's notion of *biopower*, a term he developed to explain a change in the articulation of sovereign power over the course of the seventeenth century, when the state gradually shifted from making overt decrees over the life and death of individual subjects to employing various institutions and procedures for *regulating* and *producing* life itself. Relying on newly systematized and professionalized institutions such as "the prison, the factory, the asylum, the hospital, the university, [and] the school,"[1] state power grew increasingly able to sequester, oversee, track, and train populations; in short, the state grew adept at *disciplining* the biological bodies at its disposal (i.e., its subjects or citizens), which is why Foucault calls this type of society a "disciplinary society" and why he points to the 1600s as the beginning of an era of "biopower." The organization of "scientific" knowledge over life[2] intensified in the eighteenth century and coalesced in what Foucault describes as "the concrete arrangements that would go to make up the great technology of power in the nineteenth century."[3] Today, we generally recognize this era as that of the professionalization of humanistic and scientific discourses. The effects of biopower include a docile population and disciplined workforce, perfectly suited, Hardt and Negri note, for capitalist modes of production. In the twentieth century, disciplinary societies morphed into what Foucault terms "societies of control," the primary difference of which lies in the "intensification and generalization" of institutional structures of discipline[4] such that citizens internalize disciplinary expectations and receive disciplinary "instructions" outside the walls and halls of institutional buildings, for instance through television, radio music, radio talk shows, newspapers, billboards, Internet chat rooms, and blogs.

From its earliest to its most recent forms, biopower has existed as a tool of sovereignty, that is, as a mode and weapon of the consolidating *Gestalt* of postimperialist empire. Taking biopower as a social given, Hardt and Negri focus on the related fact that every weapon generates its own form of resistance. What they call the "social flesh" of multitude—or a (trans-) population's infinite heterogeneity—can never be completely "organ-ized," or surveyed and controlled by biopower. Biopolitical potential arises from the gaps in the management of population and in the points of resistance they make possible. *Biopower*, in sum, encapsulates the fact that politics today centrally concerns the production and management of life, and *biopolitical*

1. Michael Hardt and Antonio Negri, *Empire* (Cambridge, MA: Harvard University Press, 2000), 23.

2. *Scientific* is in scare quotes because what counted (and counts) as science was (is) determined in part by these processes of organization. That is, science is both what is organized (facts, theories, conclusions) and the processes of organization (method), such that what cannot, for whatever reason, *be* organized (by result or by method) is by definition unscientific. Hence critiques of religion, of emotion, and of unique events often are structured around the impossibility of their counting in any meaningful (i.e., organizable, repeatable, "scientific") sense.

3. Michel Foucault, *History of Sexuality*, vol. 1, *An Introduction* (New York: Vintage, 1980), 140.

4. *Empire*, 23.

potential, or *biopolitical resistance*, refers to the response of multitude to empire's biopower. To assert the real biopolitical potential of evangelicals, then, is to claim that the U.S. Christian evangelical version of the story and message of the cross can be mined and deployed as a biopolitical response to the biopower of empire.

Second, the dual roles of citizen and believer—into which I wish to insert the "difference" of being-woman—engage the familiar philosophical conundrum of the one and the many, or in this case how individual and group subjectivities can be both singular and plural, both unified and riddled with difference. Hardt and Negri refuse the choice and offer a dialectical solution.[5] Each life, they insist, is both unique and yet common with others in basic constitution and shared situation.[6] Instead of theorizing society as structured by "the people," "the mass," or "the proletariat," they develop the notion of "multitude" as a social entity that is both singular (acting in common) and collective (constituted by points of irreducible difference).[7] Multitude, they claim, "tends to mobilize what it shares in common and what it produces in common against the imperial power of global capital."[8] The claim implies a dialectical social ontology. On a descriptive and structural level, multitude is what it shares in common—the organs of empire. On a revolutionary and virtual level, multitude is the galvanizing pulse that runs through and against these organs.

Just as biopower incites biopolitical resistance, so the common situation (of life, and of life under empire) incites the social and political difference (of multitude). Since the singular points of multitude all share the common situation of empire, they all *can* become points of resistance to it. Because persons and groups are already mapped on (and by) the organs of empire, they are always *both* an organized identity *and* a singularity that resists categorization. But Hardt and Negri also claim that the difference of each singularity *constitutes* the common project of democracy through the actions of multitude—and herein lies the crux of my desire to discuss habits, affiliations, and the difference of being-woman, because it seems clear that some of the habits often taken for granted about Christianity, citizenship, and gender roles somehow must be interrupted if evangelical Christians seek to be part of the struggle against empire.

5. Michael Hardt and Antonio Negri, *Multitude: War and Democracy in the Age of Empire* (New York: Penguin, 2004), 100.

6. Hardt and Negri focus primarily on human life, while I try to keep the form of life as open as possible in this chapter. Certainly all life on earth is carbon based, and all must (right now) share the common environmental fate of water, air, and soil. Equally obvious (and yet contested by some) is the common fate of nonhumans at the hands of humans. Hardt and Negri address this with respect to the common situation of global capitalism; Christians address it, if at all, under the rubric of stewardship.

7. For a collegial critique of the presumed effectiveness of this semantic difference, see Bruno Bosteels, "Logics of Antagonism: In the Margins of Alain Badiou's 'The Flux and the Party,'" *Polygraph* 15/16 (2004): 97.

8. *Multitude*, 101.

Third, Hardt and Negri's unrelenting critique of transcendence elicits the obvious question whether their project has any sympathy for Christian allies. For these Marxist theorists, sovereignty and transcendence are aligned with state, reified power, and all its attendant ills of coercion and corruption. Appeals to transcendence support the sovereignty of empire and the dominance of abstract representational politics. In contrast, they theorize the spontaneous and collective actions of multitude yielding a nonrepresentative abstraction from the common that constitutes itself through love and joyfulness.[9] Their semantics appropriate Christian language about God but direct it horizontally and immanently. In effect, they replace the sovereignty of God and the body of Christ with the power and flesh of multitude. In my abstract for this chapter I speculated that the sovereignty of God avowed by evangelicals might be made immanent, and thus made common to multitude, through the doctrine of *imago Dei* and a correlating scriptural critique of reified, power-hungry politics.

A Parable of Power

Let me begin with scripture. Recently I heard religion scholar and literary critic Roland Boer give a wonderful interpretation of Judges 9:8–15, the parable of the trees seeking a king.[10] As often happens when I hear talks involving scripture, I grew more interested in what was *not* addressed by Boer than in his own astute argument. In the parable, the trees solicit first the olive, then the fig, and finally the vine to be their king. After each refuses the office, the trees petition the bramble. The bramble responds in the language of covenant: *if* your request is truly "in good faith," then "come and take refuge in my shade," but *if not*, "let fire come out of the bramble and devour the cedars of Lebanon."[11] Boer centered his remarks on that phrase, "in good faith," and on the role of contracts and covenants in founding the rights and obligations reflected in social polity. I remained puzzled, however, by the fact that trees appeared to need shade at all. Why should the trees need "refuge" in the shade of the bramble king? Trees, after all, *provide* shade; they don't require it! Or do they?

This parable is about sovereignty—indeed, its presence in scripture reflects a debate over the desirability of kingship preserved by the chroniclers of the defeated biblical judges. The refuge granted by shade succinctly signifies the

9. For Hardt and Negri's critique of representation, see *Multitude*, secs. 3.1 and 3.2, esp. 241–47 and 290–96. They compare the decision-making process of multitude to recent cognitive research on how a brain makes decisions spontaneously and over a networked pattern of neural responses at 338–40.

10. Delivered at the Duke symposium "Singularity and Multiplicity: Recent Developments in Philosophy and Political Theory," March 26, 2005. My comments on Boer are taken from my personal notes and reflect only my interpretation of his lecture.

11. Scripture references taken from *The Jerusalem Bible* (New York: Doubleday, 2000).

persistent need for some kind of social contract between subjects and sovereign, but the fact that shade is given to those whose form *already shades* either argues for the superfluity of a king when each subject contains its own sovereignty or implies that the sovereignty of the king must itself be shaded (presumably by Yahweh). Stated as such, the parable demonstrates within scripture a basic ambivalence between state and individual (or tribal) sovereignty. Pragmatically translated to the terms of contemporary American society, the passage can evoke contradictory messages about whether to found society upon "individual" rights or upon a hierarchy that implies the sovereignty of God. This contradiction seems key in a time and place that takes for granted the linkage between Christianity and democracy. The extension of scripture to our current situation is strictly pragmatic, because the parable does not evidence a modern sense of "individual" such as that which forms the legal basis for individual rights in the United States. Rather, each tree *represents* a singularity of type (olive, fig, etc.), such that the different trees *stand for* the tribes of Israel, or perhaps they point to the irreducible variety inherent to being-human. The parable draws upon the abstracting logic of representation to image what political theory of all stripes makes clear: that material, practical, and political differences must somehow be bridged or ameliorated for the sake of social stability.

The parable of the trees puts together the guiding issues of this chapter: sovereignty and representation, organization and resistance, commonality and difference. From the multitude of internally differentiated tribes (including the almost silent and invisible difference of women) a common nation is born under the ruling, representational force of an initially unwilling king. The organization of the nation of Israel did not proceed, however, without concurrent resistance and debate. In saving traces of that cultural debate, the parable illuminates some of the material differences that fray the clean tropes of representational processes and sow seeds of skepticism about the legitimacy and superiority of theocracy. These seeds can be seen to take root in New Testament scriptures that emphasize God's *nonearthly* kingdom, the diffusion of apostolic proselytizing that resulted in a global *trans-state diaspora*, and the counterintuitive *other-* (or *un-*) *worldly messages* of the cross with respect to success, power, and wealth.

The Biopolitical Potential of Evangelicalism

Evangelical Christians who witness to and live the skepticism of tying divine to worldly power will be as subversive to empire as any nontheological group and act as a singularity within multitude. I have met self-proclaimed evangelicals who assert just this witness and skepticism—they embody a desire to delink worldly power from God's sovereignty—but I have no way of knowing whether such "evangelicals" are accepted *as evangelical* by empire-oriented evangelicals. The logic of biopolitics suggests that every organization will contain and generate its own fracturing, and many groups thrive on that dialectic between unity and dissension; but evangelical Christians identify themselves as deploying hierarchy precisely to limit horizontal dissemination of interpretations, and so it is less clear how or whether they would embrace internal dissension in this way. The parable of the trees suggests to me that evangelicals can, within the limits of scriptural interpretation, find voices and themes that can be wielded biopolitically against empire.

Recently I did speak at length with a self-proclaimed evangelical pastor from New Jersey. It was on a plane from Texas to Cincinnati after the 2004 meeting of the American Academy of Religion. He opened my mind to the possibility of socially "left" evangelicals, something I had never considered. I referred to the Christian Right's grasp for political power, and in a modern transposition of Tertullian he asked, "What does God have to do with America?" We talked of abortion, men's obligations within sexual relations, and attitudes toward the opposite gender, generally. We talked of the state's inappropriate control of marriage ("This is a matter for churches, not the state," he said). We talked of poverty, of property, and of immigration. Though I had heard of Jim Wallis and *Sojourners*, I had not connected that work to evangelicalism, in large part because of the media's other, dominant portrayal of evangelicalism as concerned primarily about sex: the purity of heterosexual marriage, the sin of homosexual relations, and the sanctity of every pregnancy from the moment of conception. I was surprised to find an evangelical I could talk with; the pastor was surprised too, I think, to find a self-proclaimed socialist woman who could quote scripture as fast as he could and who was demonstrably concerned about the physical and spiritual health of children, families, and local communities.

My experience within that conversation mirrored (reflected and inverted) some of my own presumptions about what evangelicalism is, what desires it supports, and how it envisions bridges to the nonevangelical world both within and around it. Put in the crass terms of my media-informed prejudices, I had viewed "evangelicals" as a group of Christians convened through the efforts of male leadership to discuss a theocratic agenda set by that leadership, in the desire to assert and protect a vision of God's kingdom over against the forces of evil. Expanding this stereotype to an institutional frame, I had envisioned evangelical churches as consisting of individuals united by a defined leadership, in which the latter articulates a (local or national) theocratic vision for the group and allows the unique gifts and callings of the individual members to be harnessed for this shared vision. The leaders, mostly male, stress obedience to the common vision over against individual conscience, and they justify the vision by appeals to the authority of scripture and the transcendence of God. The church coheres in its obedience around the nostalgic attraction of "traditional family values," a nostalgia that directly or indirectly works to keep women, children, and racial minorities subordinated to white male adults.

I offer this picture of evangelicals not as "truth" but as a stereotype formed both from media depictions and from my own feminist socialist wariness of hierarchy and androcentrism. Jim Wallis has written of "an almost uniform media misperception" of Christianity.[12] To the degree that self-proclaimed evangelicals live and witness a different perception of evangelicalism and thereby rope their actions to a different media image, one allied with nonevangelical facets of multitude, they are, I submit, acting biopolitically.

Certainly the common front demanded and espoused by evangelical leadership is *not* equally common all the way down a church's rank and file. Post-election shows on National Public Radio in late 2004 gave voice to numerous self-described members of evangelical churches who did not vote the way they claim they "were told" to vote (on pain of damnation) by the church leadership. Interestingly, all the callers I heard stating such disagreement with church leadership were women. These mothers and daughters were resisting the tentacles of empire that have come to inhabit their churches in America today.

One of the challenges to evangelicals concerned about the oppressions of empire, then, is the degree to which they can (practically, doctrinally, and institutionally) act against evangelicals in league with empire. To claim this ability to act biopolitically raises questions of scriptural interpretation and ecclesiology. Scripture's words against earthly power, as evidenced in books like Wallis's, give credence to the biopolitical potential of evangelicals and constitute a platform for some kind of alliance with nonevangelical groups that would not necessarily diminish their evangelical identity or community. This possibility raises questions of alliance, vision, transformation, and commonality that are not the sole purview of evangelical Christianity but form the core of political theory and political activism. How is something both itself and an other? How can evangelicals be different? How can dissension persist without destroying group unity? These are questions that the concept of multitude attempts to resolve.

The Social Ontology of Multitude

In his text *The Philosophy of Marx*, Étienne Balibar skillfully draws out how the *Theses on Feuerbach* and the *German Ideology* sketch a transindividualist ontology in which a person *is* his or her "social relations." In doing so, Balibar demonstrates how Marx rejects both realist and nominalist understandings of human essence that root identity in either universal reason or a singular soul. Since human essence *is* both plural and active for Marx, human essence

---

12. Jim Wallis, *God's Politics: Why the Right Gets It Wrong and the Left Doesn't Get It* (San Francisco: HarperOne, 2005), 3.

itself *produces the common.*[13] In other words, Balibar demonstrates that the "problem" of sameness and difference is a nonproblem for Marx: to be human is to be different *in a way that produces commonality.* Moreover, learning from the Left's political failures of 1848, Marx theorized this commonality as both shared social conditions *and* the work required for organizing a political response, and he recognized that the first did not necessarily yield the second. That is, a common economic or social plight no longer made inevitable a common political response.[14] The result of this dual commonality is social contradiction: workers *both* belong to capital *and* belong to the proletariat. Capital employs and exploits workers as individuals, and capital prevents and obstructs the unification of the proletariat collective, *which nonetheless exists.* In short, the worker is a contradiction—something both itself (capitalist employee) and its opposite (proletarian opposition). The "commonality" of the workers lies both in capital and in opposition to capital. This is not a commonality and opposition of perspective but of praxis and of material reality. Writing from a post-1989 perspective, Balibar notes, "We know that politics is both a question of ideals and a question of habits."[15] The dull repetition of habit practically and physically separates us from our dearly held ideals, a fact that resonates with a theological insight into sin but that here stands as a social and political insight into how the human collective *that we both are and are not* works against us even as it constitutes us—how being common in our organization, a commonality that gives us constancy and comfort, works against the desires of our collective flesh, our *imago Dei.*

Hardt and Negri are drawing from just this tradition of Marxian contradiction when they point to and encourage political alliance amid social opposition and when they promulgate a vision and transformation of the world wrought by common action. Like scripture, Hardt and Negri's texts can be read as parable, in this case an extended parable that reverses the vocal desire of the trees for a single sovereign. Instead, the trees long for their own democratic multitude. Inherent to capitalism are abstractions of representation that concentrate wealth and power, and these abstractions are corroborated and justified by theologies that harness the name of God for projects that fatten the rich and ignore the least of us. In response to the structural oppressions of capitalism and its theological legitimization, Hardt and Negri reject transcendence outright and develop a social ontology that stresses the singularity of persons and the networked, nonofficial facets of successful collective endeavors. In other words, the desire to resist empire—which is always also a desire to fight against the empire of/in our own bodies—yields new habits and new affiliations that Hardt and Negri encapsulate within a new ontology. They

13. Étienne Balibar, *The Philosophy of Marx*, trans. Chris Turner (New York: Verso, 1996), 29–30.
14. Ibid., 55.
15. Ibid., 77.

begin not with the vision of theocracy but with the assertion of the desire for, and unquestioned virtues of, democracy.

Because it is unquestioned in U.S. culture today, it seems pertinent to ask whether Christianity and democracy are compatible. Current evangelical theocratic impulses occur via democratic *dispositifs*, as if the fundamental disparities between democracy and theocracy could simply be elided. At the dawn of the Enlightenment, political philosophy tackled this problem in reverse. In response to religious persecution, men like Hobbes and Spinoza had empirical motivations to think their way to a *nontheocratic* basis for human sociality. To desire the absence of a theocracy is to desire the presence of social and political multitude and to desire laws not organized around a single religious framework. The centuries following these early political philosophers evidenced a slow, stretching separation, not between religion and the state so much as between dominant morality and law.

Law legislates normativity, to be sure, but the development of liberal philosophy during the early formation and expansion of capitalist modes of production yielded a perspective on law that acted as broad and oblique support for bourgeois capitalism and shied away from reliance on any one religious cosmology. Legislation functions as border control, refusing to establish once and for all what is true or false; instead, it sets up conditions under which those debates can be conducted. The one primary assumption built into the borders of U.S. law is an assumption shared by evangelicals and liberals alike, namely, the rights of private property. In recounting the global shrinking of "the commons," or shared public land, Hardt and Negri put a critique of private property at the heart of their manifesto against empire and allow us to understand the protected rights to life, liberty, and the pursuit of happiness as subordinate to the unquestioned right to property.

The right to private property typically remains implicit. What is visible are legislative and cultural battles over how to draw the limits of behavior. Thus murder is illegal (and morally wrong)—and yet if called for by military action, or in self-defense, murder is redescribed as something virtuous. The unwavering evangelical opposition to abortion, by this view, arises from an unwillingness to imagine that there ever are situations in which their perception of abortion as murder could be redescribed into something else—an unwillingness not, in my view, delinked from a rather uncontested misogyny. The halting, contested work of the centuries of "Enlightenment" have not resulted in a "secularized" refusal of religion and morality so much as in a growing acceptance of the public legitimacy of diversity of belief, perspective, and moral vision. The cultural effect of modernization was less a privatization of religion than an expansion of moral heterogeneity and a consequent pliability introduced into public and practical understandings of truth.

I would conclude, then, that democracy is *not* a Christian concept and that the struggle for democracy is not a Christian task. With even more certainty

I would submit that the lessons of history do not weigh positively on the side of theocracy. Hobbes's Leviathan is terrifying, as are all less textual dictatorships. The quest for Christian, theocratic control of public policy must be read as nothing short of reactionary. Whatever the philosophy and practical insufficiencies of liberalism, the Christian desires for justice, charity, and love cannot be incarnated in policies that elide the historical and multitudinous heterogeneities of our current national landscape. Christian love does not employ the tools of empire—or else Christ would have refused the cross and been our earthly sovereign. To the degree that Christians desire democracy, then, they desire something other than sovereignty. The desire for democracy stems from their constitution as citizens in common with other, non-Christian citizens—and in common with other, non-American citizens of other non-American states. The Christian *response* to this desire (this desire that both is and is not who we are) is what needs to be addressed, I think.

Hope for a better future elicits revolutionary and virtual claims about common life, claims that also introduce difference and dissension (as does all political and social revolution). Hardt and Negri stress the shared forces of political economy, primarily a global and intensive capitalism in which dominant forms of labor are immaterial, informationalized, and affective[16] and in which labor is pressured to be "flexible, mobile, and precarious."[17] They argue that today dominant labor produces less products than "communication, affective relationships, and knowledges,"[18] and they note how every life participates in and shares the benefits and detriments of today's intensive configuration of capital. The revolutionary aspect of this description lies in their presumption of a common desire for democracy and their link between this common desire and an active resistance to contemporary global capitalism. The virtual aspect of this revolutionary claim lies in their acknowledgment that when multitude acts, it does so seemingly spontaneously—outside of the normal, predictable channels of political action. Multitude acts from a networked, fast-paced, decentralized upsurge of desire, they say. The action is by definition counter to empire and by definition is valued as positive in light of its formation out of the virtual but active desire for democracy.

Transcendence and *imago Dei*

Hardt and Negri resist all forms of transcendence. Representational democracy, they say, conjoins unity and transcendence in a way that connects (i.e., represents) only through disconnection (i.e., abstraction).[19] The true desire for

16. *Multitude*, 108–111.
17. Ibid., 112.
18. Ibid., 114.
19. Ibid., 242. They are discussing Rousseau.

democracy, they say, entails "the very becoming divine of humanity."[20] Political action, they say, requires a fight against all "organs" of empire, including the many ways in which our very bodies and subjectivities are scripted by its reified powers.[21] It is hard for me, a liberal/socialist Christian feminist, to read their work and not view the institutions of traditional Christianity—such as that exemplified by evangelical Christians—as part of empire. Reading their work in search of ways for Christians to act biopolitically against empire sends me back to scripture, and to my former theological training, in the interest of finding resources preserved within Christian tradition that argue against its own reification—just as the parable from Judges is preserved by and against sovereignty. Recognizing that my theology will not be that of evangelicals, let me end simply with three questions, hints of which have already appeared in this essay:

First, can the doctrine of the incarnation give sustenance to an immanent flesh that signifies God's love for all creatures?

Second, can the doctrine of the *imago Dei* give impetus to recognizing and honoring what is common among all human beings and to framing the profound responsibilities we all have (Christians and non-Christians alike) as stewards of this common earth?

Third, can the universal strength of God be tied tightly to the weakness God risked on the cross so as to embrace the visible material strength of churches, but not in a way that seeks sovereignty on earth?

The dialectical power and challenge of Hardt and Negri's work is that it resists all forms of transcendence—including that of Christianity—for the sake of its unrelenting critique of sovereign power; and yet it is addressed to *everyone*, including those with Christian habits and affiliations. It is addressed to everyone *in common*. How unexpected. How Christlike.

---

20. Ibid., 285. They are commending Spinoza's political theory.
21. Ibid., 198–99 and 315.

4

Betrayed by a Kiss

Evangelicals and U.S. Empire

CHARLES W. AMJAD-ALI AND LESTER EDWIN J. RUIZ

In the aftermath of the 9/11 attacks and the invasion and occupation of Iraq, an extensive debate has emerged over the prospects and conditions for organizing opposition to the various currents of U.S. policy that advocate imperial rule. These currents share essential ends but differ on the means to achieve and consolidate a system of U.S. hegemony. What is notable is the extent to which military power and the role of the state has come to the fore, a decade after the state's eulogy was being delivered worldwide. Prior to 9/11, an emerging focus was on globalization as the dominant form of imperial rule (often framed as globalization with adjectives: neoliberal, corporate, imperialist).[1] Michael Hardt and Antonio Negri's *Empire* and *Multitude* offer one analysis that is notable for its extensive popular consumption as much as its message of a

---

1. The academic literature on this is extensive. See for example, Michael Mann, *Incoherent Empire* (London: Verso, 2003); David Harvey, *The New Imperialism* (London: Oxford University Press, 2003); and Gopal Balakrishnan and Stanley Aronowitz, eds., *Debating Empire* (London: Verso, 2003).

decentered system of imperial rule challenged by an amorphous nonpolitical formation they call "multitude."[2]

Still the reality of a U.S. empire, if not a U.S.-*led* empire, refuses to go away.[3] While appreciative of the work of Hardt and Negri, this essay takes a different, less ambitious, if implicitly critical, approach. Transforming empire requires that attention be given to the consequences of its sociopolitical and economic power and the kind of knowledge that this power has generated *in the context* of the theology that has provided, and continues to provide, the fundamental religio-moral underpinnings for empire. This theology is paradigmatically expressed in the various strands of contemporary evangelical theology.

All empires for the last five hundred years have had European roots.[4] The contemporary Euro-American history and imperial model begins with Christopher Columbus in 1492, followed by Vasco da Gama in 1498.[5] While the Western *imperium* began with Iberian Catholic colonization, the last four hundred or so years, following the "sinking of the Spanish Armada" in 1588,[6] was dominated by the emergence of northwestern European empires, mostly from Protestant countries.

Often generally unacknowledged, the United States has had a long imperial history dating back at least to the colonization of the Philippines in the 1890s. This imperial status is now being proclaimed unashamedly by many in the U.S. government. But its imperial history is well in continuity with the classical European pattern that emerged at the end of the fifteenth century and through which Europe, and by extension, European immigrant states, claimed the right to all civilizational contributions, sources, and foundations. While there have been unique expressions of this imperial project, its fundamental structures retain their European foundational values.

Every empire, whatever its *raison d'être*, is fundamentally an articulation of power. Rudyard Kipling's famous poem "White Man's Burden: The United

---

2. Michael Hardt and Antonio Negri, *Empire* (Cambridge, MA: Harvard University Press, 2000); Michael Hardt and Antonio Negri, *Multitude: War and Democracy in the Age of Empire* (New York: Penguin, 2004).

3. See generally Paul A. Passavant and Jodi Dean, eds., *Empire's New Clothes: Reading Hardt and Negri* (New York: Routledge, 2004), especially Ernesto Laclau, "Can Immanence Explain Empire?" 21–30. Cf. Mark Taylor, *Religion, Politics, and the Christian Right: Post 9/11 Powers in American Empire* (Philadelphia: Augsburg Fortress, 2005); Sharon Welch, *After Empire: The Art and Ethos of Enduring Peace* (Philadelphia: Fortress, 2004).

4. H. J. de Blij and Peter O. Muller, *Geography: Realms, Regions, and Concepts*, 11th ed. (Hoboken, NJ: John Wiley and Sons, 2004), 40.

5. Vasco da Gama is famous for his completion of the first all-water trade route between Europe and India. He set out from Lisbon, Portugal, on July 8, 1497, arriving finally in Calicut, India, on May 20, 1498.

6. While the war lingered on for at least a decade after 1588, Iberian power lost nautical and therefore also colonial imperial monopoly.

States & the Philippine Islands, 1899,"[7] with its binary of benighted natives and do-gooder colonizing Westerners, is a classic example of an unrepentant, self-aggrandizing, paternalistic raison d'être. Though a British colonialist, Kipling urged America to pursue its colonial and imperial project, while justifying the effort as a great contribution to the colonized peoples of the Philippines:

> Take up the White Man's burden—
> Send forth the best ye breed—
> Go bind your sons to exile
> To serve your captives' need;
> To wait in heavy harness,
> On fluttered folk and wild—
> Your new-caught, sullen peoples,
> Half-devil and half-child.

Michel Foucault has argued persuasively that power and knowledge are inextricably related. He makes this point in the conclusion of *The Archaeology of Knowledge*,[8] where one discovers two voices: one posed as the interrogator, from the arrogant stance of one possessing all knowledge already, and the other a respondent who is still only on the possible way to knowledge. The position of the former could be read as that of the *Cercle d'Épistémologie*[9] and the latter as Foucault himself. A more interesting reading is suggested by William Connolly's critique of the interrogator's claim. He argues that one must sort out the two voices present within Foucault himself, "recalling that both voices must be present in any text that seeks to speak to its own culture while contesting some of its patterns of insistence."[10]

Following Connolly, this essay argues that the West at its imperial best, the United States being a great example, arrogates to itself the power and privilege of the interrogator, consistently negating or demeaning the role of other peoples in civilizational, sociocultural, political, and economic history, while claiming this history as an exclusively Western possession.[11] At the same time the West is very quick to hyperbolize the imperial powers, practices, and ambitions of others and to point out their pathologies: all that is good is of

7. This was first published in an 1899 issue of *McClure's Magazine* and later in *Rudyard Kipling's Verse: Definitive Edition* (Garden City, NY: Doubleday, 1929).

8. Michel Foucault, *The Archaeology of Knowledge*, trans. A. M. Sheridan Smith (New York: Pantheon, 1972).

9. Ibid., 17n.

10. William E. Connolly, *Identity/Difference: Democratic Negotiations of Political Paradox* (Ithaca, NY: Cornell University Press, 1991), 61. See Foucault, *Archaeology of Knowledge*, 205.

11. Examples of this diminution: the ante-Nicene fathers are quickly equated with Europe despite their Asian and African origins; although almost all the Greek knowledge of the Mediterranean was preserved and passed on to the West through Muslims, they are mostly negated or at best given perfunctory recognition.

Western origin and all that is wrong is part of the larger tragic human condition which is *external* to the West.

When the colonizers first came to the Americas, they carried a theological and doctrinal certitude of God's foreordained support. In 1492, in the shadow of the *Reconquista* of Spain,[12] Isabella and Ferdinand began to support trade routes to India, which would bypass the Muslim enclosure and thus establish their own *imperium*. They found Columbus a willing executor for this task, and shortly thereafter the church. God had brought them success against the Muslims who had ruled Spain for 781 years, and God was to be their guide and succor in this new venture.

The other migration to the Americas that is hyperbolized as paradigmatic and quickly given a Reformed predestinarian justification, especially by conservative evangelical Christians, is that of the Puritans. This disaffected community experienced failures in the "New World," including the death within a year of arrival of 50 percent of those on the *Mayflower*. Despite these disasters, Puritans painted their coming to America, colonizing the native population, and taking over their land as God's preordained will for God's chosen people. Ultimately they had a similar attitude (and theology) as Columbus and the Spaniards, even though they had had very dissimilar experiences in Europe and different reasons for their journeys to the "New World."

One may ask why the Reformed tradition with its double predestinarian theology, in both the United States and South Africa for example, produced extremely unjust and malevolent polities. Proponents of this heritage have often justified their right to others' land, labor, and bodies as entitlements of God's chosen people. Non-Western peoples, they argue, are under the permanent curse of a negative predestination and therefore not entitled to their own land, culture, or future. God's chosen people, even when they expropriate the lands of the "native peoples," are without blame because this is what God intended. Therefore, neither confession of sins nor penitent behavior nor restorative and restitutive justice is required. Jewish theologian Will Herberg argues that in the United States it does not matter whether one is Jewish, Catholic, or Protestant, because in significant ways everybody falls prey to this theology and its justification.[13]

This theology dominates contemporary U.S. foreign policy: America is the righteous, blameless one because it is preordained to this hegemonic status. Any enemy is totally wrong, bereft of any goodness, because of their ontological preordained negative status and because they dare to challenge the God-

---

12. On January 2, 1492, with the conquest of Granada, the long struggle against the Moors called the Reconquista finally ended. In the same year some 170,000 Jews were expelled from Spain, and Columbus sailed for "India."

13. Will Herberg, *Protestant, Catholic, Jew: An Essay in American Religious Sociology* (Garden City, NY: Doubleday, 1955). See also Max Weber, *The Protestant Ethic and the Spirit of Capitalism*, trans. T. Parsons (New York: Charles Scribner's Sons, 1976).

given power of the United States. This blissfully uncomplicated, simplistic, and misinformed understanding of self and "enemy" takes on interesting, if amusing, forms. For example, the United States defines itself metaphorically as both David (because of its righteousness and the justness of its cause) and Goliath (for who else but one specially blessed can have the power, strength, and armor that Goliath displayed?).[14] Such schizophrenia is at times totally unbearable and for its victims an unmitigated disaster (cf. the war in Iraq, launched in 2003 and still dragging on as of this writing five years later, and the U.S. war on terrorism).

It is not as if the United States did not have other Protestant theological alternatives. That it chose this particular understanding underscores the interstructuration of power and knowledge. For example, the United States could have developed certain dimensions of Martin Luther's critical dialectics:

1. *Simul iustus et peccator*, which completely undermines any privileged claim of self being exclusively saint and the other being exclusively sinner
2. *Deus revelatus* and *Deus absconditus*, which prohibit us from claiming God exclusively for ourselves and the total lack of God for others; this dialectics also makes any claim of revelation subjected to the absconding and hidden God

Perhaps American Lutherans did not emphasize these dialectics in the political realm because they were, in Herberg's terms, equal believers, conveniently, in Reformed theology in this regard. Or perhaps the infamous Lutheran quietism and separation of realms did not allow them to participate in the public discourse.

Evangelicals, until recently, were extremely suspicious of worldly and material matters. Any preoccupation with a supposedly contaminated fallen world would lead to evil and punishment in hell. Wanting to escape the material world, they sought rebirth and a closer walk with God. Ironically, their prayers, largely petitionary, often emphasized a pious sanctified life not just to guarantee eternal life but in order to ensure a quid pro quo of tangible material success. Such success was interpreted as the definitive sign of answered prayers, as well as God's blessing and reward for piety and righteousness, ironically undercutting their professed antimateriality. If, they argue, we "strive first for the kingdom of God and his righteousness . . . all these things will be given to [us] as well" (Matt. 6:34). The kingdom of God is reduced to individual salvation, piety, and reward.

14. 1 Samuel 17, especially vv. 4–11, 41–51.

This theology has been readily extended to a national (and nationalistic) theology. God's blessing of America is thus based on its right relationship with God, its piety and righteousness. As God's chosen, the nation is a light unto the world (Isa. 42:6; 49:6, Matt. 5:14), a beacon on the mountain (Isa. 30:17), and a city on a hill (Matt. 5:14). Chosen by God, America is able to fulfill God's will and therefore to keep moving from success to success, continuously acquiring ever-expanding power, wealth, and privilege unmatched in history. Recalling Alfred North Whitehead's "misplaced concreteness" or G. W. Hegel's "bad infinity," this theology, if not ideology, is based on the *bad* covenantal theology espoused by the Puritans and continues to dominate the U.S. political psyche, but now without direct reference to God.

Recent examples of this secularized perspective include the diverse positions of Francis Fukuyama,[15] Samuel Huntington,[16] and Benjamin Barber.[17] Their positions bear striking similarities to those of the evangelicals particularly in terms of the special, almost dispensationalist, role of the United States in history, but without the notion of divine preordination. Because of this secularization, they can provide neither reasons for the emergence of this power nor an ethical ground, however dubious, for the usurpation of someone else's land, labor, or body. Understandably, following Max Weber's argument regarding the secularization of the "Protestant ethic,"[18] this secularist position is fundamentally flawed, maintaining as it does a Protestant asceticism shorn of its theological moorings while proclaiming itself to be the highest form of development. We are left not only with a debilitating "iron cage" but especially with an imagination deprived of the possibility of "the fundamentally new and better." Here Weber and Nietzsche embrace.

While the Enlightenment did not allow a simplistic religious justification for colonialism, it provided certitude through science and rationality, producing "rational" arguments for the superiority of Europeans over the benighted natives and imported slaves whose land, labor, and bodies could be stolen at will. The Enlightenment and scientific rationality, Cornel West rightly argues, provided "objective" arguments for suppressing the "other" and making that suppression scientifically permanent.[19]

15. "The End of History," *National Interest* 16 (Summer 1989): 4–18; *The End of History and the Last Man* (New York: Free Press, 1992).

16. "The Clash of Civilizations?" *Foreign Affairs* 72, no. 3 (Summer 1993): 22–28; *The Clash of Civilizations and the Remaking of the World Order* (New York: Simon and Schuster, 1996).

17. *Jihad vs. McWorld: How Globalism and Tribalism Are Reshaping the World* (New York: Ballantine, 1996).

18. *The Protestant Ethic*, n.x.

19. *Prophesy Deliverance! An Afro-American Revolutionary Christianity* (Louisville, KY: Westminster John Knox, 2002).

It is almost universally acknowledged that evangelicals[20] accepted neither the full epistemological foundations of the "scientization of knowledge" nor "Enlightenment rationality." They wanted to do two things simultaneously: first, reverse the scientific move from a *terreocentric* to a *heliocentric* universe as articulated by Galileo; second, undo the Enlightenment's reversal of the move from a *theocentric* to an *anthropocentric* universe. This move was inaugurated by Descartes' *cogito ergo sum* and later undergirded by Kant's a priori *Vernunftlichkeit*. God as Creator and originary locus of reflection and thought was replaced by humans and their rationality.

For American fundamentalists and evangelicals, these different strains culminated in Darwin's *On the Origin of Species* (1859) epitomized in *Tennessee v. John Scopes*, the so-called Monkey Trials of 1925. This debate has resurfaced regularly among evangelicals, most recently in the argument for "intelligent design" versus evolutionary theory.

To counter this form of science and the Enlightenment, as well as to defend God's role in creation, evangelicals located all true knowledge and reason in revelation as manifested in the Bible, understood as "the inerrant Word of God." All knowledge required verification by the biblical text, narrowly construed and without any "surplus of meaning," much less metaphoricity. Human rationality and knowledge are thus endowed with certainty and permanence. Because the text is perspicuous, interpretive possibilities are likewise curtailed. There is, therefore, no human input in the hermeneutical task, much less in (re)reading or (re)writing of texts. The Bible joins the Trinity in eternity.

Martin Luther's *sola Scriptura* was interpreted not as a clash with tradition and the church's teaching authority but as a counterpoint to Enlightenment and scientific rationality. Despite these critical differences, evangelicals saw themselves as the true heirs of Luther and condemned all other approaches to scripture and the hermeneutical task as "liberal." Therefore, one of their central tenets, however articulated, is the inerrancy and perspicuity of the Bible, which should not be subjected to modernist or postmodernist "relativizing" based on a use of the intellect and reason.

For the majority of U.S. evangelicals, Christianity and America are synonymous. Statements against America and the flag are regarded as blasphemous, for they understand what America does in the world as God's intervention in

20. *Evangelical* is variously defined: (1) John Stott suggests there are fifty-seven varieties of "Evangelicalism's tribes and tenets"; (2) Clive Calver talks about the "twelve tribes of evangelicalism"; and (3) Peter Beyerhaus and Gabriel Fackre name six different evangelical groupings. For a discussion of these differences, see John M. Hitchen, "What It Means to Be an Evangelical Today: An Antipodean Perspective; Part 1, Mapping Our Movement," *Evangelical Quarterly* 76, no. 1 (2004): 47–64; and "Part 2: What it means to be an Evangelical Today—An Antipodean Perspective," *Evangelical Quarterly* 76, no. 2 (2004): 99–115. For Hitchen, there are three types of "evangelicals": Confessional, Transconfessional, and Charismatic. See also Douglas Jacobsen and Frederick Schmidt's "Review Article: Behind Orthodoxy and Beyond It: Recent Developments in Evangelical Christology," *Scottish Journal of Theology* 45, no. 4 (1992): 515–41.

history, based on its true and faithful service to God, and not as an extension of some self-interested *imperium*. Unlike the Catholic view of the church as the sacrament in history, based on the metaphor of the *corpus Christi*, or the more moderate position that the church has a sacramental vocation in history, U.S. evangelicals, who mostly condemn these positions, have no problem in understanding the United States as this sacrament and part of the divine will for the world.

The recently established role of evangelicals in public life and their unrelenting attempts to control U.S. polity has produced a critical shift in their theological and ethical epistemologies. *This is not an adaptive or contextual move but a major shift in the core of evangelical theology.* Evangelicals no longer see the public square as evil and therefore to be rejected, nor do they demand an ascetic Calvinist piety unmitigated by quests for power or control of morality in public life. A few decades ago evangelicals condemned theological approaches equating the kingdom of God with the church or promoting particular social actions, social gospel movements, or liberation theologies and struggles. In recent times, however, they have plagiarized and adopted these positions themselves, without acknowledging their rightful authors, and have (pro)claimed the origins of these movements in their own heritage, warping them to fulfill a conservative moral, cultural, and political agenda.

This theological schizophrenia remains fully operational at both the personal and national levels. At the core of evangelicals' claim of a personal relationship with God is a disingenuous myopia about their extremely un-Christian and un-Christlike theology. Their theology is overtly Abrahamic and reflects a particular interpretation of the Old Testament patriarchs. It is not based on the incarnation, *kenosis*, and vulnerability of God in Christ. For while the faithfulness of Abraham and other patriarchs supposedly produced blessings of longevity, progeny, and land as a return, the same was clearly not the case with Jesus.

In fact, categorically stated, *Jesus stands in total contrast to the investment piety, with blessings as returns, that this "Wall Street theology" produces.* Jesus dies when he is in his thirties, not an old age by any standard, and he dies an unnatural and horrible death on the cross, which besides being seen as a curse, is clearly "a stumbling block . . . and foolishness" (1 Cor. 1:23). He is unmarried and there is no indication of his having any progeny. As for land, we are told clearly, "Foxes have holes, and birds of the air have nests; but the Son of Man has nowhere to lay his head" (Luke 9:58). He is even a disaster as a teacher, according to the classical male reading: after some three and a half years he is able to retain only twelve disciples, and of these one sells him to the enemy and another denies him publicly, not under duress from a soldier but to a powerless "servant-girl."[21]

21. Cf. Matthew 26:69–75 and parallels.

As for Jesus's petitionary prayer being heeded—the obvious reward of faithfulness according to evangelical theology—God does not listen, at least not in his most extremely trying existential circumstance. For it is stated, Jesus "knelt down, and prayed, 'Father, if you are willing, remove this cup from me . . .' In his anguish he prayed more earnestly, and his sweat became like great drops of blood falling down on the ground" (Luke 22:41–44). Obviously his prayer was not answered and indeed he was crucified, the source of our salvation! So unless evangelical theology ultimately wants to assert that the crucifixion is a sign of failure and therefore not Christian, its investment-based theology and understanding of petitionary prayers must be seriously reconsidered.

We also have Jesus's famous words from the cross, "Eli, Eli, lama sabachthani?"[22] revealing not only the abandonment of God but also the experience of the one crucified as central for faithfulness, rejecting at the same time the exercise of power to crucify others. Thus Christian discipleship requires that we carry our crosses. Those who are ashamed of this cross and deny it will receive a similar response: Jesus will also be ashamed of them. Evangelicals' repetitious confessions of who Jesus is become useless when they lack the understanding that our Lord had to be rejected and crucified not by ordinary humanity but by the high priest, scribes, and other leaders—that is, those in power. If we do not understand this profound doctrinal fact, we stand condemned by Jesus as Satan, despite our best and accurate confession, just as Peter was in Mark 8:27–38. Either we move our theology away from reward-based investment in God, or we have a serious crisis with our theology, Christology, and reasons for Christian praxis.

The other side of American evangelicals has been their apocalyptic emphases reflected in their multilayered millenarian arguments. This began in the European Protestant pietism and scholasticism of the seventeenth and eighteenth centuries, as part of the crisis of meaning that surfaced after the reversals discussed above. It was also a response to a special crisis after the Protestant Reformation, the Thirty Years' (Bloody) War (1618–48). This involved the Holy Roman Empire and most of the major powers and between 7.5 to 10 million deaths. So what was seen as a sign of revival of faith and a return to biblical faithfulness led to an unmitigated disaster. This produced two simultaneous movements: a piety focused largely on the soul/spirit and not the body/materiality, and a chiliastic millennialism. Despite their different circumstances, these movements substantially influenced the American evangelical revivals by focusing on predictions in the apocalyptic literature of the New and Old Testaments and trying to link them to contemporary world events.

22. Matthew 27:46, parallel Mark 15:34. This is one of the few places in the New Testament where the Aramaic words of Jesus are preserved in transliteration and then translated by the authors. One must wonder why the Gospel writers did this in these particular cases, when Jesus's normal Aramaic discourse is not preserved otherwise.

In recent years, the focus of such links has been on the Middle East, and especially events surrounding the state of Israel. There have been constant shifts in the expected timetable and the articulation of the Antichrist. To name a few of the latter: the papacy (based on the Reformation polemics); the Soviet Union and communism; even the European Union and its threat to U.S. economic power; and, most recently, Islam. That these enemies have invariably matched those defined by the American imperial state is not seen as an ideological interpolation but simply a matter of biblical interpretation. Thus we see an unmistakable convergence between evangelical theology and U.S. foreign policy interests, especially as the United States defines its enemies and thus exercises its power and domination on the world stage. One is reminded of H. Richard Niebuhr's critical appraisal of the social crisis of the 1970s: "The chief rival to monotheism . . . is henotheism or that social faith which makes a finite society, whether cultural or religious, the object of trust as well as of loyalty and which tends to subvert even officially monotheistic institutions, such as the churches."[23]

Because of their chiliastic agenda, evangelicals are apparently very concerned with world affairs, especially those readily amenable to their purposes. Paradoxically, they remain epistemologically otherworldly and use all information to make what they claim is a clear timetable for the parousia. Such a theology, however, can work only for an incredibly naive, unigenerational, egocentric, and conservative sociopolitical agenda. So while evangelicals take some world events very seriously, their theology does not have the ability to deal with ecological, social, and politico-economic issues in a way that can produce a just and sustainable intergenerational, interspecies future. Indeed, it posits an apocalypse that sees all creation and human-centered concerns for the future as superfluous because the end of the world is imminent. Evangelicals have a temporal blueprint of this future, because for them the Bible is "categorically clear."

Evangelicals in recent years have begun to enumerate their contributions to social change. These include the struggle against slavery, which is truly ironic, considering that their contemporary agenda is typified by conservatives like Jerry Falwell and Pat Robertson. The recent National Association of Evangelicals document "For the Health of the Nation: An Evangelical Call for Civic Responsibility" makes this abundantly clear. Besides its clearly nationalist focus, the document sees itself "as a milestone in the movement of the evangelicals from the insularity of a revival tent mind-set in the early 20th century to the political activism of the 21st century." Introducing the text, Richard Cizik makes a reference to William Wilberforce, Charles Finney, and

---

23. See *Radical Monotheism and Western Culture, with Supplementary Essays* (New York: Harper & Row, 1970), 11.

Lord Shaftesbury[24]—all involved in the antislavery movement—as providing the early impetus for the evangelical commitment to social justice. The reference to the long hiatus in evangelical public actions in this discourse, and to only three exemplars, who lived between 1759 and 1885, and a lack to any other person after this, is a telling statement requiring no further comment.

Even these justifications of civic responsibility ring hollow given evangelicals' fundamental theological commitment to high individualism, which underscores their total dedication to modernity. Ironically, this is reflected in their reworking of the classical Cartesian *res cogitans*, evident in both their emphatic call for personal conversion and their core requirement of personal piety and morality. The Cartesian *ego cogito ergo sum*, seen as a prerequisite of modernity, is baptized and given a Christian twist: *ego credo ergo sum*. Individual conversion, piety, and morality together become exclusive imperatives, the benchmarks of evangelical faithfulness, thus undermining the work of grace and God located at the cross. Such a decentering of the theology of the cross, the high sophistry surrounding it notwithstanding, is necessary because evangelicals do not see or have a theology that allows for a sacramental understanding of the cross in history. Nor do they grasp the profound paradigmatic value of vulnerability for others which the cross represents. The sacramental understanding of the cross sees salvation as an act of grace, and the paradigmatic value of vulnerability provides an example for faith praxis. Both these aspects of the theology of the cross challenge the reconfigured Cartesian theology of salvation and the necessity of piety and morality to achieve success and wealth based on quid-pro-quo Wall Street theology.

In the evangelical subculture, any formation of virtuous citizenry for the sake of the *polis* is severely compromised because the latter requires an organic collectivity not found in the voluntarist association that evangelicals fancy. Neither the *polis* nor the *ecclesia* can or should be reduced to the modernist myth of the voluntary association of acquisitive and possessive individuals. Evangelicals' commitment to the *polis* is thus suspect, since their personal piety and its related asceticism seek individual success, wealth, and affluence, which are always at someone else's expense. This is a fundamental reversal of the old monastic piety, which rejected affluence, required its abandonment for the sake of God, and sought the blessings of God in simplicity, poverty, and service to others. U.S. evangelicals have also abdicated the piety of martyrdom of the early church and clearly opted for the *Constantinian imperium*. This was true even when they were rejecting the *polis*. Now that they have made a commitment to taking it over, they have given up the camouflage completely, equating *regnum Dei* with the *imperium* and justifying it by citing Luke 20:20–26 and Romans 13:1–7.

24. That they have to go this far back to find a genealogy of socially concerned evangelicals is significant. For details, see www.nae.net/index.cfm.

Empire, within this frame of reference, becomes proof of its righteousness; otherwise it could not have this power. Those who lose do not lose because the empire is nasty and oppressive, and/or self-interested in worldly terms, but because God has foreordained them to be subjected, ruled, and dominated by those whom God has chosen for covenantal responsibility and steward-ship in history. Such a theology is antithetical and blasphemous to all our understandings of God, especially a God who through incarnation becomes vulnerable to history and people and dies at Golgotha on the whim of an empire and its conspirators.

Evangelical theology has three inextricably related strategies that are funda-mentally flawed:

1. proclaiming and defending the inerrancy and perspicuity of the scriptures
2. affirming a minimal to irrelevant role of humans in authorship of the biblical texts, and likewise little or no role for intellect or reason as hermeneutical tools
3. maintenance and guarding of the presumed positive fixed dogmas, based on the revelation in the Bible with no direct human agency

These strategies are based primarily on an almost Manichaean dualism and docetic theology, which ultimately rejects the materiality of the incarnated God. Therefore, that which contains God's revelation has to be divinized and set apart from the human and material world. Roman Catholics express these tendencies by making Mary, the *theotokos*, immaculately conceived (how would one preserve the divine nature and origin of Christ as the *logos tou theou*, without preserving and in fact divinizing the carrier also?). Evangelicals, despite their anti-Catholic sophistry, adhere to this tendency but change the *theotokos* from Mary to the Bible. While they insist on Mary's humanity and therefore her contaminated state, they are totally incapable of humanizing the text as *theotokos* and accepting its contamination. Evangelicals human-ize Mary and divinize the text, whereas Roman Catholics have no problem humanizing the text but end up divinizing Mary.

Both ultimately violate the orthodoxy of three *personae* and one *ousia*[25] by adding a fourth *persona* with the same *ousia* as the Father, Son, and the Holy Spirit. Not only does this contradict the central tenets of both the Nicene and Chalcedonian formulas, but it also negates any possibility of a sound *incar-national* Christology because it undermines the essential materiality that "in the flesh" presupposes.

---

25. *Homoousios*—of the same substance or essence—of Nicene and Constantinopolitan creedal formulas.

The evangelical's certainty vis-à-vis the Bible creates a demand for a similar certitude on other levels. This reproduces not only textual and confessional conservatism but also political and social conservatism, which, when wedded conveniently to the secularist ideologies of chauvinistic and cultural nationalism and then resacralized, reproduces U.S. empire. Ironically, this justification is made *in the name of the Crucified One who was himself a victim of such imperialism.*

In this sense evangelicals are like Judas Iscariot, who, though he was at the table with his Lord with the other disciples, and even dipped his bread in the same bowl as Jesus, did so having already arranged with the imperial powers and their conspirators to sell his Lord for thirty pieces of silver. This betrayal was made even more reprehensible when Judas identified the victim with a most intimate relational expression, a kiss.[26]

---

26. Matthew 26:21–25, 46–50, especially verses 24, 48 and 49, and synoptic parallels.

5

Empire-Building or Democracy-at-Work?

The Growing Influence of White U.S. Evangelical NGO Lobbying at the United Nations and in Washington, DC

JENNIFER BUTLER AND GLENN ZUBER

Covering the large global protests against the impending US-British invasion of Iraq in February 2003, a *New York Times* reporter declared, "There may still be two superpowers on the planet: the United States and world public opinion."[1] Similar to the *Times* reporter, Michael Hardt and Antonio Negri argue that after the cold war a new bipolar structure of power emerged—empire and multitude. The United States anchors the larger worldwide system of industrialized states, multinational corporations, and international economic and political agencies that constitute empire. According to Hardt and Negri, however, new forms of worldwide community and democracy arise as empire dissolves established national, ethnic, and language barriers through contact, communications, and migration. These new forms of transnational community, or multitude, are paradoxically both the result of empire and its greatest potential challenger.[2]

1. Patrick E. Tyler, "Threats and Responses: News Analysis; A New Power in the Streets," *New York Times,* February 17, 2003.

2. Michael Hardt and Antonio Negri, *Empire* (Cambridge, MA: Harvard University Press, 2000), and *Multitude: War and Democracy in the Age of Empire* (New York: Penguin, 2004).

American white evangelicals are playing an increasingly significant role in determining the balance between empire and multitude through their powerful advocacy organizations. These organizations are part of the growing influence of nongovernmental organizations (NGOs) on national governments and international agencies. For Hardt and Negri, the increasingly successful campaigns of NGOs provide a limited model of how the often powerless multitude can strongly influence the new world system at the highest levels of governance and hence challenge empire.[3] These developments have also interested international political elites and political scientists. A recent United Nations panel established to review this new development observed: "Nowadays, non-State actors are often prime movers—as with issues of gender, climate change, debt, landmines and AIDS."[4]

Over the past few decades and especially through the 1990s, the UN General Assembly held a series of world conferences designed to develop international consensus among governments on issues like human rights, women's rights, children's rights, poverty, and racism. NGO representatives gathered in parallel meetings designed to allow them to influence these governmental meetings. These NGO gatherings and the lobbying that NGO representatives engaged in prior to the UN world conferences were so well organized that NGOs had a significant influence on the texts of many of the intergovernment agreements that emerged.[5]

Bringing their own perspectives to bear on world issues, American NGOs with largely white evangelical values and constituencies have also become more active in campaigns to influence UN conferences and, more generally, U.S. foreign policy.[6] These NGOs support a range of causes, from putting "pro-family" language in UN documents to boosting America's contribution to AIDS treatments in Africa and endorsing the UN Millennium Development Goals (MDG). They are also joining creative political alliances that cut across national and religious lines to promote these causes. While often portrayed monolithically, white evangelical activism is quite diverse, making any hard-and-fast categorizations suspect. Nor can one predict whether this group will on balance provide greater support for empire or multitude.

According to George Marsden, a historian of twentieth-century American religion, *evangelicalism* can be a slippery term because it defines a loosely

3. *Multitude*, 290–312.

4. Panel of Eminent Persons on UN–Civil Society Relationships, *We the Peoples: Civil Society, the U.N., and Global Governance* (New York: United Nations Department of Information, June 2004), 1.

5. *The Third Force: The Rise of Transnational Civil Society,* edited by Ann Florini (Washington, DC: Carnegie Endowment for International Peace 2000).

6. For an overview of various kinds of religious conservative organizing at the United Nations, see Doris Buss and Didi Herman, *Globalizing Family Values: The Christian Right in International Politics* (Minneapolis: University of Minnesota Press, 2003), 19–32.

organized movement, not a religious denomination with a clearly defined membership list. In fact, the term has been used in a number of ways since 1900. Marsden broadly speaks of evangelicals as "any Christian traditional enough to affirm the basic beliefs of the old nineteenth-century evangelical consensus" that dominated American religion until the Civil War. There are five characteristics of the evangelical, including (1) using the Bible as the final authority, (2) believing in the Bible's stories of God's intervention in human affairs, (3) receiving salvation based on Christ's death, (4) engaging in missions and evangelism, and (5) experiencing a spiritually transformed life.[7] While evangelicals are traditional in their religious beliefs, they are not united behind a single political agenda—a point frequently omitted in newspaper accounts of these Christians. Newspaper reporters often incorrectly talk about the "evangelicals" behind the success of conservative politicians, implying that all evangelicals, because they are religiously traditionalist, support conservative politics. In fact, the evangelical vote is deeply divided by race and class.[8] While it is true that middle- and upper-middle-class white evangelicals tend to vote overwhelmingly for conservative politicians, that is not true for African American, poor white, and Hispanic evangelicals.

Despite the diversity within white evangelicalism, however, representatives of evangelical NGOs at the United Nations and in Washington, DC, typically pursue either socially conservative ("pro-family") or humanitarian goals. We will term these "family-focused" and "humanitarian-focused" evangelical NGOs. Moreover, since the leadership and rank-and-file of these organizations are overwhelmingly of European descent, we define them more precisely as white evangelical NGOs. Defining these groups in this way underscores that the story we are covering involves an important component, but not the whole story, of contemporary evangelical activism. The principal family-focused NGOs active at the United Nations include Focus on the Family (FOF), Concerned Women of America, and the Family Research Council, a more politically involved offshoot organization of FOF. These evangelical NGOs are connected with the U.S. Religious Right, a political movement that has mobilized large numbers of conservative evangelicals, Roman Catholics, Mormons, and others.[9] Major humanitarian-focused NGOs include World Vision, Sojourners/Call to Renewal, the International Justice Mission, and, to a lesser extent, Samaritan's Purse, as well as the National Association of Evangelicals. These

7. George M. Marsden, *Understanding Fundamentalism and Evangelicalism* (Grand Rapids: Eerdmans, 1991), 4–5.

8. Michael O. Emerson and Christian Smith, *Divided by Faith: Evangelical Religion and the Problem of Race in America* (New York: Oxford University Press, 2001), 69–91.

9. For an overview of Religious Right lobbying at the national and state levels, see Clyde Wilcox, *Onward Christian Soldiers? The Religious Right in American Politics*, 2nd ed. (Boulder, CO: Westview, 2000), 61–74.

groups organize American evangelicals and lobby governments on issues such as funding AIDS treatment in Africa.

Evangelical involvement in UN projects and conferences suggests that the political activism of family-focused NGOs tends to have the effect of supporting and benefiting from empire as defined by Hardt and Negri, while humanitarian-focused NGOs' work tends to give voice to multitude. Family-focused NGOs champion particular cultural arguments honed in American-style culture wars. Their campaigns aid empire because they often distract the international community from the deeper economic structures that result in crushing poverty. Moreover, their political successes often rely on and advocate for the logic of U.S. unilateralism. We say these NGOs "tend" to support empire, however, because the same "pro-family" rhetoric that distracts from economic issues also articulates the hopes of many in multitude for stable families. In contrast, humanitarian-focused NGOs are promoting the idea that the U.S. government should become more involved in UN-related projects designed to alleviate hunger, disease, and crushing poverty. These problems are pressing concerns to a majority of the world's population. Thus, these NGOs position themselves to represent the interests of the world's people to U.S. politicians.

Will the Real Evil Empire Please Stand Up? Identifying Empire in the Evangelical and Hardt/Negri Imaginations

Hardt and Negri and many white American evangelicals have an ambivalent view of the United Nations. Even though they come from very different starting points and employ radically different methodologies, both groups see the United Nations as a powerful institution with potential to shape world events for both good and ill. This similarity in perspective is critical, because it reveals that evangelicals, like the leftists they usually distrust, have a powerful critique against imperial arrogance within their own tradition. The focus of evangelical fears of global domination are continually shifting along with their allies and opponents. These shifting perceptions and alliances can serve the interests of either empire or multitude.

While today many evangelicals view the United Nations as potentially the oppressive end-time empire mentioned in the book of Revelation and thus do not trust its stated goal of creating international harmony, this perspective is not shared by all of them.[10] In fact, the identity of the Antichrist has changed

---

10. Tim LaHaye, Jerry B. Jenkins, and Sandi L. Swanson, *The Authorized Left Behind Handbook* (Wheaton, IL: Tyndale House, 2005), 157–63. A discussion of evangelical thought and the United Nations can be found in Buss and Herman, *Globalizing Family Values*, 19–32, and Glenn W. Shuck, *Marks of the Beast: The Left Behind Novels and the Struggle for Evangelical Identity* (New York: New York University Press, 2005), 84–85.

over time: white conservative U.S. Protestants in the last two hundred years have variously identified the Antichrist as the pope, Napoleon, theological modernism, and Hitler.[11] As the United States has grown increasingly powerful, surprisingly, prophecy writers by and large have avoided considering the possibility that America may be the corrupt empire mentioned in the book of Revelation. This has been a blind spot in their theological vision, probably because there is a powerful traditional belief among Americans that their country plays a providential role in world history.[12]

When Tim LaHaye connects the United Nations with the evil empire mentioned in Revelation in his Left Behind series, he voices the fears of many evangelicals that the United Nations will exert an imperial power over the United States. While the participation of communist countries in the United Nations used to stoke this fear, today it is the activism of socially liberal NGOs that fuels conservative suspicions. Many white evangelicals view international NGO forums as part of a conspiracy of liberal NGOs to export the Western social revolution of the 1960s and 1970s to other parts of the world, as illustrated in the case study below of the UN Special Session on Children. This attitude stands in stark contrast to Hardt and Negri's view that NGO world forums act to voice, in a limited way, the concerns of multitude. Despite their apprehensions, evangelical NGOs have been entering UN forums in the last few years. Republican Party neoconservatives, Catholic officials, and religious conservatives from the Third World have all played a role in how American evangelical involvement in the United Nations has played out.

First, some influential neoconservatives in the Republican Party have encouraged evangelicals to participate in international concerns as a counterweight to socially liberal NGOs. The Heritage Foundation, a New Right think tank, expressed their motivation this way: "Our presence will break the 'Liberals Only' roster of present NGO's—and as the skunk at the UN Party, we will be in a much stronger position to influence media coverage and public perception."[13] The growing relationship between American neoconservative intellectuals ("neocons") and conservative white evangelicals has been nurtured by New Right political leaders who recognized a potentially powerful commonality: a belief in absolute moral truths, whether one is talking about abortion, eutha-

---

11. Robert Fuller, *Naming the Antichrist: The History of an American Obsession* (New York: Oxford University Press, 1995), and Paul Boyer, *When Time Shall Be No More: Prophecy Belief in Modern American Culture* (Cambridge, MA: Harvard University Press, 1992).

12. For the history of Americans' religious self-understanding of their country, see Conrad Cherry, ed., *God's New Israel: Religious Interpretations of American Destiny*, rev. ed. (Chapel Hill: University of North Carolina Press, 1998), and Robert T. Handy, *A Christian America: Protestant Hopes and Historical Realities*, 2nd ed. (New York: Oxford University Press, 1984).

13. E-list e-mail, "Heritage Foundation Quest for U.N. Consultative Status," on file with author.

nasia, or U.S. foreign policy.[14] Viewed by many as the principal architects of the 2003 Iraq invasion, neoconservatives have argued that the United States should unabashedly use its military might to promote American-style freedom as a universal value.[15] In the words of neocons William Kristol and Robert Kagan, "The principles of the Declaration of Independence are not merely the choices of a particular culture but are universal, enduring, 'self-evident truths.'"[16]

Although neocons and politically conservative evangelicals arrive at their conclusions from different starting points, both these groups endorse a muscular moralist unilateralism in American foreign policy. Having astutely identified compatible values they share with various kinds of religious conservatives, neoconservative think tanks have helped foster a common social, economic, and foreign policy agenda. Christian Right NGOs at the United Nations are increasingly working with some of these think tanks.[17] This growing affection between conservative white evangelical and neoconservative leaders offers another window into how some forms of evangelical international activism might extend empire.

While the alliance of neocons and American evangelicals strengthens a unilateralist foreign policy, other alliances formed by evangelicals pull them in other directions. This is particularly true of the growing cooperation between American evangelicals and Vatican officials in UN forums. While many evangelicals considered various popes as the potential Antichrist before the 1960s, Pope John Paul II became an evangelical hero in the 1980s and 1990s. This is perhaps one of the most dramatic examples of the fluidity of evangelical constructs of empire. Over the past few decades, conservative evangelicals and Catholics have discovered they have more in common with one another than with their liberal counterparts.[18]

14. "The New Fusionism," *First Things*, no. 154 (June/July 2005): 22–26. For how the alliances developed among many white evangelical leaders and conservative political activists since the 1970s, see John Micklethwait and Adrain Wooldridge, *The Right Nation: Conservative Power in America* (New York: Penguin, 2004), 63–93.

15. See, for example, Nathan Glazer and Daniel Bell, "Neoconservatives Then and Now," *New York Times,* October 26, 2003, 10, and Michael Lind, "A Tragedy of Errors," *The Nation*, February 5, 2004, http://www.thenation.com/doc/20040223/lind. On the uses of American military power to establish a Pax Americana, see William Kristol and Robert Kagan, *Rebuilding America: Strategy, Forces, and Resources for a New Century*, Project for the New American Century (PNAC), September 2000, http://www.newamericancentury.org/RebuildingAmericas-defenses.pdf, and their article "Toward a Neo-Reaganite Foreign Policy," *Foreign Affairs* 75, no. 4 (July/August1996).

16. Kristol and Kagan, "Toward a Neo-Reaganite Foreign Policy."

17. The most important are the Ethics and Public Policy Center, the Institute on Religion and Democracy, and the Institute on Religion and Public Life. See Tom Barry and Jim Lobe, "The Men Who Stole the Show," *Foreign Policy in Focus*, October 1, 2002, http://www.fpif.org/papers/index.php?sort=author.

18. Robert Wuthnow, *Restructuring of American Religion* (Princeton, NJ: Princeton University Press, 1988), 132–72.

In fact, many evangelical leaders view Pope John Paul II as one of their inspirations for becoming active in the international body they so feared. Throughout the summer of 1994, the pope made a series of calls for faithful Roman Catholics to advocate conservative stances on birth control, abortion, and family at the UN International Conference on Population and Development in Cairo. John Paul II's words had direct as well as rhetorical significance, because the Holy See functions as a full member state at UN conferences. In addition to his words, the pope's strategic alliance with representatives of Muslim nations on the issue of population policy at the Cairo Conference inspired Christian Right NGOs to pursue their own alliances with Muslim governments and religious leaders.[19]

Their relationships with Catholic and Muslim political leaders and NGOs, though in some ways a marriage of convenience, has the potential to challenge and change evangelical attitudes and positions. This is especially true on the issues of U.S. unilateralism and the neoliberal economic agenda it champions. It is useful at this point to refer again to Hardt and Negri's argument that the World Trade Organization, the World Bank, and the International Monetary Fund are kinds of international regulatory agencies that constitute global empire. Hardt and Negri, like many critics on the left, charge that these regulatory agencies tend to aid the wealthiest nations and enable them to maintain their hegemony while giving lip service to slogans of economic development. Religiously conservative peoples in the Two-Thirds World as well as humanitarian-oriented evangelical NGOs (which are involved in a campaign called the Micah Challenge) might theoretically support the ideals of the family-focused NGOs, but they also sympathize with aspects of Hardt and Negri's critique of how the world economy is structured to the disadvantage of the poor. The more that evangelicals identify with American unilateralism and neoliberal economics, the harder it will be for them to build a truly global pro-family coalition.

Consequently, even as conservative evangelical leaders seek to change the United Nations, they are challenged by it. While differences plague this conservative religious alliance of evangelicals, Mormons, Roman Catholics, and Muslims, the United Nations has become a ground on which new relationships, new understandings, and possibly new worldviews might emerge.

Two Case Studies: UN Special Session on Children and the Micah Challenge USA

The following two brief case studies show the complexity of white evangelical participation in multitude and empire. The UN Special Session on Children

19. George Weigel, "What Really Happened at Cairo," *First Things*, no. 50 (February 1995): 24–31.

offers a glimpse into how the activism of socially conservative NGOs might compromise global democracy by limiting the rights of children. It also illustrates the complexity of the alliance between the United States government and the socially conservative evangelical NGOs that it claims to support. The evangelical campaign called the Micah Challenge demonstrates the diversity of evangelical interests, which increasingly extend beyond the promotion of conservative family values.[20]

1. The UN Special Session on Children

The conservative evangelical NGOs active in UN world conferences and their review processes (which generally occur every five years) are important constituents of the U.S. Christian Right. While they have been increasingly active at the United Nations since the 1994 Conference on Population and Development (Cairo), the 2002 Special Session on Children was the first UN meeting where the activism of politically conservative evangelicals in a broader Christian Right alliance had significant influence. The special session showed early on just how much political capital the Bush administration was willing to spend on satisfying Christian Right interests in the UN arena. It also demonstrated that the Christian Right could serve the interests of the Bush administration by providing a convenient smokescreen for other conservative agendas.[21]

The goal of the UN Special Session on Children was to review progress made on the Plan of Action of the World Summit for Children, adopted in 1990, and to strengthen international attention to emerging issues, including the sexual exploitation and sale of children, the use of child soldiers, and the devastating impact of the AIDS pandemic on youth and children. For the socially conservative NGOs, however, the first priority was to prevent the incorporation of any language regarding the reproductive rights of adolescents. Reproductive-health NGOs in particular wanted to add reproductive rights to the child rights platform. In many countries adolescent children marry and have children before the age of eighteen. The AIDS pandemic had made reproductive health and sex education for young adults even more urgent, since in many regions they are among the most vulnerable to HIV/AIDS.

The meeting quickly became politicized along the lines of the U.S. culture wars, drawing media attention and energy away from the other issues many governments had expressed an interest in addressing. Negotiations during the

20. For more on evangelical lobbying, see Wilcox, *Onward Christian Soldiers?* 88–95, and Allen D. Hertke, *Freeing God's Children: The Unlikely Alliance for Global Human Rights* (New York: Rowman and Littlefield, 2004).

21. This case study is documented in depth in Jennifer Butler, "A New Sheriff in Town: Christian Right Shapes US Agenda at U.N. Conference," *The Public Eye* (Political Research Associates, in Boston), Summer 2002, 14–22.

special session were grueling. They became so tense that most of the negotiating sessions were closed to NGO observers—a rare action for a UN meeting on social issues. Much of the negotiations, according to delegates and news reports, seemed to bog down on one paragraph of the negotiated outcome document—a paragraph dealing with reproductive services for adolescents · and a reaffirmation of the Beijing and Cairo conferences.

The U.S. delegation, until the final hours of negotiations, remained unwilling to compromise its conservative positions on the most hotly debated issues, which included child rights, reproductive services, the definition of family, and the death penalty for children. In the end, however, the U.S. delegation gave the most ground in the area of reproductive health and a traditional definition of the family—the areas of highest concern to the Christian Right. In retrospect, the debate over "services" appeared to be a straw man—a fabricated issue that absorbed immense attention and energy but was not actually the main agenda of the United States. While the Christian Right had full access to the U.S. delegation to the special session, including its own representatives on the delegation itself, the United States used much of its political capital to address issues that were of concern but not central to the Christian Right platform. It might be said that the U.S. government even used Christian Right concerns over abortion to cloak more controversial concerns. Less notice was given to the United States' ardent support for the death penalty and its determination to undermine support for government funding for child welfare. Given the impact of poverty on children in the United States and worldwide, this is perhaps the greatest loss suffered at the special session. The deliberations and the final results of the conference on the convention of the special session on children are an example of how polarizations within multitude can distract efforts to quell empire—in this case to reaffirm the responsibility of governments to address the economic foundations of children's welfare.

2. Micah Challenge USA

The evangelical leaders behind the Micah Challenge support UN goals to reduce poverty by 2015. They have a very different attitude toward the United Nations from that of Christian Right activist organizations such as FOF. This evangelical activism emerged out of a little-known internal discussion that has been going on since the 1960s between U.S. evangelicals and evangelicals in the Two-Thirds World regarding the social implications of Christian mission.[22] These discussions have encouraged many U.S. evangelicals to broaden their definition of Christian mission beyond evangelism alone to include the promotion of just social structures and solutions to the physical needs of the

22. Charles E. Van Engen, "A Broadening Vision: Forty Years of Evangelical Theology of Mission, 1946–1986," in *Earthen Vessels: American Evangelicals and Foreign Missions, 1880–1980*, ed. Joel Carpenter and Wilbert R. Shenk (Grand Rapids: Eerdmans, 1990), 203–32.

world's poor. This larger movement paved the way for the evangelical leaders behind the Micah Challenge to see UN agreements on poverty reduction as an opportunity to be faithful to their Christian witness by following the Old Testament prophet Micah, who called for justice for the poor.[23]

In contrast with the evangelical activism within the Christian Right, the alliance of NGOs supporting the Micah Challenge represents a global evangelical constituency, not just an American one.[24] The Baptist World Alliance, the World Evangelical Alliance, and 267 Christian relief organizations are among the participants. It is significant that these relief organizations already have experience in relieving human misery caused by poverty, hunger, and disease. This experience has brought them into direct contact with the world's poor and the policies that create such misery.

While evangelicals within the Christian Right came to the United Nations and sought to reach policymakers outside the United States, the Micah campaign emerged largely from international evangelical groups and has signed up Americans to reach other Americans. For both groups, the goal of reaching the United States is extremely important since the United States can wield great influence. Rather than encouraging the United States to take a go-it-alone approach to addressing pressing social problems, the Micah Challenge asks it to contribute to an international effort originating from UN discussions.

The campaign seeks to recruit evangelicals primarily, but other Christians as well, to call their churches and governments to do their part to see the Millenium Development Goals (MDG) of the United Nations achieved by 2015. The MDG aim to eradicate hunger, reduce child mortality, empower women, combat AIDS, improve maternal health, and ensure environmental sustainability. Peter Vander Meulen, a Christian Reformed Church official who heads Micah Challenge USA, explains that the effort "aims to mobilize 'evangelical' Christians, but we see the campaign as 'more centered than bounded.'"[25]

A number of evangelical groups, associations, and relief organizations came together in launching this international program. The World Evangelical Alliance played a particularly important role in organizing a response to the MDG. Speaking for the World Evangelical Alliance, which has three million churches, Gary Edmonds declared: "Governments are given by God and have a moral responsibility. Christians need to hold their governments responsible."[26] Evangelical organizations that signed on to help launch the U.S. phase of the campaign on May 4, 2005, included the National Association of Evangelicals,

23. C. René Padilla, "Integral Mission and Its Historical Development," Micah Challenge, http://micahchallenge.org/Christians_Poverty_and_Justice/98.asp.

24. Evelyn Leopold, "Evangelicals Push Governments on U.N. Poverty Goals," Reuters, October 15, 2004, available at http://micahchallenge.org/campaign_news/documents/160.doc.

25. "USA," Micah Challenge, http://www.micahchallenge.org/USA/.

26. Robert Parham, "Evangelicals Pledge to Hold Governments Accountable for Poverty," *Ethics Daily*, October 8, 2004, http://www.ethicsdaily.com/article_detail.cfm?AID=4864.

Association of Evangelical Relief and Development Organizations, Sojourn-ers/Call to Renewal, and Christian Reformed World Relief.[27]

At the Micah Network's first international consultation in Oxford, En-gland, in September 2001, evangelicals developed the theological framework for this campaign and called it the Declaration of Integral Mission. The au-thors reminded their fellow evangelicals that the "holistic transformation" of the person is "the proclamation and demonstration of the gospel." Simply put, "our social involvement has evangelistic consequences." They challenged evangelicals with these words:

> If we ignore the world we betray the word of God which sends us out to serve the world. If we ignore the word of God we have nothing to bring to the world. Justice and justification by faith, worship and political action, the spiritual and the material, personal change and structural change belong together. As in the life of Jesus, being, doing and saying are at the heart of our integral task."[28]

In contrast to Christian Right activities, the Micah Challenge seeks to rally the evangelical community to UN goals. Its activities and timeline are linked with several UN events and agencies.

Conclusion

The growing interest shown by white U.S. evangelical NGOs in influencing UN conference proceedings and American foreign policy will be an important story to watch in the coming few years. Most of these initiatives have just started, so we cannot say whether they will succeed or fail. What we can say is that American evangelicals have *momentum*. While family-focused NGOs are typically the kind of group that gains media attention, if any organization at the United Nations actually does, there are actually a number of evangeli-cal NGOs that receive less attention and provide an equally revealing picture of the effects of white U.S. evangelical activism. Because evangelical NGOs are acting on their values in different ways, it is hard to predict whether white evangelicalism will aid empire or the multitude in the sense that Hardt and Negri use those words. In other words, will this movement lend its resources to further the concentration of wealth and power currently taking place in the world, or will it help to articulate the concerns of the world's majority who struggle to survive?

27. "News US," Micah Challenge, http://micahchallenge.org/USA/290.asp. For an overview of one evangelical participant's perspective on the need for greater attention to world poverty issues, see Jim Wallis, *God's Politics: Why the Right Gets It Wrong and the Left Doesn't Get It* (San Francisco: HarperOne, 2005), 270–93.

28. "Overview of the Micah Challenge," http://micahchallenge.org/overview.

Many are confused and fearful when white U.S. evangelicals seek to influence NGO events and American foreign policy, because they are unfamiliar with the history, goals, and practices of this religious movement. Some evangelicals have seemingly confirmed this stereotype by employing an aggressive style of politics that strikes some as inappropriate to the cool, rational discourse expected in the diplomatic arena. However, those interested in UN proceedings need to develop a more nuanced view of evangelical activity, becoming informed of the unique characteristics of this community. Evangelicals might share particular conservative religious assumptions, but they are not all of one voice when it comes to politics, economics, and U.S. foreign policy. Those seeking to build popular support for initiatives at the United Nations or in American foreign policy should avoid thinking all evangelical activism is inevitably a kind of empire building, in the Hardt and Negri sense of those words: some of this activism is in fact a perfect example of that messy process we call democracy at work.

6

The Gospel of Freedom, or Another Gospel?

Theology, Empire, and American Foreign Policy

JAMES K. A. SMITH

In their account of empire, Hardt and Negri make a singular contribution by recognizing the passage to a new mode of empire that is unhooked from territories and (modern) nation-states and linked to a network of "flows" of a transnational market.[1] Nevertheless, the nation-state of the United States continues to play a prominent role in this new order. In this chapter, I want to suggest that what undergirds both empire and the quasi-imperialism of American foreign policy is a particular concept of *freedom*. And this has a direct link to evangelicals: on both a domestic and international level, evangelicals march eagerly under the banner of "freedom," particularly the freedom of trade and the market. Here we reach the nexus of my argument, which cuts two ways: on the one hand, I hope to demonstrate that evangelical affirmations of freedom (particularly the free market) are in fact affirmations of a heterodox, libertarian notion of freedom which ought to be rejected by the catholic (i.e., orthodox) tradition. On the other hand, I also want to suggest that Hardt and Negri's way of "being against" empire is insufficient precisely

1. Michael Hardt and Antonio Negri, *Empire* (Cambridge, MA: Harvard University Press, 2000), 166.

because they still assume a libertarian notion of freedom in their hope for "liberation."

The Gospel of Freedom: America's (Evangelical) Foreign Policy

A quick perusal of the National Security Strategy or any of Bush's State of the Union addresses will indicate that the engine that drives U.S. foreign policy is *freedom*—specifically, the export and expansion of "free regimes" as a way of fostering economic prosperity and ultimately securing peace. More specifically perhaps, what is being advocated is the expansion and imposition of *liberalism*, particularly a liberal understanding of freedom.[2] A core value of liberal democracy is a particular understanding of freedom—what we could describe, *pace* Isaiah Berlin, as "negative" freedom: independence from external restraint. To be free is to be autonomous, self-directing, and unrestrained by external conditions (and any specification of a particular, defined telos would constitute a restraint). This understanding of freedom is particularly evinced in the close, even essential, component of this desired expansion of "freedom" or "democracy": the expansion of the free market, understood as a radically laissez-faire system that encourages consumers' wants without restriction, seeks to remove all impediments to the expansion of the market, and seeks to minimize any "regulation" of corporate interest.

But what constitutes "freedom" is not at all self-evident, despite the fact that the term is usually employed without interrogation and simply equated with liberty or choice. As Reinhard Hütter has suggested: "Like a coin handled for too long by too many hands, 'freedom' has lost its clear imprint. We still circulate the coin—the more quickly and the more frequently the less it is worth. Yet we no longer know what 'freedom' means."[3] But this lack of interrogation and tacit assumption about the nature of freedom serves only to cover the fact that we take too much for granted.

In the history of philosophy and theology, there have been two dominant, and competing, concepts of freedom. One is a "libertarian" understanding of freedom that equates freedom with *freedom of choice* or the power to do otherwise (what I'll call F_L). To be free is to have (a) options to choose and (b) the ability to choose, uncoerced and unrestrained, among these options. On a certain version of this, the more options, the more free one is. Any specified

2. See John M. Owen IV, *Liberal Peace, Liberal War* (Ithaca, NY: Cornell University Press, 1997). Fareed Zakaria echoes this equation in *The Future of Freedom: Illiberal Democracy at Home and Abroad* (New York: W. W. Norton, 2003), 115.

3. Reinhard Hütter, *Bound to Be Free: Evangelical Catholic Engagements in Ecclesiology, Ethics, and Ecumenism* (Grand Rapids: Eerdmans, 2004), 112. Also see Jean-Luc Nancy, *The Experience of Freedom*, trans. Bridget McDonald (Stanford, CA: Stanford University Press, 1993), 1.

telos for human agency would constitute a restraint on legitimate options and therefore a restriction of freedom. Even the articulation of a normative good would constitute a restriction on options and therefore a restriction of freedom. To be free, then, is equated with a state of *autosovereignty*, with respect to both the power to choose and the freedom to determine one's own good. This is perhaps most powerfully formulated by John Stuart Mill: "Over himself, over his own body and mind, the individual is sovereign."[4] Thus, for Mill, "the only freedom which deserves the name is that of pursuing our own good in our own way."[5]

This conception of freedom has become so dominant that it is almost impossible for us to think of freedom otherwise. And it is particularly this notion of freedom that feeds empire and its market network. Because F_L eschews any specification of a telos as a restriction or constraint on my options, and therefore a restriction of freedom, it fosters the proliferation of choices without any valuation. This is precisely the environment necessary for the flourishing of the market, which requires endless creation of new "goods" for consumption and resists any regulation or restriction of such proliferation as a diminishment of freedom of choice (and a consequent diminishment of "prosperity"). Or, to put this otherwise, the only "Good" that can be specified is the good of prosperity, which requires precisely that we bracket any specification of "the Good" and let many *teloi* bloom (which really amounts to none).[6]

But this nonteleological conception of autosovereignty *as* "freedom" is deeply antithetical to the first affirmation of the creed (common to Jewish and Muslim faith as well): the belief that humanity is created. This is why a theology of creation, which specifies that "the orientation to an end is inbuilt," has been "offensive to moderns."[7] What the Christian (and Jewish and Muslim) theological tradition ascribes to the Creator, modern libertarian accounts of freedom ascribe to creatures. In fact, when considered theologically, F_L demands "that a free agent parallel a creator *ex nihilo*."[8] Hence I am suggesting the antithesis: to affirm libertarian, nonteleological autosovereignty (F_L) requires rejecting any relation of dependence upon the Creator.

However, there remains another option: rejecting F_L and reinscribing freedom *as* "participatory."[9] Augustine articulated this alternative account of freedom not as libertarian freedom of choice (which he linked to sin) but

---

4. John Stuart Mill, *On Liberty* (orig. 1859; London: Penguin, 1985), 69. See Q/A 1 of the *Heidelberg Catechism*.

5. Mill, *On Liberty*, 72.

6. The market, as a structure of desire, probably does operate on the basis of a kind of formal teleology but for that reason does not specify any substantive understanding of the Good.

7. David Burrell, *Faith and Freedom: An Interfaith Perspective* (Oxford: Blackwell, 2004), vii.

8. Ibid.

9. Augustine, *De civitate Dei* 22.30. This descriptor is suggested by Hütter, *Bound to Be Free*, 115. See also David C. Schindler, "Freedom beyond Our Choosing: Augustine on the Will and

rather as positive freedom *for* the Good (so I'll abbreviate as F_G). To be free is to be empowered and enabled to choose the Good. Such a conception, I will argue in the next section, stands in critical contrast to F_L.

Free to Think Freedom Otherwise: Why Evangelicals Should be Augustinians

Thus far I have suggested that F_L—which is just the concept of freedom assumed both by empire and American foreign policy—is inconsistent with the baseline orthodox confession that God is Creator of humanity, and more specifically it conflicts with the Augustinian account of participatory freedom affirmed in the catholic tradition that includes Aquinas, Calvin, and Edwards. Here I want to briefly sketch the elements of this alternative account of freedom.

David Burrell has articulated a maxim of F_G that highlights its disjunction with F_L; as he starkly puts it, "No creator, no freedom."[10] I think this maximizes the tension between F_G and F_L because it directly counters the most common modern intuitions, viz., that in order for there to be freedom, there must be no relations of dependence or external forces that might impinge upon the "free" agent.[11] So Burrell's maxim is counterintuitive in this respect but also crystallizes the core of F_G. The argument works as follows.

The primary deficiency of F_L is that it disconnects freedom from the dynamics of desire. Seeking to eliminate the theological overtones of the scholastics, especially the disruptive presence of a free Creator, modernity erected a philosophical account of freedom that (at least) ignored the presence of a Creator and instead conceived of freedom on wholly immanent grounds. This required also jettisoning any transcendence, leaving us with "a world bereft of teleology" as affirmed in medieval Christian, Jewish, and Muslim thought.[12] There are two key effects of this modern shift: (1) it denies any transcendent object of desire and thus excludes any kind of robust teleology; (2) it makes any external/transcendent dependence a compromise of autonomy. Instead, freedom now becomes a "power" that resides self-sufficiently in autonomous

---

Its Objects," in *Augustine and Politics*, ed. John Doody, Kevin L. Hughes, and Kim Paffenroth (Lanham, MD: Lexington, 2005), 84–90.

10. Burrell, "Can We Be Free without a Creator?" in *Faith and Freedom*, 35. A correlate of this maxim would be Hütter's anti-antinomian claim that there is no freedom apart from law (*Bound to Be Free*, 112 and passim).

11. A *deistic* conception of the Creator-creature relation could perhaps sustain an affirmation of both a Creator *and* F_L; but I take it that deism lies outside the purview of orthodox Christian (and Muslim and Jewish) affirmation. (This is why Burrell is particularly pointed in his critique of theists who affirm libertarian notions of freedom ["Can We Be Free," 38].) I will not argue that point here.

12. Burrell, "Can We Be Free," 41.

human agents. Freedom is thus reduced to both a radical indifference and autodetermination. Burrell sees this exemplified in Descartes but emerging most significantly in Duns Scotus.[13] For Scotus, it is the *will* that determines what one does: "The role of the intellect is to [merely] present to the will a list of possible actions from which to choose."[14] This libertarian notion of freedom implies "a radical 'indifference' before a set of options" that is coupled with a self-sufficient picture of the will as autodetermining its "free" actions.[15] Once freedom is conceived in this way, the picture "left no room for divine subvention except as a form of intervention; no way for God to empower a free act without interfering."[16] Any involvement of God in human action could only be a compromise of human autonomous agency. By choosing to preserve autodetermination and indifference, modernity could at best retain only a deistic Creator.[17] Thus I have argued that F_L and orthodox Christian confession are mutually exclusive.[18]

The libertarian emphasis on autonomy and indifference is linked to a denial of teleology, and it's because of this move that the dynamics of desire are ignored. This is also linked to a confusion about just how to think *causality* with respect to human action. By seeking to locate all "power" of "choosing" internal to the human agent, and by conceiving causality only in terms of efficient causality, F_L misunderstands the classical (and catholic) account of freedom. And it is here that the dynamics of desire are central. Burrell's case in point here is instructive. As noted above, there is a significant way in which the modern libertarian subject mimics or even replaces a free creator, or at least exhibits all the characteristics of a free creator.[19] So it is not surprising that Roderick Chisholm would suggest that the free human agent is a "prime mover."[20] The human will is a paradigmatic self-starter; it moves itself. But this allusion is instructive precisely because of the way it misconstrues Aristotle.

13. Timothy O'Connor suggests the same links between Descartes, Suarez, and Scotus in "Free Will," s.v., *Stanford Encylopedia of Philosophy*.

14. Burrell, *Faith and Freedom*, 106.

15. Ibid. Burrell also notes a somewhat Feuerbachian implication, that this conception of human freedom of choice washes back onto the conception of God such that God is free because God chooses between different possible worlds, underwriting "the [Suarezian?] fabrication of 'middle knowledge'" (107).

16. Ibid., 107.

17. This is most helpfully developed in Burrell's discussion of Al-Ghazali's radically creational account of human freedom, in *Faith and Freedom*, 156–75.

18. To properly flush this out I would have to further explore the participatory ontology that is implied by scripture and the creedal affirmation, which I don't have space for here. For a discussion, see James K. A. Smith, *Introducing Radical Orthodoxy* (Grand Rapids: Baker Academic, 2004), chap. 6. Burrell concisely summarizes when he remarks: "To characterize creation in a manner faithful to the whole of the scriptures, creator and creatures must be related by a 'non reciprocal relation of dependence'" (*Faith and Freedom*, 134).

19. Burrell, *Faith and Freedom*, vii.

20. Chisholm, "Human Freedom and the Self," quoted in Burrell, "Can We Be Free," 40.

Chisholm envisages the human will as a "prime mover" because he "presumes Aristotle's prime mover to be an initiator, a 'pusher.'" But "a coherent account of a prime mover requires that it be unmoved and that it cause whatever moves to move by being the object of desire."[21] In this respect, the prime mover is a *puller*, not a pusher; or, to put it otherwise, the prime mover, as an object of desire, is a *final* not an efficient cause. It is a mover by allure, not pressure. And this "erotic" account of human freedom, Burrell argues, does a better job of honoring the complexities of human choosings. "Does one push oneself out of bed in the morning," he asks, "or is one rather drawn by the prospect of something enticing?"[22] Unlike F_L, which reduces human beings to "mere 'choice-machines,'" F_G "offers a more phenomenologically satisfying[23] analysis" because it recognizes that "our choosings are always embedded in a rich texture of desires."[24]

Once we reject the "pusher" paradigm and honor the embedded dynamics of desire, we will have to affirm that freedom is inherently teleological, which ultimately requires that we articulate a substantive vision of "the Good." The "puller" paradigm will also help us to affirm *both* freedom *and* the Creator, and even Burrell's stronger maxim, "No creator, no freedom." In other words, the erotic dynamic of F_G requires that (a) freedom be *teleological*; (b) there be a (perceived or tacit) *normative* telos for free human action (the Good at which human action aims); and (c) the *specification* of a normative telos for human action (the triune God, according to Christian confession). Let me try to briefly unpack this.

First, the desiring paradigm of F_G allows us "to conceive of God entering into our actions without interfering," viz., as the final cause that draws out our choices and orientation. God "makes me" will something not by pushing but by pulling. "And if I cannot be pushed to will something, but only drawn to do so, not even God can cause me to do something freely, *if we are thinking of an efficient cause.* Yet God, as my sovereign good, could so draw my will as to bring me freely to consent to the end for which my nature craves. So freedom is less a question of self-determination of what otherwise remains

21. Burrell, "Can We Be Free," 40.

22. Ibid., 41.

23. By phrasing it this way, Burrell avoids the charge that this is an overly a priori account determined by, e.g., "Christian" sources like Augustine. In a way, he wants to suggest that F_G proves itself a superior account in the arena of our experience and that it is F_L which denies the "facts," as it were. I think this is a laudable tack to take, but it is also theologically legitimate (necessary?) to suggest that our account of freedom must also square with the scriptures and confessions of the church catholic.

24. Burrell, "Can We Be Free," 42. He also notes that F_G resists dualism because it roots our actions "in the world of nature." I recognize that many (theistic) libertarians are libertarians because they want to resist the determinism or compatibilism of naturalistic accounts. However, warding off the demon of naturalistic determinism does not require F_L.

undetermined than it is one of attuning oneself to one's ultimate end."[25] Thus
a transcendent "cause" *always* pulls human choice because of the embedded
dynamics of desire. This is the most formal articulation of why freedom is
teleological.

But a formal teleology is not enough, since one could then perhaps envi-
son a teleology of indifference: my choices are oriented to and "pulled by"
an end, but there is no valuation of ends. However, as David C. Schindler
has demonstrated, this could not be the case, because then we could have no
phenomenological account of why an end attracts us. The dynamics of desires
plays on an erotic attraction that attributes something attractive to the desired
(chosen) end, even if it is only "represented" as such. So the dynamics of
desire demand that the alluring ends of free actions be represented as goods;
and this requires an ultimate or intrinsic good, or at least the representation
of such. "Something that is purely optional," Schindler comments, "cannot,
strictly speaking, be intrinsically good. . . . Unless there exists some good that
is good in an absolute sense, that is, good in itself, as an ultimate end, there
can be no goods even in a relative sense."[26] The ultimate end will be, albeit
wittingly and unconsciously, linked to something like my ultimate confession.
In our preeschatological situation, there will be a plurality of such confessions
and thus a plurality of (perceived) ultimate ends. But the final assertion of
an Augustinian and Thomistic account of F_G will further specify not only a
formal teleology, nor only a formal teleology of the Good, but the concrete
and specific articulation of the triune God as *the* ultimate Good and proper
object of human desire.[27] Properly functioning desire will mean that the free
human person is oriented toward the triune God. On this account, humans
are not self-starters but "responders";[28] freedom, then, is less a matter of
"choosing" and more a matter of "accepting" a gift or "consenting" to the
in-built orientation of one's being.[29]

This does not prevent F_G from offering an account of indifference or freedom
of choice.[30] However, instead of valorizing this as the proper metaphysical
condition of freedom, F_G sees the freedom of indifference as a failure to be
properly free. The indifferent agent has averted her orientation to the Good,
which is both the source and the goal of proper freedom. "Refusing such a good
is tantamount to denying our nature," and such refusal of the Good "leads
one toward enslavement by lesser goods. Enslavement because one is only

25. Burrell, *Faith and Freedom*, 110, emphasis added (as part of an exposition of Aquinas
and Augustine).

26. Schindler, "Freedom beyond Our Choosing," 73.

27. Augustine, *De doctrina christiana* 1.5.5; Aquinas, *Summa Theologiae* 2–1.15.2 (on one's
"proper" end).

28. Burrell, *Faith and Freedom*, 150.

29. Ibid., 136–37, 110. The final clause invokes Henri de Lubac.

30. The most developed, of course, is Augustine, *De libero arbitrio*.

free to choose goods not ordered to one's final goal *via* a mistaken judgment (i.e., thinking that they are so ordered) or as a consequence of refusing one's own orientation to that good."[31] To affirm a Creator, and to refuse deism by affirming a relation of dependence upon the Creator, requires a rejection of F_L insofar as the Creator constitutes the proper Good of the human person. If we valorize freedom as mere freedom of choice, then we end up affirming the condition of a *dis*ordered soul as metaphysically normative, and we will end up describing as "free" what Christian theology describes as a state of sin. We will also end up describing the rightly ordered agent as somehow *un*free because he is not free to do otherwise.

As I hope it has become clear above, I think that evangelical faith is inconsistent with F_L. Why, then, was evangelicalism "primed," as it were, for an embrace of F_L and hence empire? Here I would suggest that contemporary evangelicalism, as heir of a certain revivalist theology, has inherited a largely negative, libertarian notion of freedom that is more closely linked with Pelagius and Jacob Arminius than to those evangelicals consider to be their predecessors: Reformers such as John Calvin and Puritan fathers such as Jonathan Edwards. In the end, I suspect the complicity of revivalism with F_L is one of the key reasons that evangelicalism has absorbed a notion of freedom that is, in fact, "another Gospel" (Gal. 1:6), owing more to Locke and Hobbes than to scripture—and that this specifically liberal understanding of freedom is fundamentally at odds with "catholic" understandings of freedom as articulated by Augustine and Edwards.[32] A more catholic, Augustinian theology of human freedom would thus call into question the notions of freedom that underwrite empire and would thus be opposed to American foreign policy's baptism of this "other gospel" of freedom.

The *Ecclesia* as Alternative Multitude

To this point, a core part of my argument has been made: insofar as Christian confession requires the rejection of F_L (for both theological reasons and

31. Burrell, *Faith and Freedom*, 109.

32. I don't mean to claim that Arminian theology necessarily entails such a political manifestation (though I do think there is a logical resonance between the two; see Edwards on "most pernicious doctrine"); rather, I am suggesting that American evangelicalism was uniquely positioned for this "chemical reaction," as it were, because of the confluence of political liberalism (driven by libertarian notions of freedom) and theological libertarianism. This raises interesting historical questions which I lack the space (and expertise) to explore. In particular, one might wonder whether America's unique role in fostering economic libertarianism (under the banner of "free markets") owes more to its revivalist heritage than to its Puritan heritage. On the other hand, there is a way in which Adam Smith's economy presumes just the kind of self-interest that Calvinists were quick to find in *all* of humanity. But whether they would then baptize that as an engine to drive economy and commerce is a different question.

concerns of justice), then evangelicals ought to also reject those policies and institutions that presume a libertarian, nonteleological account of freedom. This will include both current U.S. foreign policy and the network of market capitalism and consumerism. In this respect, we will find (perhaps surprising) agreement between an evangelical (catholic) resistance to empire and Hardt and Negri's own critique of empire. But here I arrive at the final turn of my argument: I want to further suggest that, in fact, Hardt and Negri's account of the multitude lacks the resources to really and properly resist empire precisely because they still retain F_L. Here I argue that Hardt and Negri's own critique of poststructuralist and postcolonial theory (which they take to be insufficiently radical and thus playing into the hands of the "real enemy")[33] provides a model for my critique: insofar as they fail to interrogate and oppose the concept of freedom that is at the root of empire, their own constructive proposal for resistance is insufficiently radical. The only proper alternative to the network of empire would have to be a peaceable "guerrilla" network that rejects F_L and is oriented by F_G. In order to sketch this, let's first consider the basis and goal of the multitude's resistance to empire.

In a few key pages of *Empire*, the shift from diagnosis to resistance happens very (and perhaps a little too) quickly. After Hardt and Negri provide a rigorous and meticulous analysis of the machinations of empire in parts 1 and 2, the "intermezzo" indicates a turn to considering "what type of political subjectivities might contest and overthrow the forces of Empire."[34] Simple "refusal" or withdrawal will not be enough: "What we need is to create a new social body, which is a project that goes well beyond refusal. Our lines of flight, our exodus must be constituent and create a real alternative. Beyond the simple refusal, or as part of that refusal, we need also to construct a new mode of life and above all a new community."[35] However, in this quick turn on pages 204–5—a turn from analysis of empire to "what type of political subjectivities might contest and overthrow the forces of empire"—it seems that a glaring question has not quite been answered: *Why* should the forces of empire be resisted and overthrown? Of course, on the one hand, little needs to be said: the description of the situation of exploitation, oppression, and racism under empire need little commentary to motivate opposition. This is then supplemented by the *cahiers de doléances* in *Multitude*, which spell out

33. They note, for instance, that the valorization of "difference" in postmodernism is quite amenable to the world market: "It should be no surprise, then, that postmodernist thinking and its central concepts have flourished in the various fields of practice and theory proper to capital, such as marketing, management organization, and the organization of production. Postmodernism is indeed the logic by which global capital operates. Marketing has perhaps the clearest relation to postmodernist theories, and one could even say that the capitalist marketing strategies have long been postmodernist, *avant la letter*" (*Empire*, 151). On missing the "real enemy," see 137–38.

34. *Empire*, 205.

35. Ibid., 204.

the "inequalities, injustices, and undemocratic characteristics of the global system"—specifically problems with representation, global poverty, and war.[36] In the face of such accounts, it might seem like a "foundationalist" hangup to ask for *reasons* to resist. But on the other hand, if we are to avoid the kind of relativism that Hardt and Negri rightly criticize, as well as a naive empiricism, it seems legitimate to find criteria for opposition, particularly since they also want to construct a "real alternative." It would seem that the articulation of an alternative demands concrete formulation of the criteria that would both spell out what's wrong with the regime of empire and then provide the basis for configuring an alternative.[37]

So what is really to be opposed here? What motivates refusal and resistance? Why *not* empire? Of course, at the level of "symptoms," it would seem just "obvious" that we ought to oppose servitude, exploitation, and oppression (though this clearly isn't just "obvious" to the purveyors of empire). But if we start to probe beneath the symptoms and ask what's wrong with the *system* of empire, Hardt and Negri provide only hints, but these hints are very telling. If there is something like a "root" to empire's injustices, they stem from *domination*. This is why "the refusal of work and authority, or really the refusal of voluntary servitude, is the beginning of a liberatory politics."[38] The "real alternative" that will "contest and overthrow the forces of Empire" is named a "liberatory politics" because what it opposes, above all, is domination, which is equated with "authority": thus a liberatory politics represents "the political power of refusal, the power of subtracting ourselves from the relationship of domination, and through our exodus subverting the sovereign power that lords over us."[39] What marks the multitude—that social body that is "constituted through the common name of 'freedom'"—is "its quest for autonomous self-government."[40] What the multitude resists in empire is its repression; in fact, "the action of the multitude becomes political primarily when it begins to confront directly and with an adequate consciousness the central repressive operations of Empire."[41] Thus, while the multitude is antiliberal (or at least "postliberal"),[42] it is certainly not antidemocratic. In fact, it represents a radicalization of democracy that brooks no limit on freedoms: democracy, Hardt and Negri contend, "can no longer be evaluated in the liberal manner as a limit of equality or in the socialist way as a limit of freedom but rather

36. Michael Hardt and Antonio Negri, *Multitude: War and Democracy in the Age of Empire* (New York: Penguin, 2004), 268–85.

37. This line of critique perhaps replays Alain Badiou's critique of Gilles Deleuze, where Badiou suggests that Deleuze's Spinozist line undercuts the very possibility of judgment. My thanks to Creston Davis for helpful correspondence around these questions.

38. *Empire*, 204.

39. Ibid.

40. Ibid., 350, 349.

41. Ibid., 399.

42. *Multitude*, 303.

must be the radicalization without reserve of both freedom and equality."[43] *Pace* Spinoza, such a freedom "without reserve" must be a freedom that is "absolute" and therefore refuses any authority and any teleology.[44] This must be the case because Hardt and Negri see any externality or "transcendence"—whether the transcendence of a sovereign or a god, or the externality of a determined telos—as ipso facto a restriction of freedom and therefore a compromise of the absoluteness of the multitude's freedom.[45]

What the multitude desires is absolute freedom, and what the multitude opposes in empire is its repression and restriction of freedom. But just what concept of freedom is operative in Hardt and Negri's proposal? It would seem clear, given the negative mode of formulation (freedom from restrictions), the concept of freedom that drives both their critique and their constructive vision is a most radical version of F_L. But if, as I've tried to demonstrate above, empire—as instantiated in the "world market" and served by U.S. foreign policy—is itself rooted in F_L, then it would seem that Hardt and Negri's alternative vision is still nourished by the same libertarian well. And for just that reason, their alternative is insufficiently radical insofar as it does not really oppose the root (*radix*) of empire. If the injustices of empire are in some significant way the fruit of F_L, then it's hard to see how further radicalizing F_L will redress this situation of injustice. In this way, their critique of empire is characterized by the same insufficiency as the postmodernist and postcolonial theories that they criticize because they "fail to recognize adequately the contemporary object of critique, that this, they mistake the real enemy."[46] While they chastise these theorists for "combating the remnants of a past form of domination" and failing to recognize "the new form that is looming over them in the present," we might criticize Hardt and Negri for clinging to a distinctly modern notion of freedom and thus mistakenly criticizing all forms of authority *as* domination, failing to recognize that what is at issue is not authority or teleology as such but the more complex task of evaluating and discerning the particular direction that authority takes.[47] In other words, the "real enemy" is F_L, and the way to oppose empire is not with a more radicalized version of F_L but rather with a rehabilitation of F_G.[48]

43. Ibid., 220.

44. Ibid., 221. This "absolute" democracy is also described as "pure" democracy (244) and "real" democracy (306).

45. For their equation of transcendence with domination, see *Empire*, 186, 201, 204.

46. Ibid., 137.

47. That is, oppression or repression cannot be simply identified with a situation of authority or an external "force" that shapes freedom; rather, authority structures will be oppressive to the extent that they do not empower authentic freedom (F_G).

48. It's hard for me to resist invoking Jonathan Edwards's evaluation of the F_L of his day ("Arminianism"): "I think the notion of liberty, consisting in contingent self-determination of the will, as necessary to the morality of man's dispositions and actions almost inconceivably

A further critique here could take two trajectories. First, from the standpoint of Christian theology, and therefore assuming a set of assumptions regarding the necessary situation of sovereignty and lordship that follows just from the affirmation of a Creator (not to mention more specifically christological concerns), we could easily show that Hardt and Negri's radicalized version of F_L is inconsistent with Christian confession. Such a line of critique is no doubt important and worthwhile, especially for evangelicals, but I think the lineaments of the critique are easily anticipated and need not be spelled out here. More important, such a line of critique will have little to say to Hardt and Negri, since they do not share this set of assumptions.

So I would like to briefly pursue a second trajectory, what we might describe as a more immanent or internalist line of critique. Here I want to repeat what I described as Burrell's "phenomenological" strategy above by showing that Hardt and Negri's account cannot internally sustain itself.

In particular, I would suggest that there is a certain incoherence between their account of freedom and the thematics of "desire" that organizes their account of the multitude. As they emphasize, resistance to empire requires more than refusal: it requires the construction of "a new mode of life and above all a new community."[49] This alternative community must be "equally global" and embody "a new way of living in the world," specifically constituting an alternative "through the desires of the multitude."[50] Because the multitude constitutes a "community" and is oriented by "desires," it is not surprising to hear Hardt and Negri—*pace* Aristotle and MacIntyre—invoke the notion of "habits" to provide an account of the multitude.[51] Situated "halfway between a fixed law of nature and the freedom of subjective action," habits "constitute our social nature" in community; they "create a nature that serves as the basis of life" and provide the platform for practices that make life-in-common possible.[52] But, of course, habits work in this formative way because they provide a kind of second-nature orientation to a common telos and because they are inscribed in us by discipline. And wherever discipline and telos are affirmed, F_L has been rejected. In other words, habits can be affirmed as a good only to the extent that we reject libertarian, non-teleological notions of freedom. And desires themselves operate on the basis of a teleological orientation: that is,

---

pernicious" (letter to John Erskine, August 3, 1757), quoted in George Marsden, *Jonathan Edwards: A Life* (New Haven, CT: Yale University Press, 2003), 437–38.

49. *Empire*, 204.

50. Ibid., 206, 214.

51. Admittedly, they prefer the habits of pragmatists like Dewey (*Multitude*, 198). In this sense, there is some interesting overlap between their proposal and that of Jeffrey Stout's notion of democracy *as* a tradition with its own habits and practices (see Stout, *Democracy and Tradition* [Princeton, NJ: Princeton University Press, 2004]).

52. *Multitude*, 197.

there is desire only where there is the allure and attraction of a telos.[53] In other places, Hardt and Negri seem to suggest that the multitude is characterized by just this kind of teleological orientation: "The multitude," they contend, "needs a political *project* to bring it into existence." This projection of an end then constitutes the multitude by providing "common dreams, common desires, common ways of life, and common potential that are mobilized in a movement."[54] Insofar as the multitude is constituted by habits and practices that are linked to desires, which are in turn linked to a determinate telos, then despite Hardt and Negri's stated quest to radicalize "democracy" (as radicalized F_L), the multitude must be teleological and oriented to a particular telos, which requires rejecting F_L. In other words, there is a serious contradiction in the concepts of freedom that are invoked when they describe "the absolute concept of democracy" as a "North Star that continues to guide our political desires and practices."[55] Insofar as one constitutes a "community" by practices oriented by desire, one must reject the notion of absolute freedom.

With this tension in view, it would seem that Hardt and Negri cannot so easily dispense with Augustine. While they invoke the tropes of the *City of God*—particularly Augustine's "project to contest the decadent Roman Empire" by means of a "universal, catholic community"[56]—they nevertheless emphasize their departure from Augustine precisely on the point of teleology: "Our pilgrimage on earth, however, in contrast to Augustine's, has no transcendent telos beyond; it is and remains absolutely immanent."[57] But if their account of the multitude must remain teleological, then the rejection of a distinctly *transcendent* telos is stipulated without justification, beyond the mere platitudes that "transcendental determinations of value . . . have lost their coherence" or that the city of God "has lost all honor and legitimacy."[58] Such stipulations do not constitute a warranted rejection but only a hasty dismissal. In fact, it is precisely opposition to the immanent hegemony of empire that should make us more honestly consider that perhaps transcendence (not as gnostic escape but as incarnational ground) is *necessary* for resistance.[59]

When Hardt and Negri invoke "love as a political concept"—with the offhand claim that "there is really nothing necessarily metaphysical about the

---

53. It would seem that a nonteleological desire would not be a desire but simply a voluntarist, arbitrary expression of will.

54. *Multitude*, 212–13.

55. Ibid., 241.

56. *Empire*, 207. For something of a restaging of Augustine's project that is very attentive to the imperial situation analyzed by Hardt and Negri, see Daniel M. Bell Jr., *Liberation Theology after the End of History* (London: Routledge, 2001).

57. *Empire*, 207; also see 208.

58. Ibid., 354, 396.

59. John Milbank suggests this in "Materialism and Transcendence," in *Theology and the Political: The New Debate*, ed. Creston Davis, John Milbank, and Slavoj Žižek (Durham, NC: Duke University Press, 2005), 393–426.

Christian and Judaic love of God"[60]—again, their mere stipulation does not constitute a warranted rejection. Furthermore, the New Testament claim that "we love because [God] first loved us" (1 John 4:19) does entail a metaphysical claim about the possibility of love and the kind of community in which such love—indeed as a "political concept"—would be possible. In this respect, it might be *only* Augustine's ecclesial multitude that can contest and overthrow empire. Hardt and Negri, rather than looking for St. Francis, might do better to wait for St. Benedict and the community constituted by his Rule.[61]

60. *Multitude*, 351.

61. Compare *Empire*, 413, with Alasdair MacIntyre, *After Virtue*, 2nd ed. (Notre Dame, IN: University of Notre Dame Press, 1984), 263. The point is that monastic communities obviously reject the F_L conception of freedom, since they exist as spaces where freedom is found in obedience and subjection. But there are other parallels to consider. Hardt and Negri, for instance, advocate "desertion" as a mode of resistance; this desertion involves the "evacuation of the places of power" (*Empire*, 212). In a similar way, the new monasticism movement advocates "relocation to the abandoned places of Empire." See Rutba House, ed., *School(s) for Conversion: Twelve Marks of New Monasticism* (Eugene, OR: Wipf and Stock, 2005), xii.

7

Liberality vs. Liberalism

JOHN MILBANK

Today we live in very peculiar circumstances indeed. The welfare of this world is being wrecked by the ideology of neoliberalism, and yet its historic challengers—conservatism and socialism—are in total disarray. Socialism, in particular, appears to be wrong-footed given the discovery that liberalism and not socialism is the bearer of "modernity" and "progress." If the suspicion then arises that perhaps modernity and progress are themselves by no means on the side of justice, then socialists today characteristically begin to half-realize that their own traditions in their Marxist, social democratic, and Fabian forms have been themselves too grounded in modes of thought that celebrate only utility and the supposedly "natural" desires, goods, and needs of isolated individuals.

For these reasons, there is no merit whatsoever in the contention of the aging left (Habermas, Hobsbaum, etc.) that we are faced with an abandonment of progress and the Enlightenment by a postmodern era. To the contrary, it is clear that what we are now faced with is rampant enlightenment, after the failure of secular ideologies derived from the nineteenth century—socialism, positivism, communism—that sought to some degree to *qualify* Enlightenment individualism and formalism with organicism, distributive justice, and sociohistorical substance.

Instead, in the face of a very peculiar situation, we need to take the risk of thinking in an altogether new way that will take up the traditions of socialism less wedded to progress, historical inevitability, materialism and the state and put them into debate with conservative anticapitalist thematics and the traditions of classical and biblical political thought that may allow us to see the inherent restrictions of the parameters of modern social, political, and economic reflection. Our perspective may remain basically a "left" one, but we need to consider the possibility that only a realignment of the Left with more primordial, "classical" modes of thinking will now allow it to criticize currently emerging tyranny.

This should include at its center an openness to religion and to the question whether a just politics must refer beyond itself to transcendent norms. For this reason, in what follows I have undertaken the experiment of thinking through a catholic Christian approach to the social sphere in the light of current reality, in the hope that this will have something to offer not just to Christians but to a degree also to Jews, Muslims, and people of no religious persuasion whatsoever. I do not choose to insult the latter by concealing in any way the religious grounds of what I wish to say, nor my view that a predominantly secular culture will only sustain the neoliberal catastrophe.

The documents of Vatican II, especially *Gaudium et Spes*, appear in retrospect to have been in some ways overaccepting of modern liberal democracy and market economics. This is historically understandable, since the Church needed to move beyond a previous endorsement of reactionary and sometimes absolutist monarchy and static and hierarchical economic systems linked to unequal landholding.

Today, though, we need to recognize that we are in a very different situation. First of all, recent events demonstrate that liberal democracy can itself devolve into a mode of tyranny. One can suggest that this is for a concatenation of reasons: An intrinsic indifference to truth, as opposed to majority opinion, means in practice that the manipulation of opinion will usually carry the day. Then governments tend to discover that the manipulation of fear is more effective than the manipulation of promise, and this is in keeping with the central premises of liberalism, which, as Pierre Manent says, are based in Manichaean fashion upon the ontological primacy of evil and violence: at the beginning is a threatened individual, piece of property, or racial terrain. This is *not* the same as an Augustinian acknowledgment of original sin, perversity, and frailty—a hopeful doctrine, since it affirms that the all-pervasive evil for which we cannot really account (by saying, for example, with Jean-Jacques Rousseau that it is the fault of private property or social association as such) is yet all the same a contingent intrusion upon reality, which can one day be fully overcome through the lure of the truly desirable, which is transcendent goodness (and which itself, in the mode of grace, now aids us). Liberalism instead begins with a disguised naturalization of original sin as original egotism: our own egotism which we seek to nurture, and still more the egotism of the other, against which we need protection.

Thus increasingly, a specifically liberal politics (and not, as so many journalists fondly think, its perversion) revolves around a supposed guarding against alien elements: the terrorist, the refugee, the person of another race, the foreigner, the criminal. Populism seems more and more to be an inevitable drift of unqualified liberal democracy. A purported defense of the latter is itself deployed in order to justify the suspending of democratic decision-making and civil liberties. For the reasons just seen, this is not just an extrinsic and reactionary threat to liberal values: to the contrary, it is liberalism itself that tends to cancel those values of liberality (fair trial, right to a defense, assumed innocence, habeas corpus, a measure of free speech and free inquiry, good treatment of the convicted) which it has *taken over* but which as a matter of historical record it did not invent. Rather, they derive from Roman and Germanic law transformed by the infusion of the Christian notion of charity, which in certain dimensions means a generous giving of the benefit of the doubt, as well as succor even to the accused or wicked. For if the ultimate things to be respected are simply individual security and freedom of choice (which is not to say that these should not be accorded *penultimate* respect), then almost any suspensions of normal legality can tend to be legitimated in the name of these values. In the end, liberalism takes this sinister turn when all that it endorses is the free market along with the nation-state as a competitive unit. Government will then tend to become entirely a policing and military function, as J. G. Fichte (favorably!) anticipated. For with the decay of all tacit constraints embedded in family, locality, and mediating institutions between the individual and the state, it is inevitable that the operation of economic and civil rules—which no individual has any longer any interest in enforcing (since she is socially defined only as a lone chooser and self-seeker)—will be ruthlessly and ever more exhaustively imposed by a state that will become totalitarian in a new mode. Moreover, the obsessive pursuit of security against terror and crime will only ensure that terror and crime become more sophisticated and subtly effective: we have entered a vicious global spiral.

In the face of this neoliberal slide into despotism, catholic Christianity needs once more to proclaim with the classical tradition it carries—and which tended to predict just such a slide of a "democratic" ethos into sophistic tyranny—that government is properly mixed. Democracy can function without manipulation of opinion only if it is balanced by an "aristocratic" element of the pursuit of truth and virtue for their own sake and by a "monarchic," architectonic imposition of intrinsic justice that is unmoved by either the prejudices of the few or those of the many. In addition, the church needs boldly to teach that the only justification for democracy is theological: since the people is potentially the *ecclesia*, and since nature always anticipates grace, truth lies finally dispersed among the people (although they need the initial guidance of the virtuous) because the Holy Spirit speaks through the voice of all.

But to say this is to ask that we subordinate contract to gift. A government may be contractually legitimate as elected, and its laws may be legitimate as proceeding from sovereign power, but such arrangements can still lead to tyranny—as the Nazi example and now the Bush example so clearly show. So beyond this it needs to be supposed that the truth lies with the people somewhat in the way that truth lies in the church for St. Paul: namely, that the body of Christ receives from the Holy Spirit—who is life and gift—a life of circulation which is the exchange of gifts. Different people and groups have different talents and insights—these they share for the good of the whole body. The people give their goods to the head of the church, who is Christ: in like manner, the people should give their gifts of insight and talent to the sovereign representative that acts in their name.

Inversely, the sovereign power must think of itself as distributing gifts—gifts of good governance and ordering—not simply as imposing a fiat in order to expand the utility and productiveness of a nation-state. The latter is an outrageous notion—for example, Tony Blair's racist view that Britain should accept only "skilled" immigrants and refugees who can increase the gross national product. A government that gives must pursue the intrinsic fulfillment of its citizens. To rule in this way means that the subjects of rule can participate in this ruling and appropriate its task to themselves. To be ruled renders them "subjects" even in the ontological sense, since thereby something is proposed to them that can form their own good if they respond to it. And no one is self-originated.

So in the face of the crisis of liberal democracy, catholic Christian thought (including Roman Catholic, Anglican, Orthodox, and even some Reformed strands) needs to return to certain older themes of its critique of liberalism, but for radical and not conservative reasons. The "modernity" of liberalism has delivered only mass poverty, inequality, erosion of freely associating bodies beneath the level of the state, and ecological dereliction of the earth. Now, without the compensating threat of communism, it has abolished the rights and dignity of the worker, ensured that women are treated in the workplace as well as domestic and erotic slaves, and finally started to remove the ancient rights of the individual which long precede the creed of liberalism itself (such as habeas corpus in Anglo-Saxon law) and are grounded in the dignity of the person rather than the "self-ownership" of autonomous liberal man (sic).

The only creed that tried, often valiantly, to challenge this multiple impoverishment—communism—did so only in the name of the subordination of all to the future productivity of the nation and ignored people's needs for an aesthetic and religious relationship to each other and to nature. What must rather challenge liberalism is a truer "liberality" in the literal sense of a creed of generosity that would suppose, indeed, that societies are more fundamentally bound together by mutual generosity than by contract—this being a thesis anciently investigated by Seneca in his *De beneficiis* and in modernity again reinstated by Marcel Mauss.

But considerations about gift are relevant also to a second context for contemporary social reflection. This concerns the economic realm. Today we live under the tyranny of an unrestricted capitalist market. We have abandoned the Marxist view that this market must inevitably collapse and evolve into socialism. So we have thereby abandoned immanent, secular, historicist hope. But we have also largely abandoned the social democratic idea that the capitalist market can be mitigated. Here a Marxist analysis still largely holds good: social democracy was in the capitalistic interest for a phase that required a Keynesian promotion of demand, but it was abandoned when the excessive demands of labor together with economic competition between nation-states that ensured the generation of profits, became problematic. It is true that neoliberalism has scarcely solved the problems of slow productive growth since the 1950s, but nevertheless the inherent logic of capital accumulation seems to prevent any return to social democratic solutions.

Here again, catholic social thought needs to remain true to its own genius, which has always insisted that solutions do not lie either in the purely capitalist market or with the centralized state. There is in fact no "pure" capitalism, only degrees of this. Small-scale local capitalist economies are only in truth semicapitalist, because they often exhibit a competition for excellence but not a mutually abolishing drive of companies toward monopoly (as was rightly argued by Fernand Braudel). This is because in such cases, e.g., parts of north Italy and of Germany, a certain local culture of design excellence ensures that there is *no* pursuit of production *only* to make money nor any exchange of commodities *only* determined by supply and demand and not also by a shared recognition of quality—such that supply and demand, plus the accumulation of capital for the future and offering of loans at interest for reasonable social benefit, are themselves involved in an exchange in what is taken to be inherent value and not just formal, market-determined value. (This is not at all to deny that the *debate* as to what constitutes intrinsic value will ever be completely settled.)

Given such a consideration, one can see that an element of "gift exchange" can remain even within the modern market economy. Producers of well-designed things do not just contract with consumers. The latter give them effectively countergifts of sustenance in return for the gifts of intrinsically good things, even though this is mediated by money. One can suggest that more of the economy could be like this. This requires indeed that local production of locally suitable things linked to local skills is favored. We should import and export only what we have to or else what truly can only come from elsewhere— I am not advocating asceticism but rather the true hedonism of the genuine and its interchange. If we receive only the exotic from elsewhere, then here too there can be a form of gift exchange in operation. In actual fact, global communications and transport favor this: within a global village, those in Europe wishing to receive the good gift of organically farmed coffee can pay a fair price for this, which is a countergift ensuring that producers are not exploited. (Nevertheless, one should be on guard against situations where consumers are made to pay excessively in order to compensate for inadequate investment or excessive profit-making on the part of producers.)

Examples like the economy of fair-trade coffee may not sound dramatic or decisive, and indeed they remain pathetically marginal and often compromised, but nevertheless the extension of such gift exchange bit by bit is the sure way forward rather than revolution, government action, or capitalistic solutions. Groups linking across the globe can ensure that something is given back to the earth and that genuine goods go into planetary circulation. We need once again to form systematic links between producer and consumer cooperatives, and we need to see an emergence of cooperative banking (perhaps supervised by the church, Islamic, and Jewish bodies) to regulate and adjudicate interactions between many different modes of cooperative endeavor. Only this will correct the mistake of all our current politics: namely to suppose that the "free market" is a given that should be either extended or inhibited and balanced. For if the upshots of the free market are intrinsically unjust, then "correcting" this through another welfare economy is only a mode of resignation; moreover, its task is Sisyphean and periodically doomed to go under with every economic downturn (consider the then British Chancellor of the Exchequer Gordon Brown as Sisyphus, always expostulating, puffing, and blowing . . .).

Instead, we need a different sort of market: a resubordination of money transaction to a new mode of universal gift exchange. This requires that in every economic exchange of labor or commodity there be always a negotiation of ethical value at issue. Indeed, economic value should only be ethical value, while inversely, ethical value should be seen as emerging from the supply and demand of intrinsic gifts.

For ethical value is not for Christianity just "virtue": rather it is charity, and therefore it is the forging of bonds through giving and receiving. Virtue is here *ecstasized*, and therefore its context ceases to be simply, as for Aristotle, political but rather becomes, as for St. Paul, also economic—the virtue of a new "social" in the middle realm between *polis* and *oikos* that is equally concerned with political just distribution and with domestic care and nurture (the equality of women, which stems from St. Paul even though he could not see how far it must go, has profoundly to do with this). St. Paul does not mention *arête*, though he does talk of the person who is a *phronimos*. The latter, though, is now more a giver and receiver of gifts, as Philippians especially shows. For St. Paul, in speaking of *ecclesia*, proposes a new sort of *polis* that can counteract and even eventually subsume the Roman empire—as the heirs of Abraham, Moses, and Plato must today subsume the American one. This new *polis*, as Bruno Blumenfeld shows, as with Philo, is at once monarchic, headed by Christ, and drastically democratic in a participatory sense—the people are the body of the King; the King can act only through the people. Since virtue is now newly to do with the wisdom of love, virtue with Christianity gets democratized and is indeed dispersed among the diverse gifts of the body of Christ, which as talents also need to be constantly exchanged to realize the solidarity of the whole. As much later in Christian history (the seventeenth century) Pierre Bérulle suggested (though too much in the sense of royal absolutism), human kingly rule is entirely christological, since it echoes the kenotic and deificatory exchange of worshiping and worshiped (the king manifesting in a faint degree the glory of divine rule as such) that is fused in one corpus by the incarnation.

The latter event creates a new paracosmic reality—a new order somehow embracing both God and the creation and a new order that abolishes the previous dominance and semiuniversality of the law, of Torah, *lex*, and *nomos* and so of all political process as such. The participation of the creation in God through the newly realized cosmic body of Christ ruled by the new order of love is utterly self-abandoning toward the good of the community of *esse* (as for Aquinas, there is only one divine *esse* in Christ for Bérulle). And it meets all the time with an equivalent divine kenosis: God now is—or is also and so is even in himself—simply sharing himself with the creation, and yet this by free gift of love and not by inexorable fate of immanent pantheistic process, which would tend always to appropriate the beings of the creation. As created, things exceed both temporal process and fixed form; out of these they constantly weave the exchange of *relation*, and relation persists all the way down, because the created thing is at bottom outside itself as relation to another, namely God, who gives it to be. But the God who creates affirms this within himself as generation of the Logos and affirms also the worshiping response of the creation within himself as the procession of the Holy Spirit.

Yet to this infinite good within the Trinity is added the ecstatic mysterious "extra" of finite dependence and finite worship. God, as both Philo and Bérulle in different eras said, lacks worship of himself, since he does not, as ontological rather than ontic, depend even on himself any more than he causes himself. Yet in the incarnation, suggests Bérulle, God ceases to lack even this, and in coming to share God's life we are returned by God in Christ always back to specifically finite excellence. The invisible points back to the visible as well as the other way round, as Maximus the Confessor says in his *Mystagogy*.

So with the incarnation, for all that God, it seems, can receive nothing, it happens that God comes to receive our worship of himself by joining to the personhood of the Logos our human worship. Thus, in some mysterious way, it is not that the finite receives in a unilateral way the infinite, nor that the finite returns to the infinite a unilateral praise. It is now rather true that there is an infinite-finite exchange of gifts—as St. John of the Cross affirmed was the case in his experience of deification. And in this way Christ is now King upon the earth, and so it follows that there should be always a fusion of democratic dispersal with monarchic liberality and objectivity. Indeed this should run almost in the direction of monarchic anarchy, as clearly recommended by Tolkien in the *Lord of the Rings* (no law in the Shire but an orderly echo of remote kingship). Or perhaps in the spirit of Robin Hood: like other legendary outlaws of the time of King John, he had been declared "civilly dead" (*civile mortuus*) outside the law and therefore outside humanity, with the price on his head equivalent to that of the head of a forest-wolf. He had been declared so by a feudal king who tended to reduce his rule to the self-interested formation of contracts and so was eventually restrained by the counter-contract of the baronial Magna Carta to which he was forced to submit. But Robin Hood in legend appeals to the king in exile (in later retellings this becomes John's brother Richard, away on crusade), the king of natural law from whose legal domain no living human being can possibly be excluded. It is this natural law of fair distribution and generous assistance that Robin in the forest seeks to uphold, in the knowledge that its earthly sovereign representative remains in existence and may mysteriously show up at any time.

What is the *ecclesia*? For St. Paul, it seems to be a kind of universal tribalism of gift exchange over against both local polis and universal empire. But how can this be? Gift exchange is normally of sacred things among friends. With strangers one needs formal rules of contract to ensure mutual benefit. Things exchanged here get secularized. How can one return to tribalism and exchange gifts with strangers? Well, I have already indicated that there may be a virtuous dialectic at work here: the more we become strangers, also the more—potentially at least—we become universal neighbors. We cannot achieve this as isolated individuals, but we can achieve this if across the globe localities and kinship groups still retain identity—as they tend to do, to assert themselves against anonymity—and yet ceaselessly exchange this with other groups: the way, for example, different folk musics remain themselves and yet constantly borrow from other folk musics—as English Elizabethan folk music borrowed from Celtic and Iberian sources. Today such fusion goes on of course far more.

But there is another and specifically theological point. Christianity renders all objects sacred: everything is a sign of God and of his love. Moreover, in Christ this is *shown again*, and he provides the *idiom* for rendering all sacred. Hence there need be no more neutral commodities, just as there are no more strangers—not because we are citizens, even of *cosmopolis*, but because we are sons, daughters, brothers, and sisters, in Adam and now in the new Adam, who is Christ. We are literally one kin, as the Middle Ages saw it—one kin both physical and spiritual; one kind under Christ. Thus we live by an exchange of blood, and charity is just this exchanging.

But is it? Is not charity the free *one-way* gift? But this makes love always sacrifice. But what is sacrifice, the ultimate free one-way gesture of love, for?

Surely to reestablish exchange. In this way, sacrifice by no means escapes an economy, nor should it. And yet in gift exchange, though there is equivalent return, the same thing does not come back. Something passes never to return at all. For this reason no countergift ever cancels a debt but always inaugurates a new one. In the New Testament, one finds repeated unease (in both the Gospels and the epistles) about gift exchange as something pursued for the power of the benefactor, unlike the grace of God, and yet at the same time a continued insistence that God's grace must be actively received and responded to and that the mediators of this grace, like St. Paul himself, deserve acknowledgment and support—the tension between these two stresses underlies many tortured passages in his writings.

For this reason, the gift is not a straight line, nor is it a closed circle. Rather it is a spiral or a strange loop. Beyond the law of noncontradiction, it is both unilateral and reciprocal. It spirals on and on . . . and there is no first free gift, because to give to another one must have received at least her presence. Likewise one cannot be grateful without a gesture which is already a countergift.

When one gives, for that unilateral instance one is a monarch. One stands, as it were, hierarchically above the one who cannot choose what one is going to give to him, say to him, etc. No contractual liberalism can ever bind the oscillating aristocracy of mere conversation. Likewise when one receives, for that instance one is a monarch receiving tribute, even if the roles will be reversed in the next instance. Thus to give, or to receive, is hierarchically and unilaterally to help continue a process that is nonetheless fundamentally democratic and reciprocal.

We today have totally divided reciprocal market contract from private free giving. And yet the latter remains secretly a contract, and the former is also like the crossing of two unilateral gifts whose objects in no way mingle. Our situation therefore has crazy undercurrents that go unrecognized. Giving is, by contrast, really free and liberal only where it respects and helps further to create reciprocal norms. Contract is really fair only where there is a judged equivalence of objects and also a free mutual promotion by donation of the welfare of the exchanging parties.

If all objects are sacred, then, as for primitives, they possess a kind of animated force. Objects or their equivalents must return because they have in some sense personality. And this is the ecological dimension of gift exchange. Humans identify themselves through the production and exchange of things: Marx was right. So inversely, things are imbued with the story of human comings and goings. Objects naturally carry memories and tell stories: only commodified ones do not—or they tell shameful tales that they also conceal. In a modest way, even the packet of fair-trade coffee can start again to be a mythical object with personality.

For catholic Christians, this is as it should be. Everything is sacramental; everything tells of the glory of Christ, and therefore every economy is part of the economy of salvation and every process of production and exchange prepares the elements of the cosmic Eucharist. This was true for St. Paul: his thought about grace is indissociable from his thought about the human exchange of talents and of material benefits. But the latter can be a just exchange only where there are constantly renegotiated and agreed-upon standards concerning the human common good: what should be produced and with what standards, what should be rewarded and to what degree for the sake of further beneficial (to herself and the community) action by individuals. "To each according to his needs and from each according to his means" should still be our aim; but outside a completely crass materialism the question is about legitimate and desirable needs and means and the ordering of diverse needs and means. Here the crucial paradox so often ignored by socialists (but not by John Ruskin) is that only where there is an agreed hierarchy of values, sustained by the constantly self-canceling hierarchy of education, can there actually be an equal sharing (according to a continuous social judgment as to who will most benefit from such and such a gift) concerning what is agreed to be valuable. Without such an agreement, sustained through the operation of professional guilds and associations as well as cooperative credit unions and banks, there can only be market mediation of an anarchy of desires— of course ensuring the triumph of a hierarchy of sheer power and the secret commanding of people's desires by manipulation.

For where there is no public recognition of the primacy of absolute good grounded in something superhuman, then democracy becomes impossible, for it is no longer supposed that one should even *search* for the intrinsically desirable. It follows that people can find out what they "should" desire, or even about the possible objects of desire, only from the very "mass" processes that are supposed to represent the general desires of the people. Liberal democracy is then doomed to specularity: the represented themselves only represent to themselves the spectacle of representation. This is why there is no truth in the Marxist assumption that, once freed from the shackles of oppression, people will "by reason" choose equality and justice: to the contrary, in the light of a mere reason that is not also vision, *eros*, and faith, people may well prefer the petty triumphs and superiorities of a brutally hierarchic *agon* of power or the sheer excitement of a social spectacle in which they may potentially be exhibited in triumph. This is exactly why the vast numbers of the American poor are not waiting to rise up in revolt.

We need, then, in the Europe and the world of the future, a new conception of the economy as exchange of gifts in the sense of both talents and valued objects that blend material benefit with sacramental significance. We need also to encourage a new postliberal participatory democracy that is enabled by the aristocracy of an education that seeks after the common good and absolute transcendent truth. Finally, we need to see that it is equally enabled by a monarchic principle that permits a unified power at the limit to intervene in the name of noncodifiable equity—the liberal alternative to this being the brutal exclusion of those, like the inmates of Guantánamo Bay, who escape the nets of codes and are therefore deemed to be subhuman.

Does all this sound fantastic? No, the fantastic is what we have: an economy that destroys life, babies, childhood, adventure, locality, beauty, the exotic, the erotic, people, and the planet itself. Moreover, if we refuse a profound and subtle theological social carapace, we will not in the future necessarily recover secularity: instead we may witness the effective triumph (in power if not in numbers) of religious fundamentalism and especially Protestant fundamentalism, in cynical alliance with a liberal nihilism. For the formal emptiness of the liberal market and bureaucracy is now apparent to all: its heart will be filled with something, and especially with a neo-Calvinistic creed that justifies this emptiness because cumulative success in the reckoning to oneself of its void sums is seen as a sign of favor with another eternal world that alone really matters—although that too is conceived in terms of preferential absolute success in contrast with absolute failure.

Most, including myself, have hitherto supposed that the religious conflicts in Ireland are an anachronistic echo, in a remote corner of Europe, of ancient European conflicts. But then why have they flared up again so recently (the latter half of the twentieth century) and persisted so long? Is not Ireland somewhat like the United States, where a "belated" avoidance of secular ideologies has turned imperceptibly into a foreshadowing of a time when those ideologies are exhausted? Here again, there is no progressive plot to history. What one has seen in the province of Ulster has often been a conflict between a bigoted, puritanical, and hyper-evangelical neo-Calvinism on the one hand and a largely reasonable, socially and politically aspiring Catholicism on the other. The murderous fanatics on the "Catholic" side have tended to be so for sociopolitical rather than religious reasons. Moreover, government responses to this conflict now seem, in retrospect, like dummy runs for a global suspension of civil liberties in the name of antiterrorism.

Certainly not in any straightforward fashion, but nonetheless in a real one, it could be that the Irish conflict is in fact a harbinger of a wider, future, and much more complex and many-faceted new struggle for the soul of Christianity itself—which may yet dictate the future of Europe and even of the world.

PAST

8

Historians and the Past Tense

Evangelium *and* Imperium *as Genealogies of the Concept of Sovereignty*

Patrick Provost-Smith

The relation between history and theology is first of all a problem germane to history. What is the historical significance of a doctrine within the totality of a period? According to what criteria can it be understood? These questions are difficult and debatable if, on the one hand, we cannot be satisfied with a purely literary analysis of the contents or their organization, and if, on the other, we refuse ourselves the facility of considering ideology solely as social epiphenomena, a facility which effaces the specificity of doctrinal affirmations.[1]

Michel de Certeau

Empires and Evangelicals "Past"

The kind of historical reflection that I wish to invoke here aspires to accomplish two primary objectives simultaneously: the first is to revise the

---

1. Michel de Certeau, *The Writing of History*, trans. Tom Conley (New York: Columbia University Press, 1988), 22.

historical-theoretical categories through which we most often approach the relationship of evangelicalism and empire, and the second to suggest the perimeters of another kind of genealogy that critically reflects on what Hardt and Negri understand to be the "concept of sovereignty from the perspective of colonialism."[2] Combining those inquiries, it is in the first place important to query how evangelicalism has been shaped by its own historiographical operations, and secondly necessary to ask what kinds of resources may become available to further interrogate the relationship between evangelicalism and empire in contemporary discourse once another genealogy is rendered visible. As Hardt and Negri argue, it is the colonial experience that has shaped the contemporary discourse of imperialism, and this must be a point of departure—and this surely refracts the ways in which one must engage the problems of describing or analyzing the complex relationship of evangelicalism and imperialism in the emergent American empire. Although only the contours of this genealogical problem can be explored here, analysis must take as its point of departure that the colonial projects of the European empires cannot be reduced to undifferentiated identity with the ideologies and practices of Christian evangelization of others and that the "imperial" and "evangelical" enterprises that did characterize European expansion from the sixteenth through the nineteenth centuries nevertheless occupied the same historical, geographical, and ideological space. It remains therefore impossible to invoke the concept of *imperium* absent the historical and analytic discourse of *evangelium*, and as a consequence a "genealogy of the concept of sovereignty from the perspective of colonialism" fundamentally *requires* a simultaneous genealogy of the concept of *evangelium* also from the perspective of colonialism. Some argument must follow about how the past is reconstructed for the sake of the present—and most evidently what shapes and refracts our understanding of *critique*, the practice of which lies at the heart of genealogy.

From that inaugural perspective, it is imperative to state that the very simultaneity of the discourses of *evangelium* and *imperium* in the long history of Christian thought in the West complicate the "genealogy of the concept of sovereignty from the perspective of colonialism" that forms the historical substrate of Hardt and Negri's critical project. The concept of sovereignty does not emerge from religious neutrality as advocates of the myth of the Treaty of Westphalia in 1648 as the originary moment of modern sovereignty would have us believe; nor does it emerge only, as Hardt and Negri suggest, from "the plane of immanence" and European inability to conceive of alterity.[3] Another genealogy is needed which locates the discourse of sovereignty in the framework of *imperium* from which it historically and linguistically emerged:

2. Michael Hardt and Antonio Negri, *Empire* (Cambridge, MA: Harvard University Press, 2000), 132.
   3. Ibid., 70.

the term *sovereign* (from the Italian *sovrano*) does not denote nebulous power but supreme power (*sovranitá* as *potere supremo*), synonymous with the term *imperator*—hence the prevalent use of *sovereignty* in Anglo-American political thought to translate the term *imperium*. And yet from the fourth book of Augustine's *City of God* to the neglected third and fourth books of Hobbes's *Leviathan*, how may one speak genealogically of "supreme power" without speaking of God as both possessor of that power and the One who donates "sovereignty" to those he will? No concept of *imperium* exists in either Roman or later Christian thought that is not *donated* by the gods or God. The genealogical project cannot but exist within and against that complex history of religious thought—and yet this genealogy must be accomplished by way of rigorous negation: on the one hand by refusal to collapse the discourses of *evangelium* and *imperium* to a single and undifferentiated object of inquiry, and on the other by simultaneous refusal to invoke the moralizing tone that would extract a pure and untainted Christian "gospel" from the conflicted, complex, and often spectacularly violent history of Christianity in the world, and would see only the recovery of that pure strain as necessary to remedy our current dilemmas.

Framing a "past tense" interrogation of sovereignty through the Latin terms *evangelium* and *imperium* is an overt reminder that the terms that are now invoked by the cognates *evangelicalism* and *empire* radically precede modern usage and that an approach that began with modern definitions would fail to provide a genealogy of the discursive practices from which our contemporary usage has emerged. Thus the search for a pure idea of the Christian *evangel*, unbloodied by its sojourn as *imperium Christianum* and the later colonial enterprise, will prove not only futile but disingenuously and disastrously false. As Certeau reminds us, the luxury of a purely *theological*—or for that matter *theoretical*—critique of ideology is simply not available. The turn to historiographical investigation is neither merely arbitrary nor a preference for a certain kind of disciplinary mastery. If for no other reason, history requires us to recognize that the very terms that enable contemporary discourse and that frame the realities that we wish to subject to a new kind of rigorous scrutiny are too rich, complex, contradictory, complicated, and multifaceted to be reduced to the simple theoretical categories of contemporary ideology critique—there is no "internal logic" of imperialism or evangelicalism that is not first of all a historical category. Certainly history provides us with neither historical consensus nor terms by which we may arrive at such a consensus now—and hence it is impossible to simply "define the terms" and then move on to critique and analysis. This is especially the case when the particular object of critique possesses such a rich, complex, contradictory, and complicated history as does the relationship between the Christian *evangelium* (however it is to be understood) and the contemporary and historical practices and ideologies of *imperium* (however those are to be understood). And neither may historians' work itself escape the dilemmas posed by ideology critique: as Certeau also reminds us, "the treatment of religious ideology by contemporary historiography requires us to recognize the ideologies that are already invested in history itself."[4]

These dilemmas of the "past tense" essentially serve as a call to recognize that the historical relationship between understandings of the Christian gospel and the exercise of supreme jurisdictional political power remains poorly understood and inadequately explored in contemporary conversations about globalization and the new American empire, and the theoretical work of Hardt and Negri does not fully satisfy that lack. A sustained historical critique of these terms would force us to reevaluate our contemporary usage and redraw our lines of contestation. The carrying out of that investigation is far from a straightforward enterprise, and hence the need for theoretical sensitivity coupled with the kind of historical revision and historiographical self-reflection that, while refusing to flatten the complexity of historical discourse, broadens the scope of material available for critical reflection, makes possible new genealogies, and provokes new forms of analogical analysis among what may otherwise appear to be disparate and disconnected histories.

The Production of Alterity

The two modes of inquiry situated here are connected by a common thread—the production of alterity and the historiographical and theoretical modes that obfuscate that production. Insofar as the geographical terrain that became the United States was a principal site on which conflicting "sovereignties" (English, Spanish, French, and the multiplicity of indigenous groups) and conflicting "evangelicalisms" were worked out, that common thread of inquiry requires us to recall at the very least that the history of religion in America does not solely trickle down like prosperity from the rich to the poor from New England to the South and West. Christianity arrived in the South and West through other channels, and among those—indigenous peoples, other Europeans, Africans—that constitute "other" of the normal historiographical categories of a Puritan-centered historiography, it certainly remains the reality of Spanish America. That Spain possessed the first empire on which the sun never set is a reality conspicuous by its near-absence in contemporary critical literature on religion and empires, and it is given negligible attention in Hardt and Negri's *Empire*. Although the figure of the Spanish "defender of the Indians," Bartólome de las Casas, has begun to find its place in contemporary "empire theory," this alone fails to exhaust the historical and theoretical possibilities of treating the Spanish Empire as something other than simply

4. Ibid., 21.

the embarrassing (and Catholic) prehistory of the British Empire and North American colonization. The contemporary recuperation of Las Casas remains limited to identification of the Dominican friar as the exception that proves the rule of Spanish bellicosity, or as more deeply implicated in that bellicosity than his ideological defenders would have us believe. The place of Las Casas' critique of empire for critical theorists or for North American evangelicals has yet to be substantially explored.

Contemporary evangelical historiography in North America continues to produce its own alterity, and the voice of Las Casas has yet to be recognized as one whose commitment to the Christian *evangelium* may be relevant—even analogically—to the genealogy of evangelicalism in North America. Evangelical historians and theologians often remain silent on the Spanish presence in North America precisely by taking to themselves the task of defining the contemporary discourse of "evangelicalism" in ways that consistently restrict investigation to an Anglo-American, Protestant set of terms. These terms are often then foisted upon the world in ways that silence Catholics, Hispanics, other European immigrants—in short, the "others" against which contemporary historiography often defines itself. If Certeau may be invoked again, the critical task facing historical inquiry now is to interrogate, "a structure belonging to modern Western culture [that] can doubtless be seen in this historiography: intelligibility is established through a relation with the other; it moves (or 'progresses') by changing what it makes of the 'other'—the Indian, the past, the people, the mad, the child, the Third World. Through these variants that are all heteronymous . . . unfolds a problematic form basing its mastery of expression upon what the other keeps silent."[5] As a consequence of that historiographical operation, that the "essence" of evangelicalism has been defined as pompously as some contemporary theologians have done has yet to be explored as the form of "evangelical imperialism" that such conclusions warrant: how else to account for a view in which evangelicalism is defined as that "Christianity, both convictional and behavioral, which we inherit from the New Testament via the Reformers, the Puritans, and the revival and missionary leaders of the eighteenth and nineteenth centuries"? Yet that "intelligibility" is established only by relation to the silenced multitude of other inheritors of that same New Testament—silenced so thoroughly that one may write without embarrassment that "the reason that I call myself an evangelical and mean to go on doing so is my belief that as this historical evangelicalism has never sought to be anything other than New Testament Christianity, so in essentials it has succeeded in its aim."[6] How easily that uncritically constructed Reformation-Puritan-Wesleyan genealogy becomes

---

5. Certeau, *Writing of History*, 3.

6. J. I. Packer, "The Uniqueness of Jesus Christ: Some Evangelical Reflections," *Churchmen* 92 (1978): 102; quoted in Kenneth J. Stewart, "Did Evangelicalism Predate the Eighteenth Century? An Examination of David Bebbington's Thesis," *Evangelical Quarterly* 77, no. 2 (2005): 135.

normatively descriptive not only of deeply heterogenous religious movements in diverse times and places but as itself the arbiter of essential and timeless New Testament Christianity. The "I" who "believes" is also the *sovereign* "I" who has jurisdictional power over the Christian past and over the contents of "New Testament Christianity."

Any descriptive axis that admits but "three separate meanings of the word 'evangelical' (the sixteenth-century Reformational, the eighteenth-century pietist and conversionist, and the twentieth-century fundamentalist)" tends to reinscribe precisely this kind of mastery of expression. Although the aim of such categories is to interrogate the presumed singularity of the term and demand historical and conceptual specificity, it underwrites restriction of contemporary discourse to terms defined wholly within extant narratives of the Reformation and early American Christianity. And hence the *multitude* of "others," excluded "by definition" from the construction of the past, is rendered visible—like the African or indigenous America convert of the past—only after having passed through the church doors of Wittenberg and the revival tents of nineteenth-century America.

Thus to imagine a discursive world along the axes that Hardt and Negri propose—a genealogy of sovereignty *as* the refusal of alterity—is not without its descriptive merits, and such a genealogy is enacted in too much evangelical historiography and theology to warrant otherwise. However, the move to posit the refusal of alterity at the basis of sovereignty is too quick and obliterates distinctions that rather must be made. Hardt and Negri's reading of Las Casas is most evidently a case in point: the Dominican friar's complex rendering of indigenous valorization and patrimonial prejudice is reduced to categories almost wholly derived from Tzvetan Todorov's reading of Las Casas in ways that obfuscate Las Casas' substantially more complex picture of the original encounter. A new approach to understanding the peculiar character of American evangelical and imperial discourses is imperative.

Humankind Is One and Many

As Las Casas witnessed, Christianity arrived and thrived in the Americas under the auspices of empire and—we must say now—came to act as both *decentered* and *deterritorialized* as a result of the very contest between *imperium* and *evangelium* that shaped the conquest of the Americas and the early missionary enterprises from California to Chile and came to threaten even Japan and China by the end of the sixteenth century. It is necessary to observe that it is in part through a genealogical turn to the Spanish empire of the sixteenth century and its place in the history of the Americas that those particular qualities that Hardt and Negri find descriptive of our contemporary discourse of empire emerge through a complex global history that contemporary theoretical discourse often obscures. Hence, not unlike some evangelical historians, Hardt and Negri build the heterogeneity—perhaps even *authenticity*—of the present on a predication of the descriptive homogeneity of the past. In terms of a serious inquiry into the practices of evangelization and the theoretical or theological modes that shaped those practices, even under the conditions of colonialism, it remains unacceptably reductive to name those practices unambiguously as Europeanization or homogenization. The problem of the "one" and the "many"—the problem of *humanitas*—has also been a problem of how to understand the Christian *evangelium*, even when subjected to colonial conditions.

To expand the analytic categories of Todorov's semiotics through which Las Casas has been read by Hardt and Negri is in part to recapture the range and significance of the Renaissance revival of classical rhetorical conceptions and practices. Although misconstrued in much Renaissance historiography as a "style" and "means of persuasion" alone, the particular kinds of rhetorical work recuperated often reinvigorated the ancient clash between Socrates and Isocrates over the priority or parity of rhetoric and dialectic as descriptive of human reasoning processes. While those debates cannot be explored here, it must be emphasized that epideictic reasoning of the type preferred in rhetoric (over and against the apodictic reasoning of the dialecticians) was the linguistic world through which the concept of alterity passed in early modernity. The genre of "praise and blame," to which neither Las Casas nor his Aristotelian adversary (and master rhetorician) Juan Gines de Sepulveda was a stranger, requires that neither judgments nor propositions can be collapsed into one or the other term. A perpetual tension of opposites, premised precisely on alterity, more adequately represented the world than the forced resolution of formal dialectic.

The kind of epistemological crisis occasioned by the conquest of the Americas, and debates over its justification—often fought through precisely in the terms of forensic and deliberative rhetorical modes—may be seen in part in the work of the Spanish Jesuit José de Acosta, writing a generation after Las Casas. In the aftermath of the Spanish conquest of Peru, where the exemplary status of the Roman empire as the model of antique *gloria* worthy of imitation by Spain reached its fulfillment in the bloody conquest of the Inca *imperium*, Acosta found himself at a loss to describe such a collision of *novitas* and *antiquitas*. And so in the language of those deeply familiar with the revival of Quintilian's rhetorical handbooks, Acosta opened his account of the conquest with the observation of how difficult it was to "speak aptly and to speak well" (*dicere bene et apte*) of how to "evangelize" the Indians in the context of imperial violence. The collision of terms arrived on American soil not as pure ideas or pretended timeless appropriations of New Testament Christianity rendered visible by the Reformation but embodied in the armored bodies of the conquistadors and the evangelical work of the missionary friars. Acosta reflected:

> Two things that appear among themselves so disparate, as the announcement of the gospel of peace [*annuntio evangeliae pacis*] and the extension of the sword of war [*intentatio bellici gladii*], have in our times come to be not only united but even made, legally and necessarily, to depend on one another. It is true that the condition of the barbarians that inhabit this New World, for the most part, is such that unless their ferocious customs are in some way restrained, only with difficulty would there be hope, or perhaps even none at all would come to clothe themselves in the humanity and liberty of the sons of God [*humanitatem liber-tatemque filiorum dei*]. But, on the other hand, it is proclaimed that faith itself is the gift of God, not the work of men, and because its nature is free, he who tries to impose it by force makes it entirely nothing [*nullum prorsus efficiat*]. . . . Therefore to reconcile those two things, so repugnant to one another, and make our comprehension find ways to unite them, and a diligent and active love make them coherent, is a task that surpasses all my strength and ingenuity.[7]

The sheer scale of violence that led to Acosta's epideictic juxtapositions has been the primary material from which the world of "evangelical imperialism" has been constructed. However, two things have resulted from a misunderstanding of the content and nature of the critique offered by Acosta and earlier by Las Casas. In the first place the scene is both Spanish and Catholic, and hence evangelicals have been largely content to accept the standard narratives of American religious history and Spanish bellicosity without finding their own self-understanding implicated in the controversy over the conquest of the Indies. Second, the history of evangelicalism has, by virtue of that distance, posited the problem of "empire" on the backs of the Spanish empire in a way that has allowed other European empires to function without the kind of internal critique enabled by Las Casas or Acosta. Hence the *critique* itself becomes displaced to the *other* and the consequences of critique deflected from one's own self-reflection.[8]

However, the critique of Las Casas and Acosta (in their different rhetorical modes) calls for another kind of reflection that must be taken more seriously than has been the case among evangelicals. First of all, the critique, in its forensic mode, remains always genealogical—only attention to both the aesthetic and the epistemological dimensions of rhetoric will reveal that mode of inquiry.[9] In Acosta's sense, it is the epideictic weighing of repugnant opposites,

7. José de Acosta, *De procuranda indorum salute*, ed. Luciano Perena (Madrid: Consejo Superior de Investigationes Superior, 1984), 54.

8. See Patrick Provost-Smith, "Empire and Its Critics? Andrew Porter on British Missionaries," *International Bulletin of Missionary Research* (forthcoming 2008).

9. It could be argued that Foucault, unlike Nietzsche, was insufficiently attentive to the forms of rhetorical criticism that were available to classical and Renaissance rhetoric and, further, that his understanding of genealogy as a critical enterprise would have been enriched by them.

not the apodictic mode of the dialectician which ultimately concludes with sublation and epistemic closure, that best describes the realities of the Indies. Second, Acosta provides the loci for genealogical inquiry: namely, how is it that *evangelium* and *imperium*—irreducibly opposite in their appearances and their effects—have become so embedded in the linguistic and jurisdictional world of the *imperium Christianum* that their opposition becomes occluded by the very reality of their simultaneity? Further, not only is the *evangelium* itself obliterated as a discursive category and guide for praxis by the very practices of the *imperium* under whose jurisdictional and theological authority it now finds itself, but the potential of the *evangelium* to transform human beings from bestial ferocity to love is also "made nothing" by the practices of violence. A denial of the "liberty and humanity of the sons of God," what he argues elsewhere as the basis for constituting the human being, remains the very consequence of the practice of *imperium*. Finally, evangelicals will quickly recognize Acosta's allusion to Paul's letter to the Ephesians—only Acosta invokes it for different and startling purposes from those to which evangelicals are most accustomed. The topic of faith and works here referred to is not reduced to the familiar discourse of "justification by faith alone" but is explicative of the nature of the gift itself. The *gift* is that which is utterly effaced and destroyed by violence. The *gift* remains the necessary mode for the free and unforced realization of the multitude of humanity reconciled to the One. The *gift* is *libertas* and *humanitas*, the announcement of which is *evangelium*. The *gift* is destroyed by *imperium*.

Sovereignty as Donation

Nestled within the full range of Acosta's "evangelical" critique of the Spanish empire is a genealogy of that empire's discursive practices, followed by commentary on how the ferocity of the Spanish conquest of the Americas produced the reticence to the Christian *evangelium* that later provided even further justification for the Spanish presence in the Americas. Acosta argued that in this way the indigenous peoples were more "perverted" by their encounter with the Spaniards than "converted" by the love of Christ. Acosta's own genealogical rhetoric brought the "light of the gospel" from behind the "clouds" of obfuscation and required that the Spanish empire face the reality that its "greatest sin" was the "scandal" of taking the lands, liberties, and lives of the indigenous people "in exchange" for their faith in Christ.

In Acosta's critique, the "announcement of the gospel of peace" (*evangelium pacis*) is that faith is the gift of God, not the work of men. And yet the Augustinian tradition with and against which he was obliged to work contained yet another gift of God—the donation of *imperium*. In the fourth book of The *City of God* Augustine stated, "The one true God, who never leaves the human race unattended by his judgment or his help, granted dominion to the Romans when he willed and in the measure that he willed." The potency of Augustine's reflections was not lost on another Jesuit, Alonzo Sánchez, who in 1587 arrived in Mexico from Manila, the newly founded capital of the newly conquered, colonized, and evangelized Philippine Islands, newly named in honor of the king of Spain. Lauding Philip II as the "new Constantine," Sánchez's proposal offered the monarch an opportunity to launch an armed conquest of China for the final purposes of securing the way for its evangelization.[10] His document addressed the Spanish monarch thus:

> There is offered to his Majesty the greatest occasion and the grandest beginning that ever in the world was offered to a monarch. Here lies before him all that the human mind can desire or comprehend of riches and eternal fame, and likewise all that a Christian heart, desirous of the honor of God and his faith, can wish for, in the salvation and restoration of myriad souls, created for Him, and redeemed by His blood, and now deluded and possessed by the devil, and by his blindness and wickedness.

The offer spoken of here is underwritten by the Augustinian reflection that *imperium* is the gift of God, not the work of men, lest men should boast of their great deeds. The gift of sovereignty underwrites the gift of liberty and humanity realized in the Christian *evangelium*—and the "good news" announced is that the armed conquest of China inaugurates the reign of peace overseen by the supreme power of the sovereign to whom God donates that power.[11] What greater interdependence may be found of the "gospel of peace" and the "sword of war" as simultaneous gifts of God from whom all sovereignty is derived? What more potent "genealogy of the concept of sovereignty from the perspective of colonialism" may be available for contemporary theoretical reflection?

How are we to understand this proposal? On the surface the proposal appears as an all too readily available example of what one historian has called the peculiar quality of the Spanish empire: "a close and inseparable connection between cross and crown, throne and altar, faith and empire." And the potent description of the simultaneity of *imperium* (crown, throne, empire) and *evangelium* (cross, altar, faith) indeed emerges from the account. Yet the familiarity implied by this recognition of interdependency is misleading, insofar as it has failed to probe the deeper layers of how that interdependency was refracted through the history of Christian thought about the nature of the Roman empire and how the critics of such proposals destabilized the term

10. See John Howard Yoder, *The Politics of Jesus*, 2nd ed. (Grand Rapids: Eerdmans, 1994), 1–6, for a discussion of the shifting conceptions of ethics following the conversion of the Emperor Constantine to Christiainity in the fourth century C.E.

11. Eusebius, *In laudem Constantini.*

imperium precisely by contrast with the language of *evangelium*. Acosta's critique may then be further explored as the juxtaposition of the "gospel of peace" and the "sword of war" as interdependent precisely because of historical simultaneity in Christian thought from Eusebius's reflections on the conversion of Constantine to the Spanish wars of conquest. Yet Acosta's rhetorical formulation invokes a different epistemic maneuver. Quintilian's rhetorical treatises, from which Acosta often appears to draw, posited that the power of rhetoric is "realized in act, not in effect." Hence, Acosta's epidiectic critique cuts across the very core of Sánchez's deeply providentialist arguments for the conquest of China: that in spite of Spain's admitted greed and avarice, God granted to it—through the gift of dominion over newly discovered territories to the Spanish and Portuguese monarchs offered by Pope Alexander VI after Columbus's voyages of "discovery"—an *imperium* that would be the precondition for announcing the "good news" of Christ to the indigenous peoples of the Americas. Acosta's challenge, by juxtaposing the *effects* of the simultaneous gospel of peace and sword of war, was to destabilize precisely such confidence in the result of Spanish imperial actions. The gospel as the power of persuasion and invitation could be realized only in *act*, not in *effect. Caritas* was the mode of the *evangelium pacis*, and *violentia* the mode of *imperium*—the effect of their simultaneity was the utter effacement of charity, liberty, humanity, and the good news of the gift of God. If it was true that the conquests were necessary for evangelization, Acosta countered, "it is necessary that scandals come, but woe to that man by whom they come."

So deeply had the critique of the conquest of Mexico and Peru settled into the conscience of many that Sánchez, upon his arrival in Mexico, found himself placed under house arrest by the Jesuit provincial of Mexico. He was silenced and subjected by a vow of obedience to Acosta himself until the matter could be heard in Madrid and in Rome. Alonso Sánchez did finally gain an upper hand and had his audience with Philip II of Spain, but only weeks before the loss of the Spanish Armada to English forces.

The proposal was a failure, but its deep imbrication in the realities of the conquest of the Americas is undeniably true. Hence it remains one thing to insist that there was indeed—through Las Casas, Acosta, and others—a potent "evangelical" critique of "evangelical imperialism" to be had in the Americas, but another altogether to understand its genealogical point of departure and its analytic and rhetorical movement. One ignores such proposals in the history of European imperialism at peril of misunderstanding the serious nature of the deeply religious framework that has indeed informed the concept of *imperium* both before and after the conversion of the Emperor Constantine in the fourth century and how Christian thought on the very nature of the gospel has been shaped by that encounter. More provocatively, the entire history of "just war" argumentation—certainly the language in which the conquest of the Americas and proposed conquest of China was argued—may be more closely analyzed in precisely these moments of divinely ordered mandates and donations, whether or not modern just-war theorists find such historical moments embarrassing.[12]

The New Reality of Evangelical Imperialism

One may wonder, had advocates or even critics of more recent or contemporary imperial enterprises taken up the complicated relationship of *evangelium* to *imperium* in terms similar to Spanish evangelical critics of their own empires, rather than being satisfied with the recuperation of a "pure gospel" from the "external trappings" of Roman Catholic sacramental theology and liturgical practice, whether the European empires of the nineteenth century and the American empire of the twentieth would have been possible in the same way. Hence my present foray into Spanish Catholics' "evangelical" critiques of their own "imperial" enterprises cannot leave contemporary evangelicals safely ensconced in their own self-understanding of American religious history or their own genealogical commitments. The "historical fact" of the Christianity that arrived in the Americas was precisely as Acosta described it: the "gospel of peace" and the "sword of war" inextricably linked by the ideologies and practices of evangelical imperialism. And so our current genealogical foray must echo in sensibility what the Peruvian Marxist José Carlos Mariategui said of the Spanish conquest more than four hundred years later: "The Conquista, evil as it was, was a historical fact. Against historical facts little or nothing can be done through abstract speculations of the intelligence or pure conceptions of the mind . . . a new reality has taken shape here. It is a frail reality, but it is, for all that, a reality. It would be excessively romantic to decide today to ignore it."

The new reality faced today remains but a new form of "evangelical imperialism," with ostensibly more mundane goals than the empires of the past but with infinitely more powerful weapons. Now that the language of *evangelium* as the mode of universalism has been replaced with the language of rights as universalism, the ideological substrates of ancient, early modern, and modern empires begin to appear not so disparate as advocates of the new American empire would have us believe. How much of this is underwritten by an antique concept of sovereignty or subject to the forms of evangelical critique launched by the critics of the Spanish conquest remains an open question. As for sovereignty—and all forms of *imperium*—such a concept has always been underwritten by the providence of the Roman gods or by Augustine's "true God." In either case, as Giambattista Vico certainly recognized, its genealogy is that of Roman civil theology. At what price does contemporary critical

12. Patrick Provost-Smith, *Holy War, Just War: Early Modern Christianity and the Rhetoric of Empire* (London: I. B. Tauris, 2008).

discourse embrace such a legacy? One may doubt whether the evangelicalism of much contemporary historical or theoretical reflection—replete with its own genealogies and theological commitments that obscure more than they reveal—can recover enough of the larger "past tense" of Christian thought to be capable of extracting itself from having underwritten the legacy of European and American "evangelical imperialism."

Where is the gospel realized in *act* and not in *effect*? What is the *evangelium* that is now capable of genealogical critique of the very foundations of *imperium*—or, in other words, "sovereignty from the perspective of colonialism?"

9

Empire's Future Religion

The Hidden Competition
between Postmillennial American Expansionism
and Premillennial Evangelical Christianity

Sébastien Fath

The religious notion of millennialism and the political meaning of empire share a lot in common. This has been noted by Hardt and Negri, in the parallel they draw between the postmillennial thinking of St. Augustine and today's global "empire," which they characterize as a global deregulated market with no boundaries:

> In this regard we might take inspiration from Saint Augustine's vision of a project to contest the decadent Roman Empire. No limited community could succeed and provide an alternative to imperial rule; only a universal, catholic community bringing together all populations and all languages in a common journey could accomplish this. The divine city is a universal city of aliens, coming together, cooperating, communicating.[1]

1. Michael Hardt and Antonio Negri, *Empire* (Cambridge, MA: Harvard University Press, 2000).

Defined as "the belief that at some point in the future, a messianic era of peace, prosperity, justice and fellowship will commence and last for 1,000 years,"[2] millennialism speaks of a coming global kingdom, a purpose that empires have more or less always sought to achieve. Far from being an irrational superstition, it works as an "alternative rationality"[3] that has impact on the world. Depending on the definition of millennialism, the empire's shape will be very different.

This is obvious in today's America. If we compare and confront the secular postmillennial worldviews of the neocons—and of most of George W. Bush's administration—with the evangelical premillennial emphasis, the notion of empire is translated in various ways. At first sight, similarities appear to be obvious. Bush's messianic view seems to fit quite well with evangelical missionary rhetoric. Many commentators identify both discourses as powerful imperialist weapons (see section I below). However, a closer look at the roots of both rhetorics bring into question the interpretation of a deep ideological alliance between the neocon's idea of U.S. empire and the evangelical emphasis on mission. On one hand, U.S. empire seems to be defined as a coming paradise (II). Many aspects of the worldview emphasized by Bush's administration seem to fit quite well with a postmillennial messianism in which global salvation is more or less correlated with the earthly success of the American nation. On the other hand, the evangelical view of a coming empire appears shaped by a very different ideological frame (III). Relying on a premillennial interpretation of the words attributed to Jesus Christ ("My kingdom is not of this world"), many evangelicals hold a far more pessimistic view of the political, economic, and cultural future of the global world. For them, only God's power has no limits. History itself, as ruled by sinful humans, cannot provide a global paradise. In that sense, could evangelical discourse work as an anti-imperialist force?

I. Toward a Common Empire: Evangelicals and Neocons Together?

"We are going to change the world."[4] President Bush has repeated this *mantra* several times. It can easily be understood in the U.S. messianic tradition. Messianism has always been a key component of America's civil religion. That the United States has an essential and unique mission toward the world is one of the ideas most widely shared by U.S. citizens. John F. Kennedy's inaugural

2. Richard Landes, "Millenarians and Millennialism," in *The Encyclopedia of Protestantism*, ed. Hans J. Hillerbrand (NewYork: Routledge, 2004), 3:1234.

3. Eugen Weber, *Apocalypses, Prophecies, Cults, and Millennial Beliefs through the Ages* (Cambridge, MA: Harvard University Press, 1999).

4. Quoted in Matthew Cooper, "The 12–Step Press Conference," *Time Online*, April 13, 2004. This presidential press conference was about the battle of Fallujah.

address of January 20, 1961, illustrates this messianic belief in the crucial role of America: after speaking about the "revolutionary beliefs for which our forebears fought," he asks for the blessing and the help of God, "knowing that here on earth God's work must truly be our own."[5] This emphasis on faith and new beginnings, this messianic belief in the power of Good, relates quite well to evangelical missionary rhetoric. Both engage in the Armageddon-like struggle between good and evil. It is no wonder that conservative denominations like the Southern Baptist Convention have been extremely supportive of the recent U.S. global "war on terror." This ample common ground between the freedom crusade emphasized by Bush and evangelical missionary zeal explains why neoconservatives like Eliott Abrams[6] and evangelicals appear to cooperate within the Bush's administration, in spite of the fact that neoconservatives have never been famed for their religious piety.

For both ideological camps, Europe is also an antimodel. Michael Hardt and Antonio Negri argue that the emerging empire is fundamentally different from the imperialism of European dominance. "Old Europe" is a repulsive paradigm for the neocons, just as it is a repulsive model (as too secular) for many U.S. evangelicals.[7] Similarly, the United Nations is castigated as overly bureaucratic and overly influenced by European and Two-Thirds World agendas. Suspected of weakening America's interests, the United Nations is criticized by both imperialist neocons and evangelicals. In that common view, conservatives and evangelicals just seem to be repeating history: two generations ago, dispensationalists like William B. Riley (1861–1947) and R. A. Torrey (1856–1928) considered the League of Nations to be working for the Antichrist, while a strict Calvinist like J. G. Machen (1881–1937) thought that the League of Nations usurped the attributions of a church. Far from anecdotal, this stance contributed to the rejection of Woodrow Wilson's dream.[8] For them as for many evangelicals and neocons today, the idea of empire cannot be valid outside of a certain vision of America and its religious mission.

Last but not least, George W. Bush himself is renowned as a strong Christian believer. Many secular commentators have emphasized this aspect of the president's profile, describing him as a zealous evangelical convert to whom divine calling is more important than all the rational arguments in the world. As one commentator has put it, Bush is "America's Ayatollah."[9] Since 1985

5. Quoted in Robert Bellah, "Civil Religion in America," *Daedalus* 96, no. 1 (1967): 1–18.

6. In charge of the Near East and strongly pro-Sharon, this neocon is often singled out as an effective coordinator between neocons and evangelicals in the Bush team.

7. Some leading U.S. premillennialists even consider Europe as Antichrist. See Orestis Lindermayer, "Europe as Antichrist: North American Pre-millenarianism," in *Christian Millenarianism: From the Early Church to Waco*, ed. Stephen Hunt (Bloomington: Indiana University Press, 2001), 39–49.

8. Markku Ruotsila, "Conservative American Protestantism in the League of Nations Controversy," *Church History: Studies in Christianity and Culture*, September 2003, 593–616.

9. Richard Cohen, "America's Ayatollah," *Washington Post*, April 15, 2004.

and Bush's so-called conversion experience under the influence of preacher Billy Graham, much has been said about the importance of religious faith at the White House. The president, who claims to be fond of prayer and Bible reading, has surrounded himself with several zealous Christians. One of the most famous was John Ashcroft, former attorney general, known to proclaim, "Jesus is my king,"[10] but many others have played a role in the first or the second administration, including his main speechwriter, Michael Gerson, who "puts words in Bush's mouth."[11] With such a religious background, it is fairly understandable that many have linked his worldwide unilateral politics to a kind of "Christian crusade" model.

II. U.S. Empire as Coming Paradise: G. W. Bush's White House and Its Postmillennial Messianism

However, a closer look at Bush's worldview reveals that it is far from being distinctively "Christian." In the *International Herald Tribune*, Bill Keller emphasizes that the idea that the White House is driven by fundamentalist Christianity "badly misses the point."[12] In reality, Bush's attitude might be less that of a Christian leader and more that of the high priest of a new version of America's civil religion. "Civil religion," first theorized in the U.S. context by Robert Bellah,[13] is usually defined as a way of sacralizing community identity through shared values, quite above and beyond the religious preferences of American citizens. American civil religion tends to cement a heterogeneous melting pot on the basis of shared convictions. This belief system, sustained by several rites, feasts (Thanksgiving), and public manifestations, cannot be too confessionalized. The God of U.S. civil religion is more a generic God than a distinctively Christian God. Jews, Muslims, and Buddhist Americans are supposed to commune in the U.S. civil religion.

In the case of George W. Bush's White House, this generic God seems to be identified more and more with the nation itself. This mutation is rooted in an optimistic postmillennial messianism, as if global salvation were more or less identified with the earthly triumph of America. Working in an "activist transformational" mode,[14] this postmillennial view is nothing new. It has pervaded U.S.

---

10. On the impact of evangelical faith on his career, see his autobiographies: John Ashcroft, *Lessons from a Father to His Son* (Nashville: Thomas Nelson, 1998), and *On My Honor: The Beliefs That Shape My Life* (Nashville: Thomas Nelson, 2001).

11. Judy Keen, "He Puts Words in Bush's Mouth," *USA Today*, April 10, 2001.

12. Bill Keller, "God and George Bush: How Religion Influences the President," *International Herald Tribune*, May 19, 2003.

13. See Robert Bellah, "Civil Religion in America," see *Daedalus* 96, no. 1 (Winter 1967), 1–21, www.robertbellah.com/articles.html, and his books *Beyond Belief: Essays on Religion in a Post-traditional Society* (New York: Harper & Row, 1970) and *The Broken Covenant: American Civil Religion in Time of Trial* (New York: Seabury, 1975).

14. Landes, "Millenarians and Millennialism," 1239.

political discourse for decades and even centuries. Richard Bauckham rightly highlights that in America "after the Revolution postmillennialism helped to form America's sense of national destiny, with a mission to promote democracy in the world."[15] However, the tone of this voluntarist postmillennialism is getting sharper,[16] while the distinctively Christian background fades away. Neoconservative circles, which have been deeply influenced by the philosophy of Leo Strauss, play a key role in that transformation. They are quite detached from an evangelical type of religion. As Shadia Drury outlines, their ideology might even be described as rooted in the death of God.[17] But this does not prevent them from having a different kind of faith, a strong and powerful faith in the American *imperium*. This circle of neoconservatives surrounding Bush has named one of its lobbies Project for a New American Century (PNAC).[18] An American century or an American millennium? There is no reference here to Christianity, no self-limiting principle. "What is good for America is good for the world." Although there is no intention to build a new super nation-state, contrary to old European imperialism, there is a clear imperial ambition, which is quite close—but not identical[19]—to Hardt and Negri's definition of a "*decentered* and *deterritorializing* apparatus rule that progressively incorporates the entire global realm within its open, expanding frontiers"[20] and primarily characterized as a free market built on relationships of power and exploitation.

"Infinite Justice," the initial name bestowed on military operations in Afghanistan (2001), is another example of the imperial ambition and hubris of the neocons. It gave the impression that infinite justice, a divine prerogative, now belonged to America. The absence of limitation that traditionally defined God seems now appropriate to Uncle Sam's might. The U.S. president himself quite endorsed this belief when he said in his 2004 victory speech, "When we come together and we work together, there is no limit to America's greatness."[21] These words seem to echo what Hardt and Negri specify about empire: "The concept of Empire is characterized fundamentally by a lack of boundaries: Empire's rule has no limits."[22]

---

15. Richard Bauckham, "Millenarianism," in *Dictionary of Ethics, Theology, and Society*, ed. Paul B. Clarke and Andrew Linzey (London: Routledge, 1996), 568.

16. "From Sea to Shining Sea: American Exceptionalism Is Nothing New, but It Is Getting Sharper," *The Economist* (a special issue on the United States) 8, no. 14 (November 2003): 5.

17. According to her, the postulate of the death of God is what distinguishes neocons from traditional conservatives. See Shadia B. Drury, *Leo Strauss and the American Right*, 2nd ed. (London: Macmillan, 1999; 1st ed. 1997).

18. See www.newamericancentury.org.

19. Where the neocon's idea of empire and Hardt and Negri's definition differ is that for the latter "the coming Empire is not American and the United States is not its center" (*Empire*, 384), and it would be an illusion to think otherwise.

20. Ibid., xii.

21. George W. Bush, Victory Speech, November 3, 2004.

22. *Empire*, xiv.

At the end of 2003, Richard Perle and David Frum wrote a book entitled *An End to Evil*, as if American politics were capable of coming to terms with evil today—just as the Messiah is supposed to do on the Day of Judgment.[23] Lastly, the development of "space-based weapons" and the militarization of outer space, fervently supported by Donald Rumsfeld, suggest that even the heavens are no longer off limits to the American messiah, confirming Hardt and Negri's assumption about empire's military power: "There is no longer an outside also in a military sense."[24] The impression is that only America can solve the world's problems—because of its "'global leadership.' As if it was possible to create an 'Axis of One.'"[25] The United States no longer perceives itself as the best servant of the Messiah. The sense of military and financial might that prevails in the White House puts the old Puritan God far behind the scene. During the presidential campaign, a Bush adviser said: "Just watch. . . . We'll have more money than God."[26] God's kingdom is not waiting in a remote world beyond, it is here and now, taking shape in the American Way of Life.[27]

III. "My Kingdom is not of this world": Evangelical Premillennialism as an Anti-imperialistic Force

If we compare this optimistic and secularized postmillennialism with the eschatological discourse of the majority of U.S. evangelicals, differences largely win over similarities. Even within the minority of evangelicals who endorse the postmillennial option, there is a gap between their view, rooted in the belief that only God's justice is infinite, and the Bush administration's tendency to "play the messiah." This means that although there is a tactical alliance and a partial common ground between many evangelicals and the neocons, the strategic views on the future of America and the world differ sharply. For Christian premillennialists, worldwide destruction and the return of Jesus Christ are required to save human beings and bring about a new era of peace on earth.

23. David Frum and Richard Perle, *An End to Evil: How to Win the War on Terror* (New York: Random House, 2003).

24. *Empire*, 189.

25. Gary Dorrien, "Axis of One: The Unipolarist Agenda," *Christian Century*, March 8, 2003. It is no secret that the first Bush administration has distinguished itself by its lack of diplomacy and interest in international regulations. The examples are well known. They include refusal to recognize the International Justice Court in 2002, scorning the Kyoto Agreement on environmental protection (limiting greenhouse gas emissions), questioning the Antiballistic Missile Treaty (ABM, 1972) and developing a new antimissile project (Project NMD), and so on.

26. Quoted in James Carney and John F. Dickerson, "Taking Aim at 2004," *Time*, May 5, 2003, 25.

27. This mutation has been described at much greater length in Sébastien Fath, *Dieu bénisse l'Amérique. La religion de la Maison Blanche* (Paris: Seuil, 2004)—also translated into Italian.

Relying on this premillennial interpretation of the words attributed to Jesus Christ ("My kingdom is not of this world"), the majority of evangelicals hold a pessimistic view of the political, economic, and cultural future of the global world. In the 1970s and 1980s, Hal Lindsey's hugely popular apocalyptic literature[28] emphasized that the "years preceding the Second Coming of Christ would be years of wars, disasters, and catastrophes."[29] More recently, the Left Behind series still illustrates what Richard Landes describes as a "passive cataclysmic" tendency inherent to premillennialism.[30]

This "passive" dimension of premillennialism has sometimes been exaggerated or misunderstood. This does not mean absence of social reform—far from it. Among many others, Norman Cohn has highlighted the powerful revolutionary might of premillennial chiliast movements in the Middle Ages, opposed to a postmillennial Augustinian Christendom where established church and landlords exercised strong social control.[31] The close relationship between premillennialism and a strong missionary impulse has also been noticed elsewhere.[32] Contrarily to the Augustinian postmillennial model of a "City of God" leading to medieval theocracies, regaining the premillennial eschatological kingdom has boosted Protestant mission, because the second coming of Christ was viewed as contingent upon the preaching of the gospel to the whole world, creating a feeling of urgency for proclaiming the Word. If premillennialism can be described as "passive," it is only in the sense that premillennial Christians deeply believe that redeeming human institutions is futile. They consider that they will never be able to build paradise. Only God can. The main actor of the apocalypse is God and God alone. However, this does not prevent them from action, but while they are acting, reforming, and even initiating revolutions, the premillennial discourse leaves no mystery regarding the lack of ability of sinful human beings to save themselves.

For American evangelicals, this means that there will always be a limit to America's greatness, because collective and individual sinfulness cannot provide salvation. Without the spectacular final intervention of the eschatological Savior, there is no hope for redeeming the world. This fundamental difference with the neocon's secular optimism works even among the new Christian Right, which is usually described as a close ally to President Bush. While neocons

28. Hal Lindsey's most well known book was *The Late Great Planet Earth* (New York: Bantam, 1970).

29. David S. Katz and Richard H. Popkin, *Messianic Revolution: Radical Religious Politics to the End of the Second Millennium* (New York: Hill and Wang, 1999), 207.

30. Landes, "Millenarians and Millennialism," 1239.

31. Norman Cohn, *The Pursuit of the Millennium: Revolutionary Millenarians and Mystical Anarchists of the Middle Ages*, rev. ed. (New York: Oxford University Press, 1970).

32. See Dana L. Robert, "'The Crisis of Missions': Premillennial Mission Theory and the Origins of Independent Evangelical Missions," in *Earthen Vessels: American Evangelicals and Foreign Missions, 1880–1980*, ed. Joel A. Carpenter and Wilbert R. Shenk (Grand Rapids: Eerdmans, 1990), 29–46.

firmly expected an easy victory over Iraq and radical Muslims in 2002, leading to the Middle East's glorious conversion to democracy, Pat Robertson held a far more pessimistic view. This is what he declared in Detroit: "The last thing I think we need to do is to go to war with Iraq because it will be perceived in the Arab world as an attack on Muslim people by the United States and it will not be won."[33] A more spectacular contrast between the optimistic secular postmillennialism of Bush's administration and the pessimistic religious premillennialism of evangelical and fundamentalist Christians was brought to light just after September 11. In the months that followed September 11, President Bush repeatedly stated that U.S. citizens were "good" people, rendering terrorist evil more horrendous and incomprehensible. In the mouths of Jerry Falwell and Pat Robertson, the utopian premillennial rejection of the world as it is created a very different reaction. Falwell and Robertson's apocalyptic pessimism, already familiar to former president George H. W. Bush,[34] led them to link the collapse of the World Trade Center with God's punishment for U.S. sins. Interrogated on the Christian Broadcasting Network's *700 Club* by Robertson, Falwell did not hesitate to declare that God allowed America's enemies to strike because of U.S. evil.

> The abortionists have got to bear some burden for this because God will not be mocked. And when we destroy 40 million little innocent babies, we make God mad. I really believe that the pagans, and the abortionists, and the feminists, and the gays and the lesbians who are actively trying to make that an alternative lifestyle, the ACLU, People for the American Way, all of them who have tried to secularize America, I point the finger in their face and say: you helped this happen.[35]

Robertson agreed on these comments: "Well, yes." When Falwell observed: "God continues to lift the curtain and allow the enemies of America to give us probably what we deserve," Robertson also responded: "Jerry, that's my feeling."

Whatever the moral evaluation we can make of such statements, one thing is crystal-clear: these are not the words of an optimist postmillennial neocon. No idea of a benevolent empire working for Progress, but the persistent feeling that regression, evident in an increasing public display of sinful habits,

33. Pat Robertson, "The Roots of Terrorism and a Strategy for Victory," address to the Economic Club of Detroit, March 25, 2002, available at http://www.patrobertson.com/Speeches/TerrorismEconomicClub.asp.

34. In Pat Robertson, *The New World Order* (Dallas: Word, 1991), there is a clear condemnation of the optimistic "new world order" George H. W. Bush intended to foster. Between Lucifer, the New Babylon, secular humanism, communism, and Freemasons, Robertson perceives all the signs of the end times.

35. See John F. Harris, "God Gave US 'What We Deserve,' Falwell Says," *Washington Post*, September 14, 2001, CO3.

is destroying America. The White House immediately disapproved Falwell's comments. A White House official called them "inappropriate" and added, "The president does not share those views." One can be sure that many evangelicals shared this disapproval and were shocked by Falwell and Robertson's terrible comments. But while condemning the direct relation made between a supposedly sinful liberal America and the terrorist attack, most evangelicals join in a quite pessimistic view of the present state of U.S. society. To them, America is not inherently "good." The examples of sin or evil vary considerably: all evangelicals do not tend to reduce them to abortion or gay issues (a vocal minority puts social injustice, racial prejudice, or trade policy at the top of the list). But they agree in criticizing the present society. While the neoimperial tendency to externalize evil led Donald Rumsfeld to describe Abu Ghraib abuse as "totally un-American," evangelical anthropology and eschatology are sharply at odds. Evil is part of the American society,[36] as it is part of all fallen human societies. This gap between the optimistic imperial postmillennialism shared by large sections of G. W. Bush's team and the pessimistic premillennialism defended by many evangelicals explains why the global New American Century dreamed by the neocons is not close to be endorsed per se by evangelical churches.[37]

Conclusion

"We do not lack communication, on the contrary we have too much of it. We lack creation. *We lack resistance to the present.*" When French philosophers Gilles Deleuze and Félix Guattari, quoted by Hardt and Negri,[38] emphasized this need to resist "the present," they certainly did not think about religious millennialism. However, the utopian dynamic of evangelical eschatology might work as a potent form of resistance to the injustices perpetuated or created in the coming global empire. This resistance is far from guaranteed, especially in the United States, where Protestantism and an expanding free-market nationalism easily mix together.[39] But many countercultural positions work against

36. See Ann Applebaum's comments: "Rumsfeld said yesterday that it was 'un-American' to abuse prisoners—as if Americans were still somehow exempt from the passions that grip the rest of the human race. But we aren't." Ann Applebaum, "Willing torturers," *Washington Post*, May 5, 2004.

37. Issues related to Israel are an exception. As far as the so-called Promised Land is concerned, evangelicals and fundamentalists play a direct role in shaping official policies, and their views converge strongly with neocon priorities in the Middle East.

38. *Empire*, 393.

39. To understand the process of the Americanization of God, see Mark Noll's masterpiece *America's God: From Jonathan Edwards to Abraham Lincoln* (Oxford: Oxford University Press, 2002).

the temptation of being "blinded by might."[40] In 1968, Stanley Hoffmann saw the United States as a "bound Gulliver."[41] Today, Gulliver has untied his shackles and the giant's power scorns limits.[42] In the face of the neocons' secular postmillennialism, which expects to lead the coming century, evangelical premillennialism shows that the question is not only "how the body of the multitude can configure itself as a telos," as if immanence were the only solution.[43] It remains to be seen whether worldwide evangelical networks can escape the trap of unlimited national imperialism and use their *transcendent* telos to bring an alternative, providing to the "multitude"[44] neither resignation nor disguised slavery but a genuine hope in new beginnings.

40. Cal Thomas and Ed Dobson, *Blinded by Might* (Grand Rapids: Zondervan, 1999). As former activists in the new Christian Right, these authors acknowledge that they were wrong in thinking that "America is God's favorite nation." Such thinking is "idolatrous," they say (185).

41. Stanley Hoffmann, *Gulliver's Troubles, or The Setting of American Foreign Policy* (New York: McGraw-Hill, 1968).

42. Stanley Hoffmann and Frederic Bozo, *Gulliver Unbound: America's Imperial Temptation and the War in Iraq* (Lanham, MD: Rowman and Littlefield, 2004).

43. "Our pilgrimage on earth, however, in contrast to Augustine's, has no transcendent *telos* beyond; it is and remains absolutely immanent. Its continuous movement, gathering aliens in community, making this world its home, is both means and end, or rather a means without end" (*Empire*, 207). This blunt assertion can be contested. The idea of a linear secularization of the world has been heavily relativized. See Peter Berger, ed., *The Desecularization of the World: Resurgent Religion and World Politics* (Grand Rapids: Eerdmans, 1999).

44. Michael Hardt and Antonio Negri, *Multitude: War and Democracy in the Age of Empire* (New York: Penguin, 2004).

10

Political Complexities and Rivalries
of *Pneuma* and *Imperia*

KURT ANDERS RICHARDSON

The recent burgeoning of theoretical analysis of empire can be credited to
an extent to the appearance of Hardt and Negri's book *Empire* in 2000.[1]
The authors offer penetrating interpretations of global capitalist economics,
suggesting the disappearance of boundaries between "inside" and "outside"
localities of empire. They also propose that the demise of empire will occur
through the agency of the multitude whose unique postmodern subjectivity
is engendered by this empire.[2] The book is guided by a sharp anti-imperialist
program, and yet it struggles to find a possible alternative program: "Only the
multitude through its practical experimentation will offer the models and determine when and how the possible becomes real."[3] By perceiving "empire" as a
borderless, capitalist, political reality that ideologically privileges "democracy,"

1. Michael Hardt and Antonio Negri, *Empire* (Cambridge, MA: Harvard University Press,
2000). Next to this are Niall Ferguson, *Colossus: The Rise and Fall of the American Empire*
(New York: Penguin, 2004); D. Gregory, *The Colonial Present: Afghanistan, Palestine, Iraq* (Oxford: Blackwell, 2004); Derek Harvey, *The New Imperialism* (Oxford: Oxford University Press,
2003); Alain Joxe and Sylvere Lotringer, eds. *The Empire of Disorder* (New York: Semiotex(e),
2002).

2. *Empire*, 61.

3. Ibid., 411.

a new kind of "subjectivity" emerges which wins allegiance to itself far more subtly than have earlier empires. Just when one might have thought that the era of postcolonialism had overtaken that of imperialism and its arguments, a new analysis has convincingly countered such convictions.

With the appearance of their latest book, *Multitude*,[4] some of the needed working out of suggestive statements from the first has arrived. The title is reminiscent and perhaps something of a taunt against Thomas Hobbes's deep antipathy toward "multitude" in his famous work *De Cive*.[5] In that text, "people" constitute the basis of any state, in contrast to the ungovernable and anarchic multitudinous mass from which nothing good can come. Hardt and Negri, attentive to the current American president's unilateralism and crass populism, and the latent multitude he claims to command, explore this imperialist situation and the cultural symbols that American ideologues are generating with respect to the nation's role in the world. Also, in attempting to clarify what the first book suggested with the term *revolutionary subjectivity*, the authors are searching for tendencies of global resistance that might be successful against American empire.

As the authors admit early on, twenty-first-century social movements have a disconnectedness[6] that makes their cohesiveness difficult to discern. "Multitude" is the "class" concept as they attempt to rework the Marxist tradition.[7] With the persistence of imperialistic conditions in the world, Hardt and Negri's Marxist analysis and criticism prove that this radical tradition just won't die. Given the belief by some that theorists of democracy do not adopt a sufficiently self-critical stance toward their own system, that they are unavoidably co-opted and corrupted by the values of free-market and now global capitalism, assertions over the past two decades that Marxist criticism remains valid even if its constructive political theory does not have this book as evidence for the claim. At the core of *Multitude*'s neo-neo-Marxian analysis is the identification of hegemonic structures in the new American imperialism and some proposals for finding an antidote to them.

Hardt and Negri identify the forceful shaping of culture—of qualitative over quantitative influence—as the locus of the new imperialism.[8] Immense emphasis is put upon the emergence of intellectual elites (particularly neocons), among whom are those who distinguish themselves as an entirely new class of informational power brokers over what they call "immaterial labor." Qualitatively, these elites by their very existence and skill create a new hierarchical ethos

4. Michael Hardt and Antonio Negri, *Multitude: War and Democracy in the Age of Empire* (New York: Penguin, 2004).

5. In 7.8, Hobbes distinguishes between a people and a multitude as mutually at odds and sees the latter's movements as always destructive of political order.

6. *Multitude*, 54.

7. Ibid., 103.

8. Ibid., 109.

and overall dependency. Their influence upon culture is precisely at the point where labor has crossed over from the historic status of means to social life itself.[9] This insight stems from a further implication of the loss of boundaries between inside and outside empire, between public and private life.

The power of the elites who manage immaterial labor evidence their influence in a process of making "common" every mode of labor and life on a global scale, since "they all participate in a common substance."[10] This common substance is a thoroughly technologized world, such that access to natural resources and the natural environment itself have all been determined by the biopower of these elites. The difference between this emergent social existence and that of the past is that there are no longer any marginalized classes, i.e., distinctions of same and other, inside and outside, but only singularities and commonalities.[11] Yet what they seem to ignore is that while the multitude may be formed by the networking of a technologized world, the divisions within it are pronounced and enduring.

The piece finally morphs into a work of utopian democratic theory that would achieve "the rule of everyone by everyone."[12] The authors' conviction that the cultivation of love is the only foundation for democratic sociality is an admirable one, if largely undefined. But it is not so much the utopian nature of their arguments that is problematic; many theorists of democracy employ what amounts to utopian models in explaining themselves. What is lacking is any reference to the sources of love necessary to sustain conditions of political and social survival and stability. In this chapter, I hope to offer a number of evangelical resources that could make a positive contribution in this regard.

This chapter constructively explores a number of scriptural resources according to a rubric of "evangelical biblicism," in which close readings of scripture are used to construct an ethic and a polity conspicuously in terms of Christian pneumatology. In light of these, I offer some political proposals, based on the pneumatological emphasis, as antidotes to our imperialist human culture that are integral to the Christian message though often undeveloped in Christian political theory.

Sourcing Evangelical Biblicism: Toward Democratic Polity in/against Empire

The apostle Paul, who systematizes and universalizes the message and the political program of the Christian church, orients his doctrine according to a

9. Ibid., 149.
10. Ibid., 125.
11. Ibid., 127.
12. Ibid., 307.

pneumatological principle conveyed through charismatic experience. In terms of something like a "constitution" of the church, he offers an unexpected set of arguments for a unique contribution to social/political theory. His social analogies are striking: for example, the church as the body of Christ made up of members who are equal and indispensable to one another. The church, even more pointedly, is a *polituema*, "citizenship," of a *polis*, an *ethnos*, "nation," or a *laos*, "people" (2 Cor. 6:16; Titus 2:14; also, 1 Pet. 2:9)—although in a constitutional sense, Paul envisions this new citizenship as final inclusion of Gentiles in the original but to be universalized nationality/polity that is the people of God, namely, Israel, the Jews (see Rom. 15:7–11). Paul can argue that all nations find their existence and boundary according to the divine plan for the world (Acts 17: 26). What is unique about this nationhood and its citizenship is that it is based on a bond and constitutionality of Spirit and internalized religious norms—for example, "written . . . with the Spirit of the living God . . . on tablets of human hearts" (2 Cor. 3:3; see Heb. 8:10; Ezek. 36:26).

The question of course is how such readings translate into polity and participation in the church and in the civic order of things. What have often been called "offices" in the history of doctrine—i.e., "apostles," "prophets," "evangelists," "bishops," "teachers," "presbyters," "deacons," "coworkers"— are placed side by side with "charisms" or "gifts" of healing, administration, faith, wisdom, knowledge, exhortation, and the like. The institutional is offset by the charismatic. Indeed, Paul can advocate something very close to congregational governance when he appeals to his addressees in 1 Corinthians 6:1–8 and expects that they are all competent to judge all matters of earthly disputes because they will all be made competent to judge in the world to come. His argument is really quite extraordinary in verses 2–3: "Do you not know that the saints will judge the world? And if the world is to be judged by you, are you incompetent to try trivial cases? Do you not know that we are to judge angels—to say nothing of ordinary matters?" From this passage—one of the lengthier passages on ecclesial order in the literary corpus—one senses that Paul intends for the congregation to attend to all disputable matters within the bounds of its ecclesial assembly. The means of authorization and empowerment of the *corpus fidelium* of Corinth is focused in Paul's statement in verse 11: "But you were washed, you were sanctified, you were justified in the name of the Lord Jesus Christ and in the Spirit of our God." Paul's pneumatological principle is extended to a judgment about judgment: to resort to secular courts is a failure of Christian faithfulness, in that believers' capacities for justice should be considered superior to those of any civil court.

Paul's pneumatology has anthropological and communitarian implications in the context of worship, and these can be brought into sharp relief from his

Romans epistle.[13] Paul argues for the power of the Christian message but only as it is received according to internal and external dimensions. Internally, one is to "hear" the gospel by taking it to heart (10:8); externally, one is to utter confessional witness to the reality that has been internalized. This is no less than the apostle's understanding of faith for salvation and the fundamental sacramental act (10:6–18).[14] The Romans text is of course at the core of Reformation appeals to *sola scriptura*[15] and its sacramental concentration upon the sole agency of the divine Word in salvation, *solo verbo*. This is complemented by the sole agency of the believer in appropriating this Word—no one believes for anyone else. Paul's focus on individual agency in salvation anthropologically does not take place in abstraction from ecclesial corporeality. Nevertheless, the sacramental agency of each believer on her own behalf is striking and quite radical. This leads to a second point of worship where its ethical dimension includes the political.[16]

In the text of Romans 12:1–2, Paul presents a liturgical grounding for Christian ethics. Three actions of a sacred nature are prescribed. He writes, "Present your bodies as a living sacrifice"—the operative language denotes priestly action, significantly here performed and mediated by the body of each and every Christian. The sacral language of priestly sacrifice is extended in a second prescription that what is performed is "holy and acceptable to God"—the sanctity of the gift receives divine approbation. And third, what has been performed is deemed "your reasonable/spiritual worship [*latreia*]," further highlighting the priestly nature of the action and certainly the status of the persons who perform it.

Paul is also concentrated on the ethical nature of this sacred action. The sacrificial body of the priestly believer is brought into a process of spiritual transformation that is consciousness based (*nous*) through self-abnegation (v. 3). This transformation enables the body "to approve/esteem the will of God"—using the same term that earlier denoted the divine approval of the

13. Probably the most detailed and illuminating comparative study of Hellenistic political theory and Paul is Bruno Blumenfeld, *The Political Paul: Justice, Democracy, and Kingship in a Hellenistic Framework* (Sheffield, UK: Sheffield Academic Press, 2001).

14. This is his exposition of a passage from Joel: "Everyone who calls on the name of the LORD shall be saved" (2:32; see also Acts 2:21).

15. This classic slogan is not the first instance that a claim about revelation is presupposed to be a claim about salvation: i.e., the scriptures alone (by themselves) are sufficient for gaining the knowledge and faith for salvation. It represented and represents a fundamental challenge to the ecclesial institution's claim to be the dispenser of salvation and the sole divine agent on earth. Given that, it should be noted that the canons of the catholic churches (East and West) are nuanced about their own claims in this regard.

16. For an extraordinary work of practical theology in the German context and yet written with a view to Britain—particularly Milbank, who, while drawing from mostly theologians of the past two centuries and considerations of Christian citizenship, says virtually nothing about democratic political theory and its rivals—see Bernd Wannenwetsch, *Political Worship: Ethics for Christian Citizens*, trans. Margaret Kohl (Oxford: Oxford University Press, 2004).

sacrifice itself. The connection Paul makes between reasonable/spiritual worship and the "renewing of the mind" through the sacrificial service of the body is conspicuous enough; but his emphasis is upon an ethic whereby moral decisions include human approval of God's will—a relational model of mutuality with God. What Paul has unleashed is a quite radically liberating message whose operations in the human person are pneumatologically determined. He will offer no other political or legislative principle for Christianity.

The pneumatological mutuality of Christians has contributed greatly to the evangelical transformations and political developments of the last five centuries. There is no mistaking the realization of the anti-aristocratic politics of Paul's pneumatology. But it should be recognized from virtually any political history of the West that much of what had become impossible with basis in the aristocratic principle in political relations and ecclesial authority found sources for a religious alternative in the New Testament and dissenting political theologies that finally were filtered through evangelical influences. One cannot say that evangelicals have always been at the forefront of social and political change. Indeed, because they were often minority voices in politics, they have been as prone to resistance to political change as any other Christian faction. But curiously, the biblicism that has often created the new structures of ecclesial life that characterize the history of evangelical movements keeps engendering new political resources for participation and change. One of the key exemplars of this in early American political history is Roger Williams.

Evangelical Biblicism on Political Ground

The nascent British empire of the seventeenth century provided in its first generation of American colonialists the seminal religious and political thinker on human rights in the person of Roger Williams. Having taken Anglican orders at Cambridge and also been trained by the leading English judge, Sir Edward Coke, Williams would construct the first thoroughgoing evangelical argument for a politics of unbridled religious liberty. By the time of the publication of his *Bloudy Tennent of Persecution* in 1645,[17] quickly banned, then successfully republished, then quickly banned again in England while Williams was securing the parliamentary charter for Rhode Island, the differences between his own biblicism of the civil order and that among his Reformed colleagues in Boston were set. Williams arrived in the Bay Colony in 1631 and immediately refused appointment to the Boston church because of its ties with the Church of England—on the way over, he had fully embraced Dissenting views of church and state. In the course of time, he would refuse to sign a new "oath of freemen" (1634), which instituted civil rule in all aspects of religious life

---

17. See Roger Williams, *The Bloody Tenant of Persecution for Cause of Conscience*, ed. Richard Groves and Walter B. Shurden (Macon, GA: Mercer University Press, 2002).

in the Commonwealth. John Cotton and the Bay Colony clergy put immense pressure upon Williams's supporters, and a court was convened to hear charges against him. They were offended by his claim that no civil authority had a right to rule in "spiritual matters"—not to mention his demand that colonists ought to pay the Indians for any land that they claimed as property. A law condemned anyone to banishment who denied the colony's right to punish all those who publicly broke the first table of the Ten Commandments. He was banished on October 9, 1635. His ordeal actually came in the winter, and the care afforded him by the Narragansett Indians, especially by chiefs Massasoit and Canonicus, won his survival. After establishing himself in what would become Rhode Island, Williams secured the first charter for the colony in 1644 from Parliament and established full religious liberty. The article of agreement for Rhode Island (1647) concluded with the declaration: "All men may walk as their consciences persuade them, without molestation—every one in the name of his God"—far more sweeping than the act of toleration in Maryland in 1649, where "liberty" was afforded only to Christians. Denial of essential Christian doctrines was a capital crime—consistent with the Bay Colony's legal system. Legal obligations were relegated entirely to "civil" matters.

Williams's arguments for religious liberty stemmed from the nature of faith as a voluntary act, in view of the Pauline formula "from the heart." Williams's view of this liberty as the only viable legal approach to religious matters takes on central significance for any future political theology. Perhaps one extraordinary proposition sums up his arguments as well as any with respect of religious acts once outlawed by the traditional church-state unity: "The civil laws not being broken, civil peace is not broken." In the lengthy exchange between Williams and Cotton over his book, the one civil argument for coercing religious behaviors had been the maintenance of political order. This was precisely the legal point Williams wanted to overturn.[18] He argued instead for a form of social contract and popular sovereignty as the basis for the formation of any state and its laws.

The argument was and is still radical: There is no belief that should be outlawed, since civil courts are not competent to judge in religious matters. God alone can adjudicate over the human conscience. The curious development is that the right to religious liberty secures equality before the law. In contrast to Enlightenment arguments for religious toleration, as in the case of Locke, who did not take so radical a view, Williams's arguments are entirely theological and evangelical in nature. His chief concern is the religious integrity of the human being.

---

18. In response to any claim to theo-politics based upon the Christian use of the Old Testament, Williams used the text of Ezekiel 21:26: "Thus says the Lord GOD: Remove the turban, take off the crown; things shall not remain as they are. Exalt that which is low, abase that which is high." For Williams, no justification any longer existed for theocracy until the second coming of Christ.

Williams's exegesis and political theology can begin to explain the force of the First Amendment and the atheology of the American Constitution, conceived among the Christian and non-Christian drafters as a fundamental political and religious good. Indeed, one has to wait rather a long time before one sees this extensive a theological argument in none other than the Vatican II document *Dignitas Humanae*,[19] whose principal drafter was of course the great American Catholic theologian John Courtney Murray. In this document, one finds the unmistakable evangelical arguments of Roger Williams but now entirely absorbed and finding consistency with deeply Roman Catholic theological and doctrinal sensibilities. The curious thing in all of this is that the line in the political theology of religious liberty extends through evangelical reasoning with scripture and tradition rather than through Enlightenment philosophy and reductionist theology—which in many ways made any exegetically based argument impossible.

A striking reassertion of Williams's role as founding American theorist comes from Robert Bellah. In his American Academy of Religion presidential address of 1997,[20] while celebrating the twentieth anniversary of the great multiauthored project of which he had been chief organizer (i.e., *Habits of the Heart*), he acknowledged that only one great assertion about American cultural identity had not withstood at least his own scrutiny: the contention that John Winthrop was the founding American theorist. Bellah explained that he had continued to contemplate and to struggle for understanding of the First Amendment as the great instrument of the separation of church and state, and therefore a doctrine governing religious institutions within the American public sphere. This, until he rediscovered what had always been patently evident in the language of the amendment itself, that it pertains to the rights of any and every individual citizen both not to be coerced and to be free in religious expression. It was in that moment of reawareness, Bellah states, that he recognized Williams's rather than Winthrop's influence. And it was at that moment that he realized the misguided role played by any religious body within American public life that attempted to impose its own religious norms or even to supply the nation with something he and others have been wont to call "civil religion"—or as we might term it, religionless civil piety.

Beyond Imperialist Inevitability

If Hardt and Negri and a broad spectrum of commentators and scholars are correct to assess economic and cultural globalization as empire and as a basic product of American hegemony, then evangelicals as the overwhelming

19. See John T. Ford, ed., *Religious Liberty: Paul VI and Dignitatis Humanae* (Brescia, Italy: Istituto Paolo VI, 1997).

20. See Robert N. Bellah, "Is There a Common American Culture?" *Journal of the American Academy of Religion* 66 (1998): 613–26.

Protestant majority are singularly unprepared for these political challenges. This does not mean they are not involved. They, together with many Roman Catholics, constitute significant ranks of neoconservatives in Congress and lead think tanks on public policy, let alone their own NGOs and numerous associations. At many points, evangelical political leaders are a part of the Republican elite that appear to be beyond criticism from the current White House. The further question whether all future global politics will inevitably include an empire, or, more to the point, whether successful politics always engenders imperial aspirations, cannot be addressed here. In any case, evangelicals in the main do not have the advantages of multiple generations of governance in their culture to train their future leaders by, and where they might have it, their lack of self-criticism, let alone basic Christian contrition, often cripples them in the face of so much power and wealth.

Evangelicals in America, as well as the historic churches of Roman Catholicism and Eastern Orthodoxy, provide too little in the way of well-formulated political theologies. Astute readers among their theologians are attentive to the wider intellectual conversations and journalistic queries. But as yet I find most of them somewhere between the anticolonialism of the late twentieth century and some of the latest chauvinism of Washington, DC. Much of the rhetoric that is suggestive of empire too easily serves to justify American unilateralism with the pretense of spreading democracy. One popular author offers a scenario of ridding the world of dictators by 2025.[21] Does a requisite political theology for this look like something cooked up by the Reverend Pat Robertson? Indeed, the entire subject of American empire bristles with the likelihood of ideological misstep and scandal—something that all but the most bombastic of public voices would rather avoid.

Theology is usually slow to contend with new trends in theory, political or otherwise, primarily because developing such a wider focus and subjecting it to in-depth scriptural exegesis and tradition-based analogical reflection takes time. The eruptions of new suggestions which posit the goodness of an American empire are too new to have generated well-conceived theological models. And given the theological reticence toward such an onerous task, along with the costliness, religious exhaustion, and failings of "Christian" empires in the past, this is not surprising in the least. Nevertheless, one must begin to construct such reflection, and below are a few points offered toward this end.

Pneumatological Antidotes

Democracies are polities of multiple communities and a multitude of individuals formed into a "people" by such arrangements and practices, all finding

---

21. Mark Palmer, *Breaking the Real Axis of Evil: How to Oust the World's Dictators by 2025* (Lanham, MD: Rowman and Littlefield, 2003).

common ground under proscriptive law: equal protection for the sake of co-existence. This principle of law was worked out first among Christians and their respective states. From the moment that the Peace of Westphalia (1648) took effect, the reality of Christian pluralism would determine a more general pluralism in the centuries to come, when an uncountable number of religious and moral communities were to contribute to the peaceful coexistence of the citizenries of each state. Democracy is not something evangelicals have before them to work out or reformulate.[22] What evangelicals desperately need to do is to learn the skills of democratic reasoning and political practice, and so to find their place in the common entitlement of bringing beliefs to the table of political discourse and the making of public policy.[23] This is "learning democracy," and it is required just as much on the Continent and within the global community of nations. After all, it is only since 1989 that the one truly rival political model ceased to present itself as a viable alternative—the Marxist one, the continuing relevance of its critical practice notwithstanding.

What evangelicals must do in terms of their pneumatology and their biblicism is to renew their cultivation in the wisdom and the anthropological egalitarianism this theology entails. As majority Protestants, they must not allow themselves to ignore the human rights claims of religious and ethnic minorities, but rather seek to gain the latter's confidence to assist in the constant reaffirmation of liberty of conscience. Religious liberty as the first right of the political order is established for individuals, whoever they may be, and their exercise of this right is unbounded and protected by the proscriptions of fundamental democratic law, in contrast to the bounded and limited nature of government and its prescriptive laws. Evangelicals need to consider the nature of this proscriptive, "minimalist" democratic law[24] as it defines the limits of all human authority, including the elector, the citizen, in order that that "democratic learning" can take place. The popular sovereignty behind social contracts, i.e., democratic constitutions (evangelicals think along the lines of religious "covenant" here), are intended after all to secure inalienable human

22. See such classic texts as Joseph A. Schumpeter, *Capitalism, Socialism, and Democracy* (New York: Harper, 1947); Henry Bertram Mayo, *An Introduction to Democratic Theory* (New York: Oxford University Press, 1960); and, more recently, Jürgen Habermas, *Between Facts and Norm: Contributions to a Discourse Theory of Law and Democracy*, trans. William Rehg (Cambridge, MA: MIT Press, 1999).

23. There is much working against democratic self-understanding; for example, "the ideals of democracy suggest that citizens ought to play a very substantial role in the governance of their society. The trouble is that the ideals appear quite unrealistic in a modern democratic state." Thomas Christiano, *The Rule of the Many: Fundamental Issues in Democratic Theory* (Boulder: Westview, 1996), 5.

24. Democratic states of affairs are constructed out of boundary settings for otherwise incompatible communities of belief and their incommensurable truth claims. See Adam Przeworski, "Minimalist Conception of Democracy: A Defense," in *Democracy's Value*, ed. Ian Shapiro and Casiano Hacker-Cordón (Cambridge: Cambridge University Press, 1999), 49.

rights for individuals[25] and require not only the theological justification for religious persons but particularly by religious majorities, such as evangelicals.

Pneumatology and "Democratic Learning"

There are likely many ways into democratic learning and acquisition of the competencies required to participate or to assert one's right to participate in the affairs of governance. To the extent that Pauline pneumatology is a source for this learning by means of his elevation of all believers to positions of authority in the church, evangelical Christianity can be or become one of these ways. Paul means for the church to be the primary community for Christians, outdistancing the civil state and even family. Indeed, the great letter of James posits an order of life where wealthy and powerful Christians abase themselves and poor Christians are given elevated status for a fundamentally egalitarian anthropology expressed through Christian *koinonia* (James 1:9–10).

It is more than a matter of historical record that Williams's religious thought and political action so early in the American settlements contributed fundamentally to the later nation's democratic form of government. His practice of evangelical biblicism is just as influential for evangelical ecclesiality as it was for his own time. Evangelicals will continue to participate in and cater to the development of democratic governance via their political theological reasoning. To the extent that this constructively takes place, we have instances of what Andrew Reynolds has called "constitutional medicine."[26] What is necessary along the way toward the development of evangelical proficiency in democratic participation and the practice of governing is something on the order of Larry Diamond and Leonardo Morlino's framework for gauging democratic quality,[27] no longer asking why democracy when it appears to be too liberal or too tolerant. Perhaps, as Hardt and Negri assert, empire has a certain kind of inevitability, but there are antidotes to be found, and some of them can be found among evangelical sources.

---

25. It is really quite gratifying to discover how extensively leading democratic theorists in Europe have taken ownership of just such political logic on their own terms. See, for instance, Étienne Balibar, *We, the People of Europe? Reflections on Transnational Citizenship,* trans. James Swenson (Princeton, NJ: Princeton University Press, 2004), 199.

26. Andrew Reynolds, "Constitutional Medicine: Building Democracy After Conflict," *Journal of Democracy* 16:1 (2005): 54–69.

27. Larry Diamond and Leonardo Morlino, "The Quality of Democracy," *Journal of Democracy* 15, no. 4 (2004): 20–31. Note the criteria of democratic quality: freedom, the rule of law, vertical accountability, responsiveness, equality, participation, competition, and horizontal accountability.

11

Stepchildren of the Empire

The Formation and Reformation of a Latino Evangélico *Identity*

JUAN F. MARTÍNEZ

Latinos became inexorably linked to the United States because of the U.S. government's imperial expansion and its interventions in Latin America.[1]

1. A note on the subtitle's key term: The term *evangélico* has had multiple meanings in Spanish. It was used as synonymous to *Protestant* in much of the Spanish-speaking world throughout the nineteenth and twentieth centuries. As the term *evangelical* began to define a movement, evangelical missionaries took the term with them and translated it as *evangélico*, thereby redefining the term in Spanish. This has created the multiplicity of usages for the term *evangélico* and the lack of a common term to label Protestants in Spanish. For example, José Míguez Bonino speaks of four faces of Latin American Protestantism: Ecumenical, Evangelical, Pentecostal, and Ethnic (*Faces of Latin American Protestantism* [Grand Rapids: Eerdmans, 1997]). Others continue to use the term *evangélico* in a broader sense, recognizing not only that most of the people who call themselves *evangélicos* would be identified as evangelicals but also that there are people who consider themselves *evangélicos* but not evangelical. This complexity continues in the United States, though the tendency of many to use *evangélico* as a translation of *evangelical* is changing the term. Its usage in the future will probably be affected by whether Latino and Latin American–based Pentecostal and neo-Pentecostal groups use it to describe themselves and whether or not U.S. evangelicals accept these groups as evangelicals.

This is Juan González's premise in *Harvest of Empire: A History of Latinos in America*.[2] Each of the major groups that make up the Latino community today (Mexican Americans, Puerto Ricans, Cubans, Central Americans, and Dominicans) became a part of the United States because of either the territorial expansion of the nineteenth century or military interventions during the twentieth century.

Yet, for the most part, U.S. territorial expansion was different from European colonialism in that it did not make the conquered territories into colonies. During the westward expansion, land was incorporated into the United States, and the conquered peoples (Native Americans and Latinos) entered into a relationship of internal colonialism, being treated as colonized peoples in the lands that had previously been theirs.[3] The Spanish-American War (1898) presented a more complex situation. Cuba was allowed to become independent, though with a government closely tied to the United States until the Cuban Revolution in 1959. Puerto Rico, on the other hand, became a colony in 1899 and a commonwealth in 1948. To this day Puerto Rico's status in relation to the United States remains vague, somewhere between that of a colony and full incorporation into the United States.

González's analysis dovetails well with Hardt and Negri's concept of empire. Latinos became linked to the United States because of imperialistic expansion and intervention.[4] The United States created economically and politically dependent relations with the conquered Latinos of the Southwest and with the countries of Latin America. In turn, the Latin Americans most affected by U.S. policies created migratory patterns into the United Sates. To this day those patterns reflect the impact of U.S. policy. For example, the largest Latino group is linked to Mexico, the country most affected by U.S. territorial expansion and current policies.

The migratory patterns established during the twentieth century continue to be followed in this new period of empire. Latinos, particularly the continual waves of immigrant Latinos, serve as living testimony to imperialistic U.S. policies in Latin America and "to the irreversible fact of globalization" in the age of empire.[5]

Latinos, in general, have always had an unclear place, a stepchild status, in the United States. At the time of the U.S. takeover of the Southwest (1848), they

2. Juan González, *Harvest of Empire: A History of Latinos in America* (New York: Viking, 2000).

3. For a detailed explanation of the impact of internal colonialism on Latinos in the Southwest, see Alfredo Mirandé, *The Chicano Experience: An Alternative Perspective* (Notre Dame, IN: University of Notre Dame Press, 1985).

4. In spite of its anti-imperialistic rhetoric, "Yanqui politics [in Latin America] is a strong tradition of imperialism dressed in anti-imperialist clothing." Michael Hardt and Antonio Negri, *Empire* (Cambridge, MA: Harvard University Press, 2000), 178.

5. Michael Hardt and Antonio Negri, *Multitude: War and Democracy in the Age of Empire* (New York: Penguin, 2004), 134.

were not unlike the Native Americans, people who needed to be removed from
the land to facilitate the westward migration. But for the most part Latinos were
not killed or forcibly removed from their lands. Nevertheless, U.S. laws were
used to take the land from most of them so that it could be available to the new
migrants from the East. Because most nineteenth-century Latinos lost their land,
they became a part of the disposable labor force, working for the new owners or
migrating to other places looking for work. They were treated like second-class
citizens, but they never faced the level of racism confronted by African Americans. The theological subtext used by some Protestants in the nineteenth century
reasoned that Latinos were like the Canaanites: they could not keep the land
promised to the new Israelites, the European Americans, but they could continue
in it as "hewers of wood and drawers of water."[6] Latinos were not destroyed
and isolated like the Native Americans, nor were they enslaved like the African
Americans. But they were not given the status of European immigrants. This
ambivalence was related to the fact that Latinos had European blood but they
had not migrated voluntarily to the United States. They were also Catholics, and
most were *mestizos,* of mixed European and indigenous background.

This ambivalence continued as waves of immigrant Latinos migrated to the
United States throughout the twentieth century. During World War I and World
War II, Mexican workers were welcomed because they filled the labor needs
of a country at war. But once these wars were over, the European American
majority worked to deport them and also their U.S.-born children. Throughout
the twentieth century, many economic interests in the United States developed
a dependency on migrant Latino labor, both documented and undocumented.
But attitudes toward these workers have varied depending on the economic
situation. When the economy is strong, they are welcomed or at least toler-
ated. At times the federal government has even offered special programs and/
or amnesties so that they can become an integral part of the economy. But
during economic downturns or changes, Latinos—and undocumented Latinos
in particular—become scapegoats, blamed for social and economic problems
over which they have little control. Because of conflicting social and economic
interests, the United States has not been willing to either develop a long-term
plan for legal migration nor take serious steps to stop the immigrant flow. In
the midst of the internal national debate on immigration, migration from
Latin America ebbs and flows, but it does not stop.

When the United States went to war with Mexico (1846–48), many Protestant leaders were ambivalent toward it. They opposed the direction the
country was taking and felt that the war against Mexico was not justified.[7]

6. Richard Moorefield, "The Mexican Adaptation in American California, 1846–1875,"
PhD diss., University of California, Berkeley, 1955, 2.

7. For a detailed analysis of Protestant leaders' views of the war with Mexico and of the
use of war in territorial expansion, see John Bodo, *The Protestant Clergy and Public Issues,
1812–1848* (Philadelphia: Porcupine, 1980), 216–32.

Nonetheless, many of those same leaders had a sense that if the Southwest was taken from Mexico, Protestant missionaries would find it easier to take the Protestant gospel to Catholic Mexico and other parts of Latin America. Once the Southwest became a part of the United States, several Protestant mission agencies stated a desire to evangelize the conquered Mexican population there because they could serve as a bridge for the Protestant evangelization of Latin America.[8]

The peace treaty that ended the war between the United States and Mexico (Guadalupe-Hidalgo, 1848) defined the vague status of Mexicans in the Southwest. They could migrate to the new, smaller Mexico, or they could remain and become U.S. citizens whose legal and property rights would be respected. About 100,000 remained, hoping to keep their lands and their livelihood. By 1900 most had lost both through "legal" means.

The citizenship status of the conquered Mexican population created concern among Protestant leaders because these new citizens were Catholics. Protestants were already afraid of the potential impact of Catholic immigrants from Europe on the United States. The Mexicans who were now U.S. citizens exacerbated the situation, and some Protestant mission agencies mobilized a mission effort to evangelize and Americanize these new citizens. Throughout the nineteenth century, Protestants did little mission work among these new citizens, but what they did was almost always tied to education and Americanization.

Protestant missionary efforts produced only limited results among Latinos during the nineteenth century. By 1900, Protestant denominations reported a little over 5,500 Latino members in the Southwest and a very small number on the Eastern seaboard.[9] These small initial efforts created the beginning of a new religious and ethnic identity. These new Latino *evangélicos* became a minority within a minority. They had accepted the Protestant message, which had a strong anti-Catholic component. So the Catholic majority in the Latino community saw them as traitors, both to the religion and to the ethnic identity of their ancestors.[10] But because the new Protestants were Latinos (Mexicans), many European Americans did not readily accept them either. *Evangélicos* told many stories of being persecuted by Latino Catholics, but the Protestant majority in the United States also marginalized them, making them stepchildren not only in the United States but also in the Latino community.

This new ethno-religious identity did not have a clear, cohesive center. Because Protestantism and Americanization were so closely linked, it was not

8. Juan Francisco Martínez, "Origins and Development of Protestantism among Latinos in the Southwestern United States, 1836–1900," PhD diss., Fuller Theological Seminary, 1996, 15, 104–7.

9. Ibid., 373.

10. Because being Mexican and being Catholic had been linked for several centuries, it was difficult for Latino Catholics to visualize a Latino identity that was not tied to being Catholic.

always clear what it meant to be Protestant and Latino. Some Latinos became Protestants because they wanted to Americanize, and as noted, the Protestant missionary efforts usually had a strong Americanization component. Some Latino *evangélicos* acculturated and wanted to join English-language Protestant congregations, but they were not always welcome. At the same time, if Latino *evangélicos* joined majority-culture congregations this tended to weaken Latino *evangélico* churches, because it was usually the most educated and economically secure who were most acculturated. Latino congregations lost potential leaders and financial support, condemning them to perpetual weakness.

Among many of these early converts there was a sense that conversion to Protestantism was freeing them from the "darkness" of Catholicism and its cultural limitations. "Latino converts were being asked to leave behind a culture that was somehow not as morally uplifting as the one being offered by Euro American missionaries."[11]

On the other hand, Latino churches and leaders that sought to maintain a clear *evangélico* identity had a secondary status in U.S. Protestant denominations. *Evangélicos* quickly got the message that "real" church was what European Americans did. Latino Protestant churches were imitations or even remedial programs for those who could not function in the "real" church.

Many of the early *evangélicos* paid a heavy price for their conversions. Their friends and family despised them, and they were not fully accepted by their European American coreligionists. In the midst of this complexity, *evangélicos* began to chart their own identity. This identity centered on their conversion experiences and their church communities. These small congregations, located in barrios or in small towns, reinforced the Latino Protestant identity. The members continually told their testimonies (conversion stories), reaffirmed that they had been freed from Catholicism, and built relationships with *evangélicos* in other congregations. Given their sense of "otherness" in relationship to Latino Catholics, they built a sense of being a small community of the faithful.[12] During the nineteenth and early twentieth centuries, these congregations were not unlike the Protestant churches being established in Latin America. David Maldonado, a third-generation Latino Protestant, describes his own experience and that of many other Latino Protestants of the period this way:

> To be Hispanic and Protestant of the generation reared before the civil rights movement, the Chicano Movement, and Vatican II means to have experienced

11. Arlene Sánchez-Walsh, *Latino Pentecostal Identity: Evangelical Faith, Self, and Society* (New York: Columbia University Press, 2003), 163.

12. Rubén P. Armendáriz, "The Protestant Hispanic Congregation: Identity," in *Protestantes/Protestants: Hispanic Christianity within Mainline Traditions*, ed. David Maldonado (Nashville: Abingdon, 1999), 254.

both overt racism and religious prejudice. Such attitudes led to racial segregation and religious divisions. Ethnic intolerance and religious divisions profoundly influenced this generation of Mexican-Americans. Such ethnic and religious attitudes led to the development of alternative systems of social life and religious communities that deeply influenced and shaped Mexican-American Protestants. It is no wonder that for Hispanic Protestants, ethnicity and religious identity are central to their self- and group identities.[13]

But Latino *evangélicos* had to deal with a number of issues that made their identity and that of their churches much more tenuous than that of their coreligionists in Latin America. Latinos, in general, lived in a segregated society. But their opportunities were not as limited as those of African Americans. So even before the civil rights movement, a few Latino Protestants were leaving their Latino congregations and joining the majority culture, a process that would accelerate after the 1960s. Many Latinos became acculturated enough that they could now participate in the larger religious marketplace of the United States. They were attracted to the same types of churches and religious options that were attracting their fellow citizens. Some became as secularized as any other vaguely Protestant person in the United States, while others joined English-language, mainline, evangelical, or Pentecostal churches. For many, this process has tended to also reflect a larger cultural shift so significant that it is increasingly difficult to identify anything specifically Latino about their Protestantism. Many of these people have made the shift from being Latino *evangélicos* to being U.S. Protestants of Latino descent.

New immigration from Latin America was and is both an opportunity and a challenge to Latino *evangélicos*. On the one hand, the new immigrants have always been a potential mission field. So even though Latino congregations might lose members through assimilation or secularization, they always have a pool of potential new members.

But the new immigrants have always also been a challenge for Latino *evangélicos*. Because immigrants bring new experiences and because they see their place in U.S. society differently, they tend to bring changes into Latino congregations. These changes have not always been welcomed by earlier generations of Latino *evangélicos*. As a result, Latino *evangélicos* have often established different Latino churches to serve the various segments of the Latino community.

The growth of the Latino community has also brought new religious players on the scene. Denominations that had never taken an interest in the Latino community are now establishing churches among Latinos. These denominations often continue to link Americanization and evangelization, even if this is not their overt goal. In her study of *Latino Pentecostal Identity*, Arlene

13. David Maldonado, *Crossing Guadalupe Street: Growing Up Hispanic and Protestant* (Albuquerque: University of New Mexico Press, 2001), 173.

Sánchez-Walsh states that the Vineyard movement, for example, "helps immigrants to establish a relationship with the larger evangelical world."[14] Latino immigrants are able to "accommodate to American culture" by being a part of the Vineyard.[15] Luis León takes this analysis a step further in his study of Victory Outreach:

> Evangélicos appear to offer entry into the lower North American middle class: Protestant cultural drama is mimed, that is, performed mimetically, without essence. . . . Chicano evangélicos appropriate Protestantism, inflect it and mirror it back, changing the Protestant symbolic language of North America, figuring it with distinctively Mexican-American grammars. The emergence of a Chicana/o and Latina/o middle class, of whatever religion, affects the dominant culture by creating an identifiable consumer market that demands public representation.[16]

Latin American immigration has also brought another change among Latino *evangélicos*. As the number of *evangélicos* continues to grow in Latin America, a growing number of new Latino immigrants are already *evangélicos*. Many join existing Latino congregations. But some are bringing their churches, pastors, and denominations with them. Most of these movements are Pentecostal or neo-Pentecostal and relate only marginally, if at all, with U.S. evangelicals. Many of them see the United States as a place that has lost the fervor of the gospel and needs to be evangelized. They are bringing new churches into the religious marketplace of the Latino community. Most of these churches are less than twenty-five years old. Nonetheless, some are already addressing the issues of acculturation and the "competition" from larger English-language congregations that are drawing members from their churches.

According to "Hispanic Churches in American Public Life," a study funded by Pew Charitable Trusts, as of 2002 about 20 percent of Latinos were Protestants. Though some observers of Latino Protestantism assume that *evangélico* conversions are tied to the immigration process,[17] the situation seems to be more complex. There are several countries in Latin America where the percentage of Protestants is as high as or higher than the percentage of Latino Protestants in the United States. So immigration does not seem to be a sufficient explanation for the conversions. It appears that both Latin Americans and Latinos are being drawn away from Catholicism and toward Protestantism in similar numbers.

14. Sánchez-Walsh, *Latino Pentecostal Identity*, 166.
15. Ibid., 191.
16. Luis León, *La Llorona's Children: Religion, Life, and Death in the U.S.-Mexican Borderlands* (Berkeley: University of California Press, 2004), 235.
17. Ibid., 205.

In addition, Latino *evangélicos* do not interpret their conversions as a means of acculturation or as a denial of their cultural roots. León makes this very clear:

> Rather than understanding evangélico conversion as a malinche narrative of treason and cultural abandon, los evangélicos understand themselves as continuing the essence of lo mexicano (food, language, calendar, song, place), and also availing themselves of Protestant cultural symbols of faith and material success. Mestizaje is not only a condition, a state of being, but an ongoing dialectical process of opposites that move and synthesize with each other. This movement of religious innovation has come to characterize spirituality and cultural expression in the borderlands—perhaps a rasquache spirituality.[18]

Latin American *evangélicos* have been able to define a role for themselves in their society. And that role is often supported by U.S. evangelical organizations. But Latino *evangélicos* continue in a stepchild status. If they maintain their own church structures, Protestants—and evangelicals in particular—largely ignore them. And if they become part of U.S. denominations and churches, they find that "despite the earnestness of the evangelical mission, Latinos were, and still remain, in pockets of powerlessness in churches they helped to build."[19]

European American evangelicals have usually assumed that their own experience of assimilation should be normative for all peoples in the United States. Evangelical leaders have used their own experience to interpret what impact *evangélico* conversion should have on Latino identity. They teach Latino *evangélicos* directly and indirectly that they should "subsume their ethnic identity to their religious identity because of perceived biblical mandates which suggest that race and ethnicity are no longer important."[20]

Nonetheless, Latino *evangélicos* have developed an ethnic religious identity of their own. Sánchez-Walsh recounts how that has occurred among Latino Assemblies of God, particularly those trained at the Latin American Bible Institute (LABI): "When one becomes Pentecostal, and when that process is reinforced by education, a Pentecostal identity develops as a possible alternative to any previous identity. . . . The creation of a Latino Pentecostal identity is predicated primarily on becoming Pentecostal, with residual signifiers of ethnic identity lingering, and often depending on social location, and left for others to ascertain the ethnic identities' relative strength or weakness."[21]

This account can be applied to a greater or lesser extent to most Latino *evangélicos*. They have been able to develop an ethno-religious identity among

18. Ibid., 240.
19. Sánchez-Walsh, *Latino Pentecostal Identity*, xvii.
20. Ibid., 71.
21. Ibid., 70.

each generation of new converts and/or immigrants. Because of new converts and new immigrants, new Latino churches continue to develop in most U.S. denominations. But their status seems more difficult to maintain beyond the first generation of converts. Some Latinos acculturate and are not sure they want to maintain an *evangélico* identity. Latino *evangélico* churches also continue to have an unclear status in their European American–led denominations. It is still not clear whether U.S. society in general, and U.S. evangelical churches in particular, are ready to make room for *evangélico* congregations that keep the second and third generation of *evangélicos* in their midst.

Latino *evangélico* leaders are working within their various denominations to define their identity and their place. Sánchez-Walsh calls her own denomination to create and maintain "a Latino Pentecostal identity among a variety of communities bound together by their choice to become Pentecostal and often bound by social location."[22] Latino leaders in other denominations are making the same call in their own settings.

Latino Pentecostals, particularly those denominations led by Latinos or Latin Americans, offer a different way of approaching this issue. Because they are not tied to European Americans, they are able to work at formulating a Latino *evangélico* (Pentecostal) identity outside of the pressure to subsume their ethnic identity to their religious identity. They also have to deal with their place in U.S. society. But they are not necessarily stepchildren in U.S. denominations. Most of these denominations are fairly recent, so it is not yet clear what impact they will have on a Latino *evangélico* identity.

In the midst of these formulations and reformulations of a Latino *evangélico* identity, it seems likely that, in this age of empire, Latinos will continue to migrate to the United States. Thus, even though some appear to be losing a clear Latino *evangélico* ethnic and religious identity, there are new generations of Latino *evangélicos* joining their ranks and asking the same questions about their religious and ethnic identity. Most Latino *evangélicos* will continue to define their identities in the midst of Latino churches. But others will ask the same questions in European American majority churches or in intentionally multicultural congregations.

Latinos are already having a significant impact on the Roman Catholic Church in the United States. Almost 40 percent of all Roman Catholics in the United States are Latinos. This means that Latinos are not merely one more minority within that church. They are quickly becoming the majority, and they are bringing their distinctive expressions of Catholic faith into the U.S. Catholic Church. The Roman Catholic Church is struggling to address the implications of that demographic shift in its ranks.

Latinos' potential impact on evangelicalism is much more difficult to gauge. Currently most Latino *evangélicos* are either outside of evangelical church

22. Ibid., 3.

structures or on the fringes of those structures. It remains to be seen whether evangelical denominations will allow Latino *evangélicos* a place at the table with their ethno-religious identity intact or whether assimilation will be the price of admission. But it is also not clear whether Latino *evangélicos* will decide to take on a greater role in the evangelical world on their own.

The unique stepchild status of Latino *evangélicos* will mean that it will continue to be difficult to clearly define a Latino *evangélico*. Between acculturation and new immigration, most likely that identity will be constantly in flux. But maybe that is inevitable. Speaking of Pentecostals, Sánchez-Walsh argues that "the making of a Latino Pentecostal identity needs to be remade with every generation in order to continue to grow, and, like ethnicity, religious identity is an identity one chooses."[23] As Latino *evangélicos* continue to redefine their identity, they will raise questions for U.S. evangelicals and all U.S. denominations that choose to work among Latinos. Up to now the assumption has been that Latino *evangélicos* will assimilate into existing U.S. denominations. Latinos have been perceived as the object of mission and have been greatly affected by becoming Protestants. But as their numbers continue to grow, existing U.S. denominations will need to ask themselves about the potential impact of Latinos as a growing percentage of their membership. Evangelicals in particular will need to ask themselves whether there is room under the evangelical canopy for Latino and Latin American Pentecostals and neo-Pentecostals.

Evangélicos already have a few limited spaces within the U.S. evangelical world. Most denominations have a Latino "expert" to supervise Latino congregations, and a few have elected Latinos to leadership positions, though it often appears that the Latino/a is in a token role. A small, but growing, number of evangelicals universities and seminaries are also actively recruiting Latino students; a few of these institutions are even hiring Latino faculty and/or addressing Latino issues. And at a popular level, a Latino beat and a few songs in Spanish are making it into some charismatic churches and the repertoire of some Christian pop groups.

Can *evangélicos* have a greater impact? Can they become the multitude Hardt and Negri envision? What might it look like? Because *evangélicos* are increasingly subjects, and not merely objects, of mission, they are challenging evangelical assumptions about how to do mission in the Latino community. Many of the fastest-growing Latino churches and ministries are not dependent on outside evangelical support. Evangelicals can decide to work alongside these efforts, but *evangélicos* are not waiting for evangelicals to lead or to provide financial support before they go forward.

Evangélicos are also challenging evangelicals on justice issues like immigration and bilingual education. Even politically conservative *evangélicos* are

23. Ibid., 132.

pushing evangelicals on these issues. The mere presence of undocumented *evangélicos* in evangelical churches challenges the practice of calling them criminals and wanting to "shut" the borders. The growing number of bilingual *evangélicos* in the United States also challenges the xenophobic concept that only monolingual English speakers can be good U.S. citizens.

Justo González says that Latinos challenge Christians in the United States because they have a noninnocent reading of history.[24] The theological justification of the empire is strongly supported by the evangelical reading of U.S. history that assumes the fallenness of all humanity *except for* Anglo American Protestant leaders in U.S. history. "The city on the hill" of popular U.S. mythology needs to be reread through the eyes of those who know the pain of U.S. expansionism and political expediency in Latin America. By merely telling their stories, *evangélicos* might become prophetic voices for change, if evangelicals care to listen.

Latinos, and Latino *evangélicos* in particular, are stepchildren because of the way they became part of the United States and how they converted to their new faith. But as they struggle to formulate and reformulate their identities in the midst of the impact of imperialism and empire, it remains to be seen what impact they will have on the reformulation of U.S. Protestant identity in general and evangelical identity in particular.

---

24. Justo González, *Mañana: Christian Theology from a Hispanic Perspective* (Nashville: Abingdon, 1990), 38–41.

12

Empire, Race, and the Evangelical Multitude

Jesse Jackson, Jim Wallis, and Evangelical Coalitions for Justice

ELEANOR MOODY-SHEPHERD
AND PETER GOODWIN HELTZEL

In front of a packed Riverside Church in 1967, Martin Luther King Jr. argued that the American empire was "the greatest purveyor of violence in the world today."[1] Racism, poverty, and war were identified as the three great sins of the American empire. During the final years of his life, King began to make important connections between race, the economy, and the U.S. military that together form a dangerous network of power. His prophetic discernment of the ethical problems with the infrastructure of American empire continues

---

1. Martin Luther King Jr., *The Trumpet of Conscience* (New York: Harper & Row, 1968), 24. The authors would like to thank our colleagues and students at New York Theological Seminary, especially Pearline McCrae, Anthony Rivera, Fred Sherron, Debby Washington, and David Vidal, in addition to many of the contributors to this volume, whose ongoing conversation strengthened this essay.

to be an important challenge for the United States and the churches within its borders.

Dangerous and unpredictable, empires are morphing. Hardt and Negri argue that empire now exceeds the boundaries of the nation-state through a global network of largely unregulated flows of capital.[2] While the nature of empire is changing, we are also witnessing the emergence of a multitude of social movements committed to social justice. In this new age of empire, it is vital that the U.S. evangelical movement live into the ministries of justice and reconciliation witnessed to by the Hebrew prophets and Jesus Christ.

The civil rights movement continues to be an important theological narrative for the contemporary construction and embodiment of a prophetic evangelical theology.[3] King's prophetic critique of American empire and his theological vision of "the beloved community" provide a theological framework that can simultaneously interrogate empire in its multiple forms and inspire a prophetic evangelical vision of social ethics. King's model of prophetic politics is vital to helping U.S. evangelicals live into the "beloved community," dismantling the idols of racism, materialism, and militarism.

Our chapter explores the relationship between black Protestants, white evangelicals, and the racism and economic injustice that result from current forms of empire. It is vital at this moment for evangelicals to embrace the struggle for racial and economic justice as an expression of the church's social witness and ministry of reconciliation. In this chapter we expand on Hardt and Negri's analysis of new social movements as constitutive to the emerging multitude, but we find their race theory problematic (section 1). The next two sections analyze and compare two contemporary social movements inspired by Martin Luther King Jr. and the civil rights movement of the 1960s: Jesse Louis Jackson Sr. and the Rainbow/PUSH Coalition (section 2) and Jim Wallis and Sojourners/Call to Renewal (section 3). Christian social movements like Rainbow/PUSH and Sojourners/Call to Renewal provide a new trajectory where black Protestants and white evangelicals can work together with Native Americans, Asians, and Hispanic/Latinos/Latinas for racial and economic justice for all (section 4).

---

2. Michael Hardt and Antonio Negri, *Empire* (Cambridge, MA: Harvard University Press, 2000).

3. In considering the civil rights movement as a foundational theological narrative for a contemporary prophetic theology, we are influenced by James Cone, *Martin and Malcolm and America: A Dream or a Nightmare?* (Maryknoll, NY: Orbis, 1991); David L. Chappell, *A Stone of Hope: Prophetic Religion and the Death of Jim Crow* (Chapel Hill: University of North Carolina Press, 2004); Charles Marsh, *God's Long Summer: Stories of Faith and Civil Rights* (Princeton, NJ: Princeton University Press, 1997); and *The Beloved Community: How Faith Shapes Social Justice, from the Civil Rights Movement to Today* (New York: Basic, 2005).

1. Empire, Racism, and Multitude

Hardt and Negri argue that the American empire is mediating a new form of empire: the ubiquitous "neoliberal" global economic order. One of the results of this form of economic organization is the sustained forced exclusion of the poor and many people of color in the world from the benefits of the global economy, particularly in the Global South. Hardt and Negri's theory of empire can help socially concerned evangelicals develop a clearer understanding of how the global economy is changing and currently functioning, including a gradual disclosure of who is benefiting from it and who is oppressed. In *Multitude*, Hardt and Negri refer to the ethics of empire as producing a "global apartheid":

> In the contemporary period of transition, the global interregnum, we can see emerging a new topography of exploitation and economic hierarchies the lines of which run above and below national boundaries. We are living in a system of global apartheid. We should be clear, however, that apartheid is not simply a system of *exclusion*, as if subordinated populations were simply cut off, worthless, and disposable. In the global Empire today, as it was before in South Africa, apartheid is a productive system of *hierarchical inclusion* that perpetuates the wealth of the few through the labor and poverty of the many. The global political body is in this way also an economic body defined by the global divisions of labor and power.[4]

While Hardt and Negri rightly point out that our global economic apartheid produces divisions between the wealthy and the poor in a global matrix that is "above and below national boundaries," they fail to explain the relationship of this economic oppression with racism.

Five years earlier, Richard Falk too argued that this neoliberal economic agenda has lead to a "global apartheid," imagining that if we were to think of the globe as a world-state, the only conceivable political analogue would be South Africa before freedom.[5] Thus, our world today is approximately one-fifth rich and four-fifths poor and segregated according to this economic demographic. In contrast to Hardt and Negri, Falk views the economic class distinction as being coextensive with race. The exploitation of black South Africans during the apartheid regime mirrors the exploitation of poor people of color throughout the world today. While "race" is a substantive category of analysis in Falk's account of "global apartheid," it does not play a primary role in Hardt and Negri's account.

Racism as a moral problem is domesticated in Hardt and Negri by their privileging of class struggle as the primary political problem, the heart of

4. Michael Hardt and Antonio Negri, *Multitude: War and Democracy in the Age of Empire* (New York: Penguin, 2004), 160–67. The italics are in the original.

5. Richard Falk, *Predatory Globalization: A Critique* (Cambridge: Polity, 1999), 13–23.

Karl Marx's political project. They use the language of race primarily to refer to "a new race" beyond race, a coming raceless humanity. They argue that racial discourse has undergone a shift from biological determinism to cultural determinism.[6] Following the logic of Jean-Paul Sartre, Hardt and Negri view race as a discursive construct created by the racist oppressor. In Sartre's logic, Jews are the product of the anti-Semitic imagination, just as "blacks" would be the discursive products of the white supremacist imagination in the U.S. context.[7]

Hardt and Negri's focus on race as exclusively culturally produced within Anglo European culture is problematic for several reasons. First, it allows the racial oppressors to frame racial discourse without acknowledging the personal beneficial hegemony they gain through a negative symbolization of their cultural "other." Second, it denies in a substantive way true African and African American alterity. It does not allow people of color to voice their own experience of oppression in their own unique ways. A discourse of race that emerges from African alterity has liberative potential for both the oppressed and the oppressors. Third, as Kevin Dunn has argued, Hardt and Negri's race theory leads to their spatial exclusion of Africa both discursively and economically, as it is conceived as lying outside of the smooth plan of immanence of Western Euro-American civilization.[8]

Race is undertheorized because of Hardt and Negri's economic prioritization. A more positive horizon in their race theory emerges as they connect racial consciousness with collective resistance against racial oppressors.[9] Racial identity is important only as it stimulates a collective resistance to racial oppression, mirroring paradigmatic resistance to economic oppression: "Race rises through the collective resistance to racial oppression."[10] Race gaining traction through antiracist transformative action is an important contribution to contemporary debates about race; however, the "blackness" of the Black Power movement is important to Hardt and Negri only as it names a submultitude whose "subaltern nationalism" is grounded primarily in production relations.[11] When the Black Nationalist movement achieves statehood,

6. *Multitude*, 191–92.

7. See Jean-Paul Sartre, "Black Orpheus," in *"What Is Literature?" and Other Essays* (Cambridge, MA: Harvard University Press, 1988).

8. Kevin C. Dunn, "Africa's Ambiguous Relation to Empire and *Empire*," in *Empire's New Clothes: Reading Hardt and Negri*, ed. Jodi Dean and Paul Passavant (New York: Routledge, 2004), 143–62.

9. *Multitude*, 104.

10. Ibid.

11. *Empire*, 107–8. Frantz A. Fanon describes how Europeans co-opted racial discourse as a discursive colonial management strategy to herd and contain "blacks" together as a labor group in capitalistic production. In *Empire* Hardt and Negri argue that the modern racist theory with its dubious biological basis that undergirded the subjugated black bodies of the European nation-states has been transformed into a postmodern imperial racist theory with

"blackness" immediately becomes insignificant and irrelevant to Hardt and Negri, since the movement loses its prophetic energy as an active and dynamic participant in the multitude. Race rises and falls with the changing tides of collective struggle and evaporates when the struggle for economic justice is over. In the end, race is reduced in Hardt and Negri to a class concept.

While Hardt and Negri's race theory is problematic, their vision for a world of economic equity is vital for the church's struggle for economic justice. Their methodology for achieving their vision is organizing poor people's movements for justice. While symbolizing many different things, their concept of the multitude is best understood as the poor struggling for justice. Antonio Negri writes, "Poverty is the extremely radical capacity to overturn the biopower that puts power to work so as to exploit it, exclude it and enslave it. *Poverty is the multitude in action.*"[12] It is only when the poor organize for justice that they actualize their power to create an alternative world. Organizing the poor for justice is a fundamental outworking of the "gospel of the poor" proclaimed by Jesus in Luke's Gospel. The history of the Christian church testifies to a tradition of prophetic politics that has been resolute in its commitment to organize and mobilize the power of the poor. While the civil rights movement began as a mobilization to advocate full legal and voting rights for African Americans, in the late 1960s the movement expanded out to focus on the economic empowerment of all of the poor in the United States. When social justice is discussed with evangelicals in the United States, it is vital that racial and economic justice be engaged together. We see this dual social engagement in the work of Jesse Jackson and the Rainbow/PUSH Coalition.

2. PUSHing Evangelicals: Jesse Jackson's Coalition of the Disinherited

Jesse Louis Jackson Sr., who was one of King's lieutenants and with him when he died, took up the mantle of working for economic justice for African Americans and the poor. Forged in the fires of the civil rights struggle, Jackson's program has always been executed through the lens of race, America's original sin. Best known for his Rainbow Coalition that emerged from his 1984 and 1988 presidential campaigns, Jackson spoke of his movement as a "coalition of

cultural difference as its basis and a nonhierarchical dispersal system. While they give an account of how racism has been transformed by the new imperial sovereignty of empire, they reserve moral judgment on this transformation, except where race converges with collective struggle for economic justice (*Empire*, 190–94). See Frantz A. Fanon, *A Dying Colonialism* (Harmondsworth, UK: Pelican, 1970), and *Black Skin, White Masks*, trans. Charles Lam Markhamann (New York: Grove, 1967).

12. Antonio Negri, "The Political Subject and Absolute Immanence," in *Theology and the Political: The New Debate*, ed. Creston Davis, John Milbank, and Slavoj Žižek (Durham, NC: Duke University Press, 2005), 238–39. Italics in the original.

the disinherited."[13] The language of the disinherited was biblical. It resonated with people of color, the poor, and all those who shared an American revivalist past. Jesus Christ poured out his life on behalf of the disinherited, and this is the call of Christian public theology today.

Jackson argued that the black church should support the idea of a black presidential candidate in the Democratic primaries of the 1980s because such a candidate could authentically represent the disinherited in America, including women, Hispanics, Asians, and poor whites, as well as politically open-minded whites. Drawing on the black church basis of the civil rights struggle in the 1960s, Jackson would become the consummate African American Christian coalition builder, focusing his energies on the plight of African Americans and the poor. His focus on economic justice for all God's people is an important continuation of the legacy of King and the civil rights movement. Throughout his career, Jackson has built coalitions that have taken different forms; his "coalition of the disinherited" found organizational form in the Rainbow Coalition and Operation PUSH, which merged to become the Rainbow/PUSH Coalition in 1997.

Jackson's form of prophetic black Protestantism shares a common revivalist tradition with white evangelicals. Jackson's public ministry carries on multiple streams of abolitionism, including white evangelical abolitionists like Jonathan Blanchard, John Brown, and Charles Finney and black abolitionists like Sojourner Truth, Harriet Tubman, and Frederick Douglass. If we think of prophetic evangelicalism as an antiracist, proreconciliation "Word of God" movement for love and justice in and for the world, Jackson's movement has deep resemblances to the evangelical movement. Important differences emerge in the ways that these different movements treat the problem of racism.

When asked if he was an evangelical, Jesse L. Jackson Sr. answered, "It depends on how you define it: If you mean someone who believes in the Bible, that Jesus died for our sins, and that we are to share our faith with others and join the struggle for justice in the world, Yes! I am an evangelical. However, if you are referring to the faith of white evangelicals in South Carolina where I grew up, who would not let us ride on the front of the bus, eat in their restaurants, and attend their churches, I would say No!"[14] Jackson acknowledges that there is still a tension between white evangelicals and black Christians that cannot be easily resolved through assuming a black "evangelical" identity. His response demonstrates that he can embrace the core theological values of the evangelical movement identified by David Bebbington: the Bible, the cross, conversion, and activism. It also demonstrates that his form of evangelicalism cannot tolerate other evangelicals who promote racist attitudes, systems,

13. Jesse L. Jackson, "Advantages of a Black Presidential Candidacy," *Westside Gazette*, April 28, 1983, quoted by Manning Marble, *Black American Politics: From the Washington Marches to Jesse Jackson* (London: Verso, 1995), 348.

14. Interview with Peter Heltzel, October 2007.

and practices. While there can be some agreement about theological beliefs, we live in a racist society, and this has proved extremely difficult to overcome even within white evangelical congregations.

Martin Luther King Jr.'s vision of beloved community has animated Jesse Jackson's public theology from the beginning. Jackson was inspired by the prophetic vision of King in the final years of his life, when he started to connect the dots between racism, the U.S. economy, and the military. Jackson continues in this public church tradition of systemic engagement that King embodied. Like King, Jackson thinks that the church is called to transform structures and systems, as well as influence individuals. Jackson viewed the civil rights movement as a theological narrative in which he continues to play an important role in leading after the death of King. As part of the civil rights movement's old guard, Jackson has always drawn on a black constituency that can be traced back to both liberal and conservative evangelical theological streams in the nineteenth century; however, the future of his movement will rest largely in the hands of evangelicals.

Jackson has always surrounded himself with evangelical preachers like his heir apparent, Rev. James Meeks, senior minister of Salem Baptist Church / House of Hope in Chicago and the executive vice president of the Rainbow/ PUSH Coalition. Following in the footsteps of his mentor, Meeks has become a state senator in Illinois and wields a growing amount of political influence in local, state, and national politics. As an evangelical preacher, Meeks gives an altar call every Sunday, and his church on the south side of Chicago has grown to more than seventeen thousand members. Edward Gilbreath, the black evangelical editor of *Today's Christian*, a publication of Christianity Today International, writes,

> As it turns out, a surprising number of black evangelicals have been inspired and shaped by the work of Jackson. And many of them are card-carrying members of Rainbow/PUSH. They are theology professors, parachurch leaders and senior pastors; politically, they are both Democrats and Republican. There are no hard figures on the exact number of evangelicals directly influenced by Jackson, but the anecdotal evidence points to a wide trend. . . . His true heirs will not be radical activists like Al Sharpton or others identified more by their politics than their faith. No, his successors will be honest-to-goodness Christian churchmen who, like Meeks, have a call to ministry both in and outside the church.[15]

From the evangelicals who worked with Jackson and Operation Breadbasket to those who joined his campaigns for the presidency in the 1980s to evangelicals who currently work with his Rainbow/PUSH Coalition, evangelicals are a vital part of Jackson's loyal supporters. Thus, Jackson is a symbol of a

---

15. Edward Gilbreath, *Reconciliation Blues: A Black Evangelical's Inside View of White Christianity* (Downers Grove, IL: InterVarsity Press, 2006), 115.

prophetic black Christianity with deep affinities to a prophetic evangelicalism that combines vibrant personal faith with an activist vision for social justice. Jackson's movement is unique because it grows organically from the abolition movement and civil rights movement from the position of those who were most oppressed—African Americans. As a black Christian, Jackson is lodged on the underside of a white evangelical modernity. From this vantage point, he is able to shed light on the racist regime of America through which white evangelicals were given birth.

Jackson sums up the present state of the current collective resistance struggle within the African American community as a symphony: the first movement was the struggle to end slavery; the second movement was the battle to end segregation; the third movement was the campaign to obtain full voting rights; and the fourth movement is the quest for equal opportunity through shared economic security and empowerment.

Born in Greenville, South Carolina, on October 8, 1941, Jackson grew up as a Baptist with a deep evangelical piety and has become one of the most prophetic political leaders in the African American community. While black and white Baptists in the South may have shared a conservative theological orthodoxy, politically and socially there was a large divide, if not chasm. This divide is a result of the terrible consequences of the Southern practice of slavery.

2.1. The Struggle to End Slavery

The three hundred years of chattel slavery was a time of physical, psychological, and cultural assault on the enslaved African people in the United States. Coming out of this wilderness wandering after the Civil War and experiencing white American attempts to "evangelize and educate" them, many African Americans tapped deep into the Afrocentric heritage that had long sustained their faith in the form of slave religion.[16] Slavery is the foundational experience of African American Christianity, and it means that African Americans who live in this memory of suffering will always be exiled in some sense from the Anglo American establishment, in both evangelical and old-line churches.[17] Peter Paris contends that in the perspective of black America, racism has

16. See Albert J. Raboteau, *Slave Religion: The "Invisible Institution" in the Antebellum South* (New York: Oxford University Press, 1978). See also Katharine L. Dvorak, *An African-American Exodus: The Segregation of the Southern Churches* (Brooklyn, NY: Carlson, 1991), and Melton Sernett, *Black Religion and American Evangelicalism: White Protestants, Plantation Missions, and the Flowering of Negro Christianity, 1787–1865* (Metuchen, NJ: Scarecrow, 1975).

17. Albert J. Raboteau, "The Black Experience in American Evangelicalism: The Meaning of Slavery," in *The Evangelical Tradition in America*, ed. Leonard I. Sweet (Macon, GA: Mercer University Press, 1984), 181–98; Timothy Smith, "Slavery and Theology: The Emergence of Black Christian Consciousness in Nineteenth Century America," *Church History* 41 (1972): 497–512; Mechal Sobel, *Trabelin' On: The Slave Journey to an Afro-Baptist Faith* (Princeton, NJ: Princeton University Press, 1988). See also A. G. Miller, "The Rise of African-American

been the bedrock of the American republic, shaping all dimensions of the political, economic, and social order.[18] Thus, African American slave religion also functions as a freedom movement, providing the symbols and practices for collective resistance to white supremacy.[19] Slave religion further played an important role in providing a narrative framework and safe emotional space to survive until the emancipation of the slaves.

2.2 The Battle to End Segregation

Jackson's childhood in the American South placed him in close proximity to the tragic memory of African American slavery, which lived on through the segregation and demoralization of the Jim Crow era. Segregation in the Deep South was often enforced through continued white supremacy among many Anglo American Christians, taking on its most grotesque form in the Ku Klux Klan and the White Citizens Council.[20] Because Jackson grew up on the economic and religious margins in South Carolina, he identifies deeply with the oppressed who bear the brunt of racial—and economic inequalities in the United States. He rebelled against the racial and economic apartheid in the United States, marching and protesting with King until the victory was won.[21]

2.3 The Campaign to Obtain Full Voting Rights

The civil rights community helped to fight for voting rights for African Americans, making the long journey from the three-fifths voting value of slaves for white slave owners in the antebellum South to the final ratification of the Voting Act in 1965. Maintaining this right is a constant battle. The Rainbow/PUSH Coalition is leading the ongoing effort to mobilize and educate people about the need for the renewal of the Voting Rights Act. In 2006 the Rainbow/

Evangelicalism in American Culture," in *Perspectives on American Religion and Culture*, ed. Peter Williams (Oxford: Blackwell, 1999).

18. Peter J. Paris, *The Social Teaching of the Black Churches* (Philadelphia: Fortress, 1985), 83.

19. Gayraud Wilmore writes, "From David Walker to Nat Turner, black religion in the United States—strongly fortified by the prophets of the Old Testament and New Testament apocalyptic—provided blacks with spiritual resources with which to resist oppression, if with tragic unsuccess." Gayraud S. Wilmore, *Black Religion and Black Radicalism: An Interpretation of the Religious History of Afro-American People*, 2nd ed. (Maryknoll, NY: Orbis, 1986), 72.

20. On the particularly Southern character of the struggle for racial freedom within the African American churches, see Shelton E. Smith, *In His Image, But . . . : Racism in Southern Religion, 1780–1910* (Durham, NC: Duke University Press, 1972); George Brown Tindall, *South Carolina Negroes, 1877–1890* (Columbia: University of South Carolina Press, 1952).

21. For a historic account of economic apartheid in America, see Douglas S. Massey and Nancy A. Denton, *American Apartheid: Segregation and the Making of the Underclass* (Cambridge, MA: Harvard University Press, 1993).

PUSH Coalition informed its constituents that the Voting Rights Act—the law that provided African Americans with the right to vote throughout the states that discriminated against them—had provisions that were up for renewal. The Voting Rights Act provides the basis for policing states that have tended to use various maneuvers to make it more difficult for African Americans and minorities to vote. In an age when presidential elections are decided by a very few votes, Jackson's advocacy on issues like this is vital to ensure that every vote counts and every vote is counted. As a result of the persistent efforts of Jackson and others, President George W. Bush signed a twenty-five year extension on the south lawn of the White House on July 27, 2006.

2.4 The Quest for Equal Opportunity through Shared Economic Security and Empowerment

Jackson frames his work on economic empowerment in light of the historic economic inequities in the United States along racial lines (e.g., slavery and segregation).[22] Awareness of the practice of slavery helps us understand the oppressive nature of economic organization in our country's history and present.[23] Reflections on American economic life must always emerge from the stench, the chains, the whip, the separation from family, inability to move freely and to plan ahead that lie deep within the "subversive memory" of this country. There is a substantive difference between chattel slavery in the eighteenth and nineteenth centuries and current modes of economic enslavement, yet they are dialectically both forms of economic servitude.

Through the bus boycotts during the civil rights movement, Jackson learned how to use objects like buses as "economic weapons." He translated this tactic in his work as the national director of Operation Breadbasket, the economic arm of the Southern Christian Leadership Conference (SCLC) in Chicago. Jackson led a movement that empowered black entrepreneurs and forced white business owners who continued to slight black consumers to change their relationship with local consumers. As a result of Jackson's economic tactics, he was able to find poor people well-compensated jobs and discover new markets for black-manufactured products.[24]

22. G. Frederickson and C. Lasch, "Resistance to Slavery," in *American Slavery: The Question of Resistance*, ed. J. Bracey, A. Meier, and E. Rudwick (Belmont, CA: Wadsworth, 1970); Cornel West, *Prophesy Deliverance! An Afro-American Revolutionary Christianity*, anniversary ed. (Louisville, KY: Westminster John Knox, 2002).

23. See Eugene Genovese, *The Political Economy of Slavery: Studies in the Economy and Society of the Slave South*, 2nd ed., 1st Wesleyan ed. (Middletown, CT: Wesleyan University Press, 1989); Eric Foner, *Free Soil, Free Labor, Free Men: The Ideology of the Republican Party before the Civil War* (Oxford: Oxford University Press, 1995).

24. Ronald Kisner and Warren Brown, "Will the SCLC Split Kill Dr. King's Dream?" *Jet Magazine*, January 13, 1972, 13.

These successes inspired Jackson to develop a new organization, PUSH (People United to Save Humanity), in 1971 as a "civil economics program organized in a religious setting." It had a multifaceted fifteen-point program, four of which directly address race: (1) a comprehensive economic plan for development of black people and poor people; (2) quality education regardless of race, religion, or creed; (3) economic and social relationships between the nations of Africa in order to build African-Afro-American unity; and (4) black excellence.[25] The explicit reference to race in these four objectives demonstrates a healthy synergy between racial and economic justice in Jackson's project.

In the late 1970s and early 1980s, a crisis situation developed in Chicago after Richard J. Daley's long reign as mayor of Chicago (1955–76) ended.[26] A number of political and economic issues were raised in the public mind as a result of deindustrialization, soaring unemployment rates within black neighborhoods, and downtown development. Displaced manufacturing workers were the beginning of what Hardt and Negri refer to as immaterial labor in our information age. According to Helene Slessarev-Jamir, during this period Jackson and other politicians in Chicago began a series of political compromises that advanced their political careers through assimilation into Chicago's political machine but betrayed the urban poor through an increasing focus on the black middle class.[27] With the downtown development of affluent neighborhoods and lavish service industries, manufacturers were kicked out of town and well-paying jobs became sparser. At this critical juncture, we begin to see the conflict between the effectiveness of coalitions to serve the poor and the political aspirations of leaders of the movements.

Jackson began to achieve more public success: the 1982 People's Coalition to Boycott ChicagoFest successfully protested against Mayor Jane Byrne, who had replaced two African American members of the Chicago Housing Authority with Anglo Americans, creating an Anglo American majority; black voter registration began to steadily improve; and Congressperson Harold Washington became mayor of Chicago in 1983.[28] Emboldened by these successes, in 1984 Jackson launched another organization with a broader and more inclusive membership. The Rainbow Coalition, a multiracial political organization, came into being through the momentum created in Jackson's first serious bid for the Democratic presidential nomination. The organization

25. Barbara A. Reynolds, *Jesse Jackson: The Man, the Movement, and the Myth* (Chicago: Nelson-Hall, 1975), 278–80.

26. On this transformation in Chicago politics and economic development, see Joel Rast, *Remaking Chicago: The Political Origins of Urban Industrial Change* (Dekalb: Northern Illinois Press, 1999).

27. Helene Slessarev, *The Betrayal of the Urban Poor* (Philadelphia: Temple University Press, 1997).

28. Gary Rivlin, *Fire on the Prairie: Chicago's Harold Washington and the Politics of Race* (New York: Henry Holt, 1992).

galvanized people of different races, religions, genders, and national identities. It sought to build a progressive moral consensus on both national and international political issues.

On January 15, 1996, the Rainbow/PUSH Coalition began a new project for the purpose of continuing King's work toward a more inclusive America by combining theology with the struggle for economic justice. Through research, education, and partnership, the Rainbow/PUSH Wall Street Project encourages companies to form mutually beneficial business relationships that embrace inclusion as a means of growth. The Wall Street Project has satellite offices across the nation, including New York, Washington, Los Angeles, Detroit, Chicago, Silicon Valley, Atlanta, and Houston.

2.5 The Role of the Black Church in Coalitions for Justice

The black church has been Jackson's core network over the years. However, large segments of the black church have been abandoning their historic role of being the prophetic voice for social change and leading the struggle against oppressive political and economic institutions. The church has been the institutional center of the black community, providing a spiritual community of healing and protest in a racist American culture. Black churches have embodied a radical ethic by helping to start black businesses, establishing educational institutions, strengthening family life, and providing a moral center for progressive national politics and rigorous civil rights struggles.[29] However, many new black evangelicals are neglecting this tradition of radicalism.

Even while black Americans, immigrants, and poor people are living an ongoing nightmare of poverty and limited opportunity, the black middle class and conservative black evangelicalism continue to grow. There is a serious division within the African American church between the gospel of personal piety and the gospel of social justice. Thus, the African American church, which has historically tended to be fairly unified in its theological conservatism and political liberalism, has undergone "evangelicalification" as a new generation of theological and politically conservative African Americans has emerged.[30] Gayraud Wilmore attributes this conservative evangelical movement to poor theological discernment, historical ignorance of their black ancestors, and a personal and individualistic notion of sin and redemption. Wilmore writes,

29. Jesse L. Jackson Sr., "'Sí Se Puede' Means 'We Shall Overcome,'" *Chicago Tribune*, May 1, 2006, 9.

30. *Evangelicalification* is A. G. Miller's term for people of color who assimilate into white evangelical culture without maintaining their own racial and cultural integrity. See Miller's forthcoming book on black evangelicalism, where he points to several streams of influence on this conservative black evangelical movement in the United States, including a stream from the Christian and Missionary Alliance and a premillennial dispensational stream through black ministers trained at Moody Bible Institute and Dallas Theological Seminary. Cf. William H. Bentley, *The National Black Evangelical Association* (Chicago: W. H. Bentley, 1979).

"The majority of Black preachers confuse themselves with Billy Graham and the most unenlightened versions of White evangelicalism."[31] Furthermore, Wilmore argues, the contemporary black pastors who preach only personal piety echo the theology practiced by Southern slaveholders. "They urged slaves to cling to their personal relationship with Jesus Christ, but were not to consider liberty and justice as the primary concern of the Christian church."[32] Bishop Eddie Long, the pastor of one of Atlanta's largest black churches, exemplifies this form of evangelical pietism. Long believes that African Americans must learn how to "forgive, forbear and forget" racism because they are already living in the Promised Land today. Bishop Long's response is typical of the theology shared by pastors who practice the gospel of personal piety and prosperity.

In contrast to these more conservative and pietistic forms of black evangelicalism, Jesse Jackson maintains the radical prophetic tradition of the progressive black church. Part of maintaining the prophetic tradition of the black church is deploying race as a controlling hermeneutic for social justice ministries.

Jackson's primary base has historically been African American, but its future is multiethnic, including evangelicals of all colors. Sadly, many white people—including white evangelicals—are not interested in joining the coalition. This white disinterest has intensified through the political success of the Christian Right. Moreover, it is not clear how much Jesse is really interested in white evangelicals beyond their potential to help him move his agenda. Because of politics and personalities, there is yet to be an ongoing sustained dialogue between Jackson and white evangelical leaders. However, given political realignments in the 2008 U.S. elections, there is a new opportunity for a sustained dialogue between black Christians and white evangelicals.

White evangelicals have much to learn from the Rainbow/PUSH movement. PUSH provides a paradigm of economic empowerment that is vital for the black and white evangelical church. It provides a contrast to "health and wealth" preachers like Creflo Dollar and Leroy Thompson. While Jackson has made political compromises and manifested poor personal judgment at times, he has held together a mighty coalition for justice. Jackson's credentials as a theologian, pastor, astute politician, and world leader are critical to his ability to lead at this time when the United States and the world face the challenge of a federal government that is redefining itself and functioning in ways that threaten the stability of the world. Jackson's "coalition of the disinherited" has been transformed through the decades, but he continues to be a tireless advocate for the poor, demonstrated in his advocacy for the poor affected by

31. Gayraud S. Wilmore, introduction to Gayraud S. Wilmore and James H. Cone, *Black Theology: A Documentary History, 1966–1979* (Maryknoll, NY: Orbis, 1979), 246.
32. Ibid.

Hurricanes Katrina and Rita in the Gulf of Mexico immediately following these natural disasters in 2005. As new political leaders and coalition builders emerge from the black church, they will all work on the foundation laid by King, Jackson, and many others.

3. Jim Wallis and Sojourners

Jim Wallis's commitment to social justice activism is shaped by his evangelical upbringing. A white evangelical minister raised in a Midwestern Republican family, Wallis encountered systematic white racism in his own Plymouth Brethren church. As a result he left the church for a season and joined the civil rights and peace movements of the 1960s and 1970s, then led a major late-twentieth-century evangelical justice coalition through two organizations that merged in 2007: Sojourners, established in 1971, whose mission is to offer a voice and vision for social change, and Call to Renewal, a national network of churches and faith-based groups, established in 1996 to overcome domestic poverty. Recently Wallis has been brought into more public light because of his work on the Six Point Plan as an Alternative to War with Iraq and the phenomenal success of his books *God's Politics* and *The Great Awakening*.[33]

Racial justice has also been an important animating value for Wallis. He grew up in a white community and then moved into a black community in Detroit. He observed the police brutality against African Americans and developed a righteous indignation at racial discrimination and profiling. This helped make him more conscious of the scourge of racism and helped him prioritize race in his construction of social justice.

After college, Wallis moved to Washington, DC, to start a radical urban Christian community. Inspired by the progressive, communitarian stream of Karl Barth's theology, Wallis and his friends were nourished by the writings of Jacques Ellul and William Stringfellow.[34] The antiempire ethos of this Christian social movement is reflected in the title of their first monthly publication, *The Post-American*. Wallis, together with Donald W. Dayton and others, worked out a new genealogy of evangelicalism that highlighted evangelicalism's commitment to radical justice.[35] Radical nineteenth-century postmillennialists participated in a wide variety of Christian social movements, including the

33. Jim Wallis, *God's Politics: Why the Right Gets It Wrong and the Left Doesn't Get It* (San Francisco: HarperOne, 2005), and *The Great Awakening* (San Francisco: HarperOne, 2008).

34. William Stringfellow, *A Keeper of the Word: Selected Writings of William Stringfellow*, ed. Bill Wylie Kellermann (Grand Rapids: Eerdmans, 1994).

35. Donald W. Dayton, *Discovering an Evangelical Heritage* (Peabody, MA: Hendrickson, 1976). This book is a collection of articles that Dayton wrote for *The Post-American* that served as a historical heritage for a late-twentieth-century radical evangelicalism.

abolitionist movement, the fight for child labor, and the fight for women's rights, and then protested the U.S. war with Mexico.

Wallis sees the privatization of faith embodied in fundamentalist antipolitical separatism as "the great heresy of twentieth century evangelicalism."[36] During the early twentieth century, particularly in the 1920s, evangelicalism was transformed by a number of cultural and theological factors and lost most of its radical social justice edge. The factors leading to a privatized faith were fundamentalist separatism[37] and a focus on personal morality instead of public justice.[38]

Wallis sees two contemporary options: the power politics of the Religious Right or the moral influence of the civil rights movement.[39] Having been seduced by power, the Religious Right's moral sense is assuaged through "symbols and rhetorical commitments" of the administration, while President George W. Bush's "theology of war" and establishment of an "axis of evil" continue this Manichaean heresy, according to Wallis and other religious leaders.[40] Wallis aligns himself with Martin Luther King's legacy of critiquing the failure of groups like Jerry Falwell's Moral Majority and Pat Robertson's Christian Coalition when he says, "The religious Right went wrong by forgetting its religious and moral roots and going for political power; the civil rights movement was proven right in operating out of its spiritual strength and letting its political influence flow from its moral influence."[41] The thesis of God's Politics is that faith in a personal God demands socially transformative public action, conceived as prophetic worship of the triune God. Critical to this prophetic evangelical public theology is coalition building for the common good.

Wallis, like Jackson, works out of the black social justice tradition of Martin Luther King Jr. Wallis was shaped by King's vision for a racially and economically just social order and his commitment to organizing the multitude. In God's Politics, Wallis clearly states he is working out of King's vision of beloved community: "With his Bible in one hand and the Constitution in the other, King persuaded, not just pronounced. He reminded us all of God's purposes for justice, for peace, and for the 'beloved community,' where those who are always left out and behind get a front-row seat. And he did it—bring religion into public life—in a way that was always welcoming, inclusive, and inviting to all who cared about moral, spiritual, or religious values. Nobody

---

36. Wallis, God's Politics, 35.

37. See Ernst R. Sandeen, The Roots of Fundamentalism (Chicago: University of Chicago Press, 1970), and George Marsden, Fundamentalism and American Culture (New York: Oxford University Press, 1980). On anti-intellectualism within evangelicalism, see Mark Noll, The Scandal of the Evangelical Mind (Grand Rapids: Eerdmans, 1994).

38. See Douglas W. Frank, Less Than Conquerors: How Evangelicals Entered the Twentieth Century (Grand Rapids: Eerdmans, 1986).

39. Wallis, God's Politics, 61–64.

40. Ibid., 154.

41. Ibid., 64.

felt left out of the conversation."[42] Wallis embraces and expands King's vision of beloved community, seeking to embody an antiracist, proreconciliation democratic politics.

The strength of Wallis's project is his commitment to addressing the issue of poverty. At this point he has made important headway in providing an evangelical embodiment of James Cone's claim that "theology that does not emerge from the historical consciousness of the poor is ideology."[43] Wallis views racism as "America's original" sin, an ethical starting point that he shared with Jackson. He also sees the way that racism and poverty are coextensive. As Wallis and Call to Renewal implement an ecumenical strategy to eradicate poverty it is vital that they keep racism at the center of the discussion and activism, because it is too easy to forget a rigorous analysis of the specific relations of the oppressors and the oppressed, and particularly this dynamic among whites and blacks.[44]

Public discourse often requires race not to be a central issue. In order for a person or movement to be heard, gain legitimacy, and be seen as a consensus builder, the category of race sometimes has to be displaced from its social agenda. Race is sublimated to other social issues. The problem is never personal prejudice but systematic evil. Jim Wallis is good friends with many African Americans and has empowered African American leaders within Sojourners, like Adam Taylor, who serves as senior political director; however, the racist roots of the white evangelical culture grow long and deep. Being transformed into an antiracist, proreconciliation movement means intentionally sustaining an ongoing dialogue among a multiethnic coalition that has a common goal of dismantling instituional racism.

Jim Wallis is a prophetic evangelical. Like Jackson, he sees himself working out of King's civil rights legacy. However, as a white evangelical he finds it harder to fully integrate the race critique in his writing and political project. That being said, his awareness and consistent addressing of racism are an important example to many evangelicals who are less aggressive in their antiracist, proreconciliation work. Wallis has faithfully built a powerful Christian social movement during the past four decades. Yet with his success he has had to accommodate more and more to the system. We saw such compromises in Jackson relative to his political aspirations, and we see the same potential in Wallis as he becomes a celebrity figure as a result of his tireless advocacy for justice and his compelling descriptions of a prophetic evangelical ethic.

42. Ibid., xiv.

43. James Cone, *God of the Oppressed* (New York: Seabury, 1975), 96.

44. See Wallis's chapter "Truth Telling about Race: America's Original Sin," in *God's Politics*, 307–20. Also, he has written many articles on racism in *Sojourners* during the 1990s, and Sojourners has produced many educational guides for churches on racism and antiracism trainings. Compared to that of most white evangelicals, Wallis's work on race is to be heartily commended.

4. Toward an Evangelical Theology of Justice

Rainbow/PUSH and Sojourners/Call to Renewal at their best are actualizing multitudes—"the poor in action"—to collectively resist injustice. Hardt and Negri's theory of multitude opens up a new horizon for understanding evangelicals' roles in Christian social movements. However, in the U.S. context a different strategy must be employed from the one used by Hardt and Negri, in order to help evangelicals understand the sin of racism and work against it at an institutional level.

Hardt and Negri's call for a "raceless" society resonates with King's dream of beloved community. King's three sins of the American empire—racism, poverty, and war—continue to plague America forty years after his death. King dreamed of a society of racial equality but offered a theological account of race and vision of the kingdom of God to show a way forward. Contra Hardt and Negri's optimism, this will entail an ongoing dialogue about white power and priviledge and the collective mobilization of an antiracist, proreconciliation activism committed to dismantling institutional racism.

In the U.S. context, race must continue to play a foundational role in our political theorizing and social praxis. White evangelicals like Wallis need to bear in mind our critique of Hardt and Negri: just as they sublimate race to class concerns, white evangelicals, the beneficiaries of white privilege and power, can easily sublimate racism to other moral issues. Thus, white evangelicals need to study whiteness and antiracist theory to deepen their understanding of the racial problem, while black Protestant leaders like Jesse Jackson need to be more intentional in creating forums where black Christians and white evangelicals can deepen their fellowship through work together in the task of community and national renewal.

The black and white evangelical churches have been segregated too long. It is time to develop new coalitions of justice that are not limited to traditional racial/ethnic constituencies. However, this collaborative move must be developed from the standpoint of strong respect for the particularity of different racial realities. A new alliance between progressive black and white Christians is vital to the new Christian multitude in solidarity with the poor, but it must be translated to more conservative evangelicals in both the black and the white church. Rainbow/PUSH and Sojourners/Call to Renewal are positive movements for the struggle for social justice and lasting social challenge. Through these organizations and others like them, black and white evangelicals have opportunities to overcome the racial divide and work for true economic justice for all.

13

Where Are the Pentecostals in an Age of Empire?

ELAINE PADILLA AND DALE T. IRVIN

We were visiting in the home of a local Pentecostal church leader in San Miguel, El Salvador, in the summer of 2001. The evening conversation had turned to the history of Latin American Christianity when one of the pastors asked a profoundly unsettling question: "The *conquistadores* who first brought Christianity to Latin America were Roman Catholic, I know. But where were the Pentecostals?"

The question of where were the Pentecostals has haunted the history of world evangelicalism and world Christianity for almost a century. Where do Pentecostals fit? Where do they lodge their social, political, and theological identities? Most observers, including many Pentecostals themselves, regard the movement as being a part (if now the largest part) of a more general global evangelical movement that emerged in the twentieth century to become a major force in world Christianity. The historiography of Pentecostalism has often linked "the tongues speaking movement" (as Pentecostals were often called in the early days of the twentieth century) with their near-contemporaries in North America, the fundamentalists. Indeed, most Pentecostals claim the heritage of the sixteenth-century Protestant Reformation, and the subsequent history of evangelical revivalism from which fundamentalism also emerged, as their own.

Nevertheless, the relationship between Pentecostalism and Protestant evangelicalism is more problematic than might first appear. Pentecostalism has long had an uneasy relationship with evangelicalism, especially in the United States.[1] Most fundamentalists in North America during the first decades of the twentieth century rejected Pentecostalism with its practices of speaking in other tongues and divine healing. The evangelical movement that emerged from fundamentalism in the 1940s and 1950s in the United States included Pentecostals in its major institutional formation, the National Association of Evangelicals, but only after Pentecostals had measurably toned down their distinctive hermeneutical emphasis. More recently, the alliance of Pentecostalism with evangelical Protestantism has been challenged by a number of scholars of Pentecostalism who regard the Pentecostal movement as being a distinctive form of Christian experience and not reducible to part of the evangelical wing.[2]

This latter perspective found support in an earlier ecumenical figure, Henry P. Van Dusen, a former president of Union Theological Seminary in New York. Van Dusen was an astute observer of world Christianity and not afraid to go against the grain of prevailing interpretations. In a 1958 essay in *Christianity and Crisis*, he called attention to what he termed "sectarian Protestantism" and the challenges it posed to the ecumenical movement. Among the "sectarians" Van Dusen numbered Pentecostal, Holiness, Adventist, and even Brazilian spiritualist groups. Although he also called them "evangelicals" in the essay, it was clear that he did not mean the same thing that those claiming to be evangelicals today intend when they claim to be the rightful inheritors of the sixteenth-century Protestant Reformation. The common ancestry of these "sectarians," Van Dusen noted, was in historic Protestantism. But future historians, he continued, might well look at these various movements as being part of a new reformation that took place in the twentieth century, from which has emerged "a third major type and branch of Christendom, alongside of and not incommensurable with Roman and Orthodox Catholicism and historic Protestantism, *a principal permanent variant of Christianity*."[3]

---

1. Gerald T. Sheppard, "Pentecostalism and the Hermeneutics of Dispensationalism: Anatomy of an Uneasy Relationship," *Pneuma: The Journal of the Society for Pentecostal Studies* 6, no. 2 (1984): 5–34. Donald Dayton, *Theological Roots of Pentecostalism* (Peabody, MA: Hendrickson, 1987), demonstrates persuasively the alternative theological formation that Holiness and Pentecostal movements offered to fundamentalism in North America. For a sustained exploration of Pentecostal identity that self-consciously resists its reduction to Protestant evangelicalism, see Steven J. Land, *Pentecostal Spirituality: A Passion for the Kingdom* (Sheffield, UK: Sheffield University Press, 1993).

2. See Dale T. Irvin, "Pentecostal Historiography and Global Christianity: Rethinking the Question of Origins," *Pneuma* 27, no. 1 (Spring 2005): 35–50.

3. Henry P. Van Dusen, "The Challenge of the 'Sects,'" *Christianity and Crisis* 18, no. 13 (July 21, 1958): 106, emphasis added. It is significant to note in this regard that while Van Dusen regarded "evangelicals" during the 1950s as being "sectarian," a large number of evangelicals at

In other words, while their historical roots might lie (at least in part) in the sixteenth-century Reformation, Pentecostals, along with others, could not be fitted into the existing types or branches of world Christianity and might instead constitute a principal variant.

Pentecostalism is indeed proving to be a variant stream of world Christianity. What provides its identity in categorical terms is not so much a common historical origin as a common set of practices and commitments, including an openness to "signs and wonders" and an experience of immediacy of presence of the Spirit that is baptismal in nature. The Azusa Street revival in Los Angeles in the first decade of the twentieth century is often cited in Pentecostal historiography as the origins of the global movement. Unquestionably, Azusa Street was a common point of historical convergence and emergence, but a growing body of Pentecostal scholarship recognizes that Pentecostalism cannot be reduced to its Azusa Street origins. Indeed Pentecostal leaders and practitioners have often implicitly resisted such reduction (without explicitly acknowledging that this is what they are doing) by claiming direct inspiration for their particular teachings and practices and even refusing to acknowledge any historical influences upon their own particular efforts.[4]

Historically one can point to a number of global streams of revivalism that flowed into Azusa Street, and these in turn were forged into a more or less coherent (if it was soon to prove unstable) movement and ethos, which in turn were broadcast throughout the world. Nevertheless, given the diversification of the Pentecostal movement globally, both in its initial growth throughout the world and in its successive waves of new formations (neo-Pentecostals, charismatics, and more), it makes sense to follow Ronald N. Bueno, among others, in speaking of "Pentecostalisms" rather than of one global Pentecostal movement today.[5]

According to Jean-Pierre Bastián, although Pentecostalism is usually considered to have originated in the early twentieth century in the United States,

---

the beginning of the twenty-first century regard themselves as representing the historical Protestant mainstream tradition. The question of who exactly is an evangelical, and especially what role the Holiness movement does or does not play in defining evangelicalism today, is addressed elsewhere in this volume. For our purposes, it is important simply to note that the branch Van Dusen was describing in 1958 is now generally referred to as "Pentecostal."

4. See Allan Anderson, *An Introduction to Pentecostalism* (Cambridge: Cambridge University Press, 2004), and Cecil M. Robeck Jr., "Pentecostal Origins from a Global Perspective," in *All Together in One Place: Theological Paper from the Brighton Conference on World Evangelization*, ed. Harold D. Hunter and Peter D. Hocken (Sheffield, UK: Sheffield Academic Press, 1993), 166–80. We await the long-expected definitive history of the Azusa Street revival from Professor Robeck, which promises to help clarify the relationship of Azusa Street to global Pentecostal origins.

5. Ronald N. Bueno, "Listening to the Margins: Re-historicizing Pentecostal Experiences and Identities," in *The Globalization of Pentecostalism: A Religion Made to Travel*, ed. Murray W. Dempster, Byron D. Klaus, and Douglas Petersen (Oxford: Regnum, 1999), 269.

globally it is not homogenous but variegated. As it has expanded around the world, he points out, it has transformed into indigenous movements whose ties become disconnected from their place of origin, and it has even come to contain elements that are incompatible with U.S. Protestantism. It undergoes a process of hybridity that juxtaposes diverse elements of belief, practice, and tradition. Pentecostalism is especially flexible in its integration of indigenous religious practices that reappropriate the stories of the book of Acts. In Latin America, he argues, it is a popular religion with Catholic and millennial Protestant streams flowing through it.[6]

By all accounts Pentecostalism is a rapidly indigenizing and highly contextualizing faith. Its membership is drawn from all social classes, upper class, middle class, and poor.[7] Those church leaders with whom we met in San Miguel readily called themselves *evangélico*, but what they meant by that was something much different from what North Americans intend by calling themselves "evangelicals." From the Latin American Pentecostal perspective, North American evangelicals continue to be informed by colonial sensibilities that assume theology is always imported from the Global North. For too many North American evangelicals, Latin America is a "mission" land, providing raw materials in the form of bodies to be delivered and saved but not finished goods like church identities and orthodox theological systems to be consumed. The nomenclature of *evangélico* has long been available to Latin American religious identity, and in places like Guatemala it is now becoming the dominant Latin Christian form. But it is not simply an extension of the North American experience. Something else is going on in the Latin American context.

Several of the pastors in San Miguel that evening in 2001 were from La Iglesia de los Apóstoles y Profetas (The Church of the Apostles and Prophets), a Pentecostal fellowship that was founded in El Salvador during the first decade of the twentieth century. The pastors knew of the efforts of a North American missionary that were part of their initial formation. They had no consciousness of being a North American transplant, however, and they certainly did not see their origins as being on Azusa Street in Los Angeles, USA. As far as they were concerned, their origins and history were located in Latin America

---

6. Jean-Pierre Bastian, "Pentecostalismos latinoamericanos: Lógicas de mercado y transnacionalización religiosa," in *Globalización y diversidad religiosa en Colombia*, ed. Ana María Bidegain Greising and Juan Diego Demera Vargas (Bogotá: Universidad Nacional de Colombia, 2005).

7. This is a particularly important point to make. A persistent myth in the scholarship of Pentecostalism has reduced it to a movement of the poor. The classical statement of this in North American Pentecostal studies is Robert Mapes Anderson, *Vision of the Disinherited: The Making of American Pentecostalism* (New York: Oxford University Press, 1979). Grant Wacker, in *Heaven Below: Early Pentecostals and American Culture* (Cambridge, MA: Harvard University Press, 2001), decisively refutes this notion by examining the actual class location of early Pentecostals, who, according to Wacker, match the class distribution of the general culture.

and could be read all the way back to the time of the *conquistadores*. Taking that as a guide to interpretation, we turn to the matter of Pentecostals and empire.

Pentecostalism and Empire

In its global historical formations, Pentecostalism manifests a number of elements that also characterize the new global "Empire" that Michael Hardt and Antonio Negri examine in their book by that same name. One of the identifying features of Pentecostalism in all of its global forms is a heightened experience and awareness of the divine presence of the Holy Spirit within one's own life, one's own self. The immanence of the Spirit, whether it is described as a distinctive baptism or simply a filling, results in a diffusion of power and authority throughout the Pentecostal body, both individual and collective, that coincides with the diffusion of power and authority throughout the body that empire achieves. Pentecostalism is a religion intensely and intently inscribed upon the body.[8] The power to which its adherents attest is a particular form of biopower that is often called *charisma*. Pentecostalism in all of its diverse manifestations is performative in character. It is not so much what one believes, or what one attests to, as what one has experienced, what one can testify to, that is important for Pentecostal identity. Like empire, Pentecostalism challenges older notions of authority and power in a radical way.

Also like empire, which is closely related to the economics of hyper-capitalism and globalization, Pentecostalism privileges innovation. In the latter's case, this is a result of its openness to new revelations of the Spirit. Like globalization and empire, Pentecostalism is capable of engaging in creative appropriation of a variety of signs and practices. Like empire, it relishes the paradoxes of plurality and multiplicity. By all accounts it would appear that Pentecostals should be at home within the new empire, at least as Hardt and Negri describe it. Pentecostals might even seem to be candidates for Hardt and Negri's concept of "the multitude," whose creative forces both sustain empire and are simultaneously capable of constructing an alternative organization of global flows and exchanges from within it.[9]

Here is where appearances deceive, not because the theory of empire, the multitude, or Pentecostalism is inherently flawed but because in their analysis and subsequent prescription for change Hardt and Negri fall back upon the very binary logic of the modern European Enlightenment that they so thoroughly criticize. Hardt and Negri theorize *not* from within the global horizons of

---

8. See Leslie D. Callahan, "Fleshly Manifestations: Charles Fox Parham's Quest for the Sanctified Body," PhD diss., Princeton University, 2002.

9. Michael Hardt and Antonio Negri, *Empire* (Cambridge, MA: Harvard University Press, 2000), xv.

empire but from within the historical experience of Western European civilization, specifically as it was formed in its modern period. The history that they write for empire is entirely that of Europe, of the West. They criticize the dominant "center-periphery" mode of analysis that divides the modern world into what Stuart Hall has called "the West and the Rest,"[10] arguing that the new paradigm is multicentered and pluralistic and has power diffused (however unevenly) throughout its terrain.[11] Postcolonial theory is called into account in particular for not having sufficiently moved beyond the binary mode of analysis, its utility questioned in light of the new pluralistic paradigm of power that they discern to be at work in empire.[12] Yet when they come to construct their own alternative world, one finds the only useful history of empire to be that which emanates from the West. They subtly reassert empire as a Western (as opposed to truly global) mode of imperialism by attending to its historical characteristics only as they appeared on European intellectual terrain. In doing so, they fall back into the binary opposition that they seek to move beyond precisely by privileging the West and silencing the Rest. One searches in vain through their pages for the names of colonized subjects, for historical remembrances from Asia, Africa, or Latin America, for a genealogy that is not European and white and male. Hence in the end, when we reach the point of jubilant celebration of the multitude in their work, we find that the historical identity, the constituting condition of the multitude, is only European, white, and male.

And it is at this point that we find ourselves asking once again, where are the Pentecostals? Pentecostalism refuses to be bound within this new regime of truth, which it also perceives to be a regime of death (as in "those cold, dead churches"). Infused with a radical eschatological orientation that can truly perceive a new paradigm to be at hand, Pentecostals in all of their global diversities, with varying degrees of intensity, criticize the modern for its secularism, materialism, reductionism, and lack of sanctifying imagination even as they employ the modern to their own ends.[13] Across the world, one often hears Pentecostals claiming to have a "passion for the multitude." Their intention, however, is not to leave the multitude without an identity, or with an identity imported from another part of the world. Utilizing the technologies of modernity, Pentecostalism tends to embrace the multitude precisely in order to provide participants with new identities and a sense of their own subjecthood. Pentecostalism fosters an experience of the Spirit that

10. Stuart Hall, *The West and the Rest: White Predators, Black Slavers, and the African Elite* (New York: Random House, 1975).

11. *Empire*, 334.

12. Ibid., 137–46.

13. This is the main point of Wacker (in *Heaven Below*), who explores the ambiguities of early North American Pentecostalism through the twin categories of "primitivism" and "pragmatism."

gives the people an authentic historical project in their own place. For some this is expressed through various forms of economic development and self-help (one mode being the popular and growing "prosperity teaching"). For others it is a more collective sense of community identity that comes about. Whatever the form, members of the Pentecostal multitude take on concrete histories and identities that are not merely derivative from the North or from the Eurocentic West. In short, the multitude become disciples—historical agents engaged in historical projects that lead to new forms of community in their multitudinous splendor.

Out of the Grips of the Empire: The Way the Spirit Blows

Even a multicentric model of empire knows of centers and margins. For the person at the margins, the effects of empire are the opposite of what it claims to do. Empire seeks to be centripetal in nature. At the margins, however, its effects are centrifugal. At the margins, even those elements that originated from within a seemingly homogenous whole show themselves to be dissimilar, their particularity ever more distinguishable and colorful. Empire strives for assimilation and uniformity. Its effects, however, are cacophonous.

Religion is one of the tools that empire seeks to utilize. But religion can also create the catalyzing medium for reinterpretation of originary points, becoming instead a process of authentication of the heterogeneous elements found in the whole. One can see the centrifugal effect of empire in religion among the marginalized in Latin American Pentecostalism, particularly through the eyes of a Latin American who stands at the margins of the empire, that is, the indigenous person.[14] From this perspective, one can see negotiation taking place among Pentecostals between imperialistic forces and indigenous roots, leading in subtle ways to both sociopolitical and religious subversion.

Jon Sobrino challenges empire by calling us to a "liberation of reason" that opens our minds to respond with favor and mercy on behalf of the crucified

14. For other studies on Pentecostalism in Latin America, see Walter J. Hollenweger, *The Pentecostals* (Minneapolis: Augsburg, 1972); Emilio Willems, *Followers of the New Faith: Culture, Change, and the Rise of Protestantism in Brazil and Chile* (Nashville: Vanderbilt University Press, 1967); Jean-Pierre Bastian, *Historia del protestantism en América Latina* (Mexico: CUPSA, 1990); David Martin, *Tongues of Fire* (Oxford: Blackwell, 1990); Kenneth Scott Latourette, *Desafío a los protestantes* (Buenos Aires, Argentina: La Aurora, 1957); Christian Lalive d'Espinay, *Heaven of the Masses: A Study of the Pentecostal Movement in Chile* (London: Lutterworth, 1969); Douglas Peterson, *Not by Might nor by Power* (Oxford: Regnum, 1996); David Stoll, *Is Latin America Turning Protestant?* (Berkeley: University of California Press, 1990); and Barbara Boudewijnse, André Droogers, Frans Kamsteeg, eds., *Algo más que opio: Una lectura antropológica del pentecostalismo latinoamericano y caribeño* (San José, Costa Rica: Departamento Ecuménico de Investigaciones, 1991).

peoples.[15] The liberation of reason allows for that which is truly human to be revealed. "It is the awakening to the reality of an oppressed and subjugated world, a world whose liberation is the basic task of every human being so that in this way human beings may finally come to be human."[16] The call is for a more "humane civilization" in which we place ourselves at the side of the victims.[17] To come by the side of the victims is the end to which this particular perspective beckons.

This is an end that is particularly relevant given the history of violence, repression, and torture that has been endemic to Latin America over the past century. Works such as *Las venas abiertas de América Latina* (*The Open Veins of Latin America*) by Eduardo Galeano have told the story well.[18] In El Salvador from 1932 to 1944, General Maximiliano Hernández Martínez led a regime of terror with U.S. support. Hernández Martínez ordered the massacre of thirty thousand Pipil Indians from the Izalco region. The event, called La Matanza, came after the indigenous sought help from the Communist Party against the abuses of their landlords. In 1969, peaceful demonstrations protesting the lack of employment and farming lands were once again quelled by death squads. Twice in the 1970s, the peasants were near to winning elections, and twice their efforts were quashed by the oligarchy ruling El Salvador. Right-wing death squads terrorized the people, resulting in the deaths, rapes, abductions, and disappearances of thousands of Salvadorians. Fearing communism, the U.S. government supported the oligarchy by sending $3.7 billion in military aid, the largest amount ever received by a Latin American country at the time. The result was a further increase in the death toll among Salvadorian peasants.[19]

In neighboring Guatemala in the early 1980s, President Efraín Ríos Montt, a member of a neo-Pentecostal church, sponsored a right-wing war of counterinsurgency that some regard as genocidal.[20] During that time, numerous studies focused on the *evangélico* involvement with the CIA, the acceptance of U.S. imperialism, and the escapism that this neo-Pentecostal president seemed to represent.[21] Yet subsequent research has shown that Guatemalan Pentecostalism

15. Jon Sobrino, SJ, "Awakening from the Sleep of Inhumanity," trans. Dimas Planas, *Christian Century*, April 3, 1991, 364.

16. Ibid.

17. Ibid., 368.

18. Eduardo Galeano, *Las venas abiertas de América Latina*, rev. ed. (México, DF: Siglo XXI Editores, 1980).

19. Juan González, *Harvest of Empire: A History of Latinos in America* (New York: Penguin, 2000), 133–35.

20. For a more detailed study of the life of Efraín Ríos Montt, see Virginia Garrard-Burnett, *A History of Protestantism in Guatemala* (Austin: University of Texas Press, 1999), 138–61.

21. For a brief analysis on the effects of Ríos Montt, see Abigail E. Adams, "Making One Our Word: Protestant Q'eqchi' Mayas in Highland Guatemala, in *Holy Saints and Fiery Preachers: The Anthropology of Protestantism in Mexico and Central America*, ed. James W. Dow and Alan R. Sandstrom (Westport, CT: Praeger, 2001), 207.

was more complex than this.[22] Virginia Garrard-Burnett observes that the regime of Ríos Montt was not bound by any religious delineation. Catholics and Protestants alike who were suspected of allying with the guerrillas were executed. In 1982, "thirteen members of a Quanjobal Pentecostal congregation in Xalbal, Ixcán, were burned by the army in their church."[23] Linda Green, in a study done among Kakquikel Mayan widows in Be'cal, describes Pentecostalism as a "religion of survival."[24] In the 1980s, when men in Be'cal were murdered by firing squads before the eyes of their wives and children, *evangélicos* and Pentecostals in particular offered these families a place of refuge from suffering and a space of personal control. Among these widows, in light of their struggle for survival, affiliation lines became blurry. Pentecostalism offered them a safe and joyful atmosphere where they could gain a sense of community and trust and where people lent a hand, especially in the form of male labor, so they could build their homes and plant and harvest their corn. All the while their children were still being blessed soon after birth through Catholic baptism, and the sick among them were still being seen by Mayan priests.

The Guatemalan people, particularly the indigenous, for most of the second half of the twentieth century endured extreme levels of violence and repression.[25] Repression takes many forms and can exist consciously or unconsciously. One of the forms it takes is our refusal to believe that these violent events even occurred and our denial of full presence to the victims of empire. The violence did indeed occur, but not without its victims' seeking to negotiate their way to presence. In order to account for the Latin American experience, including the experience of spiritual movements such as Pentecostalism, we must look into the negotiating practices undertaken with their violent neighbor to the north to see how they have sought to dethrone foreign forms of domination through such presence.

Subjugated Mimicry

Pentecostalism in Latin America is often interpreted through theological, social, and political definitions unsuitable for developing the image of the

22. See David Stoll, *Between Two Armies* (New York: Columbia University Press, 1993); Garrard-Burnett, *History of Protestantism in Guatemala*; Timothy Evans, *Percentage of Non-Catholics in a Representative Sample of the Guatemalan Population*, paper presented to the Latin American Studies Association, Crystal City, VA, April 1991.

23. Garrard-Burnett, *History of Protestantism in Guatemala*, 149.

24. Linda Green, "Shifting Affiliations: Mayan Widows and *Evangélicos* in Guatemala," in *Rethinking Protestantism in Latin America*, ed. Virginia Garrard-Burnett and David Stoll (Philadelphia: Temple University Press, 1993).

25. See, among other sources, Luis Cardoza y Aragón, *La revolución guatemalteca* (Antigua, Guatemala: Ediciones del Pensativo, 2004); and Gonzalo Sichar Moreno, *Masacres en Guatemala: Los gritos de un pueblo entero* (Guatemala: Grupo de Apoyo Mutuo, 2000).

marginalized with greater accuracy. In order for events to be understood, according to the reigning systems of truth, they must be compared to external parameters. The result can be a caricature of the marginalized person. More often than not, the "standard" is nothing but a dark glass that cannot fully represent what is really there. The misunderstanding, however, is not simply a malfunction on the part of the ones seeking information. The one who knows, the marginalized, reveals only what the seekers want to see. Who do the seekers see? The seekers see themselves as through a mirror and refuse the possibility of seeing the real person hiding behind the mirror.

The act of seeing as perceiving "the same but not quite" is what Homi K. Bhabha calls mimicry.[26] Mimicry is a "partial vision" of the one who excludes the other. The other, the one being marginalized, displays his or her presence in part as a metonymy, as a resemblance of the one who excludes. Mimicry "is a form of colonial discourse that is uttered *inter dicta*: a discourse at the crossroads of what is known and permissible and that which though known must be kept concealed; a discourse uttered between the lines and as such both against the rules and within them."[27]

Mimicry is a pretend game of gestures that provides the appearance of totality. Mimicry, however, does not necessarily result in the absorption of the self of the marginalized. In mimicry, there is an element of trickery or mockery that connotes subversion. There is also buried within it the cry of the repressed and oppressed. Its subversion is in the underlying trickery and mockery invisible to the eye of the forces of exclusion.[28] The marginalized person appears to be weak, a fool who is in need of constant learning and training. Even his or her speech comes forth broken, raw, and incomprehensible. In the end, however, the marginalized person is able to seize her or his rightful place as an autonomous self, relegating its source of exclusion to a place of insignificance.

In the Popol Vuh,[29] the sacred book of the ancient Mayas-Quiché, there are two characters who exemplify mimicry in an indigenous context, Huhahpú and Xbalanqué. Huhahpú and Xbalanqué are skilled flute players, singers, painters, and sculptors who become wise as a result of a life of pain, suffering, and torment. In the story that develops in book 2, these two young men are able to overcome their strongest enemies through trickery. They appear as two old men, of poor appearance and dressed in old rags. Performing dances

26. See Homi K. Bhabha, *The Location of Culture* (London: Routledge, 1994), 485–92.
27. Ibid., 89.
28. Marion Grau, drawing from the principles of Bahba on mimicry, states, "Tricksters are performers of mimicry and incarnate ambivalence." See "Divine Commerce; A Postcolonial Christology for Times of Neocolonial Empire," in *Postcolonial Theologies: Divinity and Empire*, ed. Catherine Keller, Michael Nausner, and Mayra Rivera (St. Louis: Chalice, 2004).
29. *Popol Vuh: The Scared Book of Mayas-Quiché*, trans. David B. Castledine (Col. Anzures, Mexico: Monclem Ediciones, 2001).

of the *puhuy*, the *cux*, the *iboy*, the *xtzul*, and *chitic* (names of animals), they undertake wondrous acts, like sacrificing each other and then bringing each other back to life.

The news of their dances and acts reaches the ears of Kings Hun-Camé and Vokub-Camé, longtime enemies of both them and their father. They summon Huhahpú and Xabalanqué and ask the two young men to perform before them. The kings asked them to kill a dog and then resuscitate it, to burn their house and then restore it to its original state, to kill a man and then bring him back to life, and for each young man to kill the other and then revive him. Each act is performed as requested by the kings. The hearts of Hun-Camé and Vokub-Camé, the two kings, are now filled with "an excess of desire and curiosity,"[30] and they ask to be sacrificed themselves and then be resurrected by the two young men. The two young men seize the two kings and sacrifice them, but do not bring them back to life. At the sight of such victory, everyone flees from before them. This is how the lords of Xibalbá are defeated.

The indigenous people became experts at mimicking the forces of exclusion, as exemplified in the story of Huhahpú and Xabalanqué, in order that they might successfully negotiate their identity on their own terms. The revival of the indigenous identity, called *indianismo*, has allowed for a process of negotiation that has begun to subvert five hundred years of the Spanish conquest in Latin America. Currently, Latin American countries like Venezuela have renamed October 12 from the Día de la Hispanidad (Day of Hispanicity) to Día de la Resistencia Indígena (Day of Indigenous Resistance), recognizing the absurdity of a celebration that lauded the Spanish invasion and the defeat and massacre of the indigenous people of the Americas.

The place of negotiation of excluding forces and the self is a space between realities, where opposites meet.[31] Negotiation seeks not to present indigenous identity as an expression of absolute differentiation, a people untouched by others through time; rather, it presents it as a place of struggle. This place of struggle rearticulates the past, bearing a hybrid reality of polarity. This place of negotiation is what allows us to explain how the indigenous self could have survived five hundred years of resistance against the Spanish conquest, the Christian Inquisition, landlessness, poverty, massacres, and torture.

Pentecostalism in Almolonga

Almolonga of Quetzaltenango is a small, picturesque town several hours by car north and west of Guatemala City. Nestled in a valley, Almolonga's narrow streets are lined with small houses and stores. The steep slopes of the surrounding mountains are dotted with homes set amidst cultivated plots of

30. Ibid., 81.
31. See Bhabha, "The Commitment to Theory," in *Location of Culture*, 19–39.

hillside. Covered by a mass of fog and rain, the landscape is beautiful, a sight for any eye to contemplate. The inhabitants of the town are mostly indigenous people, and most own their own homes, businesses, and land. Farming is almost entirely done by manual labor on small patches of land that sit side by side, each one belonging to a particular family, each one devoted to a particular kind of produce. This "quilted" landscape of diverse pieces belonging to each and belonging to all speaks of hard work in harmony, of a community effort that seeks no competition against one another but cooperation, an example of life that is worth following.

Almolonga is known in charismatic and Pentecostal churches worldwide through the popular video series Transformations.[32] The story of Almolonga as told in Transformations is of a revival of a whole town that began decades ago with several *evangélico* communities coming together in unity through prayer. Soon the power of the Holy Spirit was felt moving through the community. The entire town joined together to destroy what they still describe as a "local idol" that had held them in its sway. People soon began praying for their crops in the field, and the result was a miraculous increase in the growth of their produce. Extraordinarily large carrots are still offered to visitors today as signs of this continuing spiritual renewal. Crime dropped in the town to the point of there being no need for an active police force. Outside gangs have been turned away. People are not afraid to leave their doors unlocked now, visitors are still told. Even the land continues to be more productive in this experience of realized spiritual community and communion.

There is now a large neo-Pentecostal church named Iglesia Bethania in Almolonga. The congregation is constructing what will be the largest building in the town, and one sees the influences of global evangelists such as Benny Hinn as well as national Guatemalan megachurch pastors such as Cash Luna within the church. At first glance the church seems to be without concern for the suffering and the pain of the nation's recent history, to be with no memory of the past and with no immediate hope for the future beyond the goals of immediate church-growth. How does a neo-Pentecostal church like Iglesia Bethania provide an answer to the massacres that took place for nearly forty years? The key appears to be in their mimicry and negotiation. They mimic the grandeur of televangelism and megachurchism that is part of the hyper-capitalistic development of "globalization." They negotiate by focusing on their land, their community, and their significance in relation to the world, defying modernity and empire alike in the same breath.

To grasp this, one needs to see that the story of a church like Iglesia Bethania is older than it seems and that its roots are deep in the Mayan-Quiché people of Almolonga. The identity of the indigenous people is connected to their land.

32. The Transformations series is produced by George Otis Jr. and marketed by the Sentinel Group in Lynwood, WA.

The Mayans-Quiché, for example, understood creation to have been by means of ears of yellow corn. The blood of humanity was the corn that had entered women and men.[33] Creator and Maker debated and consulted one another as in a tribal council, deciding to create four men and four women, a small group of families that could be called a community.[34] Caha Paluma, Chomiha, Tzununiha, and Cakixaha were the women, who in turn were the origin of all people after them. The separation of languages happened in Tulan, among the Mayans, and not in Babel, according to their ancient wisdom.[35]

The concept of cultivated land as a sign of life has remained in the town of Almolonga. The Mayan villagers tell visitors still that it is the Holy Spirit who has transformed their agriculture and community these last twenty years. The common story is that the *evangélico* Christians in town began to seek God more fervently. They began to devote their land to God by asking the Holy Spirit to guide them in what types of seeds to plant. The Holy Spirit imparted the wisdom needed for cultivating the land. The Holy Spirit blesses the town's agriculture.

The story is not without basis. One can feel a certain communal energy in Almolonga that starts very early in the mornings. The sight of people working together for the good of everyone, first at the packing and distribution center and later at the market near the Catholic church in town, is also a radical negotiation. Some twenty-five trucks containing extraordinarily robust and healthy produce go out from this small town each day to markets in Guatemala City and elsewhere. Meanwhile the stalls that stand side by side are filled with the same fresh produce from their land, as each one sells crops to their neighbors and to villagers from nearby towns. Negotiating with the outside world, they also find community at home.

The small town of Almolonga has become the center of the world, one hears in its streets. There is a consciousness that the whole world now knows of the town's revival and is coming to study the town's spiritual form of agriculture. This sense that history began, and began again, here, in this location, in this center, causes a seismic shift in the consciousness of empire. One cannot simply tell the story of Europe and its peoples to understand this new Pentecostal body and the land, the people, among which it grows. One must tell the story from a new location.

And it is here that the question returns, where were the Pentecostals? For the story that still needs to be told is that of the massacres and terror, and not just revival and renewal. Arguably the violence in Guatemala, unlike that in some other countries in Central and South America, was uneven. Almolonga for the most part was spared the violence associated with leftist guerrillas

---

33. See *Popol Vuh* 3.1.
34. Ibid., chap. 2.
35. Ibid., chap. 3.

and right-wing death squads. Nevertheless the violence was there, as a threat if not directly as an experience, if not immediately in Almolonga certainly among the indigenous peoples who are part of the larger Guatemalan reality. The challenge confronting Pentecostals and neo-Pentecostals in Almolonga, in Guatemala and El Salvador, throughout Latin America, and everywhere on the margins of the empire is to answer this question: where, in the time of suffering and violence, were the Pentecostals?

Conclusion

Latin American countries have faced civil wars, the rule of oligarchies, and subjugation to the United States. It has been precisely during times of political and economical turbulence that Pentecostalism has grown most rapidly. Pentecostalism has grown among dislocated people who have suffered political and religious abandonment and have sustained severe socioeconomic crises. The ruling classes have embraced the modern national state formations and adopted the economic policies of global capitalism, or empire. The best lands were long ago appropriated from the poor by foreign corporations and wealthy families for the cultivation of goods that would satisfy the European and North American palate. Lands that had been owned for generations by the common people were taken, at times by force, over the last century to be exploited or even left uncultivated. Millions of *campesinos* or poor villagers were left to the mercy of landholders for the rental of, and low-wage work on, what once was their land, laboring under conditions that could almost be described as slavery. Many of them were indigenous people. Pentecostals are among them, bringing a message, an experience, and an ethos that resonates with the demoralized poor.

While Pentecostals are not exclusively poor, the poor are increasingly to be found in Pentecostal churches. The impact of Pentecostalism in society is internal and basic, an answer to human need in practical terms. Its numerical growth among the poor can mean that society at large has the potential for becoming a place where justice and goodness can prevail. The hope is that by amplifying their understanding of personal holiness into a "new secular holiness," they can become members who responsibly and creatively participate in the affairs of society.[36]

The Pentecostal identity, however, is primarily religious rather than sociopolitical in character. Pentecostals' religious experience is a personal one that is shared in community, a direct encounter with God through the outpouring of the Holy Spirit, which paradoxically most often occurs through the mediation of a pastor or evangelist. Juan Sepúlveda asserts that the emphasis on the

---

36. Juan Sepúlveda, "Future Perspectives for Latin American Pentecostalism," *International Review of Mission* 87, no. 345 (1988): 194.

work of the Holy Spirit affirms "cultural mediations other than [the] Western rational and logo-centric culture" of the Christian faith.[37] In Latin America the Pentecostal religious emphasis can be seen as stemming from a non-Western understanding of the Holy Spirit and spirits in the world.

Pentecostals perceive in the world the Spirit and spirits. Exorcisms, spiritual warfare, and healing are at the same level of their fight against Satan as alcoholism, drug addiction, prostitution, family disintegration, depression, anguish, and stress. Any social transformation for Pentecostals starts with them on their knees in fasting and prayer, with worship and even with tithing. Combating the evil forces that cripple the material world starts with spiritual victory through otherworldly weapons that are powerful enough to demolish their enemies, physical and spiritual alike.[38]

The other side of this engagement with spiritual warfare and the mixing of spiritual and material worlds in Pentecostalism are found in the growing attraction of what is called the "prosperity teaching."[39] The basic message of prosperity teaching is being broadcast from pulpits and through the electronic media by Pentecostal and charismatic preachers and evangelists across the globe. Essentially the doctrine represents the creative cross-fertilization of the classical Puritan doctrine that wealth and prosperity are "signs of election" with the Pentecostal doctrine of "Spirit-filled signs and wonders." Too often the prosperity teaching degenerates into little more than an apology for hyper-capitalism or even enters into collusion with empire's social philosophy that supports the economic agenda of globalization. But beyond this, in its emphasis on both material well-being and physical health and healing, the prosperity gospel points toward utopian hopes and possibilities that are realized in the Spirit beyond the suffering and violence that are effected by empire.

The answer to the question "Where were the Pentecostals?" might well be "In the Spirit." The utopian possibilities that they engender are not necessarily grounded in the utopian vision of empire, the modern West, or its multitudes. Pentecostals might indeed be able to escape the closure of empire upon itself, and the immanence that it proclaims regarding the multitude, through a transcendence that is nevertheless grounded in and inscribed upon the body. Their practices of mimicry make it difficult at times to tell Pentecostals from evangelicals, or Pentecostals from successful entrepreneurs. The history of Pentecostalism for this reason cannot be reduced to its modern narrative, as if it all began on Azusa Street in 1906. The story of Almolonga, which appears

37. Ibid., 191.
38. Luis A. Várguez Pasos, "La guerra espiritual en tres grupos religiosos de Yucatán, México: Neopentecostales, católicos y la Iglesia Makadesh," *Confesionalidad y Política*, (Bogotá: Universidad Nacional de Colombia, 2002), 273–94.
39. For a fuller analysis of the prosperity gospel and its spread across the world, see Steve Brouwer, Paul Gifford, and Susan D. Rose, *Exporting the American Gospel: Global Christian Fundamentalism* (New York: Routledge, 1996).

in some instances to be attaining almost mythical status in Pentecostal and neo-Pentecostal circles, points beyond its mythical origins in modernity to the mythical origins of first stories, first creations, in religion and culture.[40] The story of the suffering people serves to cut through much of the superficial analysis of Pentecostal and neo-Pentecostal churches and megachurches being offered by supporters and critics alike to point toward a prosperity that overcomes suffering. The critical issue that Pentecostals must still address more clearly, however, remains with this last concern. When it comes to the memory of violence and terror, where were and where are the Pentecostals?

40. See Charles H. Long, *Significations: Signs, Symbols, and Images in the Interpretation of Religion* (Philadelphia: Fortress, 1986), 166.

14

Intermezzo

*A Discussion between Donald W. Dayton
and Christian T. Collins Winn
about Empire and Evangelicals*

Christian Collins Winn (CCW): Don, you have been working on issues related to evangelical historiography, theology, social ethics, and identity for almost forty years. Has your involvement in the current discussion of "evangelicals and empire" been illuminating in any new ways?

Donald W. Dayton (DWD): Working on the theme of "evangelicals and empire" has been, in the words of Yogi Berra, déjà vu all over again!

CCW: In what way?

DWD: Conversations in this current project have constantly drawn me back to the dialogues in the late 1960s and early 1970s, especially those around the early days of the founding of *Sojourners* (the magazine was significantly called then *The Post-American*, because it was born in the protest against the Vietnam War and the image of the United States as the self-appointed "policeman of the world"). These debates also centered on identity and social ethics—was *Sojourners* "evangelical," "postevangelical," or something else? A high point in these discussions took place after the publication of Richard Quebedeaux's *The Young Evangelicals* (1974), which caused Carl F. H. Henry to ponder in *Christianity Today* on the "revolt on the evangelical frontiers." I argued vigorously in response that *Sojourners* was minimally "postevangelical" and maximally something new—and that its importance lay precisely in that fact.

The creative sources of the mix that was *Sojourners* (I was the first book editor) included especially Mennonite theologian John Howard Yoder, who did not think of himself as an "evangelical"; gay Barthian Episcopalian lawyer William Stringfellow; the charismatic communal movements left over from the 1960s and the Jesus Movement (the "Fisher Folk," etc.); Catholic Daniel Berrigan and the Center for Creative Nonviolence; the "new left" and the student movements of the 1960s; as well as more typical "evangelicals" like Bob Webber (already on the "Canterbury Trail") and Clark Pinnock (then dabbling in the charismatic movement in anticipation of his later fascination with the "Toronto blessing"). This is hardly an "evangelical" mix (self-identified "evangelicals" were only a part and perhaps a minority), and I don't understand how *Sojourners* can be intelligibly called "evangelical" or Jim Wallis an "evangelical minister"—as some would be inclined to do in this project.

CCW: What was it that led you to argue in the 1970s that *Sojourners* should not be seen as evangelical?

DWD: I was at the time deeply disenchanted with the label *evangelical* and was turning back to my own tradition and reappropriating the label *Holiness* to find better models of social engagement. As I look back over the four decades since, I discover that this disenchantment has, if anything, increased and deepened. I try to avoid the word whenever possible, not only because I find it distasteful but, more important, because the word has lost its usefulness and precision for any sort of careful analysis of the world we live in. Sometimes I am inclined to go so far as to argue that there is no such thing, at least in the terms of the "evangelical church" and the "evangelical movement" that seem to be presupposed by many of the contributors to this project.

It is perhaps ironic that my own disenchantment with the label has paralleled the discovery of the word by the public media. I well remember the late 1970s after *Time* magazine declared the "year of the evangelical." I began to get calls from New York media as diverse as the *Village Voice* and *Penthouse* magazine (not known for their mastery of the religious situation in the United States west of the Hudson River) wanting to know what such an animal might be. Nearly three decades later, the term now has become central to political analysis (though the media still confuse the term *evangelical* with *evangelist*). The problem now is that the word has been so thoroughly identified with a specific political ideology that it has lost any of its historical and theological richness. It is even harder today to use the word coherently than it was four decades ago when it began to fall apart for me.

I recently was interested to find that not only my distaste for the word but my suspicion that it has lost any coherent meaning was confirmed in one of George Barna's polls in late 2002. In a larger project he identified some 270 non-Christians and asked them to rank eleven professions and/or labels with a favorable or unfavorable response. At the top of the list were military officers, followed in order by ministers, "born again" Christians, Democrats, real estate agents, movie and TV performers, lawyers, Republicans, lesbians, evangelicals, and prostitutes. There are several noteworthy aspects of this list—not just that "evangelicals" outranked only "prostitutes." One is nervous about the rank of military officers and fascinated by the split between "born again Christians" and "evangelicals." But it is clear that the label *evangelical* has become "ideologized" and separated from its religious meaning. One must wonder if the word can be retrieved.

CCW: Popular misunderstanding aside, do you really find the term impossible to use in an intellectually or theologically coherent fashion?

DWD: I have long been intrigued with the intellectual problem of how one might "operationalize" the concept "evangelical" so that one might use it for statistical and sociological analysis. This is a very delicate matter. I remember some discussions among Mennonites, who discovered that if one "operationalizes" the label as *traditional* or *conservative* or *orthodox* (the synonyms that seem to be presupposed in the media today), one gets a positive correlation with racism, but if one "operationalizes" the concept as something like *devotionalism* (did you go to church this week, do you pray, do you read your Bible regularly?), one gets a negative correlation with racism. Which is "evangelical"? I'm inclined to think the latter and that whatever "evangelicalism" is, it ought not to be confused with "orthodoxy" or "conservatism." But here I suppose that I am conditioned by my own tradition of Wesleyanism. Relying on hints in the book of James (perhaps his favorite in contrast with Luther!), John Wesley often pointed out that "the Devil himself is orthodox but very far from true religion of the heart."

But I remember a similar problem in the 1980s, when the theological seminary accrediting association (ATS) spent huge amounts of money on a statistically grounded "readiness for ministry" project. The idea was to develop a questionnaire that would measure the expectations both of church families and of candidates for the ministry, so that advisers could say to seminarians something like "According to your results, you make a better Presbyterian than a Methodist, so you might want to consider switching denominations now before you get into trouble with your current denominational affiliation." After studies of the usual Roman Catholic, Lutheran, Methodist, Presbyterian, Episcopal, etc., clusters, they had a group of "nonmainstream" traditions left over that they put together and fed into the computer as "evangelical." The problem was that the group would not "compute"; that is, it did not have enough in common to give a univocal response that was at least as consistent as those of the major denominational groups. I take this as statistical evidence that there is no coherent category that can be labeled *evangelical*. The ATS did have better luck when they broke their data down into two groups, "evangelical A" and "evangelical B." One was more hard core and doctrinal with sharp edges, the other was softer, more experiential, and communal—again, differences not unlike the differences above between *orthodox* and *devotional*.

One has similar problems if one tries to think of what one might possibly mean by an "evangelical social ethic." We ran into this problem in the wake of the issuing of the Chicago Declaration of Evangelical Social Concern in the early 1970s and the founding of Evangelicals for Social Action. We had several annual meetings in which we pursued these questions. We soon discovered that a general commitment to the Bible did not give you a social ethic. One had to drop back into a particular theological tradition and its effort to articulate a particular reading of the Bible. We could find a "Reformed," Lutheran, or Anabaptist social ethic, but there was no "generic evangelical" social ethic. The category had to be broken down into a subcategory to get the mediating constructs on which one could build a social ethic. And these differences were more important than what held the larger category together, and the effort to build a common platform for "evangelicals for social action" failed—at least for many of us.

In the middle of these discussions I began to see new factors at work—like the market. I remember a trip to Calvin College and debates there in the 1970s. I was told that Calvin was "Reformed" and not "evangelical" (especially not that disgusting phenomenon called "Anglo American evangelicalism" with its prohibitions on smoking, drinking, movies, and card playing!). But I notice more recently that Calvin College, perhaps since the *New York Times* has called Wheaton College and Calvin College the Harvard and Yale of "evangelicalism," calls itself "evangelical" in its promotional material. Another interesting element on that trip was that I was told that Timothy Smith's 1950s Harvard dissertation published as *Revivalism and Social Reform* (1957) proved that "evangelicals" (this time apparently including Calvin College) had once supported "social reform." I couldn't resist noting that the very title used the term *revivalism* and was roughly equivalent to the "Anglo American evangelicalism" that had just been repudiated theologically. And I went on to note that the same movement that once denounced drinking and smoking also put a negative moral value on slavery, political despotism, and other issues that had been considered morally "adiaphorous" in the more classically "Reformed" traditions—and that one could not do substantial historical and theological work if one were going to use the label *evangelical* in such unreflective and undiscriminating ways. Again, the label does not refer to a single phenomenon.

CCW: Though you say that you do not think that the term *evangelical* is useful anymore for identifying a single coherent historical phenomenon or shared theological tradition, it does sound as though there may be some use for the term in your comments. I am thinking here of your references to "devotionalism" or what might be called "Pietism" or the "awakening movement" which was a trans-Atlantic phenomenon of the eighteenth and nineteenth centuries.

In many ways, the origin of this movement was rooted in a rebellion against the nominal Christianity of Protestant orthodoxy, which had become a useful tool to different political factions during the Thirty Years' War in Europe.

The Pietists were appalled that Christians felt justified to take up arms against other Christians simply because of creedal differences. They, especially figures like Nikolaus Zinzendorf, believed that theological discussion and conviction should be fueled by a shared center rather than concerns on the theological boundaries. This emphasis led to a different way of doing theology, which tended to be more interested in practical, biblical, ethical, and historical questions as opposed to the abstract, universal, and philosophical concerns of much Protestant orthodoxy. Concurrent with the concern with ethics and the focus on the historical was a rediscovery of the eschatological aspect of the Christian faith. Hope for the kingdom of God led many Pietists to engage with issues of social reform, take up ecumenical dialogue, and even pioneer the Protestant version of church missions, the latter sometimes with deleterious effects. Nonetheless, this engagement in hope for the transformation of the world put many of these figures on the progressive side of social movements, a fact that would seem important in regard to questions of empire.

As you have pointed out in other places, this movement and its American counterpart *can* properly be labeled "evangelical" both historically and theologically. If this history and theology were taken into account, could the term *evangelical* be recoverable and perhaps even useful for funding resistance to forms of empire?

DWD: If the term *evangelical* were to be recovered, I wholeheartedly agree that it could only be in the direction you have indicated. I had to rethink this issue when I took my first sabbatical and studied for a term at Tübingen in the 1980s. I quickly discovered that the counterparts to Sojourners (a group that edited *Unterwegs*) and "evangelicalism" had a completely different understanding of themselves from that of Americans. They looked to Pietism rather than to orthodoxy to find their roots and identity. While American theologians seemed to divide the world between "conservative" and "liberal" expressions, the German students spoke of *Gemeindetheologie* (church or community theology) and *Universitätstheologie* (academic theology), a distinction derived more from the Pietistic worldview. They could practice either, and their commitment to the category "pietism" led to serious debates about whether Kierkegaard and Schleiermacher (a "*Herrenhuter* of a higher order") were allies in their vision of Christian faith (a claim unthinkable in those circles of the United States that were reading Francis Schaeffer). They reported to me that they found incomprehensible the emerging American school of "evangelical historiography" that is now dominant. They were intrigued by the way that I was being driven back to the study of Pietism in my dissertation (published as *Theological Roots of Pentecostalism*, 1987) and helped me to understand that my book provided a more appropriate lineage of modern revivalism than did the emerging "evangelical historiography."

But even more important, my study in the German theological context enabled me to see that the German language distinguished among movements collapsed into one in English under the label *evangelical*. I learned to distinguish between *evangelisch*, the word that was used to describe the classical Protestant tradition in its struggle with late medieval Catholicism, and the modern word *evangelical*, which German had appropriated from English to describe the neo-evangelical postfundamentalist party that reads *Christianity Today* or Carl F. H. Henry and goes to Billy Graham evangelistic congresses in Berlin and Lausanne. I also learned that the "evangelical revival" of the eighteenth century yielded what was called in German *Theologie der Erweckungsbewegung* (or the "theology of the awakening movement") or perhaps just *Pietismus*, the stream with which my new acquaintances identified. I learned to distinguish E1 of the sixteenth century, grounded in Luther's struggle with Catholicism, from the E2 of the eighteenth century (articulated in opposition to "nominal Christianity" whether conservative or liberal, Roman Catholic or Protestant, or whatever), and more especially from the E3 in the twentieth century of postfundamentalist "neo-evangelicalism" (in opposition to modern liberalism). I learned that these are three different theological animals and that to use the same label in English is to invite an intellectual confusion that vitiates serious consideration of the issues.

CCW: You have mentioned that the dominant American "conservative-liberal paradigm" contributes to the diminishment of the usefulness of the word *evangelical*. Do you think rerooting the word in its Pietistic, Wesleyan, and Holiness history might help to transcend those categories?

DWD: Yes. My experience in Germany helped me to understand why the modern use of the word *evangelical* in English has come to be dominated by what I call the conservative-liberal paradigm in which the synonyms of *evangelical* are *orthodox, conservative, traditional*, etc., while the antonym is *liberal*. This derives from the constructed identity of the "neo-evangelicals," shaped by a particular understanding of the fundamentalist-modernist controversy; as refugees from fundamentalism, they decided to enter the theological and ecclesiastical arena as a form of "generic orthodoxy" in struggle against the perceived enemy of "liberalism." This conservative-liberal paradigm dominates, I am convinced, over 90 percent of the linguistic usages of *evangelical* that I read in both the popular media and scholarly academic work. The antonym is almost always *liberal*, and any other usages are suppressed and become completely vestigial. The problem is that I can't make this paradigm work in my historical and theological analysis of movements that call themselves "evangelical."

I have struggled over the years with the intellectual and historical problem of the "great reversal"—a central issue in my first book *Discovering an Evangelical*

Heritage (1976, originally articles in *The Post-American*, now *Sojourners*). "The great reversal" was a term of Timothy Smith used by David Moberg in a 1977 book by that name to describe the collapse of antebellum revivalistic reform movements into the individualized modern revivalism of Billy Graham and modern "neo-evangelicalism." The conservative-liberal paradigm gives one no help in analyzing this phenomenon; it begins to unravel, and I eventually had to give up the inherited paradigm and move to other categories of analysis in that book. Let me give an example.

I attended Houghton College (sometimes called the Wheaton of the East; both were originally founded by the denomination in which I was reared, the abolitionist Wesleyan Methodist Church; Houghton was founded to replace Wheaton after the Wesleyans lost control to separatist, perfectionist Congregationalists there). My father was later elected president of Houghton. During his presidency, we fell in conversation to discussing the pilgrimage of one of my college friends who had grown up in the Wesleyan Church but had eventually become an Episcopal priest (in this movement he was an early pilgrim on the "Canterbury Trail" that has since become so common, especially at Wheaton under the influence of Bob Webber and as a product of upward social mobility). My father lamented this movement and reflected, having only the conservative-liberal paradigm in which to think, that this poor fellow had had a proper "conservative" background in the Wesleyan Church but that he had now "gone liberal." My response was that my father did not understand his movement at all; my friend had actually "gone conservative" in that this move was a product of his growing appreciation for the classical creeds and liturgy of the Book of Common Prayer, which John Wesley had loved so much. My friend was departing from the "populist" radicalism of revivalism and was on a pilgrimage in a "conservative" direction toward more traditional forms of church life. This path of my friend is perhaps the most dominant trajectory of the young Wheaton graduates I meet. It is in many ways the natural result of the neo-evangelical decision to decide to sail under the flag of orthodoxy, but it is a phenomenon that fails utterly to be illumined by what I am calling the "conservative-liberal paradigm."

Let me give another example. When I was first learning to think about these things, I was also studying the history of the ordination of women and the rise of feminism. The "conservative-liberal paradigm" leads us to think of the ordination of women as a "liberal" agenda—one that will be advocated by the so-called liberal National Council of Churches and resisted by the so-called conservative National Association of Evangelicals. The historical reality is just the opposite. The churches of the NAE began to ordain women a century before and in much larger numbers than ever dreamt of by the churches of the NCC. Yet the "conservative-liberal paradigm" often prevents us from even noticing this fact, let alone pondering the ways in which it challenges the way we think within the "conservative-liberal paradigm." I have been in meetings where, when I refer to this fact, I am told that I am wrong, that what I am saying cannot possibly be true.

I fear that the "conservative-liberal paradigm" has the power to create realities after its own image. Again, let me illustrate with two churches born in Scandinavian Pietism, the Evangelical Free and the Evangelical Covenant Church. Originally the same movement, these churches separated in the United States in the 1880s. The Evangelical Free Church would be described probably by most thinking in the "conservative-liberal paradigm" as more conservative, even though from the beginning it ordained women (following founder Fredrik Franson's pamphlet *Prophesying Daughters*), while the Covenant Church was more traditionally Lutheran (i.e., more "liberal" in the "conservative-liberal paradigm") and did not ordain women. But in the twentieth century, the two churches switched sides on this issue. The Evangelical Free Church no longer ordains women for a variety of reasons (including sociological reasons and social evolution—as well as the fact that its twentieth-century growth was fueled by the absorption of many midwestern fundamentalist Bible churches that did not ordain women), but I am convinced that a central reason is that the conservative-liberal paradigm convinced them that to be properly "evangelical" they had to resist the practice. In this sense, the word *evangelical*, understood in the conservative-liberal paradigm, can actually become pernicious. It and the simplistic analysis of the inherited paradigm may create unfortunate social consequences.

CCW: So "evangelicals," at least the American pietistic, revivalistic version of the nineteenth century, were actually the progressives? How then did the conservative-liberal paradigm come to dominate not only popular but also scholarly discourse about evangelicalism and especially evangelical social ethics?

DWD: In regards to "evangelicalism," whatever that may be, the triumph of the conservative-liberal paradigm is based on a massive historical confusion. It assumes that it is drawing the understanding of the word *evangelical* from the fundamentalist-modernist controversy of the early twentieth century. In this I think it completely misrepresents that controversy. Even the fundamentalist-modernist controversy does not yield well to the conservative-liberal paradigm. That controversy was *essentially* a fight over eschatology; it was a fight over a new doctrine in the history of the church, dispensational premillennialism, the view that in our time is now popularized by the Left Behind series.

This is no new thesis but has been argued most forcefully by Ernest Sandeen in *The Roots of Fundamentalism* (1970). This book was largely rejected by the neo-evangelical historiography (of George Marsden and others) because it conflicted with the official version of "evangelicalism" as "orthodoxy"—though it continues to be well received by the continuing fundamentalist movement. As Marsden puts it in his history of Fuller Theological Seminary *Reforming Fundamentalism* (1987), dispensationalism was a barnacle on the hull of the good ship orthodoxy and the task of "neo-evangelicalism" was to scrape off the barnacles that had gathered during the fundamentalist era. But Sandeen argued that the phenomenon of fundamentalism itself was "dispensationalism"—or as he put it, "British millenarianism."

We are trained to understand fundamentalism as a conservative reaction to liberalism that centered on resistance to such themes as the rise of biblical criticism, modern geology, Darwinism, naturalism, and so on that climaxed in the Scopes Trial of the 1920s. But Sandeen points out that a few years before that trial, the prophecy conference movement that had advocated premillennialism in the nineteenth century organized the World Conference on Christian Fundamentals. In his keynote address, Baptist fundamentalist W. B. Riley defined "modernists" as those who "teach that the Kingdom of God is now in existence, and has been from the beginning of the world." Its "manifestation was made the more clear by the appearance of Jesus," which initiated a "renewing process [that] is to be a slow growth resulting from the preaching of the Gospel" which "will finally Christianize the world. This age, when it waxes moral, will be worthy of the name of 'Millennium,'" and "at the termination of it there will be the judgment of all men, both good and bad, and the introduction of eternity." A "modernist" by this definition is clearly a postmillennialist, and a "fundamentalist" is one Riley describes in terms of the language of dispensationalism.

Once one notices this theme many things fall into place and the fundamentalist-modernist controversy may be seen to be a fight about the nature of the kingdom of God. The "great reversal" can now be understood—as well as the reason that the "social gospel" became the symbol of "liberalism" because it advocated a doctrine of the kingdom incompatible with dispensationalism and its description of the millennium. Other issues then fall into place—all the way down to the curricula of the Bible colleges. Postmillennial evangelists of the era founded universities and liberal arts colleges, while dispensationalists founded Bible schools with their abbreviated curricula (the time is short—and why does one need all that liberal arts stuff anyway?). Even the resistance to Darwinism is illuminated by these issues. Almost all (I'm tempted to say all) of the early creationists were either Adventists or premillennialists whose "catastrophic geology" fit their more apocalyptic worldview. John Whitcomb and Henry Morris in their now classic *The Genesis Flood* (1979) argued that one must choose between the biblical worldview of "decline" (the second law of thermodynamics—that the universe is in entropy decline—goes into effect only with the fall) and the modern secular-humanist doctrine of progress.

By the way, this eschatologically oriented analysis of fundamentalism also provides a more satisfying *theological* explanation of the "neo-evangelical" emergence from fundamentalism in modern Wheaton College, Fuller Theological Seminary, *Christianity Today*, Billy Graham, etc. A college professor of mine once commented that the great intellectual task of his generation (as a "neo-evangelical") was to move beyond dispensationalism. I've tried to trace this theme in the life of Fuller Seminary (most of the early faculty were escaping from dispensationalism—like a son of the founder Dan Fuller, who made his first doctoral dissertation a critique of dispensational hermeneutics at Northern Baptist Theological Seminary, much to the concern of his father). I'm convinced that almost all the controversial themes of the "new Fuller" (after about 1970) depend profoundly on this move: "devout biblical criticism," social and cultural engagement, ecumenism, inclusive and holistic missiology, etc.

CCW: Your discussion of eschatology is very helpful for understanding the nature of the conflicts of the 1920s, and it also points to the central role that eschatology plays in questions of social engagement. This same pattern can be seen in certain forms of German Pietism, especially those that come from the Württemberg region. In that region, a realistic hope for the kingdom of God fueled a number of important movements, especially some forms of communitarianism and religious socialism.

In the case of Christoph Blumhardt (1842–1919), the spiritual father of Swiss Religious Socialism, theological and ethical engagement with social issues moved beyond simple amelioration of social ills to a calling into question the structure of the "social" itself. Blumhardt advocated a rethinking of the "social" along eschatological and communitarian lines. His vision was rooted in the conviction that the kingdom was already present in the world, and thus immanent, and at the same time was yet to come, and thus transcendent. In both its immanent and transcendent forms, the content of the kingdom was given shape by the ethics and vision of the Sermon on the Mount and the early descriptions of the believing community in the book of Acts. It was thus disruptive to the present world order, which Blumhardt believed was dominated by the empire of "mammonism," or modern global capitalism. In contrast to the vision offered by capitalism, the kingdom of God was marked by gift-giving, freedom from care, social justice, and above all, God's mercy and love.

Blumhardt's analysis of the empire of mammon was remarkably similar to what we encounter in Hardt and Negri, in that he viewed it as a global empire without a center, not merely embedded in social structures but rooted in subjectivities.[1]

Of great significance was Blumhardt's contention, arrived at after much struggle, that the kingdom could not be univocally identified with the church, Christianity, Christian culture, or even socialism. Thus, it would not be a reality open to ideological manipulation or control but could remain a theo-

---

1. See Michael Hardt and Antonio Negri, *Empire* (Cambridge, MA: Harvard University Press, 2000), 32. For Blumhardt, see Christoph Blumhardt, *Ansprachen, Predigten, Reden, Briefe: 1865–1917*, vol. 2, *1890–1906*, ed. J. Harder (Neukirchen-Vluyn, Germany: Neukirchen Verlag, 1978), 264, and Hee-Kuk Lim, *"Jesus ist Sieger!" bei Christoph Friedrich Blumhardt: Keim einer kosmischen Christologie* (Bern: Peter Lang, 1996), 66.

logical reality whose appearance was occasional and provisional. This meant that movements for social reform and change, which could be harbingers of the kingdom, were not the "thing itself" but provisional parables on the way to the final appearing of the kingdom. Also of great importance was his belief that the kingdom of God was at work not only for some special caste or group but for the whole of humanity, indeed the whole cosmos. Thus, material and spiritual resistance to the empire of mammon held significance for all of created reality and contributed in some way to the final overthrow of the present world order. Thus, Blumhardt's theology was "populist" in the most basic meaning of that term.

When we reroot the category of "evangelicalism" in Pietism and revivalism, it seems we will find more resources, like Blumhardt, for resisting the form of empire that Hardt and Negri have uncovered. Do you agree?

DWD: Yes, there are elements of retrievable histories at various stages of this process. Many of them occur in streams of "pietism," as you suggest. All of them are fragile and don't last long (except when they are institutionalized in various forms, as in the Salvation Army). In my book *Discovering an Evangelical Heritage*, I celebrated the early revivalist culture that Oberlin College and Wheaton College shared at one time. Early Oberlin contributed to making the Northwest Territory an abolitionist region, crossed racial barriers, was the first coeducational college in the world, graduated many early feminists (including Antoinette Brown, the first woman to be ordained a Christian minister), and so on. Oberlin refused to celebrate the Fourth of July and honored instead the abolition of slavery in the Caribbean, opposed wars of expansion, defended the Indian treaties, and in other ways resisted the "empire" within which it lived.

CCW: If I am right, the Oberlin tradition represented a more "postmillennial" form of eschatology. Does that form of eschatology fund forms of resistance while "premillennial" forms do not?

DWD: Not necessarily. It was mainstream missions (of the NCC type) that were more likely to confuse "civilization" and "evangelization" and thus give implicit support to forms of "empire." The modern fundamentalist missions more often presupposed dispensationalism, which draws deeply on the text of the book of Daniel with its analysis of the decline of the various empires of the world. As W. B. Riley put it in an undated pamphlet on *Daniel versus Darwin* apparently published during World War I: "This interpretation of Daniel's presents . . . the decline of nations; it portrays the catastrophe of civilization. *It presents the descent of kings!*"

This was so much the case that the University of Chicago "modernists" (Shailer Mathews and others) made this into a major critique of fundamentalism during World War I. The modernists feared that the fundamentalists put all "empires" into the same bag and failed to honor their claim of the great superiority of Western democracies. They were concerned that the apolitical character of fundamentalism might weaken American confidence in the institutions of American government and give an advantage to the Germans. (This is quite a far cry from the University of Chicago concerns in the 1980s in Martin Marty's great fundamentalism project, which seemed to make the opposite critique of fundamentalism: that it is too politically engaged. This, by the way, leads to one of the most coherent definitions of *fundamentalism* that I have been able to come up with: "It is what the faculty of the Divinity School of the University of Chicago dislikes in any given generation"!)

Actually, this critical function of eschatologically oriented movements within Christianity in the "dethroning of empires" (from Caesar on down through the ages) may be one of the most important contributions of supposedly apolitical forms of Christianity. I've been fascinated with the way this worked out in Korea and Japan during World War II. To preach the return of Christ was profoundly subversive. If Jesus is coming back and he is the King of kings and the Lord of lords, then the emperor is not. Dispensationalist preachers in Korea and Japan were imprisoned and martyred so much that there is now in Japan a "holocaust project"—a multivolume set of books celebrating the martyrs of this cause.

I remember how shocked I was in the early 1970s at a secret meeting at a retreat center in the Poconos of NCC leadership with the leaders of the Chicago Declaration, Sojourners, and so forth. It was just before the American bicentennial, and we fell into a discussion of how to celebrate that event. Claire Randall, then the head of the NCC, suggested that it should be celebrated in the National Cathedral with senators and members of Congress marching into the service alongside "heads of churches" (members of the NCC, I suppose). We *Sojourners* types with our postdispensationalist histories, our fear of "civil religion" and its impact on American culture, our struggles with the radical, Anabaptist, or left wing of the Reformation, were horrified by this proposal, which seemed to smack of all that we opposed: the instrumental use of Christian faith to prop up Western culture. Who was on the side of empire in such an event?

My, how things have changed in the last three decades! Now the issues are the "new Religious Right" and the way that this movement seems to support "empire" (at least the American one!), and most call this "evangelicalism"— especially in the media! And the critics of "empire" now seem to be associated with the NCC. I often struggle over how we got to this place. It seems a reversal of what I experienced in the 1960s and 1970s. Again, my own analysis of what is happening has to abandon the categories of "evangelicalism."

CCW: According to your analysis, eschatology is central for developing ways of resisting empire. But your examples of postmillennial Oberlin and postmillennial modernist University of Chicago come out on different sides of the same issue. Why is this?

DWD: To make sense of this contradiction requires not only eschatological categories but also sociological and class categories. I tend to see American history since the Revolution in terms of the rise of successive waves of populist religious movements that have pushed back the traditions that dominated the culture in earlier generations. Thus Methodists and Baptists began to grow in the eighteenth century to become the shapers of American culture religiously by pushing aside such groups as the Presbyterians and the Episcopalians. The Methodists organized in the United States during the Revolution, became the largest Protestant body by the time of the Civil War, founded their culture-forming institutions (universities, etc.) in the last half of the nineteenth century, and dominated American Protestantism in the twentieth century until they began to decline in the latter half, giving way to the Baptists who had grown alongside them, especially in the South.

Methodists have an interesting history on such issues as slavery. They started out highly critical of this and other aspects of American culture (materialism, etc.), but by the middle of the nineteenth century were trying to prove they were no threat to American culture as it stood (and among other acts began to expel radicals like the founders of my abolitionist Methodist church, who sounded more like liberation theologians in the face of Methodist conservatives). In the process, there began to peel off a populist lower-class protest wing (the Holiness movement) that attempted to preserve the original identification of Methodism with the poor, women, slaves, etc. But this new movement began to follow the Methodist social evolution and *embourgoisement* only a few generations behind it. The result was that by the middle of the twentieth century these parties had switched sides on most social issues. Mainstream Methodism had, at least in some influential quarters, begun to gain a critical distance from American culture just as the dissenting party was buying into it.

I tend to see what we are experiencing now as the "conservative" and culture-forming stage of this latest wave of populist movements (Pentecostals, Holiness movements, and radicals of other sorts) now pushing aside the Methodists and Baptists. One has only to look at the roots of Wheaton College, Pepperdine University, Azusa Pacific University, Regent University, Oral Roberts University, Loma Linda University, and so on, to see the new modern counterparts to Northwestern University, the University of Chicago, Southern Methodist University, and the like. This developmental stage has characteristics of a "new Religious Right" as it moves into the middle class and challenges the hegemony (even religious hegemony) of existing traditions. One might wish that this "multitude" would take a different political path, and I expect it to in the future as it regains its balance and critical distance—but then it will likely be pushed aside by the next wave.

Notice that I have almost completely avoided the categories of "evangelical" analysis, which suppress sociological and class issues and thus, I am convinced, often misread what is going on. What that analysis calls "liberal" and "evangelical" is often better seen as the overlap of the older wave (more mature and culturally engaged but often tired, characterized by critical theology and biblical studies) with a younger wave of populist religion (more vigorous but more narrowly missionally focused, characterized by uncritical or precritical theology and biblical studies). But all this will change. Just wait. One sees signs of the future at all the "evangelical" institutions even if now they are mistakenly seen merely as signs of a creeping "liberalism" (as in James Davison Hunter, *Evangelicalism: The Coming Generation*, 1993).

CCW: Would it be fair to say then that alongside a dynamic chiliastic eschatology, one must also have an ethical and social commitment that broadly echoes the Sermon on the Mount and the communitarianism depicted in Acts to fuel resistance to empire?

DWD: Yes. Awareness of social location is central to how eschatology functions, especially in relation to political structures.

CCW: It would be interesting to pursue this line of thinking further, but unfortunately we have run out of time. Thank you for your time. Your deconstruction of the accepted understanding of "evangelicalism" is enlightening, and it makes space for alternative theological and historical constructions that would appear to have more to offer to that "multitude" seeking to resist the new imperial regime.

FUTURE

15

Empire and Transcendence

Hardt and Negri's Challenge to Theology and Ethics

MARK LEWIS TAYLOR

> In time, an event will thrust us like an arrow into that living future.
>
> —Michael Hardt and Antonio Negri, *Multitude*

Michael Hardt and Antonio Negri, in their books *Empire* (2000), *Multitude* (2004), and other writings, have offered a comprehensive vision of how a "living future" might be born from a present time that is deadened by imperial networks of power. Their books are an articulate, often inspiring mélange of philosophy, literary criticism, political ontology, economic analysis—and yes, also theology, ethics, at times hortatory manifesto.

A project so comprehensive in its claims, and made in an epoch when early-twenty-first-century peoples are wrestling anew with the powers of empire, cannot help but draw the attention of theologians and ethicists to Hardt and Negri's tracing an arrow's arc toward some living future. Living future / deadened present, old eon / new eon, the birth of new being from old—all this is familiar territory to the Christian scholar. For many, Hardt and Negri may represent an all too familiar recycling of religious salvation motifs.

What is of particular importance, though, is Hardt and Negri's radical immanentalizing of the new eon. They insist that the desired "living future" emerges as a deliverance without transcendence. In fact, the spirit they propound is one that emancipates from deadening networks through a "refusal of transcendence."

I argue in this chapter that there is a mode of transcendence in the dynamism that powers the emancipatory politics of "the multitude" that Hardt and Negri present as moving into the living future. In this essay, borrowing some of Hardt and Negri's own terms, I distinguish a transcendence of emancipatory politics from two other modes of transcendence: the "transcendence of command" in authoritarian regimes and the "transcendence of ordering function" in Western capitalist and colonizing modernity. Christian discourses have long reinforced these two modes of transcendence and need still to be challenged to break with them. While the militant Christian Right may provide prominent examples of Christians reinforcing the problematic modes of transcendence that have risen to prominence in the U.S. imperial age, other Christian traditions can be just as complicit in worshiping at the altar of U.S. imperial transcendence.

If I argue that there remains a transcendence at work in the politics of organizing and struggling peoples seeking emancipation from empire, I do so not to render Hardt and Negri closet transcendentalists. Nor is it my interest to refurbish some primacy of signals of transcendence in human life which then are lifted up for an apologetic theology that tries to buffer religious and theological positions against other discourses. On the contrary, my exploration of transcendence in their work is motivated by a desire to understand wherein lies the countervailing power that enables the multitude to break with empire. It is a way to understand better the power of the "event" they see in time that might "thrust us like an arrow" into a living future.

This is one way to focus the broad interest that the works by Hardt and Negri have sparked in religious and theological conversation, as exemplified by this volume, *Evangelicals and Empire*. Whether one thinks and works out of deliberately Christian evangelical traditions (and I do not)[1] or out of others styled as liberal, postliberal, postmodern, as radical orthodoxy or liberation theology, the question of what constitutes the countervailing power of the

1. I am committed to none of the criteria of "evangelical" presented, for example, by historian Anne C. Loveland, *American Evangelicals and the US Military, 1942–1993* (Baton Rouge: Louisiana State University Press, 1996), x. Her criteria for being evangelical are three: (1) the Bible is held as the inerrant authority on faith and life; (2) salvation is experienced only through faith by undergoing a conversion experience; and (3) there is a devotion to carrying out what is viewed as "the Great Commission" attributed to Jesus in Matthew 28:19. For my own Christian faith and belief, see Mark Lewis Taylor, *Remembering Esperanza: A Cultural Political Theology for North American Praxis* (Maryknoll, NY: Orbis, 1990), and *The Executed God: The Way of the Cross in Lockdown America* (Minneapolis: Fortress, 2001).

break from empire to a living future invites alliance among theologians and ethicists of many sorts. Moreover, and just as important, the question may occasion shared venture and work between the many modes of Christian faith and the largely immanentalist or secular orientations.

The need for such alliances is great today. New coalitions across our theological, racial, class, and cultural divides are matters of great urgency. The United States, as hegemonic power on the global stage, seeks unilaterally to take on ever new imperial powers as it wages a near perpetual "war on terror." In its preemptive assault on Iraq, undertaken without real proof that Iraq was an imminent threat to it,[2] the United States initiated a war of aggression, a kind of action that even the U.S. prosecutor at the first Nuremburg trial had described as "the supreme international crime differing only from other war crimes in that it contains within itself the accumulated evil of the whole."[3] Abroad, U.S. leaders, not surprisingly, become vulnerable to international criminal proceedings;[4] at home, they become subject to indictment and impeachable offenses.[5] This supreme crime of aggressive war, along with the recent rationalizations of "aggressive interrogation" become torture, is transforming the United States into a version of the very "outlaw states" it claims to oppose.[6] As a reinvigorated system of U.S. military bases subordinates other nations to limits on their dignity and freedom, U.S. citizens at home also suffer more stringent curtailments of civil liberties, and, as the Hurricane Katrina disaster demonstrated, these occasion more virulent fusions of racial discrimination and economic neglect. In short, the situation demands that we come together around shared commitments to resist these developments.

This article develops in three sections. First, I examine Hardt and Negri's view of modernity and transcendence, in order to show how debates about transcendence are crucial to debates on empire. In particular, I track their "refusal" of transcendence. Second, I turn to Ernesto Laclau's criticisms of Hardt and Negri's view of modernity and transcendence, aiming to retrieve a notion of transcendence in the face of Hardt and Negri's trenchant "refusal" of it as always imperial. In a third section, I turn directly to Hardt and Negri's understanding of multitude, the counterimperial network of movements they identify as moving beyond empire. I will show how certain

2. Seymour M. Hersh, *Chain of Command: The Road from 9/11 to Abu Ghraib* (New York: HarperCollins, 2004).

3. Benjamin B. Ferencz, "Tribute to Nuremberg Prosecutor Justice Jackson," www.benferencz.org/taylor2.htm. Ferencz further notes: "The same view would later be confirmed by the International Criminal Tribunal for the Far East."

4. "Annual Report: Statement of Dr. William F. Schulz, Executive Director, Amnesty International USA, May 25, 2005." See www.amnestyusa.org/annualreport/statement.html.

5. See arguments, U.S. Justice Department, www.usdoj.gov/usao/iln/osc/index.html.

6. Karen J. Greenberg and Joshua L. Dratel, *The Torture Papers: The Road to Abu Ghraib* (Cambridge: Cambridge University Press, 2005).

transcending features *within* that multitude exhibit a transcendence at work in emancipatory politics.

Modernity and Transcendence—Hardt and Negri's View

Hardt and Negri's notion of transcendence emerges in tandem with a critique of modernity. This provides a backdrop for their theory of empire and of how empire might be resisted by the networking power of "the multitude." *Multitude* is their term for the fluid, writhing, transformative movements of people who, though mired in empire, will be its undoing. Modernity, for Hardt and Negri, was something like a machine for expansion across continental spaces, perduring across generations. The machine, for them, had a distinctive "apparatus," the many mechanisms of which grind away in all the different dimensions of European modernity: epistemology, metaphysics, ethics, politics. This apparatus is a "transcendental apparatus," one further distinguished by its pervasive dynamic, an "essential core" by which European systems established a global hegemony.[7]

What precisely is this essential core? For Hardt and Negri it is the tendency of modernity's key thinkers to argue for some sort of transcendence as a necessary mediation of people's experience. Here, mediation and transcendence must be thought of together. The transcendental apparatus of modernity has at its heart the view that "nature and experience are unrecognizable except through *the filter of phenomena*; human knowledge cannot be achieved except through the *reflection of the intellect*; and the ethical world is incommunicable except through the *schematism of reason*."[8] Some form of mediating apparatus "relativizes experience and abolishes every instance of the immediate and absolute *in* human life and history,"[9] an absolute in human life and history that they see as emancipatively released by the Renaissance. Hardt and Negri ask almost plaintively, "Why cannot knowledge and will be allowed to claim themselves to be absolute?"[10]

Hardt and Negri believe they know the answer. The transcendental apparatus helps contain resistance: "Every movement of self-constitution of the multitude must yield to a reconstituted order"; otherwise, so modernity fears, there would be only "subversive delirium."[11] Hardt and Negri claim that human knowledge and the will of the multitude can constitute themselves as absolute, thus to make and remake themselves and their histories. This daring assertion

7. Michael Hardt and Antonio Negri, *Empire* (Cambridge, MA: Harvard University Press, 2000), 79.

8. Ibid. (emphasis original).

9. Ibid.

10. Ibid.

11. Ibid.

they present as a hope-making rediscovery of the Renaissance's assertion of immanence. Hardt and Negri's championing of this power of immanence helped generate much of the optimism that fueled the popularity of *Empire* and the literary sensation it became at the recent turn of the millennium in 2000–2001.[12] *Empire* and *Multitude* purport to show in breathtaking sweep, historically from medieval to present times, and today across a range of disciplines in a postmodern milieu, how the multitude constitutes itself, both against the imperialism of modernity and against the more complex empire of postmodernity. The transnational empire of today is, in fact, presented as a kind of "wounded beast," a desperate elite network whose power holders at the top of a "pyramid of global constitution" are trying to stave off the multitude's resistance. "Empire itself is not a positive reality. In the very moment it rises up, it falls. Each imperial action is a rebound of the resistance of the multitude that poses a new obstacle for the multitude to overcome."[13] This is sometimes referred to as "the smoothness" of the transition from empire to multitude.

Confidence in the multitude's powers characterizes both their book and caps off the conclusion of their more recent volume, *Multitude* (2004): "The extraordinary accumulation of grievances and reform proposals must at some point be transformed by a strong event, a radical insurrectional demand. We can already recognize that today time is split between a present that is already dead and a future that is already living—and the yawning abyss between them is becoming enormous. In time, an event will thrust us like an arrow into that living future. This will be the real political act of love."[14]

The price of admission into this immanent hope, however, is, again, "the refusal of transcendence." This refusal is "the condition for the possibility of thinking this immanent power, an anarchic basis of philosophy: *Ni dieu, ni maitre, ni l'homme.*"[15] The refusal is part of a legacy of immanence. They advocate a heritage of affirming immanence that they see beginning with John Duns Scotus, who, they assert, returned to "the singularity of being," breaking the "medieval concept of being as an object of analogical, and thus dualistic predication," which had left humanity divided—broken, they would say—"with one foot in this world and one in a transcendent realm."[16] Scotus affirmed, they say, "the powers of this world and the fullness of the plane of immanence."[17] Hardt and Negri then trace an immanental liberatory line

12. Gopal Balakrishnan, introduction to *Debating Empire*, ed. Gopal Balakrishnan (London: Verso, 2003), viii.

13. *Empire*, 361.

14. Michael Hardt and Antonio Negri, *Multitude: War and Democracy in the Age of Empire* (New York: Penguin, 2004), 358.

15. *Empire*, 91–92.

16. Ibid., 71.

17. Ibid., 71, 73.

from Duns Scotus to Nicholas of Cusa, Pico della Mirandola, Bacillus, and Galileo Galilei, which then flowers in Baruch Spinoza, in whose works "the horizon of immanence and the horizon of democratic political order coincide completely."[18]

Hardt and Negri portray these propounders of immanence, though, as always in struggle. They were only a "first modernity," destined to be overrun by those whose names still typically are identified with Enlightenment and modernity: Descartes, Hobbes, Kant, Hegel, even Rousseau.[19] These constituted a "second modernity," a triumphant line that reasserted the transcendental mediations, whether by filters of perception, forms of reason, the state, or some lord or God. Together, over time and in sundry ways, these thinkers of modernity articulate a kind of architecture of sovereignty, a scaffolding of schemas of transcendence that structure the colonizing and imperial designs of modernity. It is an architecture that enables the expanding project of modernity to beat back "the liberated singularities" of the self-constituting multitude.[20] This architecture of sovereignty culminates in Hegel, for whom the development of nature and humanity in history needs a transcendent state power.

Hegel's system is presented by Hardt and Negri as a fulfillment of a long struggle to negate and harness non-European desire. This has its genesis not only in Descartes' writings (1637–44), but in the slightly earlier Francis Bacon (1609, 1622), whose writings called for a veritable holy war against colonizable peoples, who were "in their body and frames of estate, a monstrosity."[21] So modernity may have revolted against the medieval period's "transcendence of command," but instead of following early modernity's way of immanence, European modernity finally forged a brutal "transcendence of ordering function," an expansionist capitalist enterprise that both carried and expressed the modernity/coloniality that has bequeathed empire to the present moment.[22]

The multitude, and humans aspiring to end brutalities of empire building and oppression today, must dare to come out onto the plane of immanence— better, they must see that such a plane is where any who seek to be part of another world's possibility already stand. Hardt and Negri sum it up:

> The multitude today . . . resides on the imperial surfaces where there is no God the Father and no transcendence. Instead there is our immanent labor. The teleology of the multitude is theurgical; it consists in the possibility of directing technologies and production toward its own joy and its own increase of power.

18. Ibid., 73.
19. Ibid., 82.
20. Ibid., 83.
21. Sir Francis Bacon, *Of the Wisdom of the Ancients* (1609), and *Advertisement Touching on an Holy War* (1622), cited in Peter Linebaugh and Marcus Rediker, *The Many-Headed Hydra: Sailors, Slaves, Commoners, and the Hidden History of the Revolutionary Atlantic* (Boston: Beacon, 2000), 39.
22. *Empire*, 88.

The multitude has no reason to look outside its own history and its own present productive power for the means necessary to lead toward its constitution
as a political subject.[23]

Here is a radical "immanental assertion" by Hardt and Negri that situates
them in the immanental line they celebrate. It is precisely this immanental
claim that Laclau interrogates.

Laclau's Challenge

One ten-page response to *Empire* by Ernesto Laclau, a professor of political
theory at the University of Essex, stands out amid a plethora of contentious
discussions of Hardt and Negri's work, because it succinctly challenges both
historical and political dimensions of their project.[24] From Laclau's analysis,
I distill here three key critical moves made by him.

First, Laclau questions the historical interpretation of "the multitude"
that Hardt and Negri portray in early modernity. Laclau, in fact, dismisses as
"beautiful fabula!" the idea that sovereignty, with its transcendental apparatus
and systems of representation, was historically a "repressive device trying to
prevent the democratic upsurge of an unspecified multitude" (25).

Laclau points to a "far more complicated process," one that begins with
a more nuanced understanding of the social and political dynamics of early
modernity. He stresses how difficult it is to find in a postfeudal, early modern context anything like what Hardt and Negri posit as a "unified political
subject capable of establishing an alternative social order" on the plane of
immanence. On the contrary, it was "profoundly fragmented" with two sets
of powers coursing through a turbulent milieu: the "universalistic powers"
of church and empire and the more "local feudal powers." It was amid this
tumult of fragmentation, suggests Laclau, that a royal sovereignty sector and
a revolutionary bourgeois social sector rose together, *not* to repress a rising,
immanently congealing multitude (there really wasn't one, Laclau claims) but
to counter the powers that perpetuated old orders of obeisance through ever
new fragmentation of populations (25).

Laclau does seem to agree that the revolutionary character of this move in
early modernity was quickly subverted and morphed into a repressive "second
modernity." On the way to it, however, Laclau stresses that early modernity
gave birth to a phenomenon insufficiently acknowledged by Hardt and Negri:
a process of development of the idea of sovereignty, which moved from King

---

23. Ibid., 396.
24. Ernesto Laclau, "Can Immanence Explain Social Struggles?" in *Empire's New Clothes:*
Reading Hardt and Negri, ed. Paul A. Passavant and Jodi Dean (New York: Routledge, 2004),
21–30. Page references to Laclau's essay are in parentheses of the main text.

and then to "the people." It is this development that then birthed "something resembling a unitary multitude" to which Hardt and Negri give prominence (25). So the very multitude of early modernity that Hardt and Negri assume to have been repressed and beaten back by sovereignty and modernity's transcendental apparatus was, according to Laclau, in part actually a creation of dynamics of sovereignty and transcendence.

Second, and building upon his first more historical move, Laclau points toward the need for a more sophisticated reading of the immanence-transcendence distinction. In his first move Laclau suggested that sovereignty and transcendence had something to do with creating the immanental multitude celebrated by Hardt and Negri. What Laclau's second move achieves is a refocusing of the history of the assertion of immanence, so that new considerations of transcendence and politics become thinkable.

In particular, Laclau qualifies Hardt and Negri's focus on Duns Scotus (1266–1308) as the origin of the immanental line. Laclau places its start centuries earlier, in *De divisione naturae* by John Scotus Erigena (810–875). This is not just a matter of historical erudition about the origin point of ideas. No, the turn to Scotus Erigena allows another view of what was at stake in asserting a radical immanentism.

In its context, Erigena's assertion of immanence was not about secularism or resisting transcendence. It was more about how to interpret the presence of evil in world historical affairs, which was believed to be played out under divine omniscience and omnipotence. Laclau summarizes the debate, long antedating Erigena and well known to theologians today: "If God is responsible for evil, he cannot be absolute Goodness; if he is not responsible for evil he is not Almighty" (23). Erigena's response is to stake out a position holding that evil does not really exist, that evil phenomena are mere forms that God has assumed *within* history in order to bring history, and the divine itself, to a perfection. Significantly, God is hereby placed in the world-historical depths that were previously read as "evil." With God's being made internal to this world, the world in all its material, earthly—even in its distortive, ugly, violative "evil"—modalities is, at least partly, divinized.

In short, the assertion of radical immanence was not a refusal of transcendence and God-language but in fact a controversial reinterpretation of the location and modality of transcendence. That reinterpretation occurred under the pressure of human wrestling with worldly suffering and evil. All this "negativity" is seen as integral to a processual and dialectical outworking of the world's telos. This outworking, often called a "dialectical negativity" (negativity treated as one part of an unfolding world process), is at the heart of the tradition of immanence that can then be followed from Erigena to Duns Scotus (with whom Hardt and Negri begin), to the Renaissance thinkers like Pico della Mirandolo, Bovillus, and others, then to Nicholas of Cusa, Spinoza, and on to Hegel and Marx (23). The immanental way might be understood as continuing also into certain twentieth- and twenty-first-century traditions of theology and philosophy of religion: the process thought of Charles Hartshorne and Alfred North Whitehead, the existential ontology of Paul Tillich, and various reinterpretations of transcendence in feminist/ womanist, black, and liberation theologies, among others,[25] for whom evil is taken as an element of tragedy and even fault but within a divine unfolding of history and creation.

It should also be said that the present state of these discussions of "transcendence"—which has moved outside Western preoccupations with the entire transcendence-immanence binary and into more complex inter-religious settings—tends to make the whole debate about refusing or affirm-ing transcendence appear somewhat simplistic. The debate has long shifted from *whether* there are transcending dimensions of human experience to *how* those dimensions might be articulated. Laclau, who challenges the starkness of Hardt and Negri's "refusal," actually seems closer to the more complex discussions in the philosophy of religion and theology. But there's a final aspect of Laclau's challenge.

Third, and again building from the previous moves, Laclau not only rein-terprets the immanence-transcendence relation but reinterprets transcendence itself. The key to understanding this move is to recall a key feature of the previous move. Erigena's assertion of immanence entailed an interpretation of divine presence as internal to world process. What previous to the imma-nentalist assertion was an external transcendence is now via that assertion an *internal* transcendence, a transcendence internal to the world. This internal-izing of transcendence etches antagonism deep into the heart of things (God/ good versus evil, *within* history), so much so—and Laclau stresses this—that social antagonism, as a trait of historical life, could survive even in secular critics who refused God and God-language. Transcendence, now, is not only immanent to history but intrinsically bound up with senses of social antago-nism in history (23).

Laclau's main point here, regarding the book *Empire*, is that by simplisti-cally positing immanence and transcendence as opposites, Hardt and Negri not only misunderstand their relation but also propound a notion of worldly immanence without antagonism (22–23). This is problematic, says Laclau, because without a sense of social antagonism, any meaningful notion of politics is hard to think and practice. Slavery, colonization, economic exploi-tation, destruction of indigenous lands, white racism, systemic violation or curtailment of women's rights—all these might be mentioned by Hardt and Negri, as they in fact are in their texts, but theorizing them toward political

25. For an excellent critical review and discussion of contemporary notions of transcendence, especially of "transcendence *within*," treating Levinas, Dussel, Irigaray, and others, see Mayra Rivera, "Touch of Transcendence," PhD diss., School of Religion, Drew University, 2005.

projects is more difficult to do within the immanentalist milieu that Hardt and Negri weave.

This point of Laclau's challenge goes a long way, I believe, in explaining why Hardt and Negri's project has some other significant failings pointed out by other critics. These failings can be linked to a general neglect to focus social antagonism or to explore in depth the severity of that antagonism. The following neglected or insufficiently theorized antagonisms may be cited as examples of this:

- the antagonistic strife provoked by a comprehensive and brutal U.S. nationalist and militarist project[26]
- the antagonism existing between the early U.S. republic's Constitution, for which Hardt and Negri have a special reverence, and indigenous and African slave peoples, against whom the nation set itself in vigorous opposition[27]
- the antagonism at work between certain left patriarchal views of the world and contemporary feminist analyses[28]
- the antagonism between a neocolonizing Europe/USA and long-colonized peoples of Latin America, Africa, and Asia, whose perspectives rarely figure significantly in the theoretic structure of Hardt and Negri's books; Hardt and Negri do not really think across "the colonial difference" in a substantial fashion as Walter Mignolo has urged[29]

Transcendence in the Multitude

Laclau's challenge thus enables us to undertake a more complex reading of the notion of transcendence than is provided by Hardt and Negri. At the same time, however, it enables a discernment of dynamics of transcendence at work *in* the emancipatory project of the multitude, identifying better its countervailing power. This final section offers a rendering of that power of transcendence in the multitude, by first describing the more complex view of transcendence in emancipatory politics as stimulated by Laclau's challenge and, second, identifying key features of transcendence in Hardt and Negri's own discussions of the multitude.

26. Laclau, "Can Immanence Explain," 25; Carl Boggs, *Imperial Delusions: US Militarism* (New York: Garraty, 2005).

27. Peter Fitzpatrick, "The Immanence of Empire," in *Empire's New Clothes*, ed. Passavant and Dean, 47–52; Laclau, "Can Immanence Explain," 26.

28. Lee Quinby, "Taking the Millennialist Pulse of *Empire's* Multitude: A Genealogical Feminist Analysis," in *Empire's New Clothes*, ed. Passavant and Dean, 231–52.

29. Walter D. Mignolo, *Local Histories/Global Designs: Coloniality, Subaltern Knowledges, and Border Thinking* (Princeton, NJ: Princeton University Press, 2000), 49–88.

A Transcendence in Emancipatory Politics

To repeat, the transcendence within emancipatory politics is neither the "transcendence of command" that characterized medieval and feudal periods that early modernity's masses and bourgeois's rebels struggled to throw off nor the "transcendence of ordering function" that the triumphant bourgeois lords enshrined through ideologies and mechanisms of world production in a second modernity/coloniality. Transcendence within emancipatory politics has a different character. This can be delineated by taking seriously each point of what I have called Laclau's challenge.

First, a transcendence of emancipatory politics arises within the clamor and climate of resistance where diverse political agents, groups, and movements struggle with the transcendences of command or of ordering function. In the case of early European modernity, this meant a struggle through mass movement, experimentation with different political structures and leaders, the entrusting of power to key charismatic figures (kings, sovereigns) also, forging notions of "the people,"[30] and modes of representation. This helped promote the diversity of the multitude, to balance and structure its parts, so as to preserve a polity's resistance to structures of command and tyranny.

The point that Laclau leads us to underscore here is that along the way of a people's search for, or a multitude's pursuit of, political empowerment, they will not, indeed they have not historically, set themselves against all transcendence. In the late medieval period, with feudal forms being disrupted, peoples often preferred and chose princes, emergent strongmen, and secular rulers, even at times with their "transcendental apparatus," as a way to resist unwanted authority.[31] This very potential of a people to shield themselves from ecclesial authority via a secular one, however, suggests a certain popular agency, a certain will of the people, that could and did develop into fuller notions of popular sovereignty. This popular sovereignty could also be a site where more explicit theological languages of transcendence could be deployed, as among Anabaptists who invoked God as "no respecter of persons" to reinforce their populist struggle for change.[32]

The point is not that discourses of transcendence are always supportive of the emancipatory multitude. Transcendence is still a power that can be oppressive, as in the transcendence of command or as the transcendence of ordering function. Moreover, transcendence in emancipatory politics is always susceptible to deteriorating into, or compromising with, a transcendence of command (as in authoritarianism of the right and left) or the transcendence

---

30. On Hardt and Negri's alternative reading of "the people" and why they view it as problematic, see *Empire*, 102–5.

31. Owen Chadwick, *The Reformation* (New York: Penguin, 1964), 393.

32. Linebaugh and Rediker, *Many-Headed Hydra*, 82–86.

of ordering function (as in today's transnational corporate state and certain socialist bureaucratic states).

Second, if we recall Laclau's clarification about the context for asser-tions of radical immanence, we have a notion of transcendence defined by its qualitative capacity to engage, resist, and transform historical suffering and evil. The fundamental question becomes not so much whether there is a God transcendent above or outside history, but *how* God may be there in history to make an emancipatory difference amid radical suffering and evil. Or transcendence need not be about "*a* God" at all; it may focus instead on people's emancipatory experiences and social practices, which have certain qualities often spoken of as "spirit."[33] Joel Kovel, for example, writes of spirit as an experience of a "transcended self," i.e., a self emancipated from its own and others' destructive habits and cultural practices. This spirit need deploy no talk of a sovereign God or of a supernatural, transcending plane of existence, but only of a dynamism of emancipatory growth in a world of suffering and evil. As I have put it in my own work, the transcendence of spirit is not a movement "above or outside culture and history" but a move-ment into a "configuration of culture and history where something new, something creatively underivable is looked for."[34] The "new," the "creative," and the "underivable" may all be surprising, elusive, and mysterious aspects of human life, but they are intrinsic to culture and history, not extrinsic to them. The terms *transcending* or *transcendent* are not simply alternative *synonyms* for *spirit* or *spiritual*; rather, they name the dimension or power of spirit to move toward emancipation in historical, social, and natural life. They name spirit's unfolding with countervailing power under conditions of politically, psychologically, sociologically, and economically distorted ex-istence. Transcendence and transcending are ways to name the overcoming, countervailing, resistant edge of emancipatory spirit.

Third, and this is a direct implicate of the foregoing, transcendence in eman-cipatory politics is especially to be looked for in sites of social antagonism. This antagonism, recall, involves "radical disjuncture," first marked histori-cally as a distinction between the world and a God external to it, then as a distinction *internal* to history via the immanental assertion. A transcendence of emancipatory politics presumes this internalized sense of radical disjunc-ture. Here, politics' "transcendence" lies not in a looking above and away from human history and society but in embracing an antagonism of *contestation* for emancipatory ends, in pursuit of a *transformation* of structures to sustain emancipated living in society.

---

33. Joel Kovel, *History and Spirit: An Inquiry into the Philosophy of Liberation* (Boston: Beacon, 1991), 212–15.

34. Mark Lewis Taylor, *Religion, Politics, and the Christian Right: Post 9/11 Powers and American Empires* (Minneapolis: Fortress, 2005), 108.

Laclau, in *On Populist Reason* (2005), suggests that today's emancipatory politics depends on a historical condition of "failed transcendence,"[35] which would appear to be a phrase referring to this legacy of exterior transcendence being transposed into a more interior form that births social antagonism. As Laclau seems to see it, the social ground is fragmented by the internalization of the external sovereign, and this fragmenting provides a negativity in social history that is necessary for populist emancipatory action. "Failed transcendence" is "transcendence appearing within the social as the presence of an absence . . . a constitutive lack."[36] This allows organizing peoples, who need and seek emancipation, to identify certain aspects of their worlds that require resistance and others that require cooperation and solidarity.

Theologians, as well as others, may be discomfited here because Laclau's relation of transcendence to social antagonism smacks of binarism. It suggests that transcendence in emancipatory politics is dependent only, or primarily, on conditions where forces are arrayed against one another as good and evil principles (the emancipatory and the nonemancipatory). This, however, is too simplistic a reading of Laclau. Indeed, social antagonism is, for Laclau, the special fruit of the notion of transcendence. It may also be true that sites of social antagonism may be primary ones for finding traces of transcendence. But this does not mean that experiences of transcendence are only experiences of antagonism. In Laclau's own rendering of the transcendence that generates antagonism, in fact, there is a residual whisper of wholeness, i.e., a sense that the antagonism is a rupture *of* some multitudinous whole, kept in some unity. Antagonism is felt as antagonism because there is somewhere a suggestion of a certain intimacy of being and beings. That unity may be lost, or problematic, in any number of ways, but it is nevertheless remembered, giving poignancy and import to the antagonism. This interplay of oneness and rupture is what generates, I suggest, the need for Laclau to say of transcendence that it is an absence but "the *presence* of an absence." It is a "lack" but one that is "*constitutive.*" The whisper of a wholeness (disjoined, ruptured, rendered as antagonism) even may make possible—though I do not know Laclau to say this—the visions of future oneness that agents of populist struggle seek to realize.

The Multitude's Transcendence

We should not be surprised, then, that Hardt and Negri's project, especially in its intentions to present the multitude as countervailing, emancipatory power, features discursive elements of transcendence. In other words, while they rightly reject the transcendence of command and also that of ordering function, there is still an immanental transcendence of emancipatory politics.

35. Ernesto Laclau, *On Populist Reason* (London: Verso, 2005), 244.
36. Ibid., 240.

First, a transcendence of material emancipatory politics is evident in the way Hardt and Negri present the power of their "insurgent multitude." In one of the very paragraphs I quoted above to illustrate their refusal of transcendence, we can also note, now, how their respect for the multitude's "immanent labor" is referred to as an "ancient mysticism." They refer to the teleology of the countervailing multitude as "theurgical."[37] Etymologically, this means "God-working," but Hardt and Negri develop this as a sensory power, and so they speak, with Hegel, of a "material religion of the senses" or a "mythology of reason." Again, none of this constitutes a transcendence of command or of ordering function, but there is a dimension of transcendence here that invites both religious and theological analysis of the multitude's moral telos and of the materialist myths that sustain it.

Second, there is Hardt and Negri's invoking "the immeasurable."[38] This invocation should not be seized upon by theologians as some cipher for a sovereign transcendent, some infinite being. The term seems to function in Hardt and Negri's work as a kind of moving directional awareness and intention, ever pointing toward and beyond horizons and limits of the present. It is an infinite that is not outside, above, or opposed to finite historicality. On the contrary, it is in-finite, a directional, vibrant dynamism *within* finite life. Something like Tillich's notion of transcendence operates in Hardt and Negri's emancipatory politics: "Infinity is a directing concept, not a constituting concept. It directs the mind to experience its own unlimited potentialities, but it does not establish the existence of an infinite being."[39]

Intriguingly—and this is consistent with their refusal of all transcendence, which Laclau has criticized—Hardt and Negri see the multitude's nourishing "immeasurable world" *not* as a sign of transcendence but as a reaction against transcendence, which, they write, has always "abhorred the immeasurable."[40] That claim is true, though, only with respect to the transcendence of command, and especially the transcendence of ordering function. Hardt and Negri's discourse of the immeasurable is itself another form of transcendence, an immanent transcendence, one antagonistic to the world of measure and the measurable so often guarded by the hierarchies of Western transcendental forms, both in premodern/feudal absolutisms and in modern/colonial structures. They display an emancipatory transcendence at work in the "productive activity" of the multitude, as it bends toward the immeasurable with its "set of powers to act (being, loving, transforming, creating)," all in a way that "can put pressure on the borders of the possible, and thus touch the real."[41]

37. *Empire*, 396.
38. Ibid., 354–56.
39. Paul Tillich, *Systematic Theology* (Chicago: University of Chicago Press, 1951), 1:190.
40. *Empire*, 355.
41. Ibid., 357.

Negri in other writings gives fuller play to the notion of "the immeasurable."[42] If I could risk a summary of Negri's position on "the immeasurable" from his "Kairos, Alma Venus, Multitudo," I would note the term's reference to an inexhaustible, untamed power of bodies in material life to generate themselves and new conditions, and in ever new modalities: "Only the immeasurable creates a link between what has been and what is, and in the immeasurable the monads of *kairos* lean out, anxiously, over the opening of new being. So the materialist field is always projected forwards; it consists in the arrow of time and it insists in the tip of the arrow."[43] Negri seems not to acknowledge theologians' and phenomenologists' previous labors on this terrain stocked with the familiar terms of *kairos*, the eternal, and new being.[44] One gift of Hardt and Negri's work, though, is that it resituates this discourse and gives it several creative turns within a new era, a twenty-first-century period that is facing anew the forces of empire. There are several dissertations waiting to be written on what I might call Hardt and Negri's transcendental materialism—or better, perhaps, their material transcendence. Here, though, my intention is limited to a mere gesturing toward their discourse on the immeasurable as a complex site for diverse theologians' engagement.

Finally, there is an emancipatory transcendence at work precisely in a way that Laclau finds lacking, i.e., in Hardt and Negri's embrace of antagonism and social conflict. Recall that for Laclau, Hardt and Negri, in allegedly lacking a sense of antagonism, eviscerate any meaningful sense of the political (because, as Laclau argues, the political depends on focusing social antagonism for social practice). Indeed, it is true that they often write in ways that suggest that today's postmodern empire *and* the countervailing multitude work together with little sense of significant antagonism between them. Consequently, it is difficult to see why the multitude is, or needs to be, *counter*vailing at all.

It must be noted, though, that Hardt and Negri do show some signs of including social antagonism in relation to their discussions of multitude. If a theorization of social antagonism is one sign of the legacy of transcendence (albeit in secularized form), then Hardt and Negri's discourse of antagonism may reveal their entailment in the very vestiges of transcendence from which their refusal of transcendence was designed to deliver them. In their more recent work, *Multitude*, for example, they write of "exploitative forces" of empire, which work against the renewing force carried by the multitude's networking power. These forces are at work against the multitude, constantly creating divisions and hierarchies, reinforcing global control, transforming common wealth into private wealth.[45] They credit these exploitative forces with power to "constrain the multitudinous flesh," making it difficult for it to

42. Antonio Negri, *Time for Revolution* (London: Continuum, 2003), 159–82.
43. Ibid., 179.
44. Paul Tillich, *The Interpretation of History* (New York: Charles Scribner's, 1936).
45. *Multitude*, 212.

form any political project. These exploitative forces are portrayed as generating so much constraint that a "surplus" of violation is deposited in human experience, bringing into play a list of grievances (*cahiers de doleances*).[46] It is this surplus of violation that enables antagonism to be transformed into revolt. Revolt then generates political projects, or, in other terms, mobilizes "the common," intensifying the efforts of a countervailing multitude.[47]

In other words, it can be argued that Hardt and Negri have placed antagonism at the very heart of the process that generates the multitude's politics. They also discuss a multiplicity of historical movements that make up its power to be a countervailing dynamism: the 1968 revolts in Europe, the Zapatista resistance in Chiapas, Mexico, the FMLN in El Salvador, Justice for Janitors, the antiglobalization protests from Seattle to Geneva and beyond, feminist movements, the "White Overalls" movement, intifadas in Palestine, and more. These revolts and movements, and the links between them, as well as the memory of them that continues into the present, constitute a political project related to antagonism, indeed generated in part by antagonism intensified to the point of surplus. True, from the perspective of the Hardt and Negri oeuvre as a whole, this surplus antagonism does not quite have the status of what Laclau discusses as the sense of "radical disjuncture" so necessary to the political; but it is more than the smooth transition that they often articulate between destructive empire and emancipatory multitude.

Elsewhere, Hardt and Negri have brought out this antagonism by styling it as even a kind of battle between monsters. Such imagery expresses

> our need to enhance our excessive powers of transformation [as multitude] and attack the monstrous, horrible world that the global political body and capitalist exploitation have made for us. We need to use the monstrous expressions of the multitude to challenge the mutations of artificial life transformed into commodities, the capitalist power to put up for sale the metamorphoses of nature, the new eugenics that support the ruling power. The new world of monsters is where humanity has to grasp its future.[48]

With discourse such as this Hardt and Negri again mark their interest in transcendence, albeit, again, one of material emancipation. There is still their refusal of those transcendences that ground the "horrible world"—those of command and ordering function—but in this imaginative embrace of the symbolics of monsters (loving some and combating others),[49] Hardt and Negri mine some of the mythological resources of the legacy of transcendence.

46. Ibid., 268–85.
47. Ibid., 212.
48. *Multitude*, 196.
49. Ibid.

Moreover, with their discourse on a "world of monsters," we are returned, at this essay's conclusion, to a sense of our times' urgency. We are reminded of the struggle for worlds of liberation and justice, for a politics of joy, love, and peace—for life—amid powers of U.S. and transnational imperial forms. The mythologized and real "horrible worlds" of war, structured racism, torture, and neocolonialism conjure up a monstrous specter that today makes the significance of our differences pale in comparison. A sane and material apocalyptic awareness, an aspect of a transcendence of emancipatory politics, now challenges us as theologians and ethicists—whether evangelical, postliberal, neoorthodox, radical orthodox, liberal, or liberationist—to forge effective and new coalitions of thought and practice in this age of empire.

16

Empire and the Ethics of Opacity

The End of Theology and the Beginning(s) of Theological Thinking

COREY D. B. WALKER

In every case the result of an untrue mode of knowledge must not be allowed to run away into an empty nothing, but must necessarily be grasped as the nothing of that from which it results—a result which contains what was true in the preceding knowledge.

G. W. F. Hegel

But why is it necessary to defend or to celebrate reason? Why exempt it so quickly from the examination of its effects, be they ambivalent and agonizing? Why cast embarrassed glances toward the vocabulary—and the realities—of power, force, and domination? Why this rush to use the water of reason to wash the hands of so many modern-day Pontius Pilates whose beloved research "results" are frequently questioned?

Dominique Janicaud

If a tradition ceases to be the cultural terrain where creativity and the inscription of new problems take place, and becomes instead a hindrance to that creativity and that inscription, it will gradually and silently be abandoned.

Ernesto Laclau

The move to engage Michael Hardt and Antonio Negri's *Empire* and the contemporary dynamics of evangelical Christianity may strike some as a purely opportunistic endeavor.[1] Religion, let alone evangelical Christianity, is not one of the axiomatic points of departure for Hardt and Negri's theoretical elaboration of empire. Moreover, it is hard to imagine that most people, not to mention evangelical Christians, have read this massive treatise and have any knowledge of the professional status or intellectual and political project of either Michael Hardt or Antonio Negri. Now, I am not rehearsing these issues to be reductive of intellectual life in general or to be dismissive of an engagement between *Empire* and evangelicalism in particular. Quite the contrary, what this line of thinking gestures toward is a critical dimension of the (con)textual dynamics of an intellectual project that must be recognized if it aspires to be something more than a traditional theoretical exercise.[2] Given the textual acrobatics of *Empire*, the politics of the production and reproduction of knowledge in the contemporary academy, the social and symbolic capital of certain trends in advanced theoretical circles, and the material realities and theological concerns of Christian evangelicals across social formations in the United States, a critical confrontation between evangelicals and *Empire* is always already somewhat arbitrary and artificial. Notwithstanding this risk—which is the risk of any *critical* intellectual project—I will proceed to think through such an "artificial" engagement in order to better understand the contemporary terrain of religion, theory, and public life in the opening years of a new millennium.

My engagement with *Empire* and evangelicals is animated by this central question: how and in what ways can we reflexively engage Hardt and Negri's *Empire* in order to understand the multiple challenges presented by the evangelical impulse and the material and ideological consolidations of the democratic project in the twenty-first century? In grappling with this question, this essay does not turn on the axis of a critique of *Empire*, nor does it seek to justify a new form of evangelical politics or evangelical political subjectivities.[3] Rather, this essay is offered as a prolegomenon, if you will, to a much more robust project of developing a constructive theological proposal to challenge the foundations and norms of contemporary theoretical discourse that inform not only constructions of *Empire* and empire but also its evan-

---

1. The inspiration for this thought is the opening line in Theodor Adorno's *Against Epistemology*: "The attempt to discuss Husserl's pure phenomenology in the spirit of the dialectic risks the initial suspicion of caprice." Theodor W. Adorno, *Against Epistemology: A Metacritique*, trans. Willis Domingo (Oxford: Basil Blackwell, 1982), 3.

2. See Max Horkheimer, "Traditional and Critical Theory," in *Critical Theory: Selected Essays* (New York: Continuum, 1975), 188–243.

3. For critiques of *Empire*, see (for example) Paul A. Passavant and Jodi Dean, eds., *Empire's New Clothes: Reading Hardt and Negri* (New York: Routledge, 2004), and Antilio A. Boron, *Empire and Imperialism: A Critical Reading of Michael Hardt and Antonio Negri*, trans. Jessica Casiro (London: Zed, 2005).

gelical surrogates. I believe we are forced to think with, against, and beyond Hardt and Negri as well as evangelicals in examining the logic of empire that is materially and rhetorically linked with the flows of epistemic privilege that mask the neoimperial exploits and massive consolidations of global economic power of Western liberal democracies. Thus, my argument proceeds by way of an investigation into the broader phenomenon of the (re)emergence of the question of theology proper that has been placed firmly on the agenda for a variety of theoretical projects that seek to develop some form of alternative and/or radical political thought and praxis.[4] In so doing, I take the (re)turn of the theological to be a result of the following dynamics: (1) a noted revival of interest in the theological in philosophical and theoretical circles in the North Atlantic academy; (2) a marked epistemic instability within the dominant theoretical discourses as a result of a radical interrogation and undermining of the foundational claims of Western intellectual practices in the latter years of the twentieth century; and (3) an acceleration and consolidation of the epistemic and economic forces of the Western world that continue to marginalize the majority of the world's population.

The current evangelical sympathies interwoven within the articulations of the global hegemony of the West can be understood as a critical strand in the *theo-logic* of empire. Indeed, we need only to revisit the work of V. Y. Mudimbe, who reminds us of an/other example of this phenomenon more than a century ago:

> The scramble for Africa in the nineteenth century took place in an atmosphere of Christian revival: the age of Enlightenment and its criticism of religion had ended. Coleridge's phrase, "the Bible finds you," was an apt one for all Christians. In Catholic Europe, the First Vatican Council firmly reorganized Catholicism. A group of distinguished prelates even reevaluated the meaning of the so-called curse of Ham, hoping that "the interior of Africa may participate in the solemn coming joy of the Church's triumph" (*Interior Africa solemnis gaudii proximi Ecclesiae triumphi particeps fiat*).[5]

However, critical and sustained attention has yet to be given to the violent implications that are inextricably intertwined with the cartographic and epistemic

---

4. The turn to the theological can be viewed as part of the broader paradoxical (and perennial) phenomenon of the crisis of science or knowledge. This phenomenon is paradoxical in that although the certainty that underwrites "scientific" forms of knowledge is under assault, these forms of knowledge nevertheless continue to maintain a premium value in terms of their epistemic and economic guarantee. Immanuel Wallerstein has recently argued, "Faced with this urgency, many people worldwide have turned from scientist claims to knowledge to claims based on theology, philosophy, or folk wisdom." Immanuel Wallerstein, *The Uncertainties of Knowledge* (Philadelphia: Temple University Press, 2004), 14.

5. V. Y. Mudimbe, *The Invention of Africa: Gnosis, Philosophy, and the Order of Knowledge* (Bloomington: Indiana University Press, 1988), 46.

positions that inspire this theological, and by extension, political dream. In recognizing this deficiency, I will advance a critical and constructive project of theological thinking that strikes a balance between a properly reflexive theological vision of liberation in response to the demands of an ethics of opacity. The relational matrix between an epistemological project of theological thinking and an ethics of opacity interrupts any attempt at an absolute correspondence between the theological and the material in an effort to open up a new horizon for the possibility of thinking and being otherwise. As such, theological thinking comes to be defined as a radical epistemic project that breaks with the dominant episteme undergirding the theo-logic of empire by way of an ethical response in service to and solidarity with the opaque ones of modernity. Such a politics disrupts any self-recuperative, egoistic, and triumphalist politics, even a politics of the multitude.[6] The critical linkage of ethics and epistemology articulates an intricate critique of the geopolitics of theological knowledge and forms a truly revolutionary alternative that is quite suggestive for countering the "econo-epistemic" violence that is empire at the beginning of a new century.

I

"The death of God that many Europeans began to perceive," write Hardt and Negri, "was really a sign of the expiration of their own planetary centrality, which they could understand only in terms of a modern mysticism."[7] Here Hardt and Negri target a critical theme for understanding the religious malaise that challenged the nineteenth-century European mind. The death of God was not so much the end of religious belief or an end of thinking the t/Transcendent. Rather, it sounded the alarm that the rationalizing formulas that constituted the cognitive grid of the European mind were not commensurate with the new material realities and a radical reorientation was necessary in order to obtain a critical understanding of and mastery over a changing world. The situation was not so much a crisis in the confidence of the European material and intellectual project as it was a clarion call to revise the paradigmatic formulas that made and gave meaning and order to the European construction of the world. However, by unreflexively centralizing the European rational subject, Hardt and Negri fail to properly comprehend the challenge presented by the death of God to the economic and epistemic dominance of Europe—thereby missing the opportunity to challenge the hegemony of the rationalizing project of empire. Furthermore, they historicize and hypostatize "Europe" as the main locus for any critical elaboration and understanding of the development

6. See Michael Hardt and Antonio Negri, *Multitude: War and Democracy in an Age of Empire* (New York: Penguin, 2004).

7. Michael Hardt and Antonio Negri, *Empire* (Cambridge, MA: Harvard University Press, 2000), 375. Future references to this text will be cited parenthetically within the text.

of the (post)modern world.[8] Thus, contrary to their assertion of offering a "critical approach [that] addresses the need for a real ideological and material deconstruction of the imperial order," Hardt and Negri's theoretical architecture undermines the radical intent of their project and by extension facilitates the continuance of the econo-epistemic project of empire (47).

To illustrate this point further within the critical arsenal unleashed by Hardt and Negri against contemporary subversive intellectual projects, we need look no further than the authors' suspicion that "postmodernist and postcolonialist theories may end up in a dead end because they fail to recognize adequately the contemporary object of critique, that is, they mistake today's real enemy" (137). While recognizing "the value" as well as the "limitations" of these theoretical tendencies, Hardt and Negri view them as "important *effects* that reflect or trace the expansion of the world market and the passage of the form of sovereignty" (138–39). What conjoins Hardt and Negri's critique of postmodernist and postcolonialist theories with their unreflexiveness in interrogating the depth of meaning of "the death of God" for the European mind is a theoretical deficit that facilitates a willed ignorance to the very econo-epistemic conditions that animate their project. In other words, the smoothness and simplicity with which they are able to think the limits of the postcolonial and postmodern intellectual project while maintaining a theoretical Eurocentrism represents the (un)conscious desire of the traditional rationalizing process to maintain and perpetuate an ideological status quo. Indeed, if we are to truly understand the dynamics of the changing cartography of our social, political, and economic moment, what is needed is not so much a conversation with Arthur Schopenhauer's "intellectual Caliban" as an interrogation of the epistemic processes that produce the global Calibans in relation to the economic flows that bulwark the European Prospero's across space and time (81).[9] *Empire*'s deficient theoretical strategy is thus an invitation to undertake an investigation into the epistemic processes within the geopolitical flows of culture, commerce, and capital that animate not only contemporary forms of theoretical production but also, and more importantly for our project, the recent turn to the theological. It becomes incumbent upon us to unravel the logics of the theological turn prior to proffering any alternative proposals in challenging the dynamics of empire's terrain.

II

The turn to the theological in recent years has been marked by three major theoretical tendencies. The first can be characterized by a renewed interest

8. This is clearly evident in the spatial, temporal, epistemic, and material logics that in/form the chapter "Two Europes, Two Modernities."

9. On this point see Paget Henry, *Caliban's Reason: Introducing Afro-Caribbean Philosophy* (New York: Routledge, 2000).

in and deepening of the idea of the theological in contradistinction to other theoretical discourses. Such a move entails the development of alternative narrative accounts of the development of modern rationality and a repositioning of the discourse of theology from the margins to the center of contemporary intellectual discourse. Oftentimes this effort proceeds by way of a historical retrieval of certain theologians and theological ideas deemed to be distinctly "Christian" and thus assisting in bulwarking the *sui generis* gloss of Christianity's theological claims and doctrines.[10] The second tendency is shaped by a dialectical engagement between particular theological ideas and concepts and other theoretical frameworks and discourses. This move seeks to challenge the binary and dichotomous logic that separates theological formations and nontheological formations. It also blurs the boundaries between the two in seeking to facilitate a critical nexus whereby the theological is understood as being coextensive with other nontheological discourses. The final tendency argues for the efficacy of certain theological concepts and constructions without admitting the entire panoply of theological claims and commitments within its discourse. Indeed, this final tendency rejects the theological claims grounded in a transcendent guarantee and a doctrinal understanding coded in theological language and custom. The theological thus serves as a reminder of a more fundamental understanding of what can be termed a universal, humanistic understanding that informs particular constructions of the social, the political, and the economical.

Despite the revival in interest in the theological, the contemporary (re)turn is marked by a debilitating limitation. In his engagement with and critique of the work of Slavoj Žižek, William Hart develops the notion of the "imperial/ colonial model of religion."[11] This construct not only is descriptive of the general efforts of theorists who develop and deploy "evolutionary/hierarchical" models for the study of religion, but it also introduces a critical principle by which one can interrogate and critique such efforts. Hart writes, "The appellation *imperial/colonial model* of religion is apropos. For colonial modernity began with Portuguese and Spanish voyages of conquest consecrated by the Pope in the 1494 Treaty of Tordesillas. Thus conquest provides the historical context for the emergence of a theory of religion that models the hierarchical, sociopolitical relations with native peoples in the Americas, Africa, Asia, Australia, and the islands of the Atlantic, Pacific, and Indian Oceans (the bitter fruit of conquest) that were already beginning to develop."[12] According to Hart, it is the particular constellation of histories in the contact of cultures that commenced with the global transactions of culture, capital, and commerce

10. See Russell T. McCutcheon, *Manufacturing Religion: The Discourse on "Sui Generis" Religion and the Politics of Nostalgia* (New York: Oxford University Press, 1997).

11. William David Hart, "Slavoj Žižek and the Imperial/Colonial Model of Religion," *Nepantla: Views from South* 3, no. 3 (2002): 553–78.

12. Ibid., 555.

that condition and critically inform the "temporal, geographical, racial, and gendered hierarchies" within the theoretical (and material) complex of the "imperial/colonial model of religion."[13] The intellectual and material matrix that Hart codes as the "imperial/colonial model of religion" highlights an axiomatic dimension that is elided and evaded in much of the contemporary theological turn. That is, the sedimented discourses that work to ascertain, fix, and spatialize meaning turn on a coded logic that frames the discourse of theology geographically as Western, temporally as modern, and theistically as Christian. In turn, the frames of this theological discourse interpenetrate one another in an elaborate fashion so as to mask their very imbrications. The categorical evasion of the "imperial/colonial" matrix propels the (re) production of a particular sensibility of the social, political, and economic orders as ostensibly secular and modern. Such an understanding facilitates the development of "critical" forms of thought that vacate the theological dimension that is crucial in maintaining this categorical division.

The logical operations of the imperial/colonial model of religion or, to adopt the phrase developed by Walter Mignolo, the *theopolitics of knowledge*, effectively masks the (mis)recognition of the very conditions of possibility of the contemporary turn to the theological.[14] The main trajectories of the discourse of the theological in contemporary theory circulate through the registers of particular European thinkers facilitated by a strategic recourse to a European-derived and -dominated archive. The circularity and insularity of this discourse mean that there is an acute epistemic continuance with the dominant logic of the rationalist *episteme* that consolidated its power in the name of g/God, democracy, and capitalism. Such a division has fueled the (re)turn to the theological, which is always already shot through with a particular "God claim" that founds and governs the hegemonic intellectual projects and imperial exploits of the Western world.[15] What unites the current theological renaissance with the permanence of the "theologico-political" is a logic of Christianity that is always already a part of the violent subordination of the intellectual orders and social and political registers of those o/ Others who were the "end" of the new beginnings of modernity. It is through this logic that we understand that the contemporary theological turn is but a

13. Ibid.

14. Walter Mignolo articulated this concept on November 22, 2003, at the annual meeting of the American Academy of Religion in Atlanta. The theopolitics of knowledge is an elaboration of the more fundamental concept of the geopolitics of knowledge. On the "geopolitics of knowledge," see Enrique Dussel, *Philosophy of Liberation*, trans. Aquilina Martinex and Christine Morkovsky (Maryknoll, NY: Orbis, 1985), and Walter Mignolo, *Local Histories, Global Designs: Coloniality, Subaltern Knowledges, and Border Thinking* (Princeton, NJ: Princeton University Press, 2000).

15. On this point see Sylvia Wynter, "Unsettling the Coloniality of Being/Power/Truth/Freedom: Toward the Human, After Man, Its Overrepresentation—An Argument," *CR: The New Centennial Review* 3, no. 3 (2003): 257–337.

different phase of a larger and longer drama of epistemic struggle and economic violence built on the consolidations of the evacuations of the Arab, Jew, Negro, and Native and forged in the crucible of capitalist imperialism.[16] The ideological fantasy of the theological reorganizes the forces and vectors that propel the theopolitics of knowledge in its recourse to and rehearsal of the singular event of (European) Christianity and its absolute promise of a perpetual peace.

In drawing attention to this contemporary theoretical situation, which turns on an axis of the (re)turn to the theological, it is not enough for us to casually dispense with the discourse of theology in an effort to get to the r/ Real theoretical formulas and articulations that would properly place us in a position to think otherwise. We cannot simply consign the theological to a residual history of an uncritical discourse that is resistant to any type of critical theoretical elaboration or reject this discourse *tout court* as one that is incapable of confronting the conditions of its own existence Nor should we attempt to convince ourselves that only a proper construction of theology, or a singular recourse to a particular construction of Christianity which can be re/presented as evangelical, will provide us with the necessary resources to challenge this trend.[17] The theological is a critical terrain of struggle within the ideological and imperial matrix of *Empire* and empire. The (re)turn to the theological challenges us to respond by not only demystifying the logics of the dominant discursive responses to the conditions of empire but also beginning again with the construction of a certain type of responsible theological discourse that challenges the material and ideological dimensions of the theopolitics of knowledge. The necessity of a theological response carries with it a kind of ethical obligation or, rather, orientation that must account for these imbrications. Thus, in advancing my claim for a responsible theological response, I am at the same time claiming that an ethical demand is placed on the task of theology. And this ethical demand is best elaborated as an ethics of opacity.

III

I have chosen the ground of ethics in order to highlight "the very fact that ethics exist as unscientific"—that is, resistant to and restrictive of the epistemic hegemony of a strictly rationalist *episteme* proper—speaks to its critical dimension, which cannot be reduced to the disciplinary power of the

16. See Gil Anidjar, *The Jew, the Arab: A History of the Enemy* (Stanford, CA: Stanford University Press, 2003).

17. This is a critical weakness, in an otherwise admirable project, by leading evangelical thinkers and activists like Jim Wallis. See Jim Wallis, *God's Politics: Why the Right Gets It Wrong and the Left Doesn't Get It* (New York: HarperOne, 2005).

modern "scientistic" rationalizing impulse.[18] Hence the ethical question holds out the possibility of unmasking and "denouncing all myth, all mystifications, all superstitions" that inhere in a disciplinary and disciplining logic of our contemporary categorization and organization of knowledge, particularly in the North Atlantic academy.[19]

With this understanding, ethics is transformed into a critical discursive practice that evades uncritical "sentimentality and development, and pre[over] determined categories such as good and bad."[20] Ethics proper is a discourse derived from a rigorous, vigilant, and militant theoretical site of struggle. Such struggles are not merely over "values" but rather expose the "conflicts in which [groups, formations, and classes] express their means of reproducing the very struggle that creates them—and finds emancipatory expression in their practices of resistance, pleasure, and authority."[21] Ethics thus rendered is transformed into a critical terrain that fields the necessary interrogatory practices to question normative assumptions and methodological presuppositions in raising a critical consciousness within the ongoing battle to challenge the disciplinary dictates and epistemological demands of the modern organization of knowledge.

The ethics of opacity operates from a similar position, as announced by Alain Badiou: "Ethics does not exist. There is only the ethics of (of politics, of love, of science, of art)."[22] Such an ethical understanding seeks to temper the imperial strategy of traditional ethics, particular ethical formulations, traditions, and prescriptives that gather under the logics and technologies of coloniality. Indeed, "it might well be that ethical ideology, detached from the religious teachings which at least conferred upon it the fullness of 'revealed' identity, is simply the final imperative of a conquering civilization: 'Become like me and I will respect your difference.'"[23]

Inspired by the work of Charles Long, this ethical perspective establishes the critical principle that those hegemonic knowledge systems unleashed by coloniality/modernity necessarily introduce what Long calls "that 'thing' [which] must be suppressed, but the very act of suppression introduces the thing suppressed into the symbolic universe that it stakes out."[24] Long continues with recourse to the work of Paul Ricoeur, who writes, "Now defilement

18. B. Ricardo Brown, "Marx and the Foundations of the Critical Theory of Morality and Ethics," *Cultural Logic* 2, no. 2 (Spring 1999): §3.

19. Gilles Deleuze, as quoted in ibid., §5.

20. Brown, "Marx and the Foundations," §4.

21. Ibid.

22. Alain Badiou, *Ethics: An Essay on the Understanding of Evil*, trans. Peter Hallward (New York: Verso, 2001), 24.

23. Ibid., 28.

24. Charles H. Long, "Freedom, Otherness, and Religion: Theologies Opaque," in *Significations: Signs, Symbols, and Images in the Interpretation of Religion* (Aurora, CO: Davies, 1999), 199–214.

enters into the universe of man through speech, or the word; its anguish is communicated through speech. . . . The opposition of the pure and the impure is spoken. . . . A stain is a stain because it is there, mute; the impure taught in the words that institute the taboo."[25]

Within this nexus, the ethics of opacity suggest a critical site for the production and reproduction of the knowledges of those on the underside of modernity. Long writes,

> Black, the colored races, [were] caught up into this net of the imaginary and symbolic consciousness of the West, rendered mute through the words of military, economic, and intellectual power, assimilated as if by osmosis structures of this consciousness of oppression. This is the source of the doubleness of consciousness made famous by W. E. B. Du Bois. But even in these symbolic structures there remained the inexhaustibility of the opaqueness of this symbol for those who constituted the "things" upon which the significations of the West deployed its meanings.[26]

Thus, the ethics of opacity establishes a critical movement, indeed produces an ethical demand, that speaks to and is founded upon a responsibility to interrogate hegemonic epistemological production, which is "the context for the communities of color, the opaque ones of the modern world."[27] Such an ethics calls into question traditional formulations and rehearsal of ethics proper and radically calls into account "radical" formulations of emancipatory theoretical projects, i.e., scientific Marxism, dogmatic theology, Western democracy, and the host of "post-" prefixed theoretical formulations.

Such an ethics of opacity also entails, or rather prescribes, a critical intellectual practice that affirms the worth, value, and dignity of the "human." Long writes: "Octavio Paz tells us that they were filled with poets, proletarians, colonized peoples, the colored races. 'All these purgatories and hells lived in a state of clandestine ferment. One day in the twentieth century, the subterranean world blew up. The explosion hasn't yet ended and its splendor has illumined the agony of the age.'"[28] The ethics of opacity is animated by this vision in seeking to articulate the depth of meaning that is announced in these continuing events. In this sense, the ethics of opacity pushes the discourse of ethics to the limit. Accordingly, recourse to Levinas is quite appropriate when he suggests, "My task does not consist in constructing ethics, I only try to seek its meaning."[29]

25. Ibid., 204.
26. Ibid.
27. Ibid.
28. Ibid.
29. Emmanuel Levinas, *Ethique et Infini*, quoted in Simon Critchley, *The Ethics of Deconstruction: Derrida and Levinas* (Oxford: Blackwell, 1992), 4.

The ethics of opacity presents "more than an accusation regarding the actions and behavior of the oppressive cultures; it goes to the heart of the issue. It is an accusation regarding the world view, thought structures, theory of knowledge, and so on, of the oppressors. The accusation is not simply of bad acts but, more importantly, of bad faith and bad knowledge."[30] An ethics of opacity is thus defined by its critical orientation to liberation as articulated by *and* with the opaque ones. It is a critical intellectual posture that disrupts the dominant logic of coloniality/modernity in exploring the hidden and unknown, the repressed and submerged narratives, histories, and epistemologies—the *sites of opacity* that are the conditions of im/possibility of the contemporary world. Such an ethic is available because, as Long writes, "the strategies of obscuring these peoples and cultures within the taxonomies of the disciplines of anthropology as primitives or the classification of them as sociological pathologies is no longer possible."[31]

The ethics of opacity helps to structure our ability "to effect the deconstruction of the mechanisms by means of which we continue to make opaque to ourselves, attributing the origin of our societies to imaginary beings, whether the ancestors, the gods, God, or evolution, and natural selection, the reality of our own agency with respect to the programming and reprogramming of our desires, our behaviors, our minds, ourselves, the I and the we."[32] Such a move has significant implication for "reimagining our forms of life" and opens up critical possibilities for a critical return to the theological.[33]

An ethics of opacity bears a critical relation to the theological. In a crucial sense, it is the emergence and existence of the opaque ones that conditions the im/possibility of theology. Long states, "As stepchildren of Western culture, the oppressed have affirmed and opposed the ideal of the Enlightenment and post-Enlightenment worlds. But in the midst of this ambiguity, for better or for worse, their experiences were rooted in the absurd meaning of their bodies, and it was for these bodies that they were regarded not only as valuable works but also as the locus of the ideologies that justified their enslavement. . . . The totalization of all the great ideals of Western universalization met with the factual symbol of these oppressed ones."[34] The infinite meaning and depth of the "factual symbol of these oppressed ones" is the location of ethics of opacity and in turn presents to the structure the relation to the theological. Indeed, the theological thus becomes a critical process in the interrogation of this relation that cannot be evaded. The disruption announced by the ethics of opacity challenges the theological by suggesting the primacy of the method

30. Long, "Freedom, Otherness, and Religion," 208.

31. Ibid., 211.

32. Sylvia Wynter as quoted in David Scott, "The Re-enchantment of Humanism: An Interview with Sylvia Wynter," *Small Axe: A Journal of Criticism* 8 (2000): 194.

33. Ibid.

34. Long, "Freedom, Otherness, and Religion," 211.

of procedure, as opposed to the fundamental question of ontology. Here we turn our attention to the work of C. L. R. James.

Rarely is this James invoked within theological discourse. But James's 1948 text *Notes on Dialectics* can provide us with a critical orientation to the problematic that arises within the relation of the ethical and the theological as articulated here.[35] Following Lenin's 1914 example in (re)turning to a consideration of Hegel's *Science of Logic* and the implications for radical political action, James provides us with a methodological orientation for a type of theological thinking that is responsive to the demand(s) of an ethics of opacity. "Now we have established Hegel's great contribution," James writes, "in his own mind, at least to be this: that you examine, *and see that you do it*, both the things that you test and the instruments by which you test them."[36] The critical reflexivity that James highlights provides an axiomatic principle that strives to be responsive to and gestures toward a procedure for the issues raised by the presence of the "opaque ones."

Although the primary concern for James in *Notes on Dialectics* is to demonstrate the "difference and identity" of the Trotskyist and Stalinist tendencies within the highly charged Marxist-Leninist polemical debates of the second quarter of the twentieth century, he provides some formal conceptual criteria for theological thinking with an ethics of opacity.[37] James's text reminds us that there is an imperative to the practice of theological thinking:

> We shall meet it again and again, and shall take it from every point of view until we get it. Thought is not an instrument you apply to a content. The content moves, develops, changes and creates new categories of thought and gives them direction. . . . Now one of the chief errors of thought is to continue to think in one set of forms, categories, ideas, etc., when the object, the content, has moved on, has created or laid the premises for an extension, a development of thought. A philosophic cognition means a cognition in which the categories of thought are adequate to the object it is thinking about.[38]

The point James drives home is the necessity to continually engage the systems, orders, and categories of thought as one attempts to think through new intellectual and material cartographies. To try to think through new content within the horizons of *always already* established categories is to necessarily commit a categorical error. When translated to the arena of theological thinking, James's admonition provides a critical response to Long when he asks,

35. C. L. R. James, *Notes on Dialectics: Hegel, Marx, Lenin* (London: Allison and Busby, 1980).

36. Ibid., 57.

37. For a full treatment of the political and philosophical dimensions of this struggle, see John H. McClendon III, *C. L. R. James's "Notes on Dialectics": Left Hegelianism or Marxism-Leninism?* (Lanham, MD: Lexington, 2005), 41–75.

38. James, *Notes on Dialectics*, 15.

"What is the stance of a theology or a theologian when the very intellectual religious task is framed within a racist context?"[39] That is, within the intellectual and material registers of the modern world in which "the nonwhite color symbolizes and its significations have been acted upon within the modern Western world as signs of defilement and uncleanness," it is an imperative that the theological register these significations in and through the development of conceptual and analytical categories that register the "opacity of reality."[40] Such a requisite theoretical stance animates and propels the "pronouncements by the opaque ones [to] deny the authority of the white world to define their reality, and deny the methodological and philosophical meaning of transparency as a metaphor for a theory of knowledge."[41] Quoting Hegel, James writes, "'Usually no suspicion attaches to the finite forms of thought; they are allowed to pass unquestioned.'"[42] In this version of theological thinking, one must proceed cautiously, suspiciously, yet audaciously in conjuring the concepts and categories that will facilitate a nuanced and critical engagement with the depths of opacity.

James's injunction is further developed when, commenting on an extended passage from Hegel's *Logic*, he writes, "The organic life of the thought-forms, the categories, is that they develop from their own contradictions."[43] Here James describes the conditions in and through which critical forms of thought are developed. It is not a procedural application of an adequate thought-form from without that is the task, but a grappling with the contradictions of the categories in and of themselves whereby thought develops. The contradictions of the theopolitics of knowledge thus do not force us into a binary either-or problematic with respect to theological discourse. The categorical demands of opacity are critically accounted for within the space of contradiction, as a generative space for new forms of thought. In this regard, theological thinking develops with and against itself to overwhelm the static registers of a (re)turn to the theological that would resist an engagement with the opaque ones. By proceeding in this way, theological thinking "forms a discontinuity with the bad faith of the other theological models."[44] At this point "the destruction of theology as a powerful mode of discourse" always, already begins.[45]

This brief journey through James's *Notes on Dialectics* is an attempt to outline a conceptual and methodological strategy in thematizing an ethics of opacity for gaining a critical understanding of the logics and technologies

39. Long, "Freedom, Otherness, and Religion," 203.

40. Ibid., 203, 207.

41. Ibid., 207.

42. James, *Notes on Dialectics*, 16.

43. Ibid., 45.

44. Long, "Freedom, Otherness, and Religion," 209. For a response, see Anthony Bogues, *Empire of Liberty: Power, Desire, and Freedom* (Durham, NC: Duke University Press, forthcoming).

45. Long, "Freedom, Otherness, and Religion," 210.

of the theological. By turning to James and taking up some of his suggestive remarks, we are able to demonstrate the dramatic epistemological implications of this ethical orientation. On this basis we come to understand how and why the contemporary theological turn is manifested as it has been.

In his invocation of the imperial/colonial model of religion, William Hart writes, "What I will not argue is that Žižek *intends* to recapitulate the imperial/colonial model of religion. On the contrary, he stumbles into this model. He does so, precisely, because he *does not intend to*. He does not think about the ethics and politics of religion and representation at all."[46] Hart is correct in his critique of Žižek's project and, by extension, of the contemporary theological turn. According to the categories and logic that govern contemporary theoretical elaborations, it is a question not so much of intention as of the framework. Charles Long argued a similar point when assessing the theological scene a generation ago: "The designations post-Enlightenment, death of God, end of the Protestant Era, the end of ideology, which we referred to earlier, are pronouncements that have come from the intellectual orders of the sophisticated West, and they may well be the most authentic statement about their intellectual resources for the definition of the human venture."[47] I would add that a more robust critique also involves intervening in the theological (re)turn and placing into this discourse the question of an ethics of opacity and the resulting implications on the concepts and categories of thought. It is not so much a question of intentions that must be confronted as the always-already question of the *necessary* evasions and elisions that must be accomplished in order to entomb an empire's theo-logic in a modern, even radical, conceptual sarcophagus. By tracing the contours of the contemporary theological turn and offering the beginnings of a critique and corrective, we arrive at the central question animating this project: how does one proceed to construct a theological discourse proper to an ethics of opacity? In light of all that has been examined thus far, it seems appropriate now to articulate some axiomatic points of the project of theological thinking.

IV

"But what expression would freedom deriving from people who had indeed endured and overcome oppression make? If this freedom is not to be simply the sentimental imitation of the lordship-bondage structure with a new set of actors, it would have to be a new form of freedom."[48] To begin a preliminary exposition of theological thinking with Long serves as a reminder that the task before us cannot be simply derivative of other theological discourses.

46. Hart, "Slavoj Žižek and the Imperial/Colonial Model," 555.
47. Long, "Freedom, Otherness, and Religion," 210.
48. Ibid., 211.

Traditional theological ventures always already come to an end when one takes into account the absurd meanings of the bodies of the opaque ones. "These opaque ones were centers from which gods were made. They were the concrete embodiments of matter made significant in the modern world. They formed new rhythms in time and space; these bodies of opacity were facts of history and symbols of a new religious depth."[49] Thus, the formulations in the project of theological thinking must wrestle with the in/finite depth of the intellectual and material resources of opacity.[50]

"Theologies are about power, the power of God, but equally about the power of specific forms of discourse about power. These discourses are about the hegemony of power—the distribution and economy of this power in heaven and on earth—whether in the ecclesiastical locus of a pope, or more generally since the modern period, the center of this power in the modern Western world."[51] Here Long refocuses our attention on the central issue within theological discourse—the question of power and its embeddedness within dominant forms of theological knowledge. By evading the question of power and the intellectual and material economies developed in the wake of the (re)configurations of the modern world, a purely textual move within theological discourse is stripped of any critical efficacy in challenging the economic and epistemic regimes of theology proper. Long's critical project is a crucial challenge to the very norms and foundations of the projects of theology *and* theological thinking that continue to move to the rhythms of traditional theology. Put differently, the un/thinkable of the theological—what can be symbolized as g/G*d—cannot be adequately approached within the constructs and categories of a theological arena that (un)consciously rejects the legitimacy of the presence and thought structures of the opaque ones. "The opacity of God," Long writes, "forms a discontinuity with the bad faith of the other theological modes."[52] If the shift from theology to theological thinking is to produce anything more than a new semiotics trapped within the logocentric political economy of the modern world, then it must begin to wrestle with the opacity that is the foundation of the modern world. Thus, theological thinking does not "move forward to possess the theological battlefield wrested from [its] foes. . . . [It] undertake[s] the destruction of theology as a powerful mode of discourse."[53]

The project of theological thinking that I am advocating requires that we dispense with the traditional concepts and categories of theology and recent

49. Ibid.
50. My project of theological thinking has been informed by the proposals advanced by David Jasper, "From Theology to Theological Thinking: The Development of Critical Thought and Its Consequences for Theology," *Literature and Theology*, 1995, 293–305, and Carl Raschke, *Theological Thinking: An Inquiry* (Atlanta: Scholars Press, 1988).
51. Long, "Freedom, Otherness, and Religion," 209.
52. Ibid.
53. Ibid., 210–11.

formulations of theological thinking along a similar trajectory, as called for by Lewis Gordon with reference to philosophy:

> Different problems emerge in the course of philosophy as we begin to take the risk of going beyond philosophy for philosophy's sake. In some of my recent writings I have called this the teleological suspension of philosophy. And what that means is that there is a certain point in which a philosopher is constrained by the conception of philosophy in his or her time. So in the interest of truth the philosopher is willing to give up philosophy as understood within his or her time, which is paradoxical because philosophy is the pursuit of truth. And that person ends up creating a new philosophy.[54]

Gordon highlights the perplexing situation in which philosophers find themselves when their particular projects no longer find a home within the discourse of philosophy proper. It is this sentiment that frames the dilemma of the theologian as he or she seeks to engages the theological task. Following the example set by James's *Notes on Dialectics*, theological thinking must first dispense with the static categories of theology proper and begin again in the space of tension between the known and the unknown in order to exploit the opportunity for pursuing the im/possible. The im/possible is not only that which is of ultimate concern within the theological task but also the generative ground of the thought formations, categories, concepts, and constructs for the task of theological thinking. In the end, there are no guarantees regarding the possibility of creating a new theology, as the thought practices that ensue may dispense with the construct of theology as such. Moreover, the discourse that evolves may achieve such a degree of noncorrespondence with what currently travels under the banner of theology and/or the theological that some new construct may be conjured.

Theological thinking so construed need not necessarily lapse into or suggest an uncritical relativism or an unruly theoretical anarchy. To be sure, a degree of uncertainty is necessarily enveloped within this venture. But the level of uncertainty is of a generative and reflexive nature such that it animates, or rather compels, one to constantly interrogate, revise, and substantiate the arguments and claims advanced by theological thinking in dialogic relation with the conditions—both epistemological and material—of opacity. To further delineate theological thinking, one may approach this task along the following trajectory: "Evoking the memory of suffering, especially that which contradicts 'the American Dream,' is the crucial link between critical theory and theology, the political and the personal, emancipation and redemption. A socio-political theology enables a breaking through of the sense of fatedness, the raising of critical consciousness, and thus the empowering of subjects for

54. Lewis R. Gordon, "A Philosophical Account of Africana Studies: An Interview with Lewis Gordon," interview by Linda Alcoff, *Nepantla: Views from South* 4, no. 1 (2003): 147–63.

transformative social praxis."[55] In large measure it is the between that animates Karen Bloomquist's vision for an adequate sociopolitical theology that would instantiate a transvaluation of the task of theology. Analogously, theological thinking plays in the interstices between thought and experience, such that theological thinking becomes a cautious, calculated, and critical discourse on the structured chaos that is existence. Theological thinking begins, as Long so aptly articulates, "in the histories and traditions of those who have undergone the oppressive cultures of the modern period. It means that attention must be given in a precise manner to the modes of experience and expression that formed these communities in their inner and intimate lives. I don't have in mind here a romantic return to an earlier period. I am speaking of the resources that might enable us to generate another kind of meaning from the temporal-spatial existence of human beings on this globe."[56] Theological thinking commences the multiple task of critically rendering the *mysterium* of the condition(s) for the theological.

Theological thinking tempers the desire for clarity and transparency in much imperialistic theology. The quest for transparency is a quest to conquer. Georges Bataille issues the following invitation: "Every time we give up the will to know, we have the possibility of touching the world with a much greater intensity."[57] Theological thinking opens us to that which cannot be appropriated and apprehended by existing theological frameworks and systems and engages us in the materiality of the world. In interrogating the histories and traditions of the opaque ones, theological thinking highlights the fragment not in a nostalgic manner, as a remnant of a lost whole, but rather in a manner analogous to what Raymond Williams calls a "militant particularism."[58] Theological thinking eschews systems, processes, and procedures that foreclose our theological vision—that is, our theological hopes, dreams, and desires—and seeks to recapture a sense of newness and otherness that is present in the fragment. Theological thinking leverages a critical temper in theological reflection by not submitting to an imperial model of totality but leaving open the possibility of constructing more comprehensive theological conceptions.[59] It is thinking theologically as/in multiplicity. It is a radical calling to the O/other that is always already within and without.

---

55. Karen L. Bloomquist, "Toward a Theological Engagement with Working Class Experience," *Word and World* 2 (Summer 1982): 270–76.

56. Long, "Freedom, Otherness, and Religion," 210.

57. Georges Bataille, *The Unfinished System of Nonknowledge*, ed. Stuart Kendall, trans. Michelle Kendall and Stuart Kendall (Minneapolis: University of Minnesota Press, 2001), 115.

58. Raymond Williams, *Resources of Hope* (London: Verso, 1989), 249. We might also recall the notion of the fragment that is quite instructive in ethical and epistemological dimensions of the thought of Theodor Adorno and Walter Benjamin.

59. The ethics of this point is inspired by Sylvia Wynter. See Wynter, "Re-enchantment of Humanism," 188.

Theological thinking privileges a multiplicity of processes of inquiry into mundane and everyday sites of opacity. It is a critical recognition of the "inexhaustibility of the opaqueness" that forms the very foundation of the possibility of the material and theoretical project of empire.[60] Accordingly, as theologians and activists we are always already responding to the question: How do we continuously cultivate a theological thinking that is cognizant of the (in)authenticity of our theoretical concepts and categories yet attuned to the trace of the abject in giving expression to the opaque ones trying to radically transform the world?

V

Following the passage of the Fugitive Slave Act in 1850, Frederick Douglass and Sojourner Truth addressed an audience of abolitionists in Boston's Fanueil Hall. In a jeremiad against the United States, Douglass indicted and convicted American democracy for its inability to deal justly and equitably with African Americans. Douglass not only questioned the foundations of American democracy but went on to interrogate the very (im)possibility that the United States would ever "repent" and "atone" for its "sins."

Before a stunned and silenced crowd, Sojourner Truth posed a most prescient theological question to Douglass—"Frederick, is God dead?"[61]

Sojourner Truth's question brings to light the deep and complex tensions between the theological and the political in the context of empire. Indeed, Truth's question highlights the deep ambiguities regarding the viability of the theological to adequately register and articulate a full critique of democratic practices and politics, not to mention capitalist political economy. Truth's rhetorical question necessarily opens up a line of reflective investigation into the very foundational claims of the theological enterprise in relation to the existential conditions and epistemological conjurations of empire. The question "Frederick, is God dead?" requires not so much an absolute answer—as so many evangelicals would like to offer—as a deep and probing interrogation of the myriad methods, categories, norms, and substantive commitments that in/form the material and ideological constructions of empire *and* evangelicalism. Hans-Georg Gadamer reminds us, "Questioning opens up possibilities of meaning. . . . [T]o ask a question means to bring into the open. The openness of what is in question consists in the fact that the answer is not settled."[62] At stake in the openness of Truth's question is nothing less than the present and

60. Long, "Freedom, Otherness, and Religion," 204.

61. Harriet Beecher Stowe, "Sojourner Truth: The Libyan Sibyl," *Atlantic Monthly* 11 (April 1863): 473–81.

62. Hans-Georg Gadamer, *Truth and Method*, 2nd rev. ed., trans. Joel Weinsheimer and Donald Marshall (New York: Crossroad, 1989), 375, 363.

future possibility of a critical response to empire as well as a fundamental rethinking of the relation of theology and politics.

To the question posed by Sojourner Truth, "Frederick, is God dead?" the project of theological thinking responds as an ethically grounded discourse that does not privilege stock answers. This project strives to explore new avenues and opportunities for theological thinking in challenging the dictates of empire as well as the normative commitments of evangelicalism. In completing the theoretical task left undone by Hardt and Negri's *Empire*, the project of theological thinking gestures toward a new conceptual order that "recogniz[es] and engag[es] the imperial initiatives and [does] not allow them continually to reestablish order" (399). Thus, we audaciously announce the end of theology and the beginning(s) of theological thinking in service to and solidarity with the opaque ones.

Acknowledgments

I want to thank Walter Mignolo of Duke University for inviting me to contribute the initial thoughts that gave rise to this essay to the Center for Global Humanities spring 2005 workshop "Shifting the Geo-graphy and Bio-graphy of Reason." I also want to thank Anthony Bogues and the Small Axe Collective for inviting me to participate in their spring symposium at Brown University, where I was afforded the opportunity to elaborate these thoughts within a hospitable and collegial environment of committed intellectuals and activists. Parts of this paper were also presented in April 2005 at the "Mapping the Decolonial Turn" conference at the University of California, Berkeley, and the 2005 Caribbean Philosophical Association meeting in San Juan, Puerto Rico. Finally, I want to express my sincere gratitude to Reverend Mildred Best for inviting me to share my project of "Critical Theology" with the residents in the Department of Chaplaincy Services and Pastoral Education in the University of Virginia Health System.

17

What Empire, Which Multitude?

Pentecostalism and Social Liberation in North America and Sub-Saharan Africa

AMOS YONG AND SAMUEL ZALANGA

Introduction

This chapter interrogates the ideas of Hardt and Negri with regard to the possibility that Christianity in the United States and sub-Saharan Africa might serve as a catalyst for social liberation.[1] In principle, we agree with Hardt and Negri's assertion that global market fundamentalism has become a hegemonic and pervasive system, even a religion in its own right. We go further to say that the instrumental rationality underpinning capitalism has invaded the church of Christ and is transforming it in a negative way. Many churches have become like firms competing for market shares (converts). So churches develop a product (i.e., message) that appeals to the taste of consumers in general, or they specialize for a specific segment of the consumer market. Thus, while Hardt and Negri are right to see that the human struggle for liberation from the pervasive and hegemonic dominance of global market

1. See Michael Hardt and Antonio Negri, *Empire* (Cambridge, MA: Harvard University Press, 2000), and *Multitude: War and Democracy in the Age of Empire* (New York: Penguin, 2004).

fundamentalism is one of the most serious challenges of our time, as Christians we would go further and say that the church also needs to be liberated from being co-opted by this new religion of the market. Only in this way can the church further the project of social liberation rather than conspire in the causes of social oppression.

Unfortunately, however, Hardt and Negri ignore the role of faith in this broad project of social liberation. We are interested in understanding how Pentecostalism interacts with the global political economy in this conversation. Put succinctly, is Pentecostalism a medium for the operation of "biopower" in ways that prevents the oppressed from challenging their oppressors, or is it a subversive movement? Is Pentecostalism necessarily struggling to resist the virtual centers of empire, or is the movement extending the hegemony of empire? Indeed, the expression of Pentecostalism as a religious movement varies with the social structure, political opportunity structure, and level of economic development of a society. Hence we suggest that any response to this question must be empirically informed.

To explore the ramifications of Hardt and Negri's neglect of faith, we look at the increasingly influential role of Pentecostal Christianity in the Global South. We begin by summarizing some key themes from Hardt and Negri that are relevant for our argument. We then briefly examine the public role of Christianity in American society and discuss the practice of Pentecostalism in sub-Saharan Africa, especially as it has been influenced by American Christianity. We conclude by suggesting how Christianity can and should subvert any "empire" project that constitutes idolatry from a biblical perspective.

Hardt and Negri: An Overview of Relevant Themes

Hardt and Negri argue that neoliberal capitalism in the form of globalization is obliterating the legacies of imperialism (e.g., the nation-state) and creating a level playing field where market rationality is the fundamental guiding principle. In their reasoning, no one can escape the domain of capitalist hegemony. But since the new empire is "bathed in blood" and increases inequality between the few who are rich and the majority proletariat, it does not promote peace. The question then is why do people accept the violence? In partial answer to this question, Hardt and Negri maintain that "the great industrial and financial powers produce not only commodities but also subjectivities."[2] This of course means that needs, social relations, bodies, and minds of individuals in society are shaped by the industrial and financial powers of the world. By implication, this means capitalist society produces people who are socialized and brainwashed to be mere consumers. The mechanism for this socializa-

2. *Empire*, 32.

tion is through "biopower," a subtle form of manipulation that infects our brains and makes us internalize the values of capitalism. Liberal democratic societies may think they are free, but they are not because capitalism turns their day-to-day life into a "social factory."

On the prospects for social liberation, Hardt and Negri are of the view that empire makes old nationalisms based on nation-states obsolete and in doing so creates a new social space for challenging global capitalism that is not constrained by national borders. Thus opposition will now be global, and the multitude will be constituted by a plurality of groups neither related to nor in communication with each other, but each fighting the virtual expression of empire spontaneously. Hardt and Negri argue that one of the defining characteristics of the multitude is "being against." They assert, "One element we can put our finger on at the most basic and elementary level is the will to be against. In general, the will to be against does not seem to require much explanation. Disobedience to authority is one of the most natural and healthy acts. To us it seems completely obvious that those who are exploited will resist and, given the necessary conditions, rebel."[3]

But even if we grant Hardt and Negri's nonobvious assumption that human beings naturally resist exploitation, we suggest that various factors complexify the capacity for resistance. First, Hardt and Negri underestimate the role of discourse and other mediating social forces in constraining people to resist exploitation even when they recognize the fact that it takes place. This is because, we suggest, Hardt and Negri's overly theoretical approach to strategizing the social liberation of the multitude is out of touch with the reality of identity politics. They trivialize human identity and treat history as a noncritical factor in shaping the choices that people make. One would have expected them to seriously address the problem of uneven development across different regions of the world and even within regions and the implications of these for the concrete struggle for social liberation. But Hardt and Negri's proposal seems to ignore the concrete realities of inequality among and within nations.

Second, and related to the first, we suggest that the global expression of empire varies from one country to another. The structure, capacity, autonomy, and rationality of the state are directly connected to the level of penetration of capitalist rationality and mode of production in a particular society. The means available for the multitude to pursue their struggle varies with the state, nation, and level of capitalist development. If this is true, then, there is no one empire, but there is rather a plurality of empires, each intersecting with and overlaid upon others in different respects, but each nevertheless acting in particular ways in different regional contexts. And in this case, the resistances of the multitudes will also be contextually shaped by the various versions of empire that surround them.

3. Ibid., 210.

America, Empire, and the Globalization of Christianity

A closer examination of the parachurch organizations and megachurches in the United States that have been engaged in missionary work abroad shows that not only are they often Protestants and conservative but also that they have fused American civil religion and Christian commitment. Raising critical questions about this fusion runs the risk of eliciting accusations of being unpatriotic and unchristian. Still, this fusion of Americanism and Christian faith should be seen in historical perspective.

The first important development is the idea of Manifest Destiny. Throughout human history, imperial and colonial empires appealed to the workings of divine providence to justify and rationalize their colonial expansion.[4] By the beginning of the twentieth century, the fusion of Americanism and Christianity was enunciated by U.S. presidents. This divinely assigned project, as declared by various leaders of the United States, gave the nation a unique status among the nations of the world.[5]

As the fusion of Americanism with Christianity continued, it metamorphosed into a systematic theological dualism. This theology begins by glorifying and articulating the nature of the United States as a chosen nation and people, and culminates in dividing the world into two: good and evil. America represents the good and evil resides in the "other," depending on the historical moment in reference (e.g., communism or Islam). Numerous statements made by leading individuals in parachurch ministries and government affirm this theological dualism as a focal point of American Christian self-understanding and U.S. foreign policy.[6]

Unfortunately, such theological dualism ignores the need to systematically problematize and critically evaluate the relationship between American Christianity and one important domain of Americanism—that of global market capitalism. Even if American Christianity is internally decaying, and even when capitalism in America is oppressing and exploiting socially disenfranchised American citizens and the "wretched of the earth" in the Global South, there is no motivation to condemn the situation because it reflects the divine order of things. The result of the fusion of Americanism and the Christian faith is that Christianity fails to perform its prophetic role. Ironically, this theological dualism is blind to the fact that both free-market capitalism (which it

4. This development was in part an extension of the Victorian idea of the "white man's burden" to civilize the world; see Lawrence James, *The Rise and Fall of British Empire* (New York: St. Martin's Griffin, 1994).

5. See Robert Bellah, "American Civil Religion in the 1970's," in *American Civil Religion*, ed. Russell E. Richey and Donald G. Jones, 255–72 (New York: Harper & Row, 1974), and Jeffrey K. Hadden and Anson Shupe, *Televangelism, Power, and Politics on God's Frontier* (New York: Henry Holt, 1988), 272.

6. See William Martin, *With God on Our Side: The Rise of the Religious Right in America* (New York: Broadway, 1996).

embraces) and communism (usually the evil *Other*) are intellectually rooted in the same European Enlightenment that believes human rationality can discover the universal laws that can create the good society without reference to spiritual guidance.

Unsurprisingly, then, by the end of the twentieth century, one central feature of American Christian influence on the Two-Thirds world is the spread of the gospel of prosperity, free enterprise, and market capitalism. The emphasis on becoming wealthy and enjoying material success has always been part of the American dream. Interestingly, as American Pentecostals have themselves climbed up the social ladder,[7] their particular contribution to this discourse has been to provide it with a spiritual canopy. Leading Pentecostal ministers have appealed directly to the Bible in articulating their prosperity theology.[8]

What are the implications of the foregoing for the social liberation of the Global South? First, the discussion demonstrates how Americanism and American Christianity, especially in the form of Pentecostalism, lacks the ability or willingness to recognize the role of social structures and institutions as decisive causal explanations for poverty, ill health, inequality of wealth, and underdevelopment. In this view, free-market capitalism and militarism as championed by the United States have equal and positive global consequences. Thus the gospel of prosperity and free enterprise blames the victims of poverty and underdevelopment. Instead of encouraging them to use their spiritual understanding to deconstruct the foundations of poverty and underdevelopment in all their ramifications, the gospel of prosperity silences the poor and encourages them to internalize their predicament. Insofar as poverty and underdevelopment are perceived as essentially spiritual problems that are cured through faith and miracle, their persistence indicates by implication that the poor are spiritually immature and responsible for what is essentially their own spiritual condition.

Furthermore, given the fact that poverty and underdevelopment are concentrated in the Global South and wealth and prosperity have consistently been concentrated in the countries of the North,[9] philanthropy on the part of the rich countries increases their feeling of righteousness and spiritual superiority while it further disempowers the receivers of philanthropic assistance. Given the racial dimension and implications of the regional divide, philanthropy

7. E.g., Margaret M. Poloma, *The Assemblies of God at the Crossroads: Charisma and Institutional Dilemmas* (Knoxville: University of Tennessee Press, 1989).

8. See Simon Coleman, *The Globalisation of Charismatic Christianity: Spreading the Gospel of Prosperity* (Cambridge: Cambridge University Press, 2000); Milmon F. Harrison, *Righteous Riches: The Word of Faith Movement in Contemporary African American Religion* (Oxford: Oxford University Press, 2005); and Shayne Lee, *T. D. Jakes: America's New Preacher* (New York: New York University Press, 2005).

9. See Michael Todaro and Stephen C. Smith, *Economic Development* (Boston: Addison-Wesley, 2003).

from the United States reinforces the material and psychological dependence of people in the Global South on white Americans. This same logic applies to explaining poverty and social malaise experienced by some minority groups in the United States, even as it implies that white Christians in the United States are by and large people with a high degree of spiritual righteousness: of course all persons are sinners, but the sins of white Americans are sufficiently insignificant such as not to have drawn the wrath of God to curse their nation with poverty. In effect, American Christianity has developed a systematic explanation for poverty and underdevelopment grounded in the regional geography of sin concentration. This definitely will complicate any effort on the part of the socially disenfranchised of the Global South to resist or rebel against oppression by the empire. Hardt and Negri have not problematized the complex process and mechanism through which the multitudes will liberate themselves.

On the whole, then, the foregoing analysis does not lead us to believe the multitude of the Global South will automatically resist the domination perpetrated by the capitalist empire. Indeed, in some respects, especially Pentecostalism in the Global South seems to locally indigenize the goals of empire, Americanism, and the American brand of Christianity. Given what we know of the fusion of American Christianity with American secular religion, we have a situation where Two-Thirds World Pentecostals are made to internalize the social processes that dominate and oppress them. Unfortunately Hardt and Negri have overlooked the role that religion plays in either facilitating or constraining social liberation.

At the same time, we do not believe that the situation in America and the Global South as we have analyzed it necessarily has to be the way it is. Indeed, we are confident that if American Christianity, particularly Pentecostalism, can liberate itself from American secular religion and return to the original egalitarian and liberating spirit of Pentecost as portrayed in the book of Acts, it may once again engage the project of social liberation. The issue is whether Pentecostal Christians in America have the courage to pursue this original vision of Christianity given what it will cost them.

Pentecostalism in Sub-Saharan Africa: Accomplice of Empire or Subversive Movement?

We assume that both Pentecostalism and the quest for human development and social liberation are existential struggles in sub-Saharan Africa. Our hope is that Pentecostalism will contribute positively to this process of development and social liberation while still retaining its integrity as a faith and spiritual tradition. If it succeeds in doing so, we believe it has the potential of subverting the hegemony of the global capitalist empire. In this section, we present a brief analysis of Pentecostalism in Africa with particular reference to the concerns of empire. In doing this, we quickly realize that sub-Saharan Africa cannot be considered fully modern or capitalist, so what we are dealing with in this context is the transition from a premodern and precapitalist society to a modern capitalist society. This raises significant problems for Hardt and Negri's thesis, which overgeneralizes the extent to which global capitalism is rooted in different parts of the world.

Any attempt to understand the complex relationship between empire and Pentecostalism in sub-Saharan Africa will need to come to terms with Pentecostal theological discourses on the continent's high degree of poverty and underdevelopment. While Pentecostals in Africa have not provided systematic explanations for why people in certain regions of the world achieve progress and others remain relatively backward in the contemporary modern world, we can nevertheless deduce what they believe from the sermons Pentecostal ministers preach. A number of themes emerge when Pentecostal sermons are examined through the lens of empire.[10]

First, the idea of the demonic is pervasive in the Pentecostal worldview:

> The basic idea of deliverance is that a Christian's progress and advance can be blocked by demons who maintain some power over the Christian, despite his or her coming to Christ. The Christian may have no idea of the cause of hindrance, and it may be through no fault of his own that he is under the sway of a particular demon. It often takes a special man of God to diagnose and then bind and cast out this demon. Thus in the mind of many of its exponents, this deliverance is a Third stage beyond being born again, and beyond speaking in tongues.[11]

10. We acknowledge that any comprehensive study of sub-Saharan Pentecostalism cannot be limited to ideologies distilled from Pentecostal sermons. Further, we also realize that our reliance in what follows on sociological analyses needs to be balanced by other disciplinary approaches, including those of insider Pentecostal scholarship. At the same time, we proceed with the conviction that neither Pentecostal preachers nor secular sociologists who have studied African Pentecostalism are to be excluded from this conversation. For other scholarly insider perspectives on the issues in the following discussion, see Ogbu U. Kalu, *Power, Poverty, and Prayer: The Challenges of Poverty and Pluralism in African Christianity, 1960–1996* (New York: Peter Lang, 2000); E. Kingsley Larbi, *Pentecostalism: The Eddies of Ghanaian Christianity* (Dansoman-Accra, Ghana: Centre for Pentecostal and Charismatic Studies, 2001); Cephas N. Omenyo, *Pentecost outside Pentecostalism: A Study of the Development of Charismatic Renewal in the Mainline Churches in Ghana* (Zoetermeer, Netherlands: Boekencentrum, 2002); and J. Kwabena Asamoah-Gyadu, *African Charismatics: Current Developments within Independent Indigenous Pentecostalism in Ghana* (Leiden: Brill, 2004).

11. From an analysis of the sermons of Matthew Addae-Mensah, a Pentecostal minister in Ghana, by Paul Gifford, "The Complex Provenance of Some Elements of African Pentecostal Theology," in *Between Babel and Pentecost: Transnational Pentecostalism in Africa and Latin America*, ed. Andre Corten and Ruth Marshall-Fratani, 62–79 (Bloomington: Indiana University Press, 2001), quotation from 65.

Now it is important to note that such demonological discourse is common all over Africa and not only among Pentecostals. Part of the reason for this is that African indigenous religious traditions posit various levels of spiritual realities that can be manipulated by human beings through the appropriate religious rituals. In one sense, Pentecostal demonologies have emerged as a counterdiscourse that resists such traditional explanations. While we return to this point later, for now it suffices to point out that in this scheme of things demons could retard the progress of individuals and, by implication, if many individuals are obstructed from achieving their set goals, then the aggregate effect will have national and even regional consequences. Further, given the theology espoused by this Pentecostal minister, if the Christian believer struggles with centrifugal demonic powers, for the nonbeliever the situation is presumably more dismal because she or he has not even made a commitment to follow Christ. This raises question about the ability of the Pentecostal movement to create an inclusive civic community that is generally committed to the social liberation of the oppressed as a universal goal, irrespective of who they are and where they live.

Second, and following from the first, is that Pentecostals grapple with the problem of Africa's poverty in the midst of global capitalist prosperity by focusing on the role of demons in obstructing regional development.

Even some formulations of demonology can have political implications:

> One of the books on sale at this crusade (written by a Kenyan) . . . after explaining at great length that everything evil is to be explained by demonic agency, concluded that those who "do not know this cause, including a majority of Christian believers, blame the government and their leaders." In other words, no Christian who properly understood spiritual causality could blame Kenya's ills on the government. It is not irrelevant to note that the preface to this book was written by Daniel Tarap Moi, President of the Republic of Kenya.[12]

Those interested in socially liberating the oppressed in Africa from the virtual tentacles of empire cannot ignore Pentecostal demonology as a mediating social process, since in the Pentecostal perspective many postcolonial states are virtual agents and puppets of the capitalist empire. It is clear that African postcolonial elites are likely to capitalize on such demonological theology because it exonerates them and the capitalist empire they represent from significant responsibility for Africa's underdevelopment. When Kenya's problems are explained by appeal to demonic forces, the institutions and persons involved in development policy formulation and implementation at the national and global levels escape without responsibility.

12. Steve Brouwer, Paul Gifford, and Susan D. Rose, *Exporting the American Gospel: Global Christian Fundamentalism* (New York: Routledge, 1996), 177–78.

Third, Pentecostal biblicism results in interpretations of the contemporary social situation using scriptural imagery, terminology, and themes.

> And most of the continent of Africa you notice are the people of the descendants of Ham, and the things that you find in the life of Nimrod, you find all over the continent. . . . The man was actually possessed of a leopard spirit, a hunting spirit. . . . These hunting spirits affect the political life of this continent. You notice that hunters actually steal the life of the animals, and when you look at the way corruption goes on in this continent, you will see that it is a derivative of this hunting spirit. What does a man want to do when he steals eight billion dollars, ten billion dollars? . . . Then you understand that something is at work. It's not necessarily poverty only, there's a spirit behind it. These are the things that we see on this continent, and when you pray for the leaders, and you pray for the church, understand these territorial spirits and the way they operate. They affect the nations very, very strongly.[13]

Clearly Pentecostals feel the problem of economic development in Africa can be accounted for at the spiritual level, i.e., the fact that Africans are descendants of Ham, whose descendants were cursed to be slaves because he laughed when he saw his father Noah naked (see Gen. 9:20–27). Further, the high level of corruption is accounted for with the idea of territorial and "hunting spirits": unless these spirits are banished, they will hinder African economic development and social transformation. The policy implications of this demonological and theological discourse is to dismiss as irrelevant the nature of Africa's social structure and history and how that predisposes the people in the continent to corruption. Presumably too, the level of corruption is the same all over the continent because of the pervasive presence of demonic spirits. The problem is not strictly an individual or institution. It is the fight against the spirits that matters—in Pentecostal terms, "spiritual warfare." Strictly speaking, science cannot totally banish spiritual concerns and longing from human life, but does providing a theological explanation necessarily preclude the analytical utility of scientific reasoning and explanation?

Fourth, the idea of curses is another important way that Pentecostal theology accounts for the relatively slow nature of economic development and social transformation in Africa.

> Nobody comes under a curse unless he or she deserves it. "He is also under a curse, if he belongs to a nation that is under curse or lives in an area or home whose inhabitants have been cursed." The way out is to examine one's life: "if there is a curse or if there is a covenant entered into against the will of God,

---

13. From a Nigerian Pentecostal preacher, as cited in Ruth Marshall, "'God Is Not a Democrat': Pentecostalism and the Democratisation in Nigeria," in *The Christian Churches and the Democratization of Africa*, ed. Paul Gifford (Leiden: E. J. Brill, 1995), 239–60, quotation from 248–49.

or if there is a broken covenant or if a bad seed is sown or if any of the above is inherited from ancestors, unless they are revoked or cancelled they will each run their full course of consequences." Curses or covenant must be identified and revoked, and Vuha gives prayers, which effect this.[14]

Apart from the fact that this preacher's statement is somewhat contradictory and ambivalent with regard to causality, the main thrust of the argument tends to fit with the classical modernization theory argument, which accounts for underdevelopment by focusing on factors internal to the Two-Thirds World.[15] But while modernization theory aims to be systematic, this is not the case with many African Pentecostal preachers. The policy implication of the minister's assertion is vague, beyond blaming the victim, i.e., the individual, the ancestors, and the nation.

Fifth, as already intimated in the preceding, is the central role of the "anointed man of God" in dealing with spiritual, personal, and even economic problems. It is true that in theory every member of a Pentecostal church can acquire the charisma from God and use it, but in reality the charisma that God confers on certain leaders is supposed to be significantly higher. Spiritual and social transformation will come when these "anointed men of God" exorcise all the demons that exist in Africa. Indeed, Pentecostal theology assumes that individuals who are non-Christian believers will not make progress in life because of demonic forces and their unwillingness to approach the "man of God" who alone can identify and cast out the demons that are retarding their progress. Of course, since the demons operate at the spiritual realm, knowledge of their diagnoses and cure is not derivable from an application of the scientific method. Much then is in the hands of the ministers who are trusted by the masses of sub-Saharan Africa.

This leads, sixth, to a hierarchical source of power that is relatively unaccountable, since it is derived exclusively from God.

> It is often claimed that the born-again churches function as schools of democracy, since they are groups of brothers and sisters promoting equality. Many of those we considered were personal fiefdoms, held together by the personal gifts of their leaders. We noted the tendency to authoritarianism—in Uganda one pastor would not even allow members to call him Brother, and insisted on his own views being sacrosanct and unquestioned, unlike those of his followers.[16]

14. Cited by Paul Gifford, "The Complex Provenance of Some Elements of African Pentecostal Theology," in *Christian Churches and the Democratization of Africa*, 71.

15. See Philip McMichael, *Development and Social Change: A Global Perspective*, 2nd ed. (Thousand Oaks, CA: Pine Forge, 2000), and Charles P. Oman and Ganeshan Wignaraja, *Postwar Evolution of Development Thinking* (New York: St. Martin's Press, 1991).

16. See Paul Gifford, *African Christianity: Its Public Role* (Bloomington: Indiana University Press, 1998), 344.

It is considered sinful to raise critical questions about the validity of the actions, statements, or decisions of the "man of God," and thus this ecclesial structure undermines the cultivation of rational dialogue, which is integral to any social process that would bring about social liberation. In many Pentecostal churches communiqués from the minister to the congregation perpetuate this hierarchy. The decisions are made by the "righteous" who have absolute and exclusive access to truth, owing to the grace of the Holy Spirit. Our main conclusion here is that an organization that is internally undemocratic and authoritarian in its decision-making and implementation process cannot promote genuine social liberation.[17]

Seventh, the success of Pentecostal ministry is often measured by financial and material prosperity. "In 'prosperity' churches, it is most often wealth, which is the miracle designating God's chosen. Pastor Kris Okotie recently bought his wife a 0.8 million naira BMW to complement his own new Mercedes, quoting James 1:17: 'Every good gift and every perfect gift is from above, and cometh down from the Father of lights.'"[18] In a poor country like Nigeria, the monetary value of this minister's family automobile alone is extravagantly out of proportion to income distribution in the country. Interestingly, while the minister quoted the Bible to rationalize his wealth, all the wealth is generated from the congregation. To be sure, many Pentecostal ministers in Africa began their ministry in poverty, but they have gradually benefited from the highly sacrificial donations of congregational members and from affiliations with powerful and influential people in government and in North American Pentecostal networks. Yet although the money is generated in the name of God and the ministry, the decisions about how it is used and the ownership of the investment are significantly controlled by the leader of the ministry because of the personalistic and autocratic leadership style in the churches. Such successful Pentecostal leaders feel no concern about their ostentatious display of wealth, because they rationalize their behavior as glorifying God for his blessings. Many prosperous Pentecostals insulate their sources of income and success from their faith, for otherwise they would have to deal with serious ethical questions about the system from which they are benefiting.

Finally, as members of the church become wealthier or attract relatively well-to-do people, they begin to develop a distinctive upper-middle-class lifestyle that marginalizes other Christians and Pentecostals who are less fortunate.

17. This point is eloquently argued by Robert Michels's study of European socialist political parties that claim to implement egalitarian policies but are not internally democratic as social organizations; see Michel, *Political Parties: A Sociological Study of Oligarchic Tendencies of Modern Democracy* (New York: Free Press, 1962). See also Raymond A. Morrow and Carlos Alberto Torres, *Reading Freire and Habermas: Critical Pedagogy and Transformative Change* (New York: Teachers College Press, 2002).

18. Marshall, "God Is Not a Democrat," 256.

The Pentecostal revival in its early period of the 1970s developed around a doctrine of radical anti-materialism, extremely purist personal ethics, and a withdrawal not only from dominant forms of popular culture, but an attempt to achieve both institutional and moral autonomy from the state. Yet as the movement expanded, developing stronger international ties, and entering into competition for clients, this localized, retreatist community expanded from its origin among socially dominated groups of the urban poor and youth, becoming more and more associated with leading businessmen, professionals, military men, and politicians. Fellowship breakfasts at the five star Eko Le Meridien Hotel, the inauguration of groups like the Christ the Redeemer's Friends Universal, a fellowship organization of the Redeemed Christian Church of God which requires members to have a post-secondary school degree or diploma in order to join, and which publishes a monthly magazine recounting the conversion stories and received miracles of leading businessmen, military officers, politicians and civil servants, all these are part of a conscious strategy among Pentecostal churches to gain access to the "political nation."[19]

If Pentecostalism fosters the emergence and perpetuation of a petit bourgeois class, what are the broad social-cultural consequences of this on society at large and on the mission of the church? One result is an uncritical acceptance of neoliberal capitalism as an economic system, with all the human cost that this entails. The human cost of a capitalist system that has run amok is well documented in the United States.[20] The situation is even worse in peripheral capitalist societies. Surely capitalism can benefit all people if values external to it regulate its excesses, especially in cases of market fundamentalism and failure. But Pentecostalism as described above is diluting the gospel instead of using it to develop a discourse of social reform for justice and equity.

In sum, unless Pentecostals begin to provide a viable alternative to global market fundamentalism as an economic paradigm, they will be co-opted, if this has not already taken place.[21] In their attempts to honor God and reap his blessings within the capitalist global economy as we know it, Pentecostals have supported a system that makes them, wittingly or unwittingly, enemies of each other because of the competition that is at the center of the labor market. Pentecostals naively assume that they can create a genuine "Christian community" while simply subsuming their vision within the broad framework of global capitalism. In doing so, they have also come to define Pentecostal spirituality by the criterion of material success.

19. Ibid., 253–54.
20. E.g., David K. Shipler, *The Working Poor: Invisible in America* (New York: Alfred A. Knopf, 2004).
21. Walter J. Hollenweger, "Crucial Issues for Pentecostals," in *Pentecostals after a Century: Global Perspectives on a Movement in Transition*, ed. Allan H. Anderson and Walter J. Hollenweger (Sheffield, UK: Sheffield Academic Press, 1999), 176–91, esp. 190.

But these theological ideas can and should be interrogated from any number of angles. From an empirical point of view, many individuals who are not among the "righteous" by Pentecostal theological standards have succeeded in their pursuits. On the other side, there are also many Pentecostals who remain in poverty but whose Christian faith and commitment cannot be denied. Similarly, there are many nations that should not be prospering because they are not Christian nations and therefore are constrained by demonic forces, yet the economic successes of countries such as China and Japan are counterfactual evidence to this theological perspective. Finally, if Pentecostals are filled with the Holy Spirit of God as many claim to be, then why are they colluding with rather than resisting the oppressive forces of market fundamentalism? Meanwhile, others who have made no pretensions of having the transcendental power that Pentecostals claim are assiduously laboring to reform and gradually transform the soulless capitalist empire.

Concluding Remarks

There are two major lessons we want to draw as we conclude our analysis. First, we have seen that Hardt and Negri's thesis is problematized when religious and social factors are added into the mix. In our analysis, not only do the many multitudes *not* automatically resist the encroachments of empire depending on their social context, but they may even unwittingly serve the purposes of empire, depending on the religious underpinnings of their worldview. Hence when the religious element is given full consideration, the multitude is splintered ideologically, resulting in resistance to empire in some quarters but also the expansion of empire in others. Even more precisely, we find that the multitude's discourse reveals its resistance to a wide range of historical, social, political, economic, and religious forces. Sub-Saharan Pentecostal theology not only abets capitalistic enterprise but also counters the ethos of witchcraft that pervades the indigenous African mentality. This leads us to insist that any analysis of *empire* and of *multitude* will need to be multidimensional and will need to take into account the reality that different configurations of empire will elicit various responses and, with that, shape the formation of a diverse multitude.

The second lesson we have is for those of us who find ourselves within the North American and sub-Saharan Pentecostal orbits.[22] The preceding discussion suggests that we need to rejuvenate the original Pentecostal spirit and

---

22. Yong is a 1.5-generation Asian American, born in Malaysia but naturalized and educated in the United States. Zalanga is a Nigerian who came to the United States as an international student to pursue his doctorate but eventually decided to work in the country after completing his studies.

vision of Christianity.[23] In this vision, the church that partakes of Holy Communion gives expression to a radical idea of equality and a global community of faith that is united by the blood and body of Christ and transcends nationality, race, or social status.[24] While the Roman empire does not exist today, there are contemporary functional equivalents of the empire—i.e., material wealth, Americanism, or global market fundamentalism—all of which could be regarded as idolatry from this apostolic point of view. In effect, we are calling on Pentecostal Christians to desist from fusing authentic Christianity with either American civil religion or global capitalistic fundamentalism, because both ideologies—which combine into one "new world order"—contradict many core tenets of genuine Christian ethics.[25]

While we do not wish to be unduly optimistic about world Pentecostalism's capacities to resist the encroachment of the global capitalistic empire, there remain two key factors on the side of the Pentecostal multitudes which give us hope. First, being a revivalist and renewal movement, Pentecostalism tends to reproduce offspring that react to the institutionalized forms of its predecessors. Hence, rather than uncritically adopting previous American versions of Pentecostalism or Christian faith, perhaps the voices of the multitudes of Pentecostals worldwide may yet provide critical perspectives in response to current developments which can help Pentecostal Christianity regain its autonomy and prophetic role in human history and society. Subsequent generations of Pentecostals may well challenge the misdirected traditions of their foreparents, precisely because of the iconoclastic tendencies of movements seeking to follow after the Spirit's working in their own places and times.[26]

Second, and in ironic contrast to the forward- and future-looking character of Pentecostalism as just described, Pentecostalism's energy comes in part from a "backward" focus on retrieving and reexperiencing the vitality of the first generation of apostolic Christians as described in the pages of the New Testament. This means that the examples of the Son of Man who came not to

23. For a sketch of this vision, see Amos Yong, *The Spirit Poured Out on All Flesh: Pentecostalism and the Possibility of Global Theology* (Grand Rapids: Baker Academic, 2005), esp. chaps. 3–4; see also Richard A. Horsley, *Jesus and Empire: The Kingdom of God and the New World Disorder* (Minneapolis: Fortress Press, 2003).

24. See William T. Cavanagh, *Torture and Eucharist: Theology, Politics, and the Body of Christ* (Malden, MA: Blackwell, 1998).

25. See John Driver, *Kingdom Citizens* (Eugene, OR: Wipf and Stock, 1998), and Thomas D. Hanks, *God So Loved the Third World: The Biblical Vocabulary of Oppression* (Eugene, OR: Wipf and Stock, 2000).

26. Due to space constraints, we have not been able to discuss the exploding Pentecostal churches of inland China. The discourses of these multitudes resist the "empires" of communism, the official Three-Self Church, and the indigenous religious traditions of China. There is still much that we need to learn about the revival of the church in China, even as we have much to learn from them that is distinctive from sub-Saharan Pentecostalism—but these lessons will have to await another occasion.

be served but to serve others and of the early Christian communitarian ethic will never be too distant from the Pentecostal horizon. If Pentecostals can reappropriate and reembody these early Christian convictions, the movement will be subversive of the global capitalist hegemony and demonstrate that there is a viable alternative to the ethic of market fundamentalism, which is built on greed, profit, and the desires of the flesh. Instead, the vision should be one of nurturing a truly caring community that is inspired not by social Darwinism or the Chicago school of economics but by the life and teachings of Jesus, the Messiah anointed by the Spirit.

18

In Praise of Profanity

A Theological Defense of the Secular

MICHAEL HORTON

As holy assemblies were convened in the National Cathedral to rid the world of evil, with the U.S. Army band playing "Onward, Christian Soldiers" and with evangelical leaders, organizations, and even denominations playing a significant role in America's culture wars, evangelicalism is perceived more as a political constituency than as anything like a church. Frederic Jameson seems perfectly justified in concluding, "This is less to deny that there is a religious revival in course today all over the world than it is to suggest that what is called religion today (in a variety of forms, from left to right) is really politics under a different name."[1]

As legatees of the postmillennial aspirations of nineteenth-century evangelical revivalism, American Protestants share a common commitment to civil religion despite their quite different cultural and political agendas. With an Arminian soteriology and a weak ecclesiology, the church chiefly becomes an instrument of social and moral transformation. It is this fusion of cult and

1. Frederic Jameson, "The Dialectics of Disaster," in *Dissent from the Homeland: Essays after September 11*, ed. Stanley Hauerwas and Frank Lentricchia (Durham, NC: Duke University Press, 2003), 59.

culture that I want to challenge in this paper. If there is any truth to Samuel Huntington's thesis in *The Clash of Civilizations*, there can be no discussion of the relation of evangelicals and empire without a theology of the secular. In order to set up my own account of the secular, I will briefly summarize the alternatives proposed by Radical Orthodoxy (hereafter, RO), represented by John Milbank, and the work of Michael Hardt and Antonio Negri.

Lamenting the demise of a Neoplatonic, participatory ontology, Milbank reminds us, "Once there was no 'secular.' . . . Instead, there was the single community of Christendom, with its dual aspects of *sacertodium* [priesthood] and *regnum* [kingship]."[2] However, the unity of cult and culture, faith and reason, temporal and eternal orders was sundered first by nominalism, then by the Reformation, which mediated nominalism to modern political theory via the Enlightenment, reaching its apogee in Hobbes. In part, this came about "by abandoning participation in Being and Unity for a 'covenantal bond' between God and men," which in turn "provided a model for human interrelationships as 'contractual' ones."[3] Furthermore, in a dazzling historiographical feat, Milbank asserts that the absolutist hermeneutics of Spinoza and Hobbes "is really rooted in the Lutheran *sola scriptura*."[4] Concerning civil laws and punishments, "the Church . . . must have done forever with Luther's two kingdoms, and the notion that a State that does not implicitly concern itself with the soul's salvation can be in any way legitimate."[5] The link, according to Milbank, is nominalism, which surrendered reason and civic life to an autonomous realm.

Needless to say, this genealogy is threatened by reductionism and caricature.[6] Nevertheless, it attracts those who, like Milbank, seem to identify secularization (the secular as such) with secularism and the modern state—particularly liberal democracy—with the very antithesis of ecclesial reality. I think Jeffrey Stout has aptly identified this as part of the "rhetoric of excess."[7]

---

2. John Milbank, *Theology and Social Theory* (Oxford: Blackwell, 1993), 9.

3. Ibid., 15.

4. Ibid., 19.

5. Ibid., 209. At least in this early work, Milbank suggests that not even Aquinas's participatory ontology is sufficiently Christian: "[John Scotus] Eriugena's ontology, based on God as internally 'maker' and then on different degrees of participation in creation, is therefore more profoundly Christian than that of Aquinas" (425). More recent works display a greater appreciation for Thomas.

6. Contrary to Milbank's genealogy, Reformation theology does not stand in unbroken continuity with nominalism on any of the relevant points, and Milbank seems recently to have modified at least his judgments concerning Calvin in this regard in "Alternative Protestantism," in *Radical Orthodoxy and the Reformed Tradition,* ed. J. K. A. Smith (Grand Rapids: Baker, 2005). Lutheran and Reformed scholastics universally rejected the univocity of being in favor of analogy, and their allegiances range from Platonism to Aristotelianism to Ramism, Thomas, and Scotus.

7. Jeffrey Stout, *Democracy and Tradition* (Princeton, NJ: Princeton University Press, 2004), 58.

Another RO writer, William T. Cavanaugh, boldly states, "The modern state is best understood . . . as a source of an alternative soteriology to that of the Church . . . the body of the state is a simulacrum, a false copy, of the Body of Christ. The Eucharist, which makes the Body of Christ, is therefore a key practice for a Christian anarchism."[8] Christian anarchy is not chaotic but "challenges the false order of the state."[9] Once united by Neoplatonism, Milbank argues, the cultures of Judaism, Christianity, and Islam were driven apart, in the direction of nominalism (the Christian West) and "a doctrinally orthodox, scriptural, and legalistic civilization" (Islam).[10]

Along with other representatives of what has come to be called the "new traditionalism," Milbank and RO starkly oppose a participatory socialism and an atomistic radical democracy. Not only different ontologies but also different versions of socialism (one antidemocratic, the other radically democratic) distinguish these two responses to empire. The alternative I will offer here is a covenantal account of the common or profane—in other words, a thought experiment in what Colin Gunton would call a "theology of nature" as opposed to a "natural theology."[11] I will begin by laying out the rival accounts and then offer a brief summary of what a covenantal definition of "common" might look like in the age of empire and multitude.[12]

Hardt/Negri and a Secularist Account of the Secular

Profanity, the secular, the common: these have been synonyms that Christian theology has often employed (especially since the Reformation) for that which is neither divine nor demonic; neither redemptive nor autonomous, a site of God's providential order through families, neighborhoods, and wider civic associations and common callings, distinct from the church as God's site of saving grace through proclamation and sacrament. While, in my view, RO denies the legitimacy of the secular as such, Hardt and Negri deny the legitimacy of the sacred. If the secular is defined as a field of redemptive activity by RO (and, I might add, American civil religion), it is designated by these writers as a field of pure autonomy and radical immanence. Standing in the tradition of dialectical materialism, meanwhile, Hardt and Negri push the secularist logic to its conclusion: a reality that is

8. William T. Cavanaugh, "The City: Beyond Secular Parodies," in *Radical Orthodoxy*, ed. John Milbank, Catherine Pickstock, and Graham Ward (New York and London: Routledge, 1999), 182.

9. Ibid., 194.

10. John Milbank, "Sovereignty, Empire, Capital, and Terror," in *Dissent from the Homeland*, ed. Hauerwas and Lentricchia, 70–71.

11. This is the burden of Colin Gunton's *A Brief Theology of Revelation* (Edinburgh: T & T Clark, 1995).

12. I am grateful to the editors for their suggestions regarding this paper.

entirely determined by the immanent play of signs, a space of flows, with no transcendent appeals.[13]

How then are we to understand "the common" in the age of empire? Adding to the proliferating "posts" of our day, Hardt and Negri conclude that we are in a "postliberal" and "postsocialist" era.[14] "In the legal realm," they argue, "especially in the Anglo-American tradition, the concept of the common has long been hidden by the notions of public and private, and indeed contemporary legal trends are further eroding any space for the common."[15] This reduction of common space derives paradoxically from the logic of security and government control in the social sphere alongside privatization ("possessive individualism") in the economic.[16] Although they assert a difference between individuals and "singularities," the authors nevertheless fail to transcend the autonomous self ("singularities") apart from autonomously willed ("expressive") relations that are primarily economic ("communication" versus "community"). "This is not to say, of course, that all practices are acceptable (sexual violence, for example) but rather that the decision to determine legal rights is made in the process of communication and collaboration among singularities."[17]

But this raises the question of "how the 'common' can be constructed politically in our contemporary world. How can the singularities that cooperate express their control over the common, and how can this expression be represented in legal terms?"[18] No longer to be defined by "the neoliberal principle that 'everything is determined by the market,'" or by identification with the state, the common is determined by the "common interest." "In short, the common marks a new form of sovereignty, a democratic sovereignty (or, more precisely, a form of social organization that displaces sovereignty) in which the social singularities control through their own biopolitical activity those goods and services that allow for the reproduction of the multitude itself. This would constitute a passage from *Res-publica* to *Res-communis*."[19] Notwithstanding their protestations to the contrary, the authors evidence their commitments to a strong teleology of dialectical progress.

In international law, the common is increasingly undermining any contractual arrangement between sovereign nations.[20] Opposing a view of law as static and normative (archaeology) to a view of law as dynamic process ("genealogy in action"), Hardt and Negri suggest that "the common becomes

13. Michael Hardt and Antonio Negri, *Empire* (Cambridge, MA: Harvard University Press, 2000), 207–8.
14. Michael Hardt and Antonio Negri, *Multitude: War and Democracy in the Age of Empire* (New York: Penguin, 2004), 203.
15. Ibid., 202.
16. Ibid., 203.
17. Ibid., 204.
18. Ibid., 204–5.
19. Ibid., 206.
20. Ibid., 207.

the only basis on which law can construct social relationships in line with the networks organized by the many singularities that create our new global reality."[21] The authors celebrate "a theory of organization based on the freedom of singularities that converge in the production of the common. Long live movement! Long live carnival! Long live the common!"[22]

Rival accounts of "the common" are engendered by rival ontologies. Just as the ontology assumed by Hardt and Negri is sheer immanence (which RO rightly links to the notion of the univocity of being), the politics of radical democracy is carried to its logical conclusion in an antiteleological teleology and an aneschatological eschatology—a messianic structure without the arrival of any particular messiah, to borrow Derrida's expression. (Given the similarities at this point with Francis Fukayama's *The End of History*, one wonders if the two great streams of modern immanence have finally met, reconciling Hegel's left-wing and right-wing offspring.) Yet on what basis could a *legal* claim be made on behalf of an exploited worker in a Los Angeles sweatshop, or even of a victim of sexual violence—the example the authors cite? Like Derrida, Hardt and Negri offer gestures toward a vague *sensus iustitia*—a justice that Derrida at least is willing to inscribe as "Justice" with a capital J![23] Kant's transcendental categories—some of them, at least—survive the collapse of modernity when people are looking for a justification for justice. I regard these modern and postmodern versions of autonomously grounded appeals as conceptually incoherent attempts to have the fruit of Christian revelation without the tree. Nevertheless, the very fact that such appeals to "justice" are even made displays the resilience of the conscience's testimony to general revelation.

Two Cities: The Genealogy of Profanity

Without retracing the history of Christendom, I will refer to the "two kingdoms" doctrine as interpreted by Augustine and Calvin, in an effort merely to gesture toward a theology of the secular.[24] Most treatments of the two-kingdoms doctrine begin with Augustine's *City of God*, a text so rich that it has invited quite varying interpretations across the centuries. Even Hardt and Negri are attracted to the sign, even if it does not point to a transcendental signified. Like Derrida's neo-Kantian "messianic structure" without a particular

21. Ibid., 208.

22. Ibid., 211.

23. See Jacques Derrida, *Deconstruction in a Nutshell*, ed. John D. Caputo (New York: Fordham University Press, 1981), 15–19; see my further engagement with this in *Covenant and Eschatology* (Louisville, KY: Westminster John Knox, 2002), 25–28.

24. See *Empire*, 324, for an acceptable summary of the transition from classical Rome to Byzantium ("Christendom").

messiah, our authors' brief appeal to Augustine's *City of God* invites us to contemplate a pilgrimage without a destination.[25]

For Augustine, the distinction between the two cities was grounded in God's predestination of some from Adam's fallen race for salvation, leaving the rest to their just perdition.[26] Consequently, each city has its own polity, serving distinct ends through distinct means, revealing that each is determined by two different loves and therefore by two different ends and means. These are in sharp conflict.[27] Yet such comments are always balanced by an affirmation of God's preservation of the secular order. In fact, "God can never be believed to have left the kingdoms of men, their dominations and servitudes, outside of the laws of His providence."[28] Yet the earthly city is always Babylon—it is never converted, though many of its inhabitants are, into the dwelling place of God. The kingdom of God advances through the proclamation of the gospel, not through the coercive powers of the state.[29] These two cities we find "interwoven, as it were, in this present transitory world, and mingled with one another."[30] Although the earthly city is not everlasting and can never bring about true rectitude, it is of great value and service as far as it goes.[31] A Christian would then approach politics not with the question as to how the world can best be saved but how it can best be served in this time between the times.

The fact that the earthly city is transitory and dominated by self-love does not lead Augustine to a Manichaean disavowal of its legitimacy as a divinely ordained institution. Rather, such theological premises resist the pretensions of empire in their claims to ultimacy. To be sure, if a commonwealth is defined by "the weal of the people," Rome fails that test.[32] Nevertheless, this is where some admirers of Augustine stop short. Crucially, Augustine adds, "If, on the other hand, another definition than this is found for a 'people,' for example, if one should say, 'A people is the association of the multitude of rational beings united by a common agreement on the objects of their love,' then it follows that to observe the character of a particular people we must examine the objects of its love."[33] "By this definition of ours," continues Augustine, "the Roman

---

25. Ibid., 207.

26. This predestinarian grounding of Augustine's argument has been an embarrassment to Milbank, Ward, and Hauerwas. Their universalist ecclesiologies can only treat this as an incidental or intentionally mythological element.

27. *The Essential Augustine,* ed. Vernon J. Bourke (Indianapolis: Hackett, 1983), 201.

28. Ibid., 222.

29. Ibid., 208: "This city is therefore now in building; stones are cut down from the hills by the hands of those who preach truth, they are squared that they may enter into an everlasting structure."

30. Augustine, *City of God*, ed. David Knowles, trans. Henry Bettenson (New York: Penguin, 1972), 430.

31. Ibid., 599.

32. Ibid., 881.

33. Ibid., 890.

people is a people and its estate is indubitably a commonwealth"—despite its propensity for violence and internal strife.[34] Christians share in the common curse and common grace of this earthly city. While they do not bring about God's reign in the secular city by their own activity, citizens of the Heavenly City serve in anticipation of that day when "all injustice disappears and all human lordship and power is annihilated and God is all in all."[35]

The earthly city, "whose life is not based on faith," aims at a relative peace, justice, and harmony of wills—which requires compromise. Believers, who constitute "that part of the Heavenly City which is on pilgrimage," also need to "make use of this peace also" until the age to come.[36] The City of God is on pilgrimage in different earthly cities, and its citizens willingly accept the laws of the commonwealth as long as they do not violate ultimate allegiances.[37] For Augustine, then, the earthly city can be *relatively* good and just but can never arrive at *ultimate* goodness and justice: that sabbath which awaits the elect in the age to come, when affections will be rightly ordered.[38] The peace of the earthly city is to be prized, not scorned for falling short of the heavenly peace won by Christ.[39] Thus, the secular is not demonic except when it assumes the pretension of ultimate justice, truth, goodness, love, and peace.

Augustine's political theology was not as simplistic as H. Richard Niebuhr's "Christ Transformer of Culture" treatment suggests.[40] The earthly city always remains what it is: a kingdom under sin and death (the *libido dominandi*) yet preserved by God's common grace.[41] What many contemporary admirers fail to share with Augustine himself is an acceptance of the eschatologically conditioned paradox of the kingdom's current phase. To be sure, Augustine's practice did not always match his theory (any more than did the practice of his heirs), but his theory is clear enough.

While we do not have the space to treat Luther's development of the two-kingdoms doctrine, Calvin's elaboration and modification are worth considering in the light of our situation. Despite H. R. Niebuhr's heavy typecasting in *Christ and Culture*, Calvin distinguished these two kingdoms no less than Luther *yet without surrendering the civil jurisdiction to a realm of pure power*. His basis for this, as we will see, is not the assumption that this civil realm is sacred or participates somehow in the body of Christ but the belief

---

34. Ibid.
35. Ibid., 875.
36. Ibid., 877.
37. Ibid., 878.
38. Ibid., 891.
39. Ibid., 892.
40. Oliver O'Donovan, "Augustine's City of God XIX and Western Political Thought," in *The City of God: A Collection of Critical Essays*, ed. Dorothy F. Donnelly (New York: Peter Lang, 1995), 144.
41. Ibid., 146.

that it is authorized by God to exercise only a limited stewardship of the commonwealth.

Trained in some of the most distinguished circles of French humanism, Calvin wrote a commentary on Seneca's *De clementia* as his first academic treatise. "Whenever we come upon these matters in secular writers," he pleaded in the *Institutes*, "let that admirable light of truth shining in them teach us that the mind of man, though fallen and perverted from its wholeness, is nevertheless clothed and ornamented with God's excellent gifts." He continues: "What then? Shall we deny that the truth shone on the ancient jurists who established civic order and discipline with such great equity? Those whom Scripture calls 'natural men' were, indeed, sharp and penetrating in their investigation of earthly things. Let us, accordingly, learn by their example how many gifts the Lord left to human nature even after it was despoiled of its true good."[42]

Opposing what he called the "contrived empire" (Christendom), Calvin was nevertheless enough a person of his time to display contradictions similar to those of Augustine (against the Donatists) and Luther (against the peasants), yet the popular image of Calvin as the tyrant of Geneva has been thoroughly refuted by the scholarly consensus. Calvin's aim was simply to restore the proper jurisdiction of the church over its own affairs, not to rule the city council. We must recognize that we are "under a two-fold government . . . so that we do not (as commonly happens) unwisely mingle these two, which have a completely different nature." Just as the body and soul are distinct without being intrinsically opposed, "Christ's spiritual kingdom and the civil jurisdiction are things completely distinct. . . . Yet this distinction does not lead us to consider the whole nature of government a thing polluted, which has nothing to do with Christian men." These two kingdoms are "distinct," yet "they are not at variance."[43] Like Augustine, Calvin moves dialectically between an affirmation of the natural order *and* its inability because of sin to generate an *ultimate* society. The goal of common grace is not to perfect nature but to restrain sin and animate civic virtues and arts, so that culture may fulfill its own important but limited, temporal, and secular ends, while God simultaneously pursues the redemptive aims of his everlasting city.

Confusing justification before God with moral, social, and political righteousness, the Radical Reformers undermined civility between Christian and non-Christian as well as the unique message and ministry of the gospel. Responding to the Radical Reformers' insistence that a commonwealth is legitimate only if it is ordered by biblical law, Calvin declares, "How malicious and hateful toward public welfare would a man be who is offended by such diversity, which is perfectly adapted to maintain the observance of God's law!

42. John Calvin, *Institutes of the Christian Religion*, 2.2.15.
43. Ibid., 4.20.1–2.

For the statement of some, that the law of God given through Moses is dis-honored when it is abrogated and new laws preferred to it, is utterly vain."[44] After all, he says, "it is a fact that the law of God which we call the moral law is nothing else than a testimony of natural law and of that conscience which God has engraved on the minds of men."[45] Even unbelievers can rule justly and prudently, as Paul indicates even under the more pagan circumstances of his day (Rom. 13:1–7). In addition to these natural remnants, there is some concept of common grace in Calvin, "not such grace as to cleanse it [nature], but to restrain it inwardly." This grace is tied to providence, to restraint; "but he does not purge it within."[46] Only the gospel can do this.

According to Calvin, natural law can be summarized by the word *equity* (*aequitas*), which generally meant a fairness in human relations that balanced strict justice with charitable moderation. Consequently, "equity alone must be the goal and rule and limit of all laws."[47] As a natural virtue common to all people, this equity is "the perpetual rule of love," fountain of all laws. Thus, Calvin considers "pernicious and hateful of the public order" the require-ment that the laws of nations should be required to follow the judicial laws of Moses. "Surely every nation is left free to make such laws as it foresees to be profitable for itself. Yet these must be in conformity to that perpetual rule of love, so that they indeed vary in form but have the same purpose."[48] Calvin displays here a humanist appreciation for diversity of historical, cultural, and geographical conditions. To be sure, this is "thin description"; *equity* does not mandate a particular form of government (such as democracy, capitalism, or socialism). Yet this reserve is part of the genius of the concept and its appeal across a wide range of political regimes.

Love of neighbor—which includes "the most remote person . . . without distinction"—links justice and charity, "since all should be contemplated in God, not in themselves." This is what Calvin means by "equity," which requires "mutual servitude" without tyranny.[49] Calvin does not simply accept the *libido dominandi* as appropriate to the secular kingdom (Luther's tendency), but he also does not imagine that the only alternative for civic life is participation in the redemptive grace of Christ and his body. Equity, engendered by that moral law that is mediated by God through creation to everyone, fills the secular with common though not saving grace.

44. Ibid., 4.20.8, 14. The basic ligaments of Calvin's political theology can be found in 4.20.1–32.

45. Ibid.

46. Ibid.

47. Ibid., 4.20.15.

48. Ibid.

49. William Klempa, "John Calvin on Natural Law," in *John Calvin and the Church: A Prism of Reform*, ed. Timothy George (Louisville, KY: Westminster John Knox, 1990), 87, citing Calvin, *Institutes*, 2.8.55.

The principle of equity became a dominant theme among Reformed writers, particularly in the realm of civic policy. Thus, a *theological* justification for human rights could emerge that is nevertheless contrasted sharply with modern foundationalist versions (contractarian, deontological, utilitarian, and pragmatist) yet differs in key respects from the Platonist versions as well. Interestingly, David Novak argues for a version of natural law from the history of Jewish interpretation of the Noahide laws in a manner strikingly similar to this approach, contrasting a covenantal account with both the "new traditionalist" rejection of the concept and medieval as well as modern secularist notions.[50] Similarities between Novak's arguments and Calvin's may be attributed to a shared *covenantal* paradigm that can be equated with neither Neoplatonic medieval models nor modern political theory. Novak writes, "How fundamentally different all this is from seeing natural law as some sort of translation of a higher nature down to the actual affairs of human beings. In that view, there is no primary voice, but only a vision of a polity that might conform to a higher paradigm in the heavens. It is duty without an originating right/claim, for such a right/claim cannot be imagined, but only heard."[51] Jews develop their theory of rights from their own sources, he insists.[52]

This is exactly parallel to my argument. Neither a secularist nor a Platonic account of rights, nor a traditionalist rejection of rights, is proposed, but a biblically grounded theory of rights that can be articulated from our own covenantal resources, demonstrating that the very justice that nonbiblical accounts want desperately to secure is made possible only on biblical grounds. When secularists accept even a morsel of this natural law (such as the proscription of sexual violence), they are operating on the borrowed capital of this common revelation, which they deny in principle.

Without retrieving an ostensible Neoplatonic common fund from the early Middle Ages, is there nevertheless some commonly shared site of revelation not only for Judaism, Christianity, and Islam but for all human beings? Parallels between the two kingdoms account I have delineated and the theo-political arguments of Novak are suggestive. Even in Islam, according to Osman bin Bakar, however extremists may conflate categories, sharia includes both particular laws governing Muslims and laws that are regarded as universally binding as a result of a common Adamic origin.[53] Augustine spoke of "the everlasting

---

50. David Novak, *Covenantal Rights: A Study in Jewish Political Theory* (Princeton, NJ: Princeton University Press, 2000), 20. See also Novak, *Jewish-Christian Dialogue: A Jewish Justification* (Oxford: Oxford University Press, 1989), 27.

51. Novak, *Covenantal Rights*, 25.

52. Ibid.

53. Osman bin Bakar, "Pluralism and the 'People of the Book,'" in *Religion and Security*, ed. Robert A. Seiple and Dennis R. Hoover (Lanham, MD: Rowman and Littlefield, 2004), 105, 108. Nevertheless, unlike Novak, bin Bakar exploits this universal dimension as a unifying religious factor among the "religions of the book." I would argue that law, whether natural or revealed, is a unifying human factor but that the gospel is the only unifying religious factor.

law," as did his heirs.[54] The location of a core of natural law in the concept of equity seems entirely justified in our common experience, ineradicable even by modernity's pursuit of radical autonomy.[55]

Reformation theology emphasizes that while the gospel is revealed only in the proclamation of Christ (*verbum externum*), the law is the native property of all human beings (*verbum internum*), the very law of their being, which, though suppressed in unrighteousness, cannot entirely be purged from the conscience. The gospel engenders a church, while the law engenders a secular *civitas*. Precisely because the story the Bible tells about us all is true, we can appeal not to ostensibly neutral, universal foundations but to the concrete "common life" that is constituted by our being creatures of covenant.

According to O'Donovan, "John Calvin may largely take credit for conceiving and implementing a reintegration of political order and spiritual community that transformed the historical complexion of Reformation Christianity." "Even more than the later Luther, he converted the polarizations of the two-kingdoms model into parallelisms, stressing harmonization of the spiritual and temporal realms as of two communal realizations of God's will for fallen mankind, one direct and the other indirect."[56] Calvin combined "patristic, scholastic, and Lutheran theological elements with ideas and methods drawn from classical political philosophy, and humanist literary, historical, and legal scholarship."[57] In Calvin's wake, Reformed thinking not only moved toward greater refinement of its covenant theology but applied it to the social sphere, where it contributed to the evolution of early modern constitutional theory.[58]

However, the lingering meganarrative of Christendom (allegorized Israel) often kept the Reformation doctrine of the two kingdoms from being worked out in practice even in nominally Reformed lands. Despite Calvin's exegetical defense of the uniqueness of Israel's theocracy, Protestant as well as Catholic

54. Augustine, *City of God*, ed. Knowles, 873.

55. Kevin J. Hason, "Neither Sacred nor Secular," in *Religion and Security*, ed. Seiple and Hoover, 152–53. A U.S. diplomat, Hason relates, "When delegates from the fifty-eight nations of the Human Rights Commission surveyed world leaders as diverse as Mahatma Gandhi, Pierre Teilhard de Chardin, and Aldous Huxley, they found surprising agreement on a basic enumeration of rights. Yet when the Commission began its debates, the wide range of members' philosophies and religious backgrounds precluded consensus on recognizing divine revelation or natural law as the source for human rights. However, human dignity was the one foundation all parties could agree on, even countries with poor human rights records."

56. Oliver O'Donovan and Joan Lockwood O'Donovan, eds., *From Irenaeus to Grotius: A Sourcebook in Christian Political Thought, 100–1625* (Grand Rapids: Eerdmans, 1999), 662.

57. Ibid., 662.

58. The names of Johannes Althusius, John Ponet, Philippe de Morney, and other sixteenth-century Reformed theologians figure prominently in the development of modern constitutionalism. See also the research in this area by David Van Drunen in "The Context of Natural Law: John Calvin's Doctrine of the Two Kingdoms," *Journal of Church and State* 46 (Summer 2004): 503–25.

nation-states presumed that they too could enter into a national covenant with God with biblical law or canon law as the basis for public policy. Rather than a general equity derived from natural law in creation, which could be realized in a variety of political forms and laws, such nation-states pursued a legalistic application of biblical law that could not fail to end in parliamentary factions and stalemates. Thus, it was not the two kingdoms doctrine but its practical rejection that created a crisis of secular politics whose only solution to the likes of Descartes, Spinoza, Hobbes, and Kant—all the way to Rawls, Rorty, and Hardt and Negri—was to be found by appeal to universal foundations that bypassed appeals to revelation. An allegorized meganarrative evolved into a secular metanarrative of human progress which became closely identified with national destiny. Whatever new passages we are now encountering, they do not appear to have transcended this basic trajectory.

As I see it, whatever advantages secularism has taken with such secularization of political power, the latter remains a theologically justified course. It is not by resacralizing the secular in the name of Christ and his kingdom but by resecularizing it—saving it from both secularist ideology and Christian triumphalism—that we can begin again to recognize the value of equity and "the common" as something more than the war of all against all and yet something far short of the City of God that yet awaits us.

A Way Forward

In the account I offer below, there is indeed a "common interest" (what the older theologians called a *sensus communis*), and it is distinct from the *consensus fidelium* uniquely shared within the communion of saints. However, it is not self-generating, and it is more fundamentally ethical (the summons of the Other) than economic, which means that it is evoked by transcendent demands deriving from the Creator's moral character and not merely practical expediencies deriving from the creature's expressive will. Not even God can be a sovereign exception, since the divine will is determined by the divine character. This transcendent covenantal summons is subversive of modern contractual theories of nation-states but also stands over against *all* immanent claims to sovereignty, including those of individual subjects ("singularities") and their networks of communication and production. "Common interest" must be held accountable to a common revelation of God's moral will, which Christians, Jews, and Muslims have identified with a historical creation that, at least for Christians and Jews, is mediated in the form of a universal covenant distinct from the special covenant of grace. In my view, an official acknowledgment of God and this general revelation of a transcendent moral obligation are not necessary in public documents or policies in order for Christians to assume the universal covenant's validity as the justification for appealing to such categories as justice and peace.

In this light, we should envision a church that neither baptizes the secular nor washes its hands of it. Christians should be freed in their secular vocations as parents and citizens, and in their various professional callings, to love and serve their neighbors in a manner consistent with their ultimate calling as believers. Nevertheless, the church as the church is not entrusted with the transformation of the earthly city according to its heavenly archetype. The issues to be addressed in "the common" require negotiations concerning important but not ultimate claims. Sharing substantial convictions of faith and practice does not inevitably entail a particular Christian political order; conversely, sharing substantial political agreements does not engender a Christian communion. In this account, there are two covenantal communities and two "multitudes"—one founded in creation and law, the other in redemption and gospel—to which Christians belong in this age. Each has its legitimate and distinct role to play in the divine economy.

Confusing these two kingdoms undermines the integrity of the secular as such, so that biblical passages never intended to be applied to modern conditions are wrenched from their context to support poor social policy through poor exegesis. As O'Donovan warns, we cannot just mine the Bible for quotes as a gloss for our otherwise secular aspirations. "We have seen World Council of Churches documents brim over with *shalom*, evangelical Protestants become eloquent about the jubilee, and, more widely noticed than either, Exodus stride across the pages of the Latin Americans. Yet the problem of integrating them theologically has not been solved."[59] This tendency to mine the Bible for quotes is precisely how Christendom came to allegorize Israel's history as its own. This is not only the problem of Puritans and Zionists, as Milbank thinks, but the entire tradition of allegorizing Israel's history as a template for national covenants. O'Donovan adds, "To dip into Israel's experience at one point—let it be the Exodus, the promise of shalom, the jubilee laws, or, with Thomas Cranmer at the coronation of Edward VI, the reign of Josiah of Judah—and to take out a single disconnected image or theme from it is to treat the history of God's reign like a commonplace book or a dictionary of quotations." Rather, Israel's history "must be read as a history of redemption," the story of God's purposes that reach their climax in Christ, not a blueprint for the kingdoms we bring into being by our own efforts.[60]

We do not need more "Christian" influence in Washington, which in any case would only ensure a civil war between left-wing and right-wing evangelical social reformers. Rather, we need more Christianity in the churches

---

59. Oliver O'Donovan, *The Desire of the Nations: Rediscovering the Roots of Political Theology* (Cambridge: Cambridge University Press, 1996), 22.

60. Ibid., 27, 29.

and a more secular (though not secularist) influence in all areas of culture by Christians freed to pursue their secular vocations, so that the civic "multitude" enjoys a greater justice, goodness, truth, and peace than the lure of a purely immanent *libido dominandi* (however construed) would engender. If evangelicals were more Augustinian, they would be more critical of attempts to confuse the *pax Americana* with the *pax Christi*, however that confusion plays out—in either a socialist or a capitalist political idolatry. The claims of the current U.S. administration and its evangelical allies for the ultimacy of democracy and neoliberal politics would be relativized along with the claims of their more politically liberal rivals, so that the real debate could be pursued on the level of relative goods and ends.

Precisely because this appeal is to *revelation*, it is nonfoundationalist in any modern sense. It embraces the scandal of particularity. It is not the "view from nowhere," which, ironically, Hardt and Negri seem to perpetuate by their description of empire as "ou-topia." Yet precisely because this appeal is to *general* revelation, convinced that the story that this particular biblical narrative tells about the constitution of humanity in an original covenant is true, we can assume that nonbelievers will "get it," no matter how inconsistent this may be with their ultimate metaphysical convictions. Despite its suppression, the ineradicability of this revelation is the justification for our appeal to a justice between neighbors that does not justify us before God.

Democracy, like any community, is a "process of reason-exchange," as Stout observes.[61] Stout gets closer to the appropriate Christian response than do the new traditionalists, although he remains a religious skeptic:

> But one of the most important findings presented here is that Christian theological orthodoxy is not the source of the new traditionalism's antidemocratic sentiments or tendencies. . . . At a moment when orthodox Judaism in Israel and orthodox Islam around the world are struggling to sort through analogous issues, study of Christian thinkers who have connected theological orthodoxy with democratic practice is an academic topic of global significance. . . . Democracy involves substantial normative commitments, but does not presume to settle in advance the ranking of our highest values. Nor does it claim to save humanity from sin and death. . . .
>
> Yet it holds that people who differ on such matters can still exchange reasons with one another intelligibly, cooperate in crafting political arrangements that promote justice and decency in their relations with one another, and do both of these things without compromising their integrity.[62]

Since the churches themselves are divided along cultural, racial, and political lines today, simply identifying with the church over against the world

---

61. Stout, *Democracy and Tradition*, 283.
62. Ibid., 298.

is hardly a panacea.[63] Here once again, the Emersonian religious skeptic Stout appears more illuminating than some Christians who see the church as the only savior of "the common." "If a personal God exists and chooses to interact with us," he reasons, "then our relationship with God, according to the theory just given, should be capable of giving rise to obligations. If God issues commands to us, these will qualify as a kind of social requirement." This sounds a lot like a divinely revealed covenant rather than the modern social contract. "The theory holds that the goodness of the social bond is essential to giving obligations their force." All of this, says Stout, may still be objectionable to religious skeptics like himself, but at least it isn't metaphysical. It makes ontological claims that yield important convictions in favor of human rights.[64]

If Hardt and Negri are right about our having passed from the era in which debates over nation-states mattered (and their case seems fairly solid), the suggestions I have offered are nevertheless just as relevant for today's conditions of empire. Challenging what he calls the "rhetoric of excess," Stout concludes,

> The theological antidote for this rhetoric of excess, at least from a mainstream Augustinian perspective, has always been to stress that God not only created this world, but also declared it good, and remains its gracious ruler despite the temporary triumphs of sin. If the world is essentially good, but thrown out of whack by sin, the fitting response to it is not rejection, but an ambivalent mixture of affirmation and condemnation. . . . You are still making a difference when you are engaged in a successful holding action against forces that are conspiring to make things worse than they are.[65]

And whatever fascinating and important passages of Babylon lie before us, they pale in significance compared to the pilgrimage of the saints to their everlasting City.

63. Ibid., 299.
64. Ibid., 260.
65. Ibid., 58.

19

The Future of Evangelical Theology in an Age of Empire

Postfoundational and Postcolonial

MABIALA KENZO AND JOHN R. FRANKE

The Anglo American evangelical church has long been the leading influence in the development of evangelical expressions of church and theology throughout the world. The prominence of the United Kingdom and the United States in the political situation of the past century, coupled with the material largesse entailed by this prominence, served to secure this leading role for Anglo American evangelicalism in the formation and development of the global evangelical church. The central role of the United States in the global and economic empire articulated by Michael Hardt and Antonio Negri has enabled this hegemony to continue after the demise of nationalistic imperialism. The centrality of the Christian religion to the American myth has ensured an important role for American evangelicalism in this new empire. However, the dramatic growth of Christianity in the Global South has raised some probing questions and challenges for American evangelicalism concerning its position in the global church as we enter a new century. Here we focus on the challenges for North American evangelical theology as it faces this situation.

The thoroughly contextual nature of theology, while often acknowledged, has yet to take hold of the discipline as it is generally practiced in North American evangelical Protestantism. It is our conviction that this situation is due in large part to two factors. First, there is the enduring propensity of conservative evangelical thinkers to embrace the characteristics and tendencies of modernity in the task of theological formulation, particularly those of foundationalism. Second, the same evangelical thinkers tend to consistently overlook the fact that they belong to a dominant culture, which affects their theology and its reception in non-Western contexts. This essay will suggest a postfoundational, postcolonial model for the theological task. Such model takes seriously the contextual nature of all human knowledge and the ecumenical vocation of the practice of theology. While remaining faithful to core Christian commitments, it draws on the insights of postmodern and postcolonial theories from the perspective of evangelical and ecumenical orthodoxy. We will begin with a consideration of the postfoundational character of this approach to theology before turning our attention to the ways in which it is, and must be, postcolonial.

Postfoundational Theology

In the modern era, the pursuit of knowledge was deeply influenced by Enlightenment foundationalism. In its broadest sense, foundationalism is merely the acknowledgment that not all beliefs are of equal significance in the structure of knowledge. Some beliefs are more "basic" or "foundational" and serve to give support to other beliefs that are derived from them. Understood in this way, nearly every thinker is in some sense a foundationalist, which means such a description is unhelpful for grasping the range of opinion in epistemological theory found among contemporary thinkers. However, in philosophical circles *foundationalism* refers to a much stronger epistemological stance than is entailed in this general observation about how beliefs intersect. At the heart of the foundationalist agenda is a desire to overcome the uncertainty generated by the tendency of fallible human beings to error and the inevitable disagreements and controversies that follow. Foundationalists are convinced that the only way to solve this problem is to find some means of grounding the entire edifice of human knowledge on invincible certainty.

This quest for complete epistemological certitude, often termed *strong* or *classical foundationalism*, has its philosophical beginnings in the thought of the philosopher René Descartes. Descartes sought to reconstruct the nature of knowledge by rejecting traditional medieval or "premodern" notions of authority and replacing them with the modern conception of indubitable beliefs that are accessible to all individuals. This conception of knowledge became the dominant assumption of intellectual pursuit in the modern era. In terms of a philosophical conception of knowledge, foundationalism is a theory concerned with the justification of knowledge. It maintains that beliefs must be justified by their relationship to other beliefs and that the chain of justifications that results from this procedure must not be circular or endless but must have a terminus in foundational beliefs that are immune from criticism and cannot be called into question. The goal to be attained through the identification of indubitable foundations is a universal knowledge that transcends time and context. In keeping with this pursuit, the ideals of human knowledge since Descartes have tended to focus on the universal, the general, and the theoretical rather than on the local, the particular, and the practical.

In spite of the hegemony of this approach to knowledge, Nancey Murphy notes that it is "only recently that philosophers have labeled the modern foundationalist theory of knowledge as such."[1] This means that while this approach to knowledge has been widely influential in intellectual thought, it has been *assumed* by modern thinkers rather than explicitly advocated and defended. In light of this, Murphy suggests two criteria in the identification of foundationalism: "first, the assumption that knowledge systems must include a class of beliefs that are somehow immune from challenge; and second, the assumption that all reasoning within the system proceeds in one direction only—from that set of special, indubitable beliefs to others, but not the reverse."[2] The goal of this foundationalist agenda is the discovery of an approach to knowledge that will provide rational human beings with absolute, incontestable certainty regarding the truthfulness of their beliefs. The Enlightenment epistemological foundation consists of a set of incontestable beliefs or unassailable first principles on the basis of which the pursuit of knowledge can proceed. These basic beliefs or first principles must be universal, objective, and discernible to any rational person apart from the particulars of varied situations, experiences, and contexts.

This conception of knowledge came to dominate the discipline of theology as theologians reshaped their construals of the Christian faith in accordance with its dictates. In the nineteenth and twentieth centuries, the foundationalist impulse produced a theological division in the Anglo American context between the "left" and the "right" in which liberal and conservative theologians, while maintaining opposing material positions, can also be viewed as working out theological details from two different sides of the same modernist foundationalist coin. However, this classical form of foundationalism is in dramatic retreat, as its assertions about the objectivity, certainty, and universality of knowledge have come under fierce criticism.[3] As J. Wentzel

1. Nancey Murphy, *Beyond Liberalism and Fundamentalism: How Modern and Postmodern Philosophy Set the Theological Agenda* (Valley Forge, PA: Trinity Press International, 1996), 13.

2. Ibid.

3. John E. Thiel, *Nonfoundationalism* (Minneapolis: Fortress, 1994), 37.

van Huysteen observes, "Whatever notion of postmodernity we eventually opt for, all postmodern thinkers see the modernist quest for certainty, and the accompanying program of laying foundations for our knowledge, as a dream for the impossible, a contemporary version of the quest for the Holy Grail."[4] One of the central concerns of the postmodern quest for a chastened approach to knowledge is found in the rejection of both the classical foundationalist approach to knowledge *and* its intellectual tendencies.

Postmodern theory raises two related but distinct questions to the modern foundationalist enterprise. First, is such an approach to knowledge *possible?* And second, is it *desirable?* These questions are connected with what may be viewed as the two major branches of postmodern hermeneutical philosophy: the hermeneutics of finitude and the hermeneutics of suspicion. However, the challenges to foundationalism are not only philosophical but also emerge from the context of Christian theology. Merold Westphal suggests that postmodern theory, with respect to hermeneutical philosophy, may be properly appropriated for the task of explicitly Christian thought on theological grounds: "The hermeneutics of finitude is a meditation on the meaning of human createdness, and the hermeneutics of suspicion is a meditation on the meaning of human fallenness."[5] In other words, many of the concerns of postmodern theory can be appropriated and fruitfully developed in the context of the Christian doctrines of creation and sin.

Viewed from this perspective, the questions that are raised by postmodern thought concerning the possibility and desirability of foundationalism are also questions that emerge from the material content of Christian theology. Questions from both sources lead to similar conclusions. First, modern foundationalism is an impossible dream for finite human beings, whose outlooks are always limited and shaped by the particular contexts from which they emerge. Second, the modern foundationalist emphasis on the inherent goodness of knowledge is shattered by the fallen and sinful nature of human beings, who desire to seize control of the epistemic process in order to empower themselves and further their own ends, often at the expense of others. The limitations of finitude and the flawed condition of human nature mean that epistemic foundationalism is neither possible nor desirable for created and sinful persons. This double critique of foundationalism suggests the appropriateness of postfoundationalism for an approach to the task of theology that is in keeping with the Christian tradition.

A postfoundationalist approach to knowledge does not demand that knowledge systems include a class of beliefs that are immune from criticism; rather, all beliefs are subject to critical scrutiny. It also maintains that reasoning within

4. J. Wentzel van Huysteen, "Tradition and the Task of Theology," *Theology Today* 55, no. 2 (July 1998): 216.

5. Merold Westphal, *Overcoming Onto-theology: Toward a Postmodern Christian Faith* (New York: Fordham University Press, 2001), xx.

the system proceeds not in only one direction but rather moves conversationally in multiple directions. This suggests a metaphorical shift in our understanding of the structure of knowledge from that of a building with a sure foundation to something like a web of interrelated, interdependent beliefs.[6] Further, the ideals of human knowledge in nonfoundational and contextual approaches place emphasis on the local, the particular, and the practical rather than on the universal, the general, and the theoretical. According to William Stacy Johnson, postfoundationalist approaches to theology "share a common goal of putting aside all appeals to presumed self-evident, non-inferential, or incorrigible grounds for their intellectual claims."[7] They reject the notion that among the many beliefs that make up a particular theology there must be a single irrefutable foundation that is immune to criticism and provides the certain basis upon which all other assertions are founded. In postfoundationalist theology all beliefs are open to criticism and reconstruction. This does not mean that postfoundational theology eschews convictions, only that such convictions, even the most long-standing and dear, are subject to critical scrutiny and therefore potentially to revision, reconstruction, or even rejection.

One of the significant entailments of a postfoundationalist theology is its inherent commitment to contextuality, which requires the opening of theological conversation to the voices of persons and communities who have generally been excluded from the discourse of Anglo American theology. It maintains without reservation that no single human perspective, be it that of an individual or a particular community or theological tradition, is adequate to do full justice to the truth of God's revelation in Christ. Richard Mouw points to this issue as one of his own motivations for reflecting seriously on postmodern themes: "As many Christians from other parts of the world challenge our 'North Atlantic' theologies, they too ask us to think critically about our own cultural location, as well as about how we have sometimes blurred the boundaries between what is essential to the Christian message and the doctrine and frameworks we have borrowed from various Western philosophical traditions."[8] The adoption of a postfoundationalist approach to theology mandates a critical awareness of the role of culture and social location in the process of theological interpretation and construction. From the perspective of the ecumenically orthodox Christian tradition, postfoundationalist theology seeks to nurture an open and flexible theology that is in keeping with the local and contextual character of human knowledge while remaining thoroughly and distinctly Christian.

6. See, for example, Willard V. O. Quine and J. S. Ullian, *The Web of Belief* (New York: Random House, 1970).

7. William Stacy Johnson, *The Mystery of God: Karl Barth and the Postmodern Foundations of Theology* (Louisville, KY: Westminster John Knox, 1997), 3.

8. Richard Mouw, "Delete the 'Post' from 'Postconservative,'" *Books and Culture* 7, no. 3 (May/June 2001): 22.

The sociology of knowledge reminds us that all forms of thought are embedded in social conditions, and while this does not mean that those conditions unilaterally determine them, it does point to the contextual nature of theology. It is not the intent of theology simply to set forth, amplify, refine, and defend a timelessly fixed orthodoxy. Instead, theology is formulated in the context of the community of faith and seeks to describe the nature of faith, the God to whom faith is directed, and the implications of the Christian faith commitment within the specific historical and cultural setting in which it is lived. Because theology draws from contemporary thought-forms in theological reflection, the categories it uses are culturally and historically conditioned. Moreover, because the context into which the church speaks the message of the gospel is constantly changing, the task of theology in assisting the church in the formulation and application of its faith commitments in the varied and shifting context of human life and thought never comes to an end. As Garrett Green notes, "Like all interpretive activity, theology will therefore be historically and culturally grounded, not speaking from some neutral vantage point but in and for its human context. One corollary is that the theological task will never be completed this side of the Eschaton, since human beings are by nature historical and changing."[9] Thus, the contextual and ongoing task of theology is best characterized by the metaphor of pilgrimage. This understanding of theology as a nonfoundational, contextual, and ongoing enterprise that takes shape in the midst of particular circumstances suggests the local character of the discipline and leads to a consideration of the significance of postcolonialism for evangelical theology in the age of empire.

Postcolonial Theology

Born in the context of Western imperial expansion and nurtured by the rise of what Hardt and Negri call "Empire,"[10] Anglo American evangelical theology has grown accustomed to conceiving itself as the center around which other evangelical theologies orbit. Although Anglo American evangelical churches have played a leading role in promoting contextualization in their "mission fields," those outposts and peripheries of the metropolitan center, they have generally failed to recognize the extent to which their own theology is contextual. This attitude has done nothing but perpetuate Western hegemony. If evangelical theology is to become a cradle of dialogue for the promotion of a truly ecumenical spirit of interaction, interanimation, and interpenetration between the West and the Global South, Anglo American churches need to

9. Garrett Green, *Imagining God: Theology and the Religious Imagination* (San Francisco: Harper & Row, 1989), 186.

10. Michael Hardt and Antonio Negri, *Empire* (Cambridge, MA: Harvard University Press, 2000).

come to terms not only with the contextual nature of their own theology but also with the impact of colonialism and its aftermath on those from the Global South, for whatever theology those from the Global South bring to the table will be affected by the experience of colonialism and its aftermath.

Concern for colonialism and its aftermath has produced a discipline, "postcolonial studies," that deals with the state of postcoloniality and the theory of postcolonialism. *Postcolonialism* designates a critical practice whereby the political and cultural experience of the marginalized periphery is developed into a general theoretical position "set against Western political, intellectual, and academic hegemony and its protocol of objective knowledge."[11] Michel Foucault's work has exerted a significant influence on the development of postcolonialism. Two of its key ideas constitute postcolonialism's starting point: first, both subjectivity and knowledge are determined by the conditions of one's existence; and second, knowledge as a discursive practice is essentially linked to the exercise of power and control.[12]

In his seminal work *Orientalism*,[13] Edward Said makes use of Foucault's insight to argue that the Orient does not exist except in the imaginary of the West, which created it to serve as its Other.[14] The barbaric, irrational, pagan, and mysterious Orient became part of the discourse of legitimation of the colonial enterprise.[15]

In exposing the genealogy of the concept of the Orient, Said and other postcolonial thinkers join hands with postmodernists (especially poststructuralists) in denouncing the cultural power dynamics at work in modern epistemology, which seeks to master being by forcing it into a binary opposition of "same/other, spirit/matter, subject/object, inside/outside, pure/impure, rational/chaotic."[16] Further, postcolonialism, which is borne by a sense of homelessness and a feeling of alienation, presents itself as a space-clearing gesture and an identity-constructing strategy.[17] It offers an alternative between radical fundamentalism, whereby the Global South would violently reject everything Western in the name of liberation and return to its precolonial past, and complete assimilation, whereby difference, alterity, and otherness would be violently erased in the name of a unifying sameness. With the realization that

11. Robert Young, *Postcolonialism: An Historical Introduction* (Oxford: Blackwell, 2001), 65.

12. Michel Foucault, *The Order of Things: An Archaeology of the Human Sciences* (New York: Random House, 1970), xxii.

13. Edward W. Said, *Orientalism* (1978; reprint New York: Vintage, 1994).

14. V. Y. Mudimbe makes a similar point in relation to Africa in *The Invention of Africa: Gnosis, Philosophy, and the Order of Knowledge* (Bloomington: Indiana University Press, 1988).

15. Ania Loomba, *Colonialism/Postcolonialism* (London: Routledge, 1998), 20.

16. Catherine Keller, Michael Nausner, and Mayra Rivera, *Postcolonial Theologies: Divinity and Empire* (St. Louis: Chalice, 2004), 11.

17. Bill Ashcroft, Gareth Griffiths, and Helen Tiffin, *The Empire Writes Back: Theory and Practice in Post-colonial Literature*, 2nd ed. (New York: Routledge, 2002), 8–9.

these two alternatives are not only impossible to achieve but also undesirable, postcolonialism adopts the language of the West, which it inflects in order to make it "bear the burden"[18] of the marginalized. Through mimicry, pastiche, parody, or bricolage, postcolonial criticism subverts the Western discourse of legitimation and creates at the margins of the West spaces of emancipation where alterity is celebrated. Only, unlike modern spaces that are centered, coherent, and unified, postcolonial spaces are hybrid and in-between spaces, crossroads, borderlands, or *fronteras*.[19]

In *Empire*, Hardt and Negri question the relevance of this postcolonial strategy, arguing that the current paradigm, which is post-postmodern, renders postmodern and postcolonial theories inadequate and useless.[20] They contend that imperialism has morphed into empire. In its new configuration, induced by capital globalization, empire shares the ideals of postmodernism. For instance, as the new global form of sovereignty, empire has neither global center nor fixed boundaries. It includes rather than excludes the Other, and it thrives on difference. As such, empire is a nonplace, an "*ou-topia*" where everything is connected with everything else.[21] Thus, with this new enemy, distinctions among economic, political, and cultural spheres is blurred as they all come under the regime of biopower.[22] Yet Hardt and Negri end their work on an optimistic note in which they prophetically envision an eschatological earthly city beyond empire that will be brought about by the multitude, that is, the "universality of free and productive practices," which they oppose to the limited sphere of imperial democracy configured as a "people," an organized particularity that defends established "principles and properties."[23]

In calling attention to the new configuration of empire and its particular challenges, Hardt and Negri make a significant contribution to the current debate concerning our time. However, for all of its erudition in the identification of postimperialist forms of empire, the proposed response still reads like an attempt at yet another metanarrative. Despite its obvious postmodern tone and sensitivity, *Empire* is a dialectic march with a predictable telos, much like Hegel's *Phenomenology of Spirit*. While Hardt and Negri carefully define the concept of multitude to emphasize its multiplicity, it still remains a universal concept that homogenizes the effect of empire on its victims. In the face of empire, in its imperial forms or in the forms described by Hardt and Negri, the postcolonial struggle continues. Empire does not render postcolonial criti-

18. James Baldwin, quoted by Chinua Achebe, *Morning Yet on Creation Day* (New York: Doubleday, 1975), 62.

19. Keller, Nausner, and Rivera, *Postcolonial Theologies*, 3.

20. *Empire*, 137–38.

21. Ibid., xii, 190.

22. Ibid., 41.

23. Ibid., 316.

cism irrelevant as long as its effects are inflected differently according to race, gender, or location.

Postcolonial strategies have made their way into the praxis of theology as well. Postcolonialism in theology is a space-clearing gesture and an identity-constructing strategy in much the same way that it is in philosophy, the arts, and literature. Postcolonial theologies are essentially discourses of otherness that embody a desire to exercise the "right to difference."[24] They apply such postmodern strategies as pastiche, bricolage, mimicry, and hybridity to produce vernacular theological constructs. Hence postcolonial African theologians inflect the Nicene language of *ousia, homoousios, monogenes*, and *hypostaseis* in such a way that it also conveys the image of Christ as "Chief," "Ancestor," "Master of Initiation," "Healer," or "Elder Brother"—that is, images under which Christ is worshiped in local faith communities in Africa.

Postcolonial theologies are not without their problems. Just as postmodernism has taught us to be content with the regional, the local, and the vernacular, postcolonial theology runs the risk of becoming localized to the point of idiosyncrasy. As Gayatri Spivak argues in "Can the Subaltern Speak?" the defense of the local and the vernacular can conceal other forms of oppression.[25] Such images as Christ as a traditional Luba chief, the *Mwadia-Mvita* or the *Cilobo*, that is, the chief warrior whose countless arrows never miss their target, or the *Mukokodi-wa-ku-muele*, "the one who never trifles with the hatchet, the one whose hatchet never fails to strike home,"[26] may indeed conceal forms of local oppression and encourage gratuitous violence. Thus one needs to oppose these images with others such as the image of a chief seated on the poor person's mat. Not only Western metanarratives need deconstruction but African narratives as well.

As the ranks of evangelical churches swell with Christians from the Global South, evangelical theology is poised to serve as that space of interrelation, interanimation, differentiation, dialogue, and exchange where different perspectives are both deconstructed and reconstructed through contact with one another. However, for this to happen certain preconditions have to be met. First, evangelical theology needs to rethink the virtue of marginality. The Christian church initially developed at the margins of both Roman and Jewish centers. However, over time and through mimicry it began to act as the center. Developments both in the West and in the Global South indicate that the Constantinian captivity of the church may finally be coming to an end. The church, and particularly the evangelical church, has to learn anew to

---

24. Tite Tiénou, "The Right to Difference: The Common Roots of African Theology and African Philosophy," *African Journal of Evangelical Theology* 9 (1990): 24–34.

25. Gayatri C. Spivak, "Can the Subaltern Speak? Speculation on Widow-Sacrifice," *Wedge*, 1985, 120–30.

26. François Kabaselé, "Christ as Chief," in *Faces of Jesus in Africa*, ed. Robert J. Schreiter (Maryknoll, NY: Orbis, 1991), 103–15.

live at the margins of empire. A church at the margins is decentered; it has no mother church, only localized contextual churches living in solidarity with one another. Second, evangelical theology needs to theologize the in-betweenness of Christian living. Christians are resident aliens whose life in the space in-between is full of ambiguities. The promise of the eschaton as a space of unmediated knowledge and permanence of being relativizes all constructs of God, subjectivity, or reality within the space in-between.

Finally, evangelical theology needs to liberate the creative potential of the concept of hybridity. It is quite easy to reduce the concept of hybridity to syncretism, which represents the effort to unite opposing principles. In its positive sense, hybridity is the persistence of difference in unity. Life in the church is life together-in-difference modeled on the triunity of Father, Son, and Holy Spirit. As such, hybridity stands for resistance to hardened differences based on binary oppositions and the refusal to absorb all difference into a hegemonic plane of sameness and homogeneity,[27] just as it stands for openness to being nurtured by the Other. According to Emmanuel Levinas, the Other cannot be thematized or conceptualized, suppressed or possessed. Instead, in the face of the Other—in the strangeness of the Other, the Other's irreducibility to the I—we glimpse the epiphany of transcendence.[28]

Conclusion

Our awareness of the local character of theology suggested by a postfoundational and postcolonial approach raises a challenge for the practice of an appropriately catholic theology. How do we do theology that is not simply accommodated to our own cultural assumptions and aspirations? Lesslie Newbigin has addressed this question by observing that while the ultimate commitment of the Christian theologian is to the biblical story, such a person is also a participant in a particular social setting whose whole way of thinking is shaped by the cultural model of that society in ways that are both conscious and unconscious. These cultural models cannot be absolutized without impairing the ability to properly discern the teachings and implications of the biblical narrative. Yet as participants in a particular culture, we are not able to see many of the numerous ways in which we take for granted and absolutize our own socially constructed cultural models. Given this state of affairs, Newbigin maintains that the unending task of theology must be to be wholly open to the biblical narrative in such a way that the assumptions and aspirations of a culture are viewed in its light in order to find ways of

27. Ien Ang, "Together-in-Difference: Beyond Diaspora, into Hybridity," *Asian Studies Review* 27, no. 2 (2003): 141–54.

28. Emmanuel Levinas, *Totality and Infinity: An Essay on Exteriority*, trans. Alphonso Lingis (The Hague: Kluwer, 1991).

expressing the biblical story in terms which make use of particular cultural models without being controlled by them. He concludes with the assertion that this can be done only if Christian theologians are "continuously open to the witness of Christians in other cultures who are seeking to practice the same kind of theology."[29] Only through such openness will North American evangelicals be able to participate in the subversion of empire and bear faithful witness to the kingdom of God.

29. Lesslie Newbigin, "Theological Education in a World Perspective," *Churchman* 93 (1979): 114–15.

20

Evangelicalism and/as New Constantinianism

Globalization, Secularity, and the Heart of the Gospel

PAUL LIM

"Evangelicalism as the new Constantinianism?" is the main idea to be investigated in this chapter as the multifarious realities of North American evangelicalism—its belief structure as regards contemporary political contexts—are subjected to scrutiny vis-à-vis a similar metanarratival structure, the new *Empire* and the *Multitude*, two recent "academic best sellers" (which, in this case, is not oxymoronic) by Antonio Negri and Michael Hardt.[1]

In the first section, a critical engagement with the ideological trajectory and substantive threads of argumentation of the Negri-Hardt thesis will be given;[2] in the second section, I will propose the necessity for broadening the semantic range of the word *evangelical* to accommodate the global realities

---

1. Michael Hardt and Antonio Negri, *Empire* (Cambridge, MA: Harvard University Press, 2000), and *Multitude: War and Democracy in the Age of Empire* (New York: Penguin, 2004).

2. By this phrase I mean the overall ideological thrust contained in *Empire* and *Multitude*.

that present themselves right here in North America; in the final section, a tertium quid for the future of evangelicalism vis-à-vis *Multitude* and *Empire* will be given, a global ecclesial order that emphasizes a concrete movement from xenophobia to *philoxenia*.

There is hardly any need to rehearse the litany of panegyric given to *Empire* and *Multitude*, heralded most memorably by Slavoj Žižek, who said that *Empire* merits being considered "a rewriting of the *Communist Manifesto* for our time" or a literary harbinger for the Huxleyan world *redivivus*. *Empire* offers a trenchant critique of the regimes of power, be they nation-states, imperialisms of all sorts, and of the post–cold war dominance of America. On the rubble of all toppled—or soon to be toppled—ideologies and systems stand both the empire and the only group of unlikely heroes who possess the singular will to challenge, indeed overcome, its concatenating bondage: the multitude. In an obvious sense, what distinguishes *Empire* and *Multitude* is their virtual absence of pessimism or dark foreboding of apocalypticism. Whether one ends up agreeing with the Negri-Hardt thesis or not, it is a significant milestone, both within Marxist and neo-Marxist scholarship and within the œuvre of postmodern political-cultural theories.

Empire and *Multitude* as Metacritique

According to *Empire*, the seemingly invincible force is the "invisible hand" of market-driven capitalism, destabilizing and rendering largely ineffectual the reality of nation-states and making economic issues the sole existential question for the dawning of a new global order.[3] In this section, two main critiques will be given vis-à-vis the Negri-Hardt thesis. First, their emphatic certitude regarding "no transcendence" within our world-system and the radical immanentizing trajectory will be analyzed. Second, their Manichaean-Pelagian ontology will be evaluated and will show itself to be a pragmatically unviable system.

Critics with such wide-ranging ideological perspectives as Brian C. Anderson and Johann Hari have written of the highly unrealistic and ethereal character of Negri and Hardt's joint project. Hari writes: "It's not just that this preacher of Empire has not clothes; he is living in an intellectual nudist colony."[4] Alan Wolfe averred that *Empire* "cares as little for logic as it does for empirical reality."[5] How accurate is its portraiture of the global situation as having transcended transcendence? According to Ernesto Laclau, "*Empire* . . . makes immanence its central category and the ultimate ground of the multitude's

---

3. *Empire*, 219–350.
4. Johann Hari, "The Nostalgic Revolutionary," *Independent*, August 17, 2004, 7.
5. Alan Wolfe, "The Snake," *New Republic*, October 1, 2001.

unity."[6] The impossibility of politics within the framework of *Empire* has been pointed out both by Anderson, a neoconservative ideologue, and Laclau, whom I would call a chastened neo-Marxist/socialist, in great detail.[7]

"Today there is not even the illusion of a transcendent God," and the "multitude today . . . resides on the imperial surfaces where there is no God the Father and no transcendence": so assert Hardt and Negri. Before we take a look around the shifting bounds of the global religio-cultural context, let us examine the philosophical issues raised by that statement and how this undergirds the edifice of *Empire*. The foregoing assertion of the utter extinction of a transcendent deity is similar to Nietzsche's comment in "The Madman," in *Gay Science*, where he proclaims the death of God:

> "Where has God gone?" he cried. "I shall tell you. We have killed him—you and I. We are his murderers. But how have we done this? How were we able to drink up the sea? Who gave us the sponge to wipe away the entire horizon?. . . . Do we not hear anything yet of the noise of the gravediggers who are burying God? Do we not smell anything yet of God's decomposition? Gods too decompose. God is dead. God remains dead. And we have killed him. . . . Who will wipe this blood off us? With what water could we purify ourselves? What festivals of atonement, what sacred games shall we need to invent? Is not the greatness of this deed too great for us? *Must we not ourselves become gods simply to be worthy of it?* There has never been a greater deed; and whosoever shall be born after us—for the sake of this deed he shall be part of a higher history than all history hitherto.[8]

All the rhetorical flourish and eloquence notwithstanding, one has to ask both the writers of *Empire* and Nietzsche himself whether it still remains true: the putrefaction of God and the erasure of that memory of transcendence from the collective human memory. Hardt and Negri locate the incipient crack in the seamless ontology of Being within the Christian-Platonist system—which inexorably ushered in the movement toward secularization—in the univocity of being propounded by Duns Scotus.[9] In a key section called "The Revolutionary Plane of Immanence," Hardt and Negri argue that secularization is "only a symptom of the primary event of modernity: the affirmation of

6. Ernesto Laclau, "Can Immanence Explain Social Struggles?" *Diacritics* 31 (Winter 2001): 3–10, here 3.

7. Brian C. Anderson, "The Ineducable Left," *First Things*, no. 120 (February 2002): 40–44; Laclau, "Can Immanence Explain Social Struggles?" See also Laclau's book *On Populist Reason* (London: Verso, 2005), in which he corrects what he perceives to be the structural flaws of both *Empire* and *Multitude*.

8. Friedrich Nietzsche, *The Gay Science*, ed. Walter Kaufmann (New York: Vintage, 1974), 125, 181–82, emphasis added.

9. This is technically incorrect. It was John Scotus Erigena (ca. 810–ca. 877) who taught this, albeit for radically different purposes and trajectory. See his *Periphyseon: De division naturae*, trans. I. P. Sheldon-Williams (Washington, DC: Dumbarton Oaks, 1987), especially libs. 3–4.

the powers of *this* world, the discovery of the plane of immanence. 'Omne ens habet aliquod esse proprium'—every entity has a singular essence. Duns Scotus' affirmation subverts the medieval conception of being as an object of analogical, and thus dualistic predication—a being with one foot in this world and one in a transcendent realm."[10] This omnibus treatment of the rise of immanentism takes us on a breathtaking tour of European intellectual history, giving us a taste of Nicholas of Cusa, Pico della Mirandola, Bovillus, Bacon, and Galileo, ending up with Spinoza, whose pantheistic philosophical perspectives collapsed all distinction so that the "horizon of immanence" and "the horizon of the democratic political order coincide completely."[11] This genealogy of "manifest destiny" of the multitude, starting with Scotus and ending with Spinoza, has one major problem. "It gives us," as Laclau avers, "a truncated narrative."[12]

Laclau then places the need for a "planar distinction" between that of God (primarily *transcendent*) and that of creation (primarily *immanent*) *within* theology, for theological purposes, not as planting a seed for secular subversion. However, the subversion indeed followed suit, reaching its zenith with Hegel and his pupil Marx, as the providential "invisible hand" of Adam Smith was replaced by the utterly immanent hands of multitudes amid—and after—much class and economic struggle and suffering.[13] The immanentized telos of the multitude would be the total extermination of all vestiges of transcendence.[14]

However, Laclau's main critique is to question the existential and political viability of just such a proposal: the "postulate of the *homogeneity* and *unity of the multitude* as an historical agent."[15] Moreover, telescoping the far more complex history of political thought in early modern England to a mere half-paragraph,[16] Hardt and Negri neglect to revisit the *topoi* of the theological justification given for the rise of the British civil wars, the unprecedented regicide (à la the charge that Charles I was the "man of blood"), the Interregnum of Oliver Cromwell (during which Hobbes's *Leviathan* was written), and the restoration of monarchy and episcopacy. The idea that sovereignty was an "essentially repressive device to prevent the democratic upsurge of an unspecified multitude" thus becomes problematized rather quickly.

10. *Empire*, 71.
11. Ibid., 73.
12. Laclau, "Can Immanence Explain Social Struggles?" 4.
13. See, especially, vol. 1 of Karl Marx, *Capital: A Critique of Political Economy*, 3 vols., trans. Ben Fowkes (New York: Penguin, 1990), pt. 3, chap. 10; pt. 4, chap. 15; pt. 8, chaps. 28–30, for gripping depictions of the suffering of laborers which largely occasioned the writing of *Das Kapital*.
14. Laclau, "Can Immanence Explain Social Struggles?" 5.
15. Ibid.
16. *Empire*, 84.

What of the idea of the evaporation/extinction of the transcendent deity once again? Here the emergence of global Christianity has falsified the Hegelian immanentizing of the Spirit, in that the Hegelian phenomenology of the Spirit has now received a face. In Philip Jenkins's *The Next Christendom*—which is, much like *Empire* and *Multitude*, an academic best seller—both the hemispheric shift in global Christianity and Christianity as a major force to be reckoned with world geopolitics are painstakingly chronicled. Lamin Sanneh, a professor of history and religious studies at Yale, has also pointed to how the postcolonial and global landscape of Christianity has opened to full bloom in the very century when the death and decomposition of God—as presaged by Nietzsche—was to occur.[17] Moreover, David Martin of the London School of Economics has questioned the putative inevitable and self-evident secularization thesis, while Pippa Norris, in her *Sacred and Secular: Religion and Politics Worldwide*, also identifies the increased/increasing role to be assumed by religion, particularly Islam and Christianity, in global politics.[18] The virtually synonymous nature of secularization and the European Enlightenment has also been questioned. Gertrude Himmelfarb's *The Road to Modernity* portrays a slightly different trajectory of the "inevitable secularity" thesis, arguing that the Anglo American Enlightenment is to be distinguished from the French version in that the *philosophes* were much more antagonistic toward revealed religion than their Anglo American counterparts were.[19]

Hardt and Negri exude a contagious confidence in the multitude, in contradistinction to the cultural elites and power brokers who are the great beneficiaries of the current biopower of capitalism. Tapping the resources of the disenfranchised and demonized, Hardt and Negri want to recruit a motley crew of individuals all of whom converge in their angst regarding the existing sociocultural and political infra- and superstructure. "One element we can put our finger on," write Hardt and Negri, "is *the will to be against*. In general, the will to be against does not seem to require much explanation. Disobedience to authority is one of the most natural and healthy acts."[20] This singularity of rebellion is almost axiomatic for Hardt and Negri, and they see their prophetic task as to cure the dispossessed's "inability to identify the enemy." For them, the enemy is global

17. Philip Jenkins, *The Next Christendom: the Coming of Global Christianity* (Oxford: Oxford University Press, 2002); Lamin Sanneh, *Whose Religion Is Christianity? The Gospel beyond the West* (Grand Rapids: Eerdmans, 2003).

18. David Martin, *On Secularization: Towards a Revised General Theory* (Burlington, VT: Ashgate, 2005), 141–56; Pippa Norris, *Sacred and Secular: Religion and Politics Worldwide* (Cambridge: Cambridge University Press, 2004). See also Scott Thomas, "The Global Resurgence of Religion and the Changing Character of International Politics," in *Christ and the Dominions of Civilization*, ed. Max L. Stackhouse and Diane B. Obenchain (Harrisburg, PA: Trinity Press International, 2002), 110–38.

19. Gertrude Himmelfarb, *The Road to Modernity: the British, French, and American Enlightenments* (New York: Alfred A. Knopf, 2004).

20. *Empire*, 210.

capitalism, with its impeccable sense of control over all of its denizens, which, while promising—and even delivering—a good life, sucks the marrow of their vitality in "being-against," the sine qua non of the Negrian Prometheus.[21]

However, can a headless multitude really survive? Can a radically imma-nentist version of a global order truly obtain? Hardt and Negri have said:

> Empire represents a superficial world, the virtual center of which can be accessed immediately from any point across the surface. If these points were to constitute something like a new cycle of struggles, it would be a cycle defined not by the communicative extension of the struggles but rather by their singular emergence, by the intensity that characterizes them one by one. In short, this new phase is defined by the fact that these struggles do not link horizontally, but each one leaps vertically, directly to the virtual center of Empire.[22]

The fragility of unity around the generic theme of "being against," contra Hardt and Negri, needs to be taken fully into account. Alasdair MacIntyre's *Whose Justice? Which Rationality?* has a tremendous heuristic value for utopian promulgators such as Hardt and Negri. Is "being against" really a sufficient warrant for a peaceful dismantling of empire?

Political mediation, adjudication, representation is desperately needed lest the movement of multitude degenerate into a veritable pandemonium. Are Hardt and Negri proposing a freeze on the computer systems of all political, financial, and educational—the Foucauldian triumvirate of guardians of all social order—branches of the world empire? Could the singular will of "being against" not also lead to an internal fissure within the multitude, generating yet another renegade multitude, and ending up with the reductio ad absurdum of an eternally conflictual mode of human existence, with no telos and no shalom? This point had been anticipated by Laclau: "The present proliferation of a plurality of identities and points of rupture makes the subjects of political action essentially unstable and thus makes impossible a strategic calculation that covers long historical periods."[23] This point is worth dwelling on a bit. Let us do a thought experiment, following the proposal of gathering a horde of people whose apparent—and as we shall see, real—reason for being in the multitude was "being against."

Let us assume that in this particular group there are a number of irrecon-cilable binary oppositions: homophobes and homosexuals, xenophobes who strongly resent foreigners and a group of "undocumented" nomadic workers, Islamic terrorist and right-wing Americentric militia, and so on—you get the picture. Could we really marshal a significant "new majority" multitude as the basis of global politics? Does this notion not manifest a simple disregard, if not for the inveterate and incorrigible nature of our enmity and suspicion

21. Ibid., 211.
22. Ibid., 58.
23. Laclau, "Can Immanence Explain Social Struggles?" 7.

toward others, then at least for the multiplicity of hatreds, the binary dialectic of which may converge precisely within the circle of this multitude?

Moreover, it seems unlikely, given the singular thread of "being against" as the only point of convergence for this multitude, that the trajectory of these "new barbarians'" "affirmative violence" could be the same. The philosophical-cum-anthropological ontology espoused throughout *Empire* and *Multitude* is what I would call a coalescence of Manichaean Pelagianism. It is Manichaean in that it posits an ontology of dualism: a perduring coexistence of good and evil, with no eschatological hope of the victory of the good over the evil; it is intrinsically conflictual, the mode of a perennial "being against" befitting the paradigm of Negri-Hardt. Moreover, it is Pelagian since Negri and Hardt do not take seriously the pervasive reality of our "selfish genes." A cursory reading of Richard Dawkins's *The Selfish Gene* could have compelled Hardt and Negri to grapple with the fact that humans are intrinsically selfish and are often prone to violate the terms of the "Prisoner's Dilemma," thus making likely a collapse of any metaproject of "being against" the empire. Negri and Hardt's ontology of convergence of angst, plus their confident assumption that such a convergence could be maintained without political representation and manipulation, seems hardly realistic. Once again, that is precisely the focus of Laclau's critique, encapsulated in his title, "Can Immanence Explain Social Struggles?" The answer given by Laclau and by the present author is an emphatic *no*.

Building on the critique of Laclau and on the Christian exegetical tradition in Revelation 7:9–17, I would like to offer a biblical—and this is not always coterminous with *evangelical*—counterperspective, which I would call a "headed eschatological multitude":

> After this I looked, and there was a great multitude that no one could count, from every nation, from all tribes and peoples and languages, standing before the throne and before the Lamb, robed in white, with palm branches in their hands. They cried out in a loud voice, saying,
> > "Salvation belongs to our God who is seated on the throne, and to the Lamb!" . . .
> Then one of the elders addressed me, saying, "Who are these, robed in white . . . ? . . . These are they who have come out of the great tribulation; they have washed their robes and made them white in the blood of the Lamb.
> > For this reason they are before the throne of God,
> > > and worship him day and night within his temple,
> > > and the one who is seated on the throne will shelter them.
> > They will hunger no more, and thirst no more;
> > > the sun will not strike them . . .
> > for the Lamb at the center of the throne will be their shepherd,
> > > and he will guide them to springs of the water of life,
> > and God will wipe away every tear from their eyes.

What is intriguing is an unmistakable convergence of the utopian ideal of Negri-Hardt and that of this vision in the Apocalypse of John: the closure of struggles, the cessation of victimization and marginalization. The Christian tradition, however, has always affirmed that this multitude is a "headed" one, in that the Lamb is the agent both of cleansing—and conferring of a new identity that inverts the categories of "being against" and "being for"[24]—and of leading to paradise. John's vision bespeaks an ontology of peace, purchased precisely through "the blood of the Lamb," which thus takes seriously the prevalent reality and ontology of violence yet proposes the reality of a christocentric transcendent solution through the horizon of immanence. Thus John provides a metacritique superior to that of Negri-Hardt, despite their well-targeted critique of market-driven capitalism as the grossly insufficient and ill-equipped ideology and ontology for a new global order. As Laclau has demonstrated well, immanence *alone* cannot account for social struggles.

Evangelicalism as Neo-Constantinianism?

There has been an implicit assumption, hitherto rarely challenged and often unnoticed, in both the liberal and the conservative versions of Christianity that "a democratic state ought to and is able to serve as a primary vehicle of the good God will accomplish through God's church in the world."[25] However, since 9/11 and more acutely since the reelection of George W. Bush as U.S. president, critics have increasingly used the opprobrious term *Constantinian* or *Constantinianism* to describe a breaching of the line of separation between church and state. As most of the contributors to this volume have echoed this sentiment, this criticism deserves a closer scrutiny.

The current cultural fascination with Constantine (AD 288?–337) comes from two contrasting sources: one from an immensely popular novel by Dan Brown, *The Da Vinci Code,* and the other from more high-brow academic discussions on the putative betrayal of pristine Christianity by Constantine's sanctioning of Christianity and its meteoric hegemonic rise. Elizabeth DePalma Digeser and H. A. Drake, with their revisionist sketches of Constantine, have contributed to this historiographic debate recently by challenging the idea of the French Enlightenment *philosophes* that religion is antithetical to reason and constitutive of intolerance. In fact, Digeser elevates the crucial—and hitherto seldom noticed—role played by a Christian apologist, Lactantius, in articulating a theory of religious freedom as an intrinsic part of religious

24. More on this crucial concept of "christocentric inversion" anon, in the third section of this essay.

25. Allen R. Hilton, "Who Are We? Being Christian in an Age of Americanism," in *Anxious about Empire: Theological Essays on the New Global Realities,* ed. Wes Avram (Grand Rapids: Brazos, 2004), 154–55.

belief and thus possibly proscribing the trajectory of persecution. More recently, Robert Louis Wilken has continued with the historiographic revision by giving a more traditional "defense of Constantine."[26]

The label *Constantinianism* and the obloquies that follow have less to do with the emperor's new religion or the putative obsequiousness of Eusebius's panegyric of Constantine than with the co-optation of the church by the state—in other words, the Caesaropapism perhaps best represented in Henry VIII and the ensuing Erastianism in England. It would seem initially strange that there is a confluence of the language of Constantinianism and the supposed rise of evangelical influence on Capitol Hill, which makes a number of people, including some—though not all—evangelicals, nervous about the future of the American religio-political landscape. Is evangelicalism really the culprit for all the wrongs and abuses in American politics and global realities, as some imply? Might it perhaps be an overattribution for evangelicalism to be given responsibility for most of the wrongs committed by hawkish neoconservative Americans, by both sides? I believe the jury is still out on this contentious issue.

There does seem to be a fallacy of overattribution on the part of liberal elites. Threatened—indeed scared—as they were by the prevalence of the "unthinking and uncouth" red state *mentalité*, coupled with the Machiavellian *realpolitik* of Karl Rove, whose political savvy led him to tap into the social conservatism of the *hoi polloi* in America, certainly including white, middle-class, midwestern evangelicals, they have tended to make an intense and perhaps even intentional identification of the Religious Right with the second Bush administration. That alliance has been perhaps one of the most unexpected political gambits on the part of the Bush brain trust, but it is more than that. It seems clear, from all accounts, that President Bush is a self-confessing Christian, and it seems also clear that the liberal argument that equates his personal faith with taking "our troops to war in Jesus's name" is problematic.[27]

In a recent article, Stephen H. Webb challenges the targeting of evangelicals as those who commit the most heinous political sins, justifying them in the name of God. Three issues raised by Webb's critique of the lacerating rebuke heaped on the putative collusion between American evangelicalism and empire of Big Brother America are worth considering. First, Webb correctly identifies "the political complexity of the issue [which] suggests that too many Christians have merely adopted the liberal orientation of the academy in place of thoughtful theological analysis. After all, it is far from clear what impact the

26. Elizabeth DePalma Digeser, *The Making of a Christian Empire: Lactantius and Rome* (Ithaca, NY: Cornell University Press, 2000); H. A. Drake, *Constantine and the Bishops: The Politics of Intolerance* (Baltimore: Johns Hopkins University Press, 2000), 19, 21, 24–28, 71–74; Robert Louis Wilken, "In Defense of Constantine," *First Things*, no. 112 (April 2001): 36–40.

27. Stephen H. Webb, "On the True Globalism and the False, or Why Christians Should Not Worry So Much about American Imperialism," in *Anxious about Empire*, ed. Avram, 122.

American empire will have on the world."[28] The second issue is the tendency among some Christian constructive theologians to be against "all nation-states [as] illegitimate" expressions of the political will, divinely ordained or humanly construed. The third is a rather traditional—and this in a nonpejorative sense—doctrinal and existential construal of the providential ordering of the world. Webb argues, "Sectarian arguments about the Constantinian captivity of the church, while provocative, often go too far in dismissing the providential ways that God has used governments to spread the gospel."[29]

Two more issues on evangelicalism deserve a closer look. The first issue is a definitional one. The editors of this volume have written of the "political consolidation of conservative evangelicals in America," expecting most readers to know the referent of the term *evangelicals*. However, isn't *this* evangelicalism the basically suburban, midwestern white religiosity, as opposed to the evangelicalism that is urban and nonwhite—primarily African American (or increasingly, African), Hispanic, and Asian? What of their "nonoppressive" worldviews? Moreover, as Lamin Sanneh, Timothy Tennent, and Philip Jenkins have made clear, the epochal shift of the epicenters of global Christianity to the Southern Hemisphere cannot be disregarded; in these parts of the world, Christianity is generally "evangelical" in its theological trajectory, yet reconstructed within postcolonial contexts. Perhaps it is high time for North American evangelicals to learn from their sisters and brothers from the non-Western world about "non-Constantinian" ways of worshiping God and celebrating God's presence in this world.

The landscape of American evangelicalism itself is changing. With the hemispheric shift in world Christianity and with the increasing number of immigrants in the United States, many of whom adopt "America's religion," Christianity, the typical profile of an American evangelical is no longer white, suburban, and midwestern; it could very well be Haitian, urban, and northeastern, as it is often the case for where I live, Boston. Critics who use *evangelical* as a catchall term for all Christians with relatively conservative sociotheological perspectives as being equally guilty in co-opting the state to be the handmaiden of the church are in need of a more nuanced awareness of the increasingly complex American religious topography. The authors of a recent book, *A Many Colored Kingdom*, compellingly argue for a missional approach to Christian education and spiritual formation since the context of the evangelical church in America has changed so dramatically.[30] If one were to judge by *Time* magazine's "The Twenty-five Most Influential Evangelicals" (published January 30, 2005), American evangelicalism would be a predominantly white, middle-class, midwestern phenomenon, with Wheaton,

28. Ibid., 123.
29. Ibid., 124.
30. Elizabeth Conde-Frazier, S. Steve Kang, and Gary A. Parrett, *A Many Colored Kingdom: Multicultural Dynamics for Spiritual Formation* (Grand Rapids: Baker Academic, 2004).

Illinois, as its mecca—but such a view betrays the changing dynamic of this significant global religious force, localized so prominently in America. Thus the charge that evangelicalism *always and inevitably equals* Constantinianism needs some further qualification.

Allen R. Hilton's thought-provoking essay "Who Are We? Being Christian in an Age of Americanism" raises the differences of ontology between the state and church: of self-protection as regards the state and of self-giving as regards the church. Not only different ontologies but also perhaps a different goal for each domain needs to be considered. It is almost tautological to argue that a nation-state's raison d'être is its own benefit and survival. The ontology of peace for a state, however it's defined and parsed out, must have its citizens as its primary beneficiaries and limit its boundaries to them. It is *polis* and not *ekklesia*.[31] While the state is constitutionally structured to extend its protection to its citizens, the church has different marching orders. The state operates—indeed has to operate—out of an ontology of conflict. Although the eventual aim of any state is peace, the path of procuring it is inevitably laden with violence, even if for self-protection. This is a point raised by Jean Bethke Elshtain.[32] As Hilton has argued, there is an increasing trend within American evangelicalism: the rise of evangelical NGOs, which intentionally bypass the "route of Constantine" to deliver relief supplies to states experiencing material deprivation and disasters, thus once again refusing a reductionistic identification of evangelicalism *as* Constantinianism.

Is a Tertium Quid Possible?

As I finished this essay, news of France's social unrest and xenophobic hysteria made the cover of the *Economist* (issue of November 12–18, 2005), which deplored "France's Failure." Social catastrophes of this sort bring a greater sense of foreboding than even major natural disasters such as earthquakes, tsunamis, and alphabetized hurricanes, for they seem harder to understand and ameliorate. French nationalists and second-generation Muslim immigrants had in common one thing: "being against." To argue that they *can* and *will be* united in the "headless immanentist multitude" would be considered a case of utter political naiveté or, worse yet, a sinister plot to engender even greater violence, affirmative or negative. The global movement of peoples, deemed salutary by Hardt and Negri in *Empire*, comes at a great price. Throughout

31. For a fascinating rhetorical analysis of President Bush's speech on March 17, 2003, in which he articulated the doctrine of preemption vis-à-vis Iraq as an illustration of the primary responsibility of a nation-state to its citizens, see Allen R. Hilton, "Who Are We? Being Christian in an Age of Americanism," in *Anxious about Empire*, ed. Avram, 152.

32. Jean Bethke Elshtain, "International Justice as Equal Regard and the Use of Force," in *Anxious about Empire*, ed. Avram, 129–44.

the world, xenophobia is on the rise. The famed Italian journalist Oriana Fallaci, in her best-selling books *The Rage and the Pride* (2002), and *La forze della ragione* (2004), calls for the mass removal of recent immigrants—most of whom are nonwhite Muslims—so that Europe's cultural hegemony and religious purity can be restored. Patrick Buchanan's *The Death of the West* singled out "immigrant invasions" as the explanatory matrix for the slow decline and demise of America and Europe.[33]

Is there then a better way, a tertium quid of some sort? I do think there can be: redemptive hospitality. Over against the proposal of Negri-Hardt with its unrealistic celebration of "the nomadic," and likewise over against those of Fallaci and Buchanan, let us adopt the biblical model, as best encapsulated in Hebrews 13:1–2: "Let mutual love continue. Do not neglect to show hospitality to strangers, for by doing that some have entertained angels without knowing it." What the NRSV renders as "hospitality to strangers" is the Greek term πηιλοχενια, from which we get the word *philoxenia*, love of strangers. Redemptive hospitality is a biblical injunction. Xenophobia is a given in our world. So how do we move from xenophobia to philoxenia? Redemptive hospitality is the key to overcoming our inveterate sense of xenophobia. However it is construed, it seems the neo-Marxist ideologies of *Empire* and *Multitude* fail to generate this type of religious imagination.[34] But to the extent American evangelicals embody ecstatic philoxenia, the real possibility of avoiding the co-optation of the church by external agents exists, be it a nation-state (thus avoiding Constantinianism) or an ideology of a fascist or Marxist variety (thus avoiding the danger of overenculturation of the gospel).[35] The "constitutional basis" for the *ekklesia* is for the sake of others. While seeking one's own good is entirely justifiable and indeed warranted for the *polis*, the church needs to demonstrate something bigger than the logic of self-seeking survival.

Hardt and Negri, and before them Marx, have witnessed not only the church's impotence but also its complicity in advancing the agenda of the powerful, the privileged, and the cultural elite, and given this, their distaste for or apathy toward religion as a globally transformative force is understandable.

33. Patrick J. Buchanan, *The Death of the West: How Dying Populations and Immigrant Invasions Imperil Our Country and Civilization* (New York: St. Martin's Press, 2002).

34. On redemptive hospitality, see Hans Boersma, "Irenaeus, Derrida, and hospitality: On the Eschatological Overcoming of Violence," *Modern Theology* 19 (2003): 163–80; Reinhard Hütter, "Hospitality and Truth: The Disclosure of Practices in Worship and Doctrine," in *Practicing Theology: Beliefs and Practices in Christian Life*, ed. Miroslav Volf and Dorothy C. Bass (Grand Rapids: Eerdmans, 2001), 206–27. However, the best volume in this theme in a global context is Anselm Kyongsuk Min, *The Solidarity of Others in a Divided World: A Postmodern Theology after Postmodernism* (Edinburgh: T & T Clark, 2004).

35. Indeed, Andrei Rublev's icon of the Trinity is titled *Philoxenia*, signifying that the only source of our overcoming of xenophobia is the triune God. However, the *agent* of demonstrating the triune nature of God is a person whose life is being re-formed by the prevenient and prevalent grace of God, in this case Abraham.

Hilton puts it scathingly, yet all too accurately: "The Christian community has not been fully formed by this example" of existing for the sake of others "in its nearly two-millennia-long history. In fact, Christian groups have shown a discouraging capacity for disastrous failure."[36] So the call for the diverse groups that constitute "evangelicals" in America is for both clear recognition of the danger of the church's co-optation by an empire with a head other than Christ the *Pantokrator* and an unrelenting insistence that Christ is "the one Word of God which we have to hear and which we have to trust and obey in life and in death," as Karl Barth wrote in the Theological Declaration of Barmen. This one Word supersedes the multitude of words of Negri and Hardt, as well as Buchanan and Fallaci.

36. Hilton, "Who Are We?" 154.

21

Love in Times of Empire

Theopolitics Today

MARIO COSTA, CATHERINE KELLER, AND ANNA MERCEDES

People today seem unable to understand love as a political concept, but a concept of love is just what we need to grasp the constituent power of the multitude.[1]

Love News

Love is what we need? What unexpected news from the secular left. For even in its religious auxiliaries, the left has sternly reduced "love" to "justice" or "liberation." "Christian love," when not a straight front for domination, has seemed to us a swamp of sentimentality, draining off the positive political energies of the prophetic tradition. Of course, progressive Christians allowed love some free play in the dissident zones of sex, privileging the rhetoric of *eros* over the New Testament *agape*.[2] The politics of sex, however, has functioned

---

1. Michael Hardt and Antonio Negri, *Multitude: War and Democracy in the Age of Empire* (New York: Penguin, 2004), 351.
2. See Virginia Burrus and Catherine Keller, eds., *Theologies of Eros: Transfiguring Passion at the Edge of Discipline* (New York: Fordham University Press, 2006). Or, earlier, Rita Nakashima Brock, *Journeys by Heart: A Christology of Erotic Power* (New York: Crossroad, 1988). With reference to Hardt and Negri's love-concept in *Empire*, see Catherine Keller's "The

as a set of single issues, falling dangerously short of "love as a political concept." Yet recently, especially since the 2004 U.S. election, love has been poking
up among the fragments of progressive movements. Whether in the counsel
to continue to do and to teach what we love rather than to despair, or in the
attempt to learn new skills of compassion for the recalcitrant U.S. submul-
titudes known as "the swing vote," "middle America," or "moderate Christians," the political potentiality of love is being reconsidered.[3] Facing empire,
we are thrown back upon the motive-force of love. The authors of this essay
find hope in this throwback. We examine the biblical basis and theological
promise of love as a progressive political force. In order to make a constructive
theopolitical contribution to the thematic of this volume, we draw the incipient love-doctrine of Hardt and Negri into resonance with the gospel symbol
of love, whose echoes they delicately solicit.

There are three major senses of *evangelical*: the oldest means simply of the
evangel, "gospel" or "good news," and thus "gospel-based"; the second, based
in the Reformation and current German usage, signifies merely "Protestant";
the third, often confused with fundamentalism, refers to the recent U.S.-based
phenomenon of politically conservative, biblicist Christianity. We situate ourselves within the older meanings, even as we engage the multiplying mass of the
"born-again" third. While an unstable majority of self-designated evangelical
Christians lend votes and legitimacy to the new U.S. empire, none would deny
that a Christian involvement in national politics must conform to gospel values.
However, there seems to be confusion about what those gospel values actually are. This is odd, as the Jesus of the Gospels is unambiguous as to the top
priority. It can be nothing but the so-called Great Commandment: "Love the
Lord your God with all your heart, and with all your soul, and with all your
strength, and with all your mind; and your neighbor as yourself."[4] These are
his key hermeneutical citations of the Hebrew scriptures.[5] His distinctive spin,

---

Love of Postcolonialism: Theology in the Interstices of Empire," in *Postcolonial Theologies:
Divinity and Empire*, ed. Catherine Keller, Michael Nausner, and Mayra Rivera (St. Louis:
Chalice, 2004).

3. For instance, among the brave progressive voices that publicly articulated both grief and
hope in the immediate aftermath of the 2004 election were a couple of wise articles posted on
the November 11 Alternet. Both reached into a love-discourse unfamiliar among progressive
secular venues: one asked, "What's our job? To dedicate our lives to preserving and passing on
what we love, so that if things ever get sane again there'll be something left" (Michael Ventura,
"Dancing in the Dark," *Austin Chronicle*). Another argued that while many "God-fearing"
individuals are outside our range, "religious Americans who believe in a loving God share many
of our values." To reach them, "we have to reach into our hearts, as we slowly recover from the
heartbreak of Nov. 2, and rediscover our own capacities to appreciate people who, as things
stand, really do threaten what we most value: our planet's health, our civil liberties, our commitment to a government that cares for its people" (Vivan Dent, "From the Heart"). A "love of
the enemy" as outreach to the swing vote?

4. Matthew 22:37–9; Luke 10:27; Mark 12:29–31.

5. Leviticus 19:18 and Deuteronomy 6:5.

however—his unique, indeed original contribution, which would presumably be of special interest to all evangelical Christians—is the text so unpopular when Christians go to war: "But I say to you, Love your enemies and pray for those who persecute you."[6]

It was to "the multitudes," the *ochloi*, the poor and marginal, that the Jesus of the Gospels preached his radical desire for an improbable world.[7] If Hardt and Negri invoke the "multitude" today, in its still unrealized potential for a love-driven coalition for a "new humanity," we wonder if the originative love-teaching can remain altogether sublimated, superseded by political theory. How shall we communicate with the specifically Christian multitude within the United States, now, without it? That collective, however, seems strangely locked into a popular culture of violence, its politics of friend versus foe blessed by a theology of the born-again versus the damned. Analyzing the legitimacy the National Association of Evangelicals has conferred upon U.S. military imperialism since September 11, 2001, Andrew Bacevich concludes that "were it not for the support offered by several tens of millions of evangelicals, militarism in this deeply and genuinely religious country becomes inconceivable."[8] How can this imperial version, this inversion, of the love-imperative be so intractably potent? How could the texts of underdog-love become the pretext for empire-building? How does the power of love flip into the love of power? How does "love the enemy" get replaced by "eradicate them"?

If progressive Christianity has so far failed to make a serious dent in Christian militarism, with its familiar ferment of fear, hate, and violence, our aim here is not to denounce militant evangelicals but to announce the evangel of love in times of empire. In the present context, the annunciation takes the form of a tripartite meditation on Christian love—as elemental force in the face of enmity, as agapeic risk in the face of apocalyptic certainty, as the erotic kairos in the face of the poor.

Of Enemies and Elemental Love

"It's fun to shoot some people." "You got guys who . . . ain't got no manhood left anyway. So it's a hell of a lot of fun to shoot them." Speaking out was Lt. Gen. James N. Mattis of the U.S. Marine Corps. Chastened by his superior and inspiring reactions such as "How terrible! How insensitive!" Lieutenant General Mattis found a defender in the conservative Christian

---

6. Matthew 5:44.

7. On the biblical *ochloi* as South Korean *Minjung*, see Jürgen Moltmann's *In the End—the Beginning: The Life of Hope*, trans. Margaret Kohl (Minneapolis: Fortress, 2004).

8. Andrew Bacevich, *The New American Militarism* (Oxford: Oxford University Press, 2004), 146.

magazine *World*.[9] There columnist Gene Edward Veith derides those who were shocked by the lieutenant general's call to have fun shooting and killing. Veith reminds readers that "there is a pleasure in battle. . . . Excitement, exhilaration, and a fierce joy . . . go along with combat." Some soldiers testify to this pleasure; others feel differently. Veith wants readers to appraise Mattis's fun "from a Christian point of view." The question: "Should a Christian soldier take pleasure in killing people?" His answer: war-making is precisely the work of killing people, and "there is nothing wrong with enjoying one's work."

Most evangelical Christians would abhor Veith's position: a little gospel alarm goes off. Love (killing) the enemy? Yet perhaps we should not be too fast to judge. Veith touches an uncomfortable truth: if war unleashes a primal energy in some of its participants, a sporting excitation shared vicariously by many noncombatants back home, who would begrudge this pleasure to those who are doing our dirtiest work for us?[10] Public pleasure in vicarious violence supports DC and Hollywood. The predictable gospel-based peace-making seems nice, tired, lame. Virtue without the *vir*. No elemental energy. No fun. Besides, Christendom has routinely reenergized itself through manful violence.[11] It is the Gospels that carry the great world symbol of the vicarious benefits of violence, slick with the blood of its nonviolent victim. The cross after Constantine was wielded in defense rather than defiance of empire, and the blood of the Lamb mingled with the gore of Christian crusades and *conquistas*.

Has progressive Christianity (or the secular left) yet grasped the connection between violence and passion—the craving for contact with elemental energies, open to chaos? In the meantime, the religio-political right, obsessed with order, skillfully manipulates the fear and the craving. It channels the excitation of violence through the imaginary of apocalypse, with its vision of an Evil to be countered by all-out holy war. Ironically, the messianic warrior of Revelation, the single most anti-imperial figure of the ancient world, became the great defender of empires that John of Patmos would have marked, like Rome, as the Whore of Babylon: whether Holy Roman, Spanish, British, or now, truly apocalyptic in its weaponry, American.[12] If the religio-political right taps the excitation of apocalypse—a book tone-

---

9. February 26, 2005, cited in Martin E. Marty, "Fun for Christian Soldiers?" *Sightings*, March 7, 2005.

10. *War Is a Force That Gives Us Meaning*, after all. (This is the title of a book by Chris Hedges, published in 2003 by Anchor.)

11. The elemental energy of evangelical militarism is captured by David S. Gutterman's analysis of the Promise Keepers movement as primal, masculinist, antipolitical, and antidemocratic. See "Promise Keepers: Delivering Brothers from Democracy," in *Prophetic Politics: Christian Social Movements and American Democracy* (Ithaca, NY: Cornell University Press, 2005), 94–128.

12. See analysis of this religio-political configuration in Catherine Keller's *God and Power: Counter-apocalyptic Journeys* (Minneapolis: Fortress, 2005); also *Apocalypse Now and Then* (Boston: Beacon, 1996).

deaf to the priority of love—the nice Jesus of the old mainline is helpless in the face of it.

Traditionally, enemy-love is read as a call to exceptional personal virtue, meant for the supererogation of the few—something like celibacy. Such exceptionalism has rendered any practice of love apolitical. Indeed, for common sense it laces the entire spectrum of Christian love, from love of God to love of the neighbor (whether friend, stranger, or enemy) with a sentimental moralism, begging to be complemented by the loveless excitation of apocalyptic violence.[13]

But let us consider the actual text of enemy-love. In the Gospel of Matthew it is situated within the Sermon on the Mount, the first great address of Jesus to "the multitudes." This is in other words no counsel of intimate moralism: it is a call to the widest possible public. "Love your enemies" does not somehow mandate a self-abnegating extreme or self-martyring position; rather, it is offered as an argument *against* an extreme, against the routine polarization of social convention: "You have heard that it was said, 'You shall love your neighbor and hate your enemy,' but I say to you, Love your enemies and pray for those who persecute you."[14] Far from a private gesture, Jesus's radical love preaching is a lure cast out to the multitude, an attempt to create mass movement, to shift the course of history: beginning where each member of the multitude can, no matter how powerless, always begin —in self-transformation, the activation of our singular gifts. "Be perfect [*teleios*] as your heavenly Father is perfect" belongs to the same context and is another text conventionally sidelined as supererogatory—or eschatological— impossibility.[15] Rather it is a shocking call to our Godlikeness, inconvenient for a Protestantism concerned to keep Creator and creature ontologically separate as a way of emphasizing sin and thus our passive dependence upon a unilateral grace. Jesus's attempt at a radical activation of the *imago Dei* suggests by contrast a call to collective action, to the self-actualization of the multitude. The Greek *teleios* does not imply flawlessness or finality but rather a wholeness, maturity, or fulfillment that lodges eschatology in the present tense: the *kairos*, as we shall see. In its synoptic context, it is precisely enemy-love, not replaceable by any private love of God, the demand for a

---

13. The single "love" allusion in Revelation is tellingly begrudging: "I reprove and discipline those whom I love. Be earnest, therefore, and repent" (Rev. 3:19). But the text is uninhibited in the opposite direction: "Yet this is to your credit: you hate the the works of the Nicolaitans, which I also hate" (Rev. 2:6).

14. "You shall love your neighbor and hate your enemy" (Matt. 5:43). Where would the *ochloi* have heard this? Nothing like it occurs within Jewish scripture. Where it does occur, it may have held considerable interest for these specifically Galilean multitudes: in the Dead Sea Scrolls, the text of the Qumran community with which Jesus's old mentor John the Baptist was associated. So then his utterance directly counters the intensified apocalyptic dualism of good and evil that had emerged in the intertestamental period as a response to occupation by a foreign empire.

15. Matthew 5:48.

new relation to the most difficult strangers or neighbors, which is posed as the test and actualization of this "perfection." Thus, the address to the *ochloi* performs the possibility of a new way, a new world—to be initiated by a new sort of subject.

As Hardt and Negri call to the postmodern multitude: "Become different than you are! These singularities act in common and thus form a new race, that is a politically coordinated subjectivity that the multitude produces. The primary decision made by the multitude is really the decision to create a new race, or rather, a new humanity."[16] This new humanity, read through Matthew 5:43–44, can take place only within the space of a gracious deconstruction of any rigid "right" versus "wrong" (or "right" versus "left"). Otherwise, all primal force is sucked and circulated between the poles of good and evil, of "loving the neighbor" and "hating the enemy," draining human, creaturely interdependence of its vitality, consuming hope in fantasies of annihilation. Thus the humanization of the enemy—what else does "love" here mean?— requires de-demonization and understanding, not fondness or agreement. In this sense enemy-love may be indispensable to any progressive politics: otherwise our humanity, along with our would-be coalitions, remains divided against itself.

Intriguingly, it is in the context of the enemy-love proposal that the Sermon on the Mount testifies to a divine refusal of *any* received good-evil boundary: the God we are invited to emulate is said to make the "sun rise on the evil and on the good, and sends rain on the righteous and on the unrighteous."[17] Where with a radical moral imperative we might expect a heightened anthropomorphism, the text performs instead this elemental gesture, inscribing upon divine love the signs of *nonhuman* nature. To be Godlike, *teleios*, then, is to take part in a cosmic, indiscriminate love; it is to practice the solar radiance, the fertilizing rain, of love out of bounds.

Does such boundless care render meaningless all moral striving, resistance to oppression, distinctions of just and unjust? Hardly. It renders them *relative*, subject to the neighborly interdependence of all creatures. Human good is presumed, expected, practiced—in the very repetition, the *persistence* of a streaming, indiscriminate *agape* that at once exceeds justice and makes it possible. In emulation of its inhuman excess, we reclaim our Godlikeness. This love is rewarding. But I do not "love" now to pig out later in heaven. The rewarding telos of this love unfolds in its insistent permeation of this shared world. Like the rain and the sun. Like embracing atmosphere, sustaining soil, force of gravity. Of course, the elemental ecology of creation has remained on the whole foreign to the anthropocentrism of Christian sensibility, as it

16. *Multitude*, 356.
17. Matthew 5:45.

remains also to Hardt and Negri, and indeed most postmodern theory so far.[18] Yet, as eros, this love lures its own materializations.[19]

Elementality, charged with the energies of nonhuman nature, saves love from sentimentality. This love seems to be recharged, indeed electrified, by the collapse of moral dualism, ethnic purity, or identity politics into the "self-transformation, hybridization, and miscegenation" of the multitude.[20] In the connections of difference, it reaches toward always-more-extensive relationship, more intensive reciprocity. So is it possible that in this very elementality the theological opposition between a merely divine *agape* and a merely human *eros* collapses?[21] Traditionally, only an agapeic one-way love, not passionate desire, can be divine. The agapeic generosity is readily construed as a one-way grace; *eros* desires something back from the other, desires the desire of the other, and drives toward reciprocity. Yet the gospel makes no such distinction. A fruitful politics of love—an empire-resistant love—will take place, we suspect, only in a reclamation of the gospel *agape* as including an erotic elementality of desire. God desires passionately; God-love is no patronizing condescension that loves us only for our sake.[22] Dynamic currents of relation circulate between all creatures, affecting us all, affecting God. In this force field crackles an energy otherwise channeled into the sick righteousness of violence. As love, therefore, with its elemental, *non*human scope, it tests itself on the *in*humanity of the enemy and the obstreperousness of the neighbor.

18. There are intriguing exceptions such as Bruno Latour, *Politics of Nature: How to Bring the Sciences into Democracy* (Cambridge, MA: Harvard University Press, 2004).

19. "Lure" here echoes process theology's Whiteheadian notion of the "divine eros," registering as possibility in the genesis of every event and drawing upon a nonomnipotent force of persuasion rather than coercion. See John B. Cobb Jr. and David Ray Griffin's *Process Theology: An Introductory Exposition* (Louisville, KY: Westminster John Knox, 1976), particularly chap. 3, "God as Creative-Responsive Love."

20. *Multitude*, 356.

21. This theological opposition has been given one of its most forceful articulations in Anders Nygren's now classic, but nevertheless problematic, *Agape and Eros*, trans. Philip S. Watson (Philadelphia: Westminster Press, 1953). Although Nygren is right to point out the obvious—that *agape* is the preferred New Testament word used for love—he too quickly jumps to the conclusions that only *agape* is divine love and, more narrowly, that *agape* is a form of love unique to Christianity. By challenging the opposition between *agape* and *eros*, we aim to allow for the inclusion of the divine in a broader range of love relations, ones both erotic and agapeic. Moreover, such relations are open to Christians and non-Christians alike. From the point of view of our theopolitics, as we will make clear in what follows, at stake here is the recognition that love is a multidimensional elemental force, one that gives and wants, one that is human and divine. Such love has the potential to bring about real political change.

22. Feminist theology particularly has striven to counter the condescending power drives of the agapeic model, seeking to liberate a more embodied *eros*. See especially Brock, *Journeys by Heart*.

The Gift of Agape: Love as Political Act

The release of love begins in God's agapeic gesture. Agape takes upon itself the risk of initiation. Within an alienated, oppressive world, where our interdependence with all human and nonhuman creatures has been occluded by sin, someone has to start the transformation. Someone has to begin to become different. Someone has to break the cycle of friend-foe polarities. In any given deadlock, someone must take the chance of novelty. So to initiate is to risk—not to seek!—self-sacrifice. To initiate love is the agapeic risk and, therefore, involves a moment of one-way flow. This is not a unilateralism of love or politics, however, but the initiation of reciprocity. For the initiation is an invitation into relationship.

A theopolitics of agapeic love finds stimulation in a suggestive passage toward the end of *Multitude*: "Both God's love of humanity and humanity's love of God are expressed and incarnated in the common material project of the multitude. We need to recover today this material and political sense of love, a love as strong as death."[23] Although Hardt and Negri are by no means articulating a theology—despite this scriptural theologoumenon, presuming a historical allegorization of the erotic love of the Song of Songs[24]—this passage lends itself to our own biblical hermeneutic. The elemental force of love—a love as strong as death and thus a counterforce to death—can be materially and politically constituted through the reciprocal and cooperative love between God and the creation. Love follows two trajectories: one flows from God to the creation, the other from the creation back to God. Traditionally, the former trajectory has been identified as *agape* (divine love) and the latter as *eros* (human desire). On the basis of this difference these two forms of love have been put in opposition to one another. We acknowledge the semantic and affective difference between agape and eros, even as we stress their inseparability: God's love for the creation is both agapeic and erotic, as is the creation's love for God. Further, we think the coincidence of these two dimensions—giving and desiring—is necessary if love is to find expression in material and political projects, indeed if love is to be a transformative force in history.

God's love for the creation is classically exemplary, particularly as it is manifested in giving. And yet, contrary to some traditions, the power of this love does not show itself in brute force and domination. Although God's agapeic giving—in its excess and generosity—marks a certain unilateral moment in the economy of love, it is so inasmuch as it initiates a desire in the other, a desire for reciprocity between God and the creation, and subsequently a desire for reciprocity within the creation. As an expression of love, God's "gift" is purposeful and intentional, given in anticipation of its reception. It is in this appropriateness that the gift initiates a relationship between the giver and the

23. *Multitude*, 351–52.
24. Song of Songs 6:8.

receiver. This, not its divinity, is what distinguishes agape as a form of love: love is given to the other as other, for the well-being of the other. This is not a love that seeks to control others (not an expression of omnipotence) but a love that risks its own vulnerability in giving freely of itself, in taking ever again (like the sun and the rain) the first step in initiating relationship.

This would then hold true of human love for God—a loving that loves *like* God. Jesus's teaching regarding the greatest commandment tells us exactly how one is to love God: with one's whole being, which includes all one's "strength." Here we catch a glimpse of the force of love. Christianity, however, has not yet realized the meaning of this strength, a strength altogether different not just in degree but in kind from omnipotence. To love with all one's strength the God who is the giver of life and all the gifts that sustain life is to love with a love as strong as death. To love God, therefore, cannot be separated from a love of God's gifts, for to love the gift is to love the giver, just as to love the giver necessarily entails loving the gift. *To destroy life and the conditions of life—be it through murder, war, or ecological destruction—is to demonstrate ingratitude toward God; it is to reject the abundant gifts of the Creator.*[25] But just as ingratitude manifests itself in action, so love must be construed beyond mere sentiment. If what we seek here is a love as strong as death, then this is a love that makes itself felt in action, a love where action and feeling are inseparable. Which is to say that a love as strong as death is not passive, is not a private, interior affair between "me and my God." To love with strength is to love *with the material resources available.* To love with all one's strength is also to love those resources—that is, the created world. These resources in all their diversity are charged with a certain elementality because they are the very elements that sustain and energize life. Thus, a love of life is a life of love. This is the core of what Hardt and Negri call "biopolitics"—a politics that affirms, even celebrates, life. To love life cannot be separated from a life that materially manifests such love; to love life cannot be separated from loving the other and giving of oneself to the other.

According to Jesus, the love for God is realized in love for the neighbor; this is the heart of the greatest commandment. If the release of love begins in a vertical gesture, from God to the creation, such love is consummated in its horizontal dispersal—from one individual to the other, the "neighbor"— and only thereby is truly a love for God. Love of neighbor too has its own strength. As the initial divine gesture of agapeic love is realized (materially and concretely) through the repetition of this initiating gesture in agapeic love of neighbor, divine love is always at work in human agape. Thus, a love as strong as death is not anthropomorphic; rather, it is the nonhuman involved

---

25. How readily an otherworldly distortion of Christianity has thought it could love God and disdain God's gifts, which amounts to the most insidious ingratitude.

and at work in the human. It is the persistent surge of divine love that imbues human agape with its elemental force, its strength.

As a motivating force for political action, agapeic love is not without familiar dangers, however. Christianity has too often perverted God's love, thwarting the elemental inclusivity such that God's mercy extends only to the "righteous" while God's justice is exercised only on the "wicked."[26] A human love patterned on this model permits and justifies human violence toward others in the name of God and Christ. Thus, Christian power trumps Christian love, politics, and the core message of the gospel. A political movement that claims the power of God as the justification of its methods, that claims, therefore, that the outcome of its acts is determined in advance by God, is dangerous (and all too common). Whatever relations that might obtain between God and humanity do not bring with them a guarantee regarding the future outcome of any political act, just as the multitude itself cannot determine in advance the outcome of its movements. Thus, an important dimension and consideration of a theopolitics of love is eschatology. The eschatological dimension of love considered here, however, is interpreted by way of the Gospel, not the Apocalypse.

In Mark's account of Jesus's teaching of the greatest commandment, the scribe's acknowledgment of the priority of the commandment impresses Jesus, who claims that the scribe is "not far from the kingdom of God."[27] What of this proximity? There is little doubt that the kingdom of God signifies a realm of love, a potentiality to be realized in this world as well as in a world "to come." But whereas apocalyptic eschatology aims beyond this world, the eschatology implied here aims into the world in order to transform it. It seems to be the recognition of the priority of love that brings the scribe near to the kingdom of God and brings the kingdom of God closer to realization. Might this proximity enter into the political movement of the multitude? If some critical Christian mass were to recognize the radicality of the love-command, an agapeic love freed from the narrow restraints of morality, no longer exercised as a means of absolving oneself from debt to God, might its elemental force of love be released into the world? For the future is indeterminate, and thus the political act of love and the political movements of the multitude cannot be separated from a certain eschatological expectancy. Yet this expectation is not a foreclosure of the future but *an openness to it*. This openness to the future demands that political action will be open to revision, that it will change its tactics in the light of the always-shifting and always-changing context of global relations.

---

26. This, of course, is just one more example and manifestation of the friend-foe binarism discussed above.

27. Mark 12:34.

Despite their rejection of a form of eschatology that predicts the future outcome of political action in advance and thus forecloses the future, Hardt and Negri's thought hardly excludes eschatological reflection.[28] Their vision for a better world is a vision of something other, collectively unprecedented, yet to come. For us, it supports a hope for a graced outcome of this political project of love. This formulation challenges certain evangelical apocalyptic eschatologies where the end time is indeed already determined: where we are just awaiting, or even violently hastening, the day of its arrival. Out of love, our theopolitics rejects such a view. "Time is split between a present that is already dead and a future that is already living—and the yawning abyss between them is becoming enormous. In time, an event will thrust us like an arrow into that living future. This will be the real political act of love."[29] If this real political act is future oriented, the "thrust" into the future of the multitude is animated in part by the streaming agapeic love that risks its present by giving itself to that future. But the real political act of love is also vitalized by desire, by the eros for a future whose freedom, liberation, and emancipation can be realized for all forms of life. So now we consider the erotics of insistence on political transformation.

A Kairotic Erotics

"*Kairos* is the modality of time through which being opens itself, attracted by the void at the limit of time, and it thus decides to fill that void."[30] Already Negri's words carry erotic tones: attraction, opening, filling. And this eros leads to birth: *kairos* is for Hardt and Negri a distinct moment of generativity, the "moment of rupture" able to "create a new world."[31]

Christian love, we are suggesting, can fund such a kairotic moment only when potent enough to resist the titillations of violence, to arouse creative energy. Only an agape charged with the productive powers of eros has a chance of luring the Christian multitude from its seduction by empire. At the same time, the reintroduction of eros into agape prevents the construal of God's love as a unilateral act of sovereign grace; rather, in love God is drawn into tender exchange. Agape ever infused with fresh streams of eros conveys the elemental, exciting character of God's love for us and of the love stirred in us by God. The erotic dimensions of divine love—what A. N. Whitehead, riffing on Plato's *Symposium*, called "the Eros of the Universe"— help to "flesh out" its carnal proximity. Scriptural stories describe the ways God comes so near as to shine, crackle, and flow in the elements, indeed to

28. See in particular, *Multitude*, 357.
29. Ibid., 358.
30. Antonio Negri, *Time for Revolution* (New York: Continuum, 2003), 152.
31. *Multitude*, 357; see Negri, *Time for Revolution*, 152–58.

become flesh. Not only giving, this divinity is shown *desiring* our participation so much as to display jealousy when we do not respond, wild fecundity when we do.

Emulation of this divine eros is no less risky—though perhaps no more—than mimesis of the agapeic initiation. After all, in eros distinct neighbors coalesce, identifying closely with each other, loving both self and other in an almost simultaneous love. Such intimate spaces of heightened vulnerability provide fruitful ground for growth, transformation, creativity. Yet the risks of abuse and violence are also at their highest. Those who follow their own deep desire to draw near and feel the response of the other, in the private or public arena, may meet with devastation. The Gospels tell the story of a God who insistently works for life even when Jesus's vulnerability is exploited. While in the light of Easter we are encouraged to persist in the theopolitics of divine desire, the outcomes of our eros remain ambiguous. Perhaps it is precisely the embedding of eros within agape (rather than the clear separation which Christian theology has preferred) that will enable the erotic to tend toward productivity rather than destruction.[32]

Erotic love working productively—as agape's most insistent desire—is exemplified in the thematics of poverty both in the Christian scriptures and in Hardt and Negri's work. It is poverty that Matthew's Jesus emphasizes in the practice of love. When Jesus encounters a young person who claims to have kept the great commandments, he tells this young man to go and give away all his possessions to those who are poor and then to come and follow him. Jesus insists on agapeic generosity but also on a particular intimate coalition, here specifically with the poor. Yet the young man goes away grieving, for he owns many possessions.[33]

When Hardt and Negri write about poverty, they do so with the understanding that the poor are key agents in the multitude, and even an immanent presence of divinity, as "god on earth."[34] For writers so resistant to theology, they place great faith in the poor. Negri describes the poor as the strongest "biopolitical" subjects, most capable of productive societal change.[35] Those who know impoverishment must persist in producing ways of life alternative to the ways of empire, because the ways of empire only exclude

32. For a recent effort to rethink the relationship between eros and agape that puts desire at the heart of a productive excess rather than a destructive lack, see Mario Costa, "For the Love of God: The Death of Desire and the Gift of Life," in *Theologies of Eros*, ed. Burrus and Keller.

33. Matthew 19:16–23. Similarly, James 2:8–9 implies that any practice of partiality between the poor and rich negates the practice of the greatest commandment. And the Lukan Jesus offers the parable of the good Samaritan in order to illustrate the practice of the greatest commandment, a parable in which loving the neighbor requires association with the downtrodden (Luke 10:29–37).

34. Michael Hardt and Antonio Negri, *Empire* (Cambridge, MA: Harvard University Press, 2000), 157.

35. Negri, *Time for Revolution*, 194, 209, 260.

them.[36] Impoverishment of all sorts presents the most focused insistence on cooperation, and as many who study the downtrodden have noted, those in impoverished situations reveal an astoundingly focused energy for coalition and for life.[37] Thus the coalitions of the poor offer a clear illustration of "counterpower"[38] to empire, not because they show so well how to suffer and stay poor but because they show so elementally what it is to live, to intend to keep on and get out, to rise up together and walk on to a brighter hope. To borrow Negri's image (one that he surely borrowed from Hebrew scripture), the poor initiate the "exodus" out of the expansive power of empire, parting the seas of empire by their "living labor," or in other words, their "love."[39] The eros beats strongly in this love: the impoverished work in carnal coalition, insisting on a future.

Yet here again, poverty also illustrates the vulnerable location of people in intimate proximity. Poor areas are often crime-ridden areas. The insistence on a better life, erotic in its fervor, too often forces its way, making demands with violence and crime. The odd claim of eros: where vulnerability is high, the potential for the birthing of a new world is also high, especially where eros is secured within the agapeic gesture. Just as Mary's surprising yes affirms the erotic proposal of the divine, so everyday people answer yes to coalition, though the risks are high, and in so doing they move their neighborhoods forward to a new day.

The theopolitical eros of the poor differs significantly from any "love of the poor" where the poor are the object of the love of the rich; it is rather the poor's own love, the brawny love born in the place of poverty itself. Light in the darkness does not come from Christian charity to the poor; light comes from the poor's ingenuity in loving and living against all odds. Theirs is an "amorous innovation,"[40] a courageous and loving push into a new day. They do not present themselves as a group to be sentimentalized; there is nothing sentimental, proper, or even "decent"[41] about the grit of poverty. Rather, they call, like Matthew's Jesus, for those who would follow the exodus toward *kairos* to turn over all their possessions and start walking alongside the *ochloi*. They call us, quite elementally, to coalition. It seems that too often most of us would rather turn away grieving.

36. Ibid., 195, 197–98.

37. See especially Traci C. West, *Wounds of the Spirit: Black Women, Violence, and Resistance Ethics* (New York: New York University Press, 1999); Ivone Gebara, *Out of the Depths: Women's Experience of Evil and Salvation* (Minneapolis: Fortress, 2002); and Melissa Raphael, *The Female Face of God in Auschwitz: A Jewish Feminist Theology of the Holocaust* (London: Routledge, 2003).

38. See *Empire*, 66.

39. Negri, *Time for Revolution*, 241, 258–61.

40. Ibid., 260.

41. See Marcella Althaus-Reid, *Indecent Theology: Theological Perversions in Sex, Gender, and Politics* (London: Routledge, 2000).

Christian love for the poor has become erotic when the "Christian" and the "poor" are no longer a distinct subject and object but have become so close that the space between them blurs and each benefits from the rich subjectivity of the other. The benefit can be at once mutual: whose pleasure do we seek, our own or the other's? When it is good we both are fulfilled, or I am fulfilled in your fulfillment, or vice versa, and I can barely tell the difference: a hair's-breadth. The neighbor is loved "as the self" when love is practiced not out of any effort to do the right thing but rather like the inhalation and exhalation of one's own breath: it is its own reward.

For those U.S. Christians who have been so enamored by empire that love for the other as the self seems much more like piety than breath, perhaps a good start toward coalition would be a deep breath of the common air of the empire's impoverished. In order to breathe the air of the people who cannot afford to drive themselves to work, one might consider riding the bus; in order to ride the bus one might need to move to a neighborhood serviced by a bus line. We can get out of our cars and onto the bus, to breathe alongside those who are always creating new ways to survive, new spaces in which to breathe.[42] We can breathe the bus exhaust with them until we begin to blur together with the crowd on the bus: an erotic, messy closeness, with potential for anguish and for birth. Not accidentally, the elemental ecology of the earth is better served by such a practice. And one day we may find ourselves resisting the bad conditions of the bus, not in pity for "those people who take the bus" but with anger on our own behalf—on their behalf—anger for *all of us* on the bus. We are in love, for the neighbor as for the self.

When our agape is infused with eros, the coalescing of our differences becomes fecund: we pulse with vital energy, expanding, opening, and generating new being and new energy. Such erotic fecundity, we suspect, drives the biopolitical production of the multitude: Negri writes of how the multitude "dilates" and opens to new space and new time.[43] It is as though the multitude lifts up its luminescent newborn on the edge of a smoggy age when all time and space has come under the surveillance of empire. Letting such light shine, Christians in this age of empire have a sort of "kairotic erotics" to practice, soon and often. Secure within the trustworthy persistence of agapeic love, we can risk an insistence on bright hope and pleasure all around. Engaged in such an erotic insistence, we might nurture the fecundity of diverse coalitions in ways both arduous and ardent, slipping between self and other such that loving the other as the self is our daily labor and our daily delight.

42. A good companion for the way is Heidi B. Neumark, *Breathing Space: A Spiritual Journey in the South Bronx* (Boston: Beacon, 2003).
43. Negri, *Time for Revolution*, 185, 212.

A Theopolitics of Love

Only when conceived in its multidimensionality can love realize its potential as a political force in history, a force strong enough to challenge and subvert the current global empire—from the inside, indeed the *heart*. If Christianity is yet—almost too late—to become "good news" to the poor, the suffering, the subjugated, it will ground itself in the gospel priority of agape. Then it might have the chance of its kairos, its cosmic incarnation, its enfleshment in history. In a different but not Christ-free context, Hardt and Negri write that "we need to learn what this flesh can do." They cite Maurice Merleau-Ponty, reminding us that "the flesh is not matter, is not mind, is not substance. To designate it we should need the old term 'element,' in the sense it was used to speak of water, air, earth, and fire. The flesh of the multitude is pure potential, an unformed life force, and in this sense an element of social being, aimed constantly at the fullness of life."[44] In the elemental Spirit of this flesh, loosening itself from the bounded bodies of its own failed ecclesiologies and politics, another *ekklesia* lives, has perhaps always lived, and may yet, as it never has, come into its own. In time.

If a postmodern theopolitics is to be truly evangelical, it will, we have argued, firmly root itself in the gospel priority of agape. This radical agape will not be reduced to a mere ethical imperative or social justice issue. Rather, *the agapeic gesture initiates erotic relatedness*. We propose that an evangelical politics demonstrate the *persistent* flow of agapeic energy that continuously reinitiates love, on the one hand, and an erotic *insistence* on justice, on the other, that desirously exceeds self-interest even as it transforms it. If now, perhaps out of desperation, religious and irreligious moderates, liberals, and progressives begin to work with more discipline together, with persistence and insistence, beyond mere flare-ups of trendy resistance, a counterapocalyptic coalition can emerge.

Together, we experiment with the politics of a love whose shadow is not hate but uncertainty. Indeed it recognizes its ciarascuro of partners in all who would share the fullness of life. It becomes possible to extend a certain elemental love, intensified by acute vulnerability, across the gulf to the future.

---

44. *Multitude*, 193. For an ecotheological rendering of the four elements by way of a biblical pneumatology, see Mark Wallace, *Finding God in the Singing River: Christianity, Spirit, Nature* (Minneapolis: Fortress, 2005).

Afterword

Michael Hardt and Antonio Negri

We are grateful to the editors and authors of this volume for their generous, thoughtful, and challenging engagements with our work. We had hoped that writing these articles would generate not just disagreements but also serious reflection on the problems we have struggled with. These essays are excellent examples of the kind of sympathetic and critical reactions that we wished for.

Evangelical Challenges to Evangelicals in Power

One of the central accomplishments of these essays is to challenge the common understandings of what it means to be evangelical today by insisting on the significance of both evangelical traditions of theological interpretation and the history of evangelical political engagement. We must admit that this really has little to do with us since we are not evangelicals (nor Christians, for that matter). That does not prevent us from recognizing, however, the importance of such an ideological operation of demystification and contestation. This is ever more important today, since, as many of the essays point out, evangelicals are now in power. Not only are there evangelicals in the White House and throughout the U.S. political structure who claim to act on their faith when they promote right-wing and militaristic policies, but also evangelical churches, missionary projects, and NGOs are playing significant (and largely reactionary) political roles throughout the world, particularly in Africa, Latin America, and Asia. Such facts inevitably create the public impression that evangelicals as a whole constitute a repressive political force that supports the U.S. government's military deployments and its projects for global domination.[1] In this context, therefore, it is very significant that many of these essays demonstrate that a strong current of evangelicals (even if they are a minority) has a different political orientation.

Some of the essays—particularly the contributions by Jim Wallis, Lester Ruiz and Charles Amjad-Ali, Jennifer Butler and Glenn Zuber, Sébastien Fath, and Donald Dayton and Christian Collins Winn—show how alternative evangelical traditions can contest today's dominant evangelical politics and illuminate how strongly some evangelicals have challenged militaristic powers in the United States in the past. One group of authors—including Helene Slessarev-Jamir and Bruce Ellis Benson, Juan Martínez, Patrick Provost-Smith, and Eleanor Moody-Shepherd and Peter Heltzel—emphasize the racial and social differences among evangelicals as a point of strength. Two of the essays—those by Elaine Padilla and Dale Irvin and Amos Yong and Samuel Zalanga—extend these questions specifically to the contemporary politics of Pentecostals. As a whole these authors demonstrate that the theological basis of evangelicalism requires a politics of liberation and that evangelical groups have struggled in the past and indeed could struggle today in the United States against militarism and for the liberation of the multitude. We consider this project of evangelicals challenging "the evangelicals in power" extremely important—just as important, for example, as the efforts of Jews to articulate their dissent from the repressive policies of the Israeli state on theological and political grounds, and as efforts of Muslims similarly to challenge the most dominant reactionary tendencies within Islam.

Analogies with Ancient Empires

Many of the essays in the collection take up the analogy between the current empire and ancient ones, particularly Rome and Byzantium. Kurt Anders Richardson's essay, for example, makes this link explicit. It is clear, of course, and these authors are very aware of this fact, that the relationship between Christianity and the ancient empires cuts two ways. On the one hand, Jesus, the Evangelists, and early Christians generally can be considered as an anti-imperial force insofar as they were persecuted by the Romans and created a movement to oppose or escape from its power. The analogy for some suggests, then, that Christians or Christian theology can today serve similarly as

---

1. William Connolly emphasizes the close relationship between evangelicals and capitalism: "The right leg of the evangelical movement is joined at the hip to the left leg of the capitalist juggernaut." See "The Evangelical-Capitalist Resonance Machine," *Political Theory* 33, no. 6 (December 2005): 869–86, at 874.

protest and resistance against the domination of U.S. power.[2] On the other hand, Christianity has its own imperial pasts, which the editors and several of the authors group under the rubric of Constantinianism. The contemporary analogy here is primarily with the Christians (particularly evangelicals) in power in the U.S. government and the centrality of their religious faith in political projects of national and global domination. So we have an interesting rhetorical situation in this collection in the sense that there is a sort of competition between two analogies with ancient empires that pose Christians on opposite sides of the relationships of domination. In essence, this rhetorical alternative corresponds to one of the general arguments of the collection as a whole that we mentioned earlier, that whereas the dominant group of U.S. evangelicals—in the government, in NGOS, and other institutions—generally serve today repressive political forces, they could (and some evangelicals already do) operate as a force of resistance.

We should point out, however, that our use of the analogy between the contemporary situation and the ancient empires is quite different than the analogies in these essays. We refer to ancient Rome, rather than the modern imperialisms of the European nation-states, as part of an argument that the empire in the process of formation today will be global in scope and cannot be ruled by a single center or nation-state. This empire is like ancient Rome in that it has indefinite, expansive boundaries and that it constantly incorporates hybrid populations rather than fixing exclusive identities. It is unlike the ancient empire, however, in that it has no emperor and no Rome, no central point that can dictate imperial power. One aspect of our claim, in other words, is that the United States, although it is certainly the most powerful nation-state in many respects, is not capable today of dictating global political, military, economic, and cultural affairs. In our view the attempts of the current U.S. government to act like an imperialist power and unilaterally control global affairs have proven to be an unqualified failure. One index of this failure is the inability of the U.S. government in Afghanistan and Iraq to pacify the population through military force and occupation, create stable markets for profit, and impose its political order. Another index, which reveals the domestic face of the failure, is the disaster that followed Hurricane Katrina, revealing the exacerbated racialized poverty in the United States, the collapsing social infrastructure, and generally the incapacity to devote sufficient resources to the "home front" when conducting foreign adventures. Our argument, which is much too long to repeat here, is that what is forming today and what we will face in the future is not a new U.S. imperialism but rather a much broader and more complex form of global domination.

2. For an example of the use of this analogy, see Mark Lewis Taylor's excellent indictment of the death penalty and the U.S. prison system: *The Executed God: The Way of the Cross in Lockdown America* (Minneapolis: Fortress, 2001).

This does not mean, we should be clear, that we think people should not protest against and resist the murderous and tragic policies and projects of the U.S. government. That those within the United States do so is all the more important, just as it is necessary that evangelicals challenge the evangelicals in power. Our analysis requires, first of all, that we look at forces of control beyond the United States and its government to recognize the functioning not only of other dominant nation-states but also of capitalist corporations, supranational institutions, NGOs, and other powers. The overestimation of the capacities of the U.S. government implies an underestimation of other forces of domination. Second, our analysis should serve as a warning against lodging one's hope and faith in the idea that a future, virtuous government of the United States (or any other nation-state) will save us. The liberation from this empire and the formation of an alternative to it cannot and will not take a national form.

The Immanence of the Multitude

Several of the authors in the collection—including Gail Hamner, James Smith, Mark Taylor, and Michael Horton—highlight our insistent attack on the various forms of transcendence and our proposal of a politics of immanence. This is for us a crucial issue and one that illuminates a significant difference between our thought and most Christian (or religious) frameworks for politics. Allow us first to explain the basic context in which we see the alternative between transcendence and immanence in political thought and practice, and then proceed to engage the complexities that some of the authors raise.

To begin it might be useful to return to early modern European political theory and remember that the primary figures of authority and power there are derived directly from the theological tradition. When authors in the seventeenth and eighteenth centuries speak of the king or the sovereign or the state as being a "god on earth" they are directly drawing on the theological figures of authority as analogies or models for the secular power. Carl Schmitt may be right, in this sense and for this limited tradition of thinking, to say that every figure of sovereignty relies on a theological conception. The figure of a transcendent ruling power was in this sense merely transferred from religious to secular forms and institutions. When we criticize and mark our opposition to the tradition of political transcendence, then, we are referring to all those figures of authority that "stand above" society and impose their control, whether they be religious or secular. We are merely insisting that society be able to organize itself with no superior power ruling over it. This would be a politics of immanence in its simplest form. Such a proposition does not seem to us in itself very radical or controversial. And furthermore a politics of immanence is the only valid definition of democracy. Monarchy and aristocracy pose the king or the elect few in the transcendent position above society. Democracy is the only political form that refuses all such transcendence and allows only the play of immanent forces. We have tried to articulate the concept of the multitude as such an immanent and autonomous form of association, composed of innumerable differences and crisscrossed by conflicts but able, nonetheless, to organize itself as society.

Our experience has been that although many Christians share our basic political vision in principle, the conflicts between this notion of a politics of absolute immanence and at least some versions of Christian theology can pose stumbling blocks. Consider, for example, an experience that one of us had recently when speaking about our notion of the politics of the multitude at a theological seminary. After the lecture a member of the audience expressed her sympathy with our project but then objected that we overestimate the power of people. We are weak when we act on our own, she explained, and we are strong only when we confide ourselves in and are guided by a power that stands above us, God's power. This exchange with the audience member gives a clear example of the distinction between a politics of immanence and one of transcendence. And this is one of those moments when, despite a deep sense of sympathy, we simply have to part company, because we do indeed maintain that the multitude on its own can have enormous power, wisdom, and virtue without the guidance of a higher power of any kind—finally, that the multitude is capable of ruling itself. We do not mean, of course, that this power is spontaneous and immediate. We have to work together to organize and form the multitude.

John Milbank's essay in this volume is a more sophisticated and erudite version of the question from the audience member that poses the need for transcendent guidance. Milbank's central premise is that common people do not necessarily act in the interests of equality or justice, nor even for their own liberation, and thus they must be led by an elite. This premise, of course, is a red herring, which should be contested from both the theoretical and empirical perspectives. Theoretically, no one should question the fact that the spontaneous actions of mobs can have horrible consequences and that the masses can act to oppress others and even reinforce their own oppression. And certainly we have no belief in the natural goodness and virtue of all. But political action is not merely the spontaneous expression of natural faculties; it is a collective training, a labor of organization and cooperation that needs no external guiding force standing above it. These capacities of the multitude for self-organization and collective intelligence are what Milbank does not recognize, and without them he can see only the potential for irrationality, injustice, and violence. "This is exactly why," he writes, "the vast numbers of the American poor are not waiting to rise up in revolt." Such a statement, of course, invites an empirical response too, because there are indeed large numbers of the poor and exploited in the United States and throughout the world who are continually experimenting with new forms of resistance and revolt, from small daily practices to large-scale movements. It would be easy to produce a long catalog of examples from welfare rights movements in the United States to landless movements in Brazil, and from New Orleans protests against government actions after Hurricane Katrina to the Paris suburb revolts in the summer of 2005. There is no doubt that each of these movements is incomplete and imperfect, that none of them is capable on its own of successfully overthrowing the oppressive global system we face—and that some of them might at times even be counterproductive—but that is not reason to dismiss them altogether. One must instead work with them to help make them more adequate to their task of liberation.

Milbank's argument has the great virtue of clarifying the political stakes in these theoretical discussions about immanence and transcendence. The democratic interactions of the multitude, he concludes, must be led and ruled by a minority that stands above it—an aristocracy that guarantees the reference to the transcendent norms of truth and virtue and a monarchy that ensures justice. (And it is useful to keep in mind that for Milbank there is a direct connection between the transcendent norms implied in Christian theology and the transcendent political power that he believes should rule over the multitude.) Such a "mixed government," of course, ruled by an elite that stands above society, is no democracy at all. This is exactly the kind of argument that we intend to oppose when we critique transcendence and propose a politics of immanence.

Mark Taylor's essay in this volume also treats the political stakes in transcendence, but he approaches them in a way that is much more complex and more useful than Milbank's. He makes two extremely important contributions to this discussion: first, distinguishing between two forms of transcendent power and, second, indicating how some aspects of a democratic project of the multitude might themselves be considered to be transcendent. He makes clear that at times the battle cry in our books for immanence against transcendence presents a divided scene too simple for the argument we want to conduct.

We agree entirely with Taylor's first distinction between a "transcendence of command" and a "transcendence of ordering function," even if we would prefer slightly different terms. It seems to us that there has been excessive scholarly focus in recent years on the concept of sovereignty, drawing primarily on theorists in the line from Thomas Hobbes to Carl Schmitt. (And to the extent that we ourselves have participated in this trend, please consider this also as a self-critique.) This is what Taylor calls the transcendence of command, a sovereign power that stands outside the law—or, perhaps, both inside and outside the law—creating a permanent state of exception. One problem with this focus on sovereignty is that it often leads to an apocalyptic view of power relations, collapsing all forms of modern power into fascism. In effect, too many of the contemporary discourses on power seem to be replaying the

European (primarily German) debates of the 1930s. The second problem is that this excessive focus on sovereignty has tended to eclipse the powers of capital and property, along with the legal system that supports them. Sovereignty is, in fact, always based in and interwoven with legal norms and procedures. Taylor calls this second form of power the "transcendence of the ordering function," but we would prefer to call it a juridical and capitalist transcendentalism. The terminological shift from transcendent to transcendental can help indicate a shift in theoretical focus, which we could express, in a kind of philosophical shorthand, as moving from Hobbes to Kant. The ordering function is carried out primarily by the transcendental rule of law and property. This focus on the transcendental forms of power gives us a view that is less dramatic and catastrophic but actually highlights more clearly the forms of resistance that are emerging within its structures. In short, then, we are happy to agree with the distinction that Taylor marks and would add to that a call to move away from an excessive focus on the transcendent forms of sovereignty and pay more attention to the transcendental juridical structures that accomplish the ordering function.

Regarding Taylor's second point, our disagreement with him might be primarily terminological. He claims, following Ernesto Laclau, that there are and should be elements of transcendence in the multitude. In one sense it is impossible to disagree. The multitude after all has goals and desires, it arrives at decisions, and it is structured by forms of organization. From a certain perspective these could all be considered elements of transcendence. We have written about such situations, for example, by using paradoxical terms to indicate the complexity of the matter. For instance, we have at several points written of a "materialist teleology of the multitude." We use that term to indicate that struggles are always organized by desire and always create new norms through their practice. But this is a strange kind of teleology because no telos stands at the end and pulls the process forward. There is no end point but merely a vector that extends from the present in the direction of the desire of the multitude. One could certainly say that this materialist teleology and similar formulations indicate elements of transcendence in the multitude. We do not see, however, what is gained by such a statement. The risk of such formulations, in fact, is that they could mask or confuse the difference between resistance and power and thus make it seem that there is no way to go beyond the limits of power, be they transcendent or transcendental.

The materialist teleologies that we read in the constitution of the political action of the multitude have an epistemological foundation that resides in the imagination. When the political desires and constituent powers extend in time to construct new institutions and forms of life, they follow a telos that the imagination has designed. The materialist teleology of political action demonstrates in filigree the imaginative tension of reason. This is not a matter of renewing in Kantian fashion the bonds of transcendentalism and blocking modes of life and forms of knowledge at the level of the intellect. On the contrary, this involves liberating the imagination (in a Spinozian way) as the fabric of the coming world. But didn't Kant too, in his *Critique of Judgment*, liberated from the bureaucratic philology of absolute idealism, try to reach the intense power of this imaginative function?

Despite the great philosophical interest of these nuances in the meaning of the transcendent and the transcendental, we find ourselves more concerned in the end with the kind of confusions that they introduce. To our ears, when someone calls for elements of transcendence in the multitude, that sounds too much like calling for a vanguard to lead it, for a select population to stand above and rule over it—a call, in other words, for the kind of transcendence that Milbank wants. Perhaps the pressures of these practical and political uses of the terminology are too strong to allow us to be comfortable with Taylor's subtle philosophical distinctions.

This brings us to love—and the fascinating reflections by Mario Costa, Catherine Keller, and Anna Mercedes that conclude the volume—because love too is best understood as an immanent encounter. The political concept of love that interests us, in other words, is neither the love of a creator that stands above and looks down on its creatures nor that of those creatures for their transcendent creator. It is instead the power of creation that resides and is born again and again in the encounters between and among us. And indeed the love that these authors explore seems to us also intimately tied to the materialist powers of the imagination. This love is the fundamental power of the multitude, a power that convinces us that the multitude is indeed capable of ruling itself with no transcendent, guiding force that stands above it.

List of Contributors

Charles W. Amjad-Ali is Martin Luther King Jr. Professor of Justice and Christian Community and professor of Islamic studies and Christian-Muslim relations at Luther Seminary.

Bruce Ellis Benson is professor of philosophy and chair of the philosophy department at Wheaton College in Illinois.

Jennifer Butler is the executive director of the Faith and Public Life Resource Center in Washington, DC.

Christian T. Collins Winn is assistant professor of biblical and theological studies, Bethel University.

Mario Costa is completing his PhD in theological and religious studies in the Caspersen School at Drew University.

Donald W. Dayton taught theology and ethics at Northern Baptist Seminary, Drew University, and Azusa Pacific University.

Sébastien Fath is senior researcher at the National Center for Scientific Studies (CNRS) and teaches at the University of Paris—IV (Sorbonne).

John R. Franke is professor of theology at Biblical Seminary.

M. Gail Hamner is associate professor of religion at Syracuse University.

Michael Hardt is professor of literature and romance studies at Duke University.

Peter Goodwin Heltzel is assistant professor of theology at New York Theological Seminary.

Michael Horton is professor of theology at Westminster Seminary, California.

Dale T. Irvin is president and professor of world Christianity at New York Theological Seminary.

Catherine Keller is professor of theology at Drew University.

Mabiala Kenzo is professor of theology at Canadian Theological Seminary.

Paul Lim is assistant professor of the history of Christianity at Vanderbilt Divinity School.

Juan F. Martínez is assistant dean for the Hispanic Church Studies Department and associate professor of Hispanic studies and pastoral leadership at Fuller Theological Seminary.

Anna Mercedes is a PhD candidate at Drew University.

John Milbank is research professor of religion, ethics, and politics at the University of Nottingham.

Eleanor Moody-Shepherd is associate dean and professor of ministry at New York Theological Seminary.

Antonio Negri is an independent researcher and writer. He has been a lecturer in political science at the University of Paris and professor of political science at the University of Padua.

Elaine Padilla is a PhD candidate at Drew University in the field of sociology and religion.

Patrick Provost-Smith is assistant professor of the history of Christianity at Harvard Divinity School.

Kurt Anders Richardson is a member of the theology faculty at McMaster University in Canada.

Lester Edwin J. Ruiz is academic dean and professor of theology and culture at New York Theological Seminary.

Helene Slessarev-Jamir is Mildred M. Hutchinson Professor of Urban Ministries at Claremont School of Theology.

James K. A. Smith is associate professor of philosophy at Calvin College.

Mark Lewis Taylor is professor of theology and culture at Princeton Theological Seminary.

Corey D. B. Walker is assistant professor in the department of Africana Studies at Brown University.

Jim Wallis is president and executive director of Sojourners.

Nicholas Wolterstorff is Noah Porter Professor Emeritus of Philosophical Theology, and Fellow of Berkeley College, Yale University. He is currently a senior fellow at the Institute for Advanced Studies in Culture, University of Virginia.

Amos Yong is professor of systematic theology at Regent University School of Divinity.

Samuel Zalanga is associate professor of sociology at Bethel University.

Glenn Zuber recently completed a PhD in American Studies and Religious Studies at Indiana University (Bloomington).

Index

Note: The editors wish to thank James F. DiFrisco for compiling the index.